# Money Laundering, Terrorist Financing, and Tax Evasion

Aretha M. Campbell

# Money Laundering, Terrorist Financing, and Tax Evasion

## The Consequences of International Policy Initiatives on Financial Centres in the Caribbean Region

palgrave
macmillan

Aretha M. Campbell
University of Salamanca
Salamanca, Spain

ISBN 978-3-030-68875-2 ISBN 978-3-030-68876-9 (eBook)
https://doi.org/10.1007/978-3-030-68876-9



This Palgrave Macmillan imprint is published by the registered company Springer Nature Switzerland AG
The registered company address is: Gewerbestrasse 11, 6330 Cham, Switzerland

*I dedicate this work to my Lord and Saviour Jesus Christ who has made it all possible for me to complete this journey despite the many obstacles I encountered along this way. I am truly an example that with You, anything is possible.*

*To Larry, you've been my rock and my support throughout this entire process. You've strengthened and encouraged me continuously. I am forever grateful to have you in my life.*

# Foreword

This book is a breath of fresh air, and therefore it is a special honour to have been asked to write this foreword to it.

The reader is in for a treat, because the author gives an analysis of four financial centres in the Caribbean—The Bahamas, Bermuda, the British Virgin Islands and the Cayman Islands—which helps to sweep aside the popular stereotypes and reveals the sophistication and the impressive evolution of compliance and transparency within these jurisdictions which rival those of financial centres anywhere.

The book begins by showing that, while globalization of the world economy fostered the growth of these centres, they too share the concerns of the international community to find solutions to the three phenomena of money laundering, terrorist financing and tax evasion ("the three phenomena"). Although these phenomena are considered in this book, they are not conflated in any way, and each one is given a balanced treatment. Hence, as the reader turns the pages, it is apparent that it is a gross misrepresentation simply to dismiss the four countries as jurisdictions of light regulation and supervision, less stringent reporting requirements, and less stringent trading restrictions, especially when change accelerated after 2000. The true picture is not so simple as that.

Interestingly, the book also looks at the other side of the coin. It examines the three phenomena from the perspectives of both the United States and the European Union, by scrutinizing the challenges facing law enforcement authorities related to drug trafficking, money laundering and organized transnational crime groups.

In a comprehensive sweep of the landscape, the book reviews the standards set by the Organization for Economic Cooperation and Development (OECD), the Global Forum on Transparency and Exchange of Information for Tax Purposes, as well as the US and EU in relation to combating tax evasion. Notably the measures include exchange of information on request, foreign accounts tax compliance legislation, common reporting standards, and the European Union code of conduct.

Then, the reader is also invited to step out of her or his bubble and to see the world from the perspectives of The Bahamas, the Cayman Islands, Bermuda and the BVI, attempting to be agile and flexible in response to aggressive policy initiatives introduced by the Financial Action Task Force (FATF) to counter money laundering and terrorist financing. This analysis relates to the period 2007–2012, when each jurisdiction underwent their third mutual evaluation report conducted by the Caribbean Financial Action Task Force (CFATF). The famous or infamous Forty Recommendations of the FATF are reviewed in a comparative analysis of the four jurisdictions.

The policy initiatives instituted by the Global Forum, the OECD, the US and EU to counter tax evasion were no less aggressive. A close examination is conducted regarding the period 2010–2016, which coincided with the introduction or implementation of the Global Forum's Exchange of Information on Request, the US Foreign Account Tax Compliance Act (FATCA), the OECD Common Reporting Standard (CRS), and the EU Code of Conduct on Business Taxation. These initiatives are also reviewed in a comparative analysis of the four jurisdictions.

What was the collateral damage? What were the consequences of these aggressive initiatives for the economies of these jurisdictions? Although the first eight chapters are necessary, eye-opening precursors, it is with great anticipation that one reads the final and concluding chapter. It is entirely worth the wait.

The author has chosen to write about the four jurisdictions as a case study. The lesson is emphatically that all countries do not fit the same mold. Even among the four, there are significant differences of substance and emphasis that are ably presented in the book.

But, important commonalities should not be overlooked. Climate change, related disasters such as hurricanes of unprecedented ferocity, and now Covid-19 have increased the importance of their financial sectors for their survival. They are largely dependent on tourism and financial services to generate foreign exchange earnings. Before Covid-19, with mature tourism infrastructures supporting large numbers of stopover and cruise visitors per annum, tourism is the largest driver of the economic activity.

Generally secondary only to the dominant tourism sector, the financial sector contributes significantly to each country's GDP, directly impacting domestic employment and expenditure, and also other important sectors, such as construction, and wholesale and retail trade. People have dropped out of the middle class, as better paying jobs in the financial sector have been lost.

Meanwhile, the financial sectors of developed countries, though often larger and more complex, are not materially different from those of many developing countries. The differences are largely of scale and magnitude and not of quality. The financial sectors of developed countries also consist of commercial banks, savings banks, trust companies, offshore banks, insurance companies, development banks, publicly controlled pension funds, housing corporations, public savings banks, private pension funds, cooperative societies, credit unions and their respective regulators, just as developing countries.

Hence, the pejorative sting of terms, such as "offshore centre" and even "international financial centre" and variants of those terms used to distinguish these places from regular financial centres, is based on the notion unsupported by data that tax evasion, terrorist financing, and other criminal activities are particularly prevalent and uncontrolled there. Another factor is the small geographic or population size of these jurisdictions. These considerations even compel some observers to conclude that these developing countries have no business being financial centres at all.

But, these jurisdictions are indeed financial centres. As this book points out, no additional qualifier is needed. They are not a new invasive species. Such existential attacks are unwarranted and really deplorable. There is no evidence that criminal elements are any more prevalent in the so-called offshore centres than there are "onshore". All financial centres have offshore sectors that may vary in size and intensity. But, under adverse external circumstances, these centres have mustered the resilience to continue to focus on finance as a continuing source of growth and development, and to change and adapt.

But now, we witness the international politics of constantly shifting goal posts, as so-called supranational organizations with limited self-serving memberships constantly impose increasing demands on weaker countries. One reasonably surmises that the end game is to eliminate any competitive advantage of the weaker jurisdictions so that international financial flows return to developed countries and are invested instead in places like Delaware, Hawaii, Nevada, and Wyoming, none of which satisfy the high standards imposed on developing countries.

Moreover, courts have been almost entirely removed from the equation. As opposed to the experience of more than five decades following World War II, few cases now come to trial in the twenty-first century, in defence of the financial sectors and of the economic development of these countries.

It is said that the three-hundred-pound gorilla is the room is the reduced tax receipts of developed countries allegedly caused by these financial centres. Therefore, much collateral damage has been done to these countries in the name of so-called harmful tax competition.

However, financial centres contribute very significantly to economic growth. Centres with well-developed financial systems tend to grow faster over time, and the evidence suggests a cause and effect relationship. Financial development is not simply an outcome of economic growth, but is a catalyst for growth.

Therefore, this book is a small but significant step towards changing and one day controlling the narrative about the offshore sectors in these jurisdictions.

It has been a pleasure to have collaborated with Aretha Campbell in the recent past on an article appearing in the Commonwealth Lawyer. It is also a pleasure to see her spread her wings and soar towards a future of hope for countries that are too often misunderstood.

Miraflores/Nassau, The Bahamas — Peter D. Maynard
November 2020

# Preface

This book represents the work undertaken to satisfy the requirements of my PhD thesis. It is intended for academics, researchers and students interested in understanding the problem of money laundering, terrorist financing and tax evasion, the international solutions to these problems, and the impact of international policy initiatives against these phenomena on the legal systems, institutions, offshore business sectors and economies of financial centres located in offshore jurisdictions in the Caribbean region.

This book is organized into nine chapters. The first chapter is a comprehensive introduction to the topic looking at the reason why offshore jurisdictions in the Caribbean have established financial centres, their role in contributing to money laundering, terrorist financing and tax evasion, and the events which pushed the international community to institute measures to counter these phenomena. In the second chapter, a detailed overview of the four main financial centres in offshore jurisdictions in the Caribbean is undertaken. These centres include, The Bahamas, the Cayman Islands, Bermuda and the British Virgin Islands. A look at the general profile of each centre, including an overview of their offshore financial sectors and the anti-money laundering and anti-tax evasion regimes instituted by each jurisdiction prior to 2000 are undertaken. Chapter 3 takes a look at the problem of money laundering from both the US' and EU's perspectives. It discusses globalization and the challenges associated with money laundering and terrorist financing, and reviews the incentives which pushed the international community to take action. This chapter also looks at the organization designated with the responsibility to deal with these phenomena, and its approach to tackle both issues. The fourth chapter examines the factors which facilitate tax evasion. A look at the challenges faced by tax authorities in countering this phenomenon, particularly as it relates to tax heavens and globalization is discussed. This chapter also discusses the incentives which contributed to pushing the agenda forward in the international arena to address the problem of tax evasion, as well as the organization and specific countries which took on the task to deal with this issue, and the key tools implemented by each to combat it.

Chapter 5 looks at international initiatives introduced by the FATF and the Basel Committee on Banking Supervision (BCBS) as solutions to the problem of money laundering and terrorist financing. An in depth review is undertaken of the Forty Recommendations to determine the role this standard play in countering money laundering and terrorist financing. Conclusions are drawn based on the findings. Chapter 6 reviews the standards set by the OECD, the Global Forum, as well as the US and EU to determine the roles they play in combating tax evasion. Specifically, an examination is conducted of the three principal functions each standard play in promoting transparency in the legal systems and institutional measures of the four jurisdictions, in implementing backstopping measures as preventative mechanisms to mitigate the risks associated with tax evasion, and in establishing effective exchange of information through fostering national and international cooperation. The standards examined in this chapter include, exchange of information on request (EOIR), foreign accounts tax compliance act (FATCA), common reporting standard (CRS), and the European Union Code of Conduct. Chapter 7 analyses the measures implemented by The Bahamas, the Cayman Islands, Bermuda and the BVI in response to international policy initiatives introduced by the FATF to counter money laundering and terrorist financing. This analysis is conducted for the period 2007 to 2012, which coincides with the timeframe in which each jurisdiction underwent their third mutual evaluation report (MER) conducted by the Caribbean Financial Action Task Force (CFATF). We examine these measures using a comparative analysis approach and observe the resulting trends to determine the impact of the Forty Recommendations on the legal systems and institutions of these four jurisdictions.

Chapter 8 examines the response of The Bahamas, the Cayman Islands, Bermuda and the BVI to international policy initiatives instituted by the Global Forum and the OECD, in addition to the US and EU, to counter tax evasion. The period reviewed for this analysis is between 2010 to 2016, which coincides with the introduction of EOIR by the Global Forum, FATCA by the US, CRS by the OECD, and the standard implemented by the EU Code of Conduct on Business Taxation. An examination of the measures implemented by each jurisdiction is undertaken, and in a comparative analysis, the trends are analysed to determine the impact of these standards on the legal systems and institutions of these four Caribbean islands. In Chapter 9, we look at the dis-articulation and misportrayals of 'offshore', raise questions regarding the knowledge produced about the international financial ecosystem; and carry out an analysis of the consequences of international policy initiatives against money laundering, terrorist financing and tax evasion on the business of the offshore financial sectors in The Bahamas, the Cayman Islands, Bermuda and the BVI. An examination of the effects of this sector on the economies of these four jurisdictions is also conducted. The period used for this part of the analysis is from 2011 to 2019 based on available data. Each jurisdiction is then ranked from least to most adversely affected based on our findings. Conclusions are then drawn based on the overall results of our analysis.

Salamanca, Spain

Aretha M. Campbell

# Acknowledgements

A special thank you to my Ph.D. tutors, Dr. Victoria Maria Muriel Patino and Dr. Fernando Rodriguez in the Department of Applied Economics in the Faculty of Law at the University of Salamanca, for helping me establish a firm foundation in this discipline, which has been key to producing this monograph. I am grateful to you for all your help in directing and supervising my thesis. Your collaborative efforts and guidance have been both insightful and illuminating.

My sincere thanks to Dr. Nicolas Garcia, Coordinator of my doctoral program, "Estado de derecho y gobernanza global," for always being open and willing to help me in any way possible during my time at the University of Salamanca. I truly appreciate your support.

I would also like to thank Dr. Don Marshall, Director and Senior Fellow at the Sir Arthur Lewis Institute of Social and Economic Studies at the University of the West Indies, Cave Hill, Barbados, for his contribution to the conceptualization of final chapter of this book. Your time, effort and commitment to this project have been invaluable and immensely appreciated. I've been very fortunate to have worked with you.

Finally, I am very grateful to Dr. Peter D. Maynard, Head of the Law Department at the University of The Bahamas for writing the forward to this book. Your time and dedication to this work is highly valued and deeply appreciated.

# Contents

# Abbreviations

| | |
|---|---|
| AEOI | Automatic Exchange of Information |
| AIM | Approved Investment Manager |
| AML | Anti-Money Laundering |
| AML/CFT | Anti-Money Laundering and Countering Financing of Terrorism |
| AMLR | Anti-Money Laundering Regulations (2008) |
| AMLTFCOP | Anti-Money Laundering and Terrorist Financing Code of Practice, 2009 |
| ATA | Anti-Terrorism Act |
| ATFA | Anti-Terrorism (Financial and Other Measures) Act 2004 |
| BEPS | Base Erosion Profit Shifting |
| BIS | Bank of International Settlement |
| BISX | The Bahamas International Securities Exchange |
| BMA | Bermuda Monetary Authority |
| BSFB | The Bahamas Financial Services Board |
| BSX | Bermuda Stock Exchange |
| BVI | British Virgin Islands |
| CAA | Model Competent Authority Agreement |
| CBB | Central Bank of The Bahamas |
| CCG | Code of Conduct Group in Business Tax |
| CDB | Caribbean Development Bank |
| CDD | Customer Due Diligence |
| CFATF | Caribbean Financial Action Task Force |
| CFT | Countering the Financing of Terrorism |
| CICAD | Inter-American Drug Abuse Control Commission |
| CIMA | Cayman Islands Monetary Authority |

| | |
|---|---|
| CITIA | Cayman Islands Tax Information Authority |
| CPI | Consumer Price Index |
| CRPL | Confidential Relationships (Preservation) Law |
| CRS | Common Reporting Standard |
| CSX | Cayman Stock Exchange |
| CSP | Corporate Service Providers |
| CSPBA | Corporate Service Provider Business Act 2012 |
| CTITF | United Nations Counter-Terrorism Implementation Task Force |
| CTS | Common Transition System |
| DAR | Detailed Assessment Report |
| DEA | Drug Enforcement Administration |
| DITC | Department of International Tax Co-operation |
| DNFBP | Designated Non-Financial Businesses and Professions |
| DTT | Double Tax Treaties |
| EIA | External Insurance Act, 2009 |
| EOI | Exchange of Information |
| EOIR | Exchange of Information on Request |
| FATF | Financial Action Task Force |
| FCSPA | Financial and Corporate Services Providers Act |
| FDI | Foreign Direct Investment |
| FFI | Foreign Financial Institution |
| FIA | Financial Investigation Agency |
| FIU | Financial Intelligence Unit |
| FMSA | Financing and Money Services Act |
| FSC | Financial Services Commission |
| FSRB | FATF Style Regional Body |
| FTRA | Financial Transaction Reporting (Amendment) Act, 2014 |
| GDP | Gross Domestic Product |
| Global Forum | Global Forum on Transparency and Exchange of Information for Tax Purposes |
| GN | Guidance Notes on the Prevention and Detection of Money Laundering and Terrorist Financing |
| GNP | Gross National Product |
| GoB | Government of The Bahamas |
| GoCI | Government of the Cayman Islands |
| GoVI | Government of the Virgin Islands |
| HIRE | Hiring Incentives to Restore Employment Act |
| IBC | International Business Company |
| ICA | International Cooperation (Tax Information Exchange Agreements) Act 2005 |
| ICB | Insurance Commission of The Bahamas |
| ICIJ | International Consortium of Investigative Journalists |
| ICRG | International Co-operation Review Group |

| | |
|---|---|
| IFA | Investment Funds Act |
| IGA | Intergovernmental Agreements |
| ILS | Insurance Linked Securities |
| IMF | International Monetary Fund |
| IOSCO | International Organization of Securities Commissions |
| IRP | Incident Response Plan |
| IRS | International Revenue Service |
| ISIN | International Securities Identification Number |
| ITA | International Tax Authority |
| LDC | Limited Duration Company |
| LLC | Limited Liability Company |
| MAL | Monetary Authority Law |
| MCAA | Multilateral Competent Authority Agreement |
| MER | Mutual Evaluation Report |
| MLAT | Mutual Legal Assistance Treaty |
| MMOU | Multilateral Memorandum of Understanding |
| MOU | Memoranda of Understanding |
| MTA | Money Transmission Agent |
| MTB | Money Transfer Business |
| MVTS | Money or Value Transfer Service |
| NAMLC | National Anti-Money Laundering Committee |
| NC | Non-Compliant |
| NCCT | Non-Cooperative Countries and Territories |
| NFE | Non-Financial Entities |
| NPO | Non-Profit Organization |
| OAS | Organization of American States |
| OECD | Organization of Economic Cooperation and Development |
| OFC | Offshore Financial Centre |
| PC | Partially Compliant |
| PCCL | Proceeds of Criminal Conduct Law |
| PEP | Politically Exposed Person |
| POCL | Proceeds of Crime Law |
| PP | Percentage Point |
| PRG | Peer Review Group |
| PRP | Peer Review Process |
| PTC | Private Trust Company |
| PWC | PricewaterhouseCoopers |
| SAC | Segregated Account Company |
| SCB | Securities Commission of The Bahamas |
| SIA | Securities Industry Act, 2011 |
| SIBL | Securities Investment Business Law |
| SIR | Securities Industry Regulations, Act 2012 |
| SLoB | Statute Law of The Bahamas |

| | |
|---|---|
| SMART Fund | Specific Mandate Alternative Regulatory Test Fund |
| STR | Suspicious Transaction Reports |
| SXA | Stock Exchange Authority |
| TIA | Tax Information Authority |
| TIA Law | Tax Information Authority Law |
| TIEA | Tax Information Exchange Agreement |
| TIN | Tax Identification Number |
| TOR | Terms of Reference |
| UK | United Kingdom |
| UN | United Nations |
| UNDCP | United Nations International Drug Control Programme |
| UNODC | United Nations Office on Drugs and crime |
| US | United States |
| VAT | Value Added Tax |
| VISTA Trust | Virgin Islands Special Trust Act |
| WTO | World Trade Organization |

# List of Tables

CHAPTER 1

# Introduction

The proliferation of Offshore Financial Centres (OFCs) in the 1960s and 1970s in the Caribbean region did not happen by chance. The provision of offshore financial activities was for the most part strategically developed overtime and has become a key component for Caribbean economies. These countries, generally small economies, vulnerable to exogenous shocks, began developing initiatives in the agriculture sector and gradually shifted towards tourism, but its growth has been insufficient to maintain a sustainable gross national product per capita (Suss et al. 2002). The establishment of OFCs presents an alternative to achieve greater real growth (Suss et al. 2002). The economic benefits range from employment creation, increase spending within the local economy and a rise in government revenues (Suss et al. 2002), to positive growth in other sectors, such as tourism, construction, retail and wholesale trade, resulting in a more favourable climate for foreign direct investment (IMF 2017; Butkiewicz and Gordon 2013).

The rise in the offshore finance sector has concurred with and to a great degree has accelerated globalization as it exists today (Christensen and Kapoor 2004). Globalization and the adoption of economic policies by developed countries have resulted in the relaxation of exchange controls, deregulation of banks and technological changes, which allow



A. M. Campbell, *Money Laundering, Terrorist Financing, and Tax Evasion*, https://doi.org/10.1007/978-3-030-68876-9_1

funds to be transferred instantaneously around the globe. The role played mainly by OFCs is said to aid in facilitating the movement of capital around the global resulting in a higher degree of capital mobility. Their function in aiding global capital mobility is also perceived to be linked to certain risks including increased vulnerability of financial systems to sudden changes in international capital flows due to the transmission of banking and financial crisis. Additionally, given their unique characteristics, such as zero or low taxes on income, no withholding taxes and prevailing banking confidentiality provisions, in addition to their flexibility in the use of trusts and other product offerings, OFCs became increasingly popular in attracting capital not only from wealthy individuals and companies from onshore jurisdictions and developing countries in emerging markets, but their popularity is also said to have come about due to individuals seeking to exploit them to carry out criminal activities (Sikka 2003). Intricate corporate structures and a network of transactions, in addition to nominees and regulators unwilling to cooperate are noted to have become part of the investigative process undertaken to trace monies hidden in OFCs. Concerns regarding secrecy have been mentioned as the cause leading to increased difficulty in investigations and prosecutions due to the fact that most offshore havens are presumed to depend on international finance that values secrecy (Sikka 2003).

The movement associated with the war on drugs and the proceeds generated from narcotic trafficking during the early 1970s have led to an entire new industry to combat money laundering (Alldridge 2008). Concerns over money laundering have gradually evolved from dealing with drug-related crimes and bank regulations in the 1980s and early 1990s, to confronting organized crime in the financial sector and acquisitive crimes in the professional sector, to eventually dealing with terrorist financing in the early 2000s (Alldridge 2008). According to the IMF, the scale of transactions associated with money laundering is estimated to be between 2% and 5% of global GDP, which is equivalent to approximately $800 billion to $2 trillion US dollars per annum. Given its scale, the potential risks associated with money laundering at a micro-level are its ability to corrupt and destabilize markets and small economies. At a macro-level, its impact can result in: (i) sudden shifts in the demand for money; (ii) a higher level of risk to the soundness of banks; (iii) a negative impact on legitimate financial transactions; and (iv) a higher degree of volatility in the global flow of capital and foreign exchange rates as a result of cross-border asset transfers. Socially and politically, money laundering inflicts pain on its victims and leads to a deterioration in the social fabric of society.

Likewise, terrorism is said to be a serious threat to global peace and security and undermines their core values per the United Nations. Terrorism not only bears the high cost of human lives lost and the millions of persons who are affected by it, but its acts undermine the stability of governments and cripple their ability to provide economic and social development. Additionally, the continuous evolving methods used by terrorist groups make the threat of terrorism complex and difficult to deal with. Given that terrorist acts are global in nature, they require close collaboration of governments, regional and international organizations to work together to combat it.

According to the Financial Action Task Force (FATF), if left unmanaged, money laundering and terrorist financing can have negative economic impacts on businesses. They can also have negative effects on the economic development of financial centres in developing countries with ineffective anti-money laundering measures as they can be perceived as being strongly influenced by organized crime. This eventually over time can significantly hinder sustainable economic growth. It concludes that success in money laundering negatively affects the integrity of financial systems, democratic institutions and society at large, and undermines the very fabric of democracy and the rule of law.

International organizations such as United Nations and Organization of American States (OAS) have concluded that money laundering and terrorist financing originating from crimes considered to be serious in nature, undermine the principal soundness and strength of the financial sector and government systems throughout the world. In a testimony given before US Congress, the Deputy Secretary of the US Department of Treasury described the detrimental effects of money laundering and terrorism on foreign governments, the US financial system, its diplomatic relationships with foreign countries and its promotion of serious crimes, as a serious challenge that pose a severe threat to the US and the rest of the world (Schroeder 2001).

The economic liberalization of capital mobility cross-borders has also led to national tax systems grappling to protect their tax base from tax avoidance schemes undertaken by wealthy individuals and profit laundering activities carried out by transnational businesses (Christensen and Kapoor 2004). Tax competition has caused many governments to reduce tax rates on the income of non-residents, in an effort to entice portfolios and foreign direct investments per Christensen and Kapoor. Confronted with these dilemmas, governments in both developed and developing countries have taken recourse measures including reallocating their tax load from capital to labour, even though from the perspective of employment creation, this measure is considered regressive and also counter-productive. Additionally, in response to increasing fiscal pressures, many governments have not only gotten rid of and privatized services, but have also been quickly pulling back on their pledge of welfare provisions (Christensen and Kapoor 2004).

Although the World Trade Organization (WTO) has employed immense political pressure to follow through with the trade and fiscal liberalization of the Washington Consensus, there has not been enough political commitment to the redesign of international tax policies with regard to information exchange, as well as to the definition of the international tax base. This is said to have created opportunities for businesses to take advantage of existing legal vacuums between nation states through the use of mainly OFCs to carry out aggressive tax avoidance schemes including transfer pricing, re-invoicing, thin capitalization, special purpose vehicles, corporate inversions and the use of suspicious foundations, trusts and charitable entities (Christensen and Kapoor 2004). The *Panama Papers* highlighted the manipulative tax schemes and consequential damages to developing countries as well as to their domestic resources (Zaidi et al. 2017). The global money laundering and tax evasion schemes that were revealed as a result of the leak of the Panama Papers have led to mounting pressure surrounding mainly OFCs and brought to the forefront the urgent need to enhance transparency and due diligence (Zaidi et al. 2017).

Given the magnitude of financial transactions that pass through offshore jurisdictions has increased to such an extent, some authors argue that OFCs cannot be considered insignificant any longer to the global economy. It is a necessity solely on the basis of economic efficiency that offshore finance be subject to more transparency, effective scrutiny and regulation (Christensen and Kapoor 2004). According to these authors, in addition to techniques used to launder profits by transnational companies, most schemes associated with tax avoidance and tax evasion are purported to include the use of foundations, offshore trusts, charities, international business corporations, holding companies, special purpose vehicles and artificial transactions. The growth in tax avoidance schemes is viewed as having developed along with the use of tax competition as a means of enticing inward investments through the use of tax holidays, export processing zones, fiscal subsidies, accelerated depreciation rates and preferential tax terms (Christensen and Kapoor 2004). Offshore finance centres or tax havens are said to be deeply embedded in and represent a substantial portion of global capitalism, although they are not reflected in conventional economic analysis (Hampton 1996 as cited in Christensen and Kapoor 2004). The products offered by OFCs are viewed as conduits to facilitate the means by which transnational companies withdraw themselves in part or in whole from taxes and also from regulatory regimes that are nationally based. Offshore finance centres are regarded as providing transnational companies with a considerable tax advantage compared to their nationally based competitors. This competitive advantage is viewed as one which creates an uneven playing field, and as a result, it is perceived to give rise to market distortions (Christensen and Kapoor 2004).

Tax evasion has proven to be a multi-facet challenge for tax authorities and law enforcement officials. According to Tavares, tax evasion restricts the amount of revenue raised by countries, resulting in their inability to implement policies in key areas such as social, economic, cultural and other sectors of society. It also undermines a government's ability to promote welfare and social programs (Tavares 2013). It takes away from the integrity of democratic institutions and creates a feeling of distrust by citizens in their view of a democratic government. Tax evasion also promotes social inequality and widens the gap between wealthy and non-wealthy citizens, as it allows tax evaders to avoid their civic responsibilities while at the same time placing the tax burden on middle- and lower-class citizens.

Tax evasion also promotes participation in corrupt activities by financial institutions, authorities, politicians, etc., for their own benefit. For instance, to increase their profits, banks may be encouraged not to adhere to certain rules, and authorities may choose to overlook this error to increase their position of power. Finally, the asymmetries of tax rates and tax authorities among member states in the European Union help to facilitate tax evasion. Establishing a holding company in a jurisdiction which offers nil or nominal taxes, lite regulations and supervision, incentivizes corporations to participate in tax evasion. This unfair tax competition is harmful to such member states, particularly during periods of economic recession among certain member countries, as it substantially reduces the tax revenues they so desperately need (Tavares 2013).

The negative impacts that tax policies in one country can have on tax systems in other countries at both the corporate income and personal investment income levels have become a principal concern for G7 countries. Specifically, in situations where tax incentives are implemented by one country with the underlying objective to attract capital which composes the tax base of another country. Harmful tax competition overtime has proliferated the increase in harmful tax practices. Developing standards that are internationally recognized to combat harmful tax practices became of utmost importance to G7 countries, while at the same time providing leeway to allow countries to develop their own tax systems independently. Equally so, money laundering and terrorism have also become high on the agenda list of governments of the G7 countries.

Global intervention came in 1989 through the establishment of theFATF. Formed by the Ministers of the G7 Summit, the FATF objectives were to establish standards and promote the implementation of regulatory, legal and operational measures that are effective for countering money laundering, the financing of terrorism and other relevant threats posed to the integrity of the global financial system (FATF 2012). In this regard, the FATF Recommendations established a comprehensive framework of measures that are consistent for countries to adopt in order to counter money laundering and terrorist financing (FATF 2012). To support the national implementation of the FATF Recommendations and supplement its goals and objectives, the Basel Committee on Banking Supervision released its revised 2012 Basel Statement of Principles (an amendment of its 1988 original version), which consists of a set of guidelines for banks conducting business cross-borders to adhere to in order to combat money laundering and terrorist financing, and to protect and ensure the soundness of the global financial system (BIS 2017).

Global intervention for tax evasion came by way of the OECD, through its work carried out by the Global Forum on Transparency and Exchange of Information for Tax Purposes (the Global Forum). The Global Forum plays a key role in implementing the international standards set by the OECD for the Exchange of Information on Request (EOIR) and Automatic Exchange of Information (AEOI) via common reporting standard (CRS). Other policy initiatives were also instituted by the US, by way of Foreign Account Tax Compliance Act (FATCA), and the EU, via the EU Code of Conduct. These international agreed standards and national policies on tax transparency serve as the measure by which jurisdictions are assessed for compliance purposes. International cooperation by way of these rules on transparency and effective exchange of information has increasingly been relied upon by tax authorities worldwide over time. These two components are key elements to ensure that taxpayers at an individual and corporate level do not use tax havens to shelter their income and assets, and that correct taxes are paid in the relevant country (OECD 2016).

Consequently, these international policy initiatives pose important questions about the future of OFCs in the Caribbean region. Among them, questions related to the impact of global policy initiatives on the legal systems and institutions of OFCs, and the consequences of these international measures on the business of the offshore banking sector in OFCs, and inevitably on their local economies, are critical to the future of OFCs in the region. This book presents an overview of the four main OFCs in the Caribbean region. It discusses the problems and dimensions of money laundering, terrorist financing and tax evasion, and the international solutions to counter each of these phenomena. It will also examine the effects of these global policy initiatives on the legal systems and institutions, and offshore financial sector in The Bahamas, the Cayman Islands, Bermuda and the BVI. It also analyses the impact of the offshore financial sector on the domestic economies of these jurisdictions, and discusses the results of this investigation.

This book is based on my PhD thesis. The methodology used to compile the book is derived from the guidelines developed in collaboration with my PhD tutors during my research period at the Universidad de Salamanca. Our approach consisted of five steps. The first involved introducing the theme under discussion in a holistic manner, stating the problem, explaining the objectives of the research, its importance, the questions it aims to answer, and the methodology it will use to accomplish its objectives. The second step involved providing a comprehensive background overview of the financial systems of the four main offshore financial centres in the Caribbean. This includes a review of their profiles, an overview of their offshore financial industry and details of their AML/CFT framework and legislative regime to counter money laundering and tax evasion prior to 2000. In step three, a literature review is undertaken dealing with the issue of money laundering and terrorist financing, the challenges of dealing with both, taking into account the effects of globalization, and the incentives and responsibility of the international community to address these issues. A similar approach is undertaken to address the issue of tax evasion in a separate chapter.

In step four, an analytical assessment is conducted on the principal policy initiative against money laundering and terrorist financing, examining the following strategic tactics embedded in the Financial Action Task Force's Recommendations to: (i) compel national action to increase transparency; (ii) implement backstopping measures aimed at reinforcing national governance to prevent money laundering and terrorist financing; and (iii) apply additional measures to strengthen national institutions with a view to increasing international cooperation. This approach was also undertaken to address the international solution to tax evasion in a separate chapter. In step five, an in-depth analysis is conducted to assess the impact of this international policy initiative against money laundering and terrorist financing on the legislative systems and institutions of each of the four offshore financial centres in the Caribbean. The same approach is undertaken to evaluate the impact of policy measures against tax evasion on the legislative systems and institutions of these four offshore financial centres in a separate chapter. To conclude this research, a further analysis is conducted to examine the consequences of these policy initiatives on the offshore financial sector of each jurisdiction, looking at specific areas such as: (i) banking and fiduciary services; (ii) corporate services; (iii) securities and investment services; and (iv) insurance services. An additional analysis is undertaken to determine the impact of the offshore financial sector on the local economies of each jurisdiction. A further discussion is carried out to explain the results of this research findings, and lastly, conclusions are drawn based on the results of these findings.

This research is based on a qualitative analysis of the legal instruments and institutions implemented by these four jurisdictions in response to global policy initiatives, and on a comparative quantitative analysis on the consequences of these policy measures on the offshore banking sector in these four countries, and on their respective economies. To examine the legal instruments and institutions instituted by each jurisdiction in response to money laundering and terrorist financing policy measures, the period used for this analysis will be from 2007 to 2012, which coincides with the third mutual evaluation report (MER) conducted by the Caribbean Financial Action Task Force (CFATF) for each jurisdiction. The information used for this analysis includes the MERs published by the CFATF, literature produced by the FATF, along with the annual financial reports and special reviews published by the central banks and government institutions in each country. The MERs used in this analysis are the latest available for all four jurisdictions. Whereas for tax evasion, the period used for this analysis is from 2010 to 2016, which corresponds to the time when key international and national policy initiatives were introduced by the OECD, the Global Forum, the US and the EU. The information used for this analysis includes the peer review reports prepared by the OECD, literature published by the OECD, along with the annual financial reports and special reviews published by the central banks and government institutions in each country.

To conduct the analysis on the consequences of international policy initiatives against money laundering, terrorist financing and tax evasion on the offshore banking sector in each jurisdiction, the period used will be from 2011 to 2019 based on available data. This period was chosen because it falls outside the spillover effects of the 2008 financial crisis, it is also the most recently available data, and it incorporates the results of the impact stemming from the third MER, as well as the measures taken by each jurisdiction to satisfy the deficiencies highlighted in their respective reports. This period also takes into consideration the results of the impact deriving from policy initiatives instituted by the Global Forum, the OECD, the US and EU to counter tax evasion, and to a great degree, the results of the actions undertaken by each jurisdiction in response to these measures, given the recent occurrence of these events. The data used in this analysis will be obtained from the annual financial reports and special digests and reviews published by the central banks and various governing institutions in each country. The segments which will be examined include banking and fiduciary services, corporate services, securities and investment services, and insurance services.

A further quantitative analysis is also conducted to determine the effects of the offshore banking sector on the local economies of these jurisdictions. This is done by analysing the impact of the sector on critical data related to employment, spending by offshore operations within each local economy, and revenues generated by the governments of these countries from the offshore banking sector. The same period (2011–2019) is also used for this part of the analysis based on available data. Conclusions are drawn based on the results of this analysis.

## References


Alldridge, Peter. 2008. Money laundering and globalization. *Journal of Law and Society* 35 (4): 437–463.

Basle Committee on Bank Supervision. 2017. *Sound Management of Risks Related to Money Laundering and Financing of Terrorism*. Bank for International Settlements.

Butkiewicz, J., and L. Gordon. 2013. The Economic Growth Effect of Offshore Banking in Host Territories: Evidence from the Caribbean. *World Development* 44. https://doi.org/10.1016/j.worlddev.2012.09.017.

Christensen, John, and Sony Kapoor. 2004. Tax Avoidance, Tax Competition and Globalization: Making Tax System Justice a Focus for Global Activism. *Accountancy Business and the Public Interest* 3 (2): 1–16.

FATF. 2012. *International Standards on Combating Money Laundering and the Financing of Terrorism & Proliferation—The FATF Recommendations*. Financial Action Task Force. https://www.fatf-gafi.org/media/fatf/documents/recommendations/pdfs/FATF%20Recommendations%202012.pdf.

IMF. 2017. *The Bahamas Selected Issues*. IMF Country Report no. 17/315. International Monetary Fund. https://www.imf.org/.

OECD. 2016. *Exchange of Information on Request. Handbook for Peer Reviews 2016–2020*. OECD Publishing. https://www.oecd.org/tax/transparency/global-forum-handbook-2016.pdf.

Schroeder, William R. 2001. Money Laundering: A Global Threat and the International Community's Response. *FBI Law Enforcement Bulletin* 70 (5). https://www.coursehero.com/file/11601296/cj394laundering.

Sikka, Prem. 2003. The Role of Offshore Financial Centres in Globalization. *Accounting Forum* 27 (4): 365–399. https://doi.org/10.1046/j.1467-6303.2003.t01-2-00111.x.

Suss, Esther C., Oral H. Williams, and Mendis Chandima. 2002. *Caribbean Offshore Financial Centers: Past, Present, and Possibilities for the Future*. IMF Working Paper WP/02/88, International Monetary Fund. https://www.imf.org/external/pubs/ft/wp/2002/wp0288.pdf.

Tavares, Rui. 2013. *Relationship Between Money Laundering Tax Evasion and Tax Havens*. The Special Committee on Organised Crime, Corruption and Money Laundering (CRIM) 2012–2013. https://www.europarl.europa.eu/meetdocs/2009_2014/documents/crim/dv/tavares_ml_/tavares_ml_en.pdf.

Zaidi, Syed Haider Ali, Xin-Yu Wang, Sardar Ahmad, Tan-Xue Ping, and Meng Qi. 2017. Panama Papers and the Dilemma of Global Financial Transparency. *International Journal of Modern Research in Management* 1 (2): 18–35. http://www.ijournalmrm.com/article/12/panama-papers-and-the-dilemma-of-global-financial-transparency.

CHAPTER 2

# Offshore Financial Centres in the Caribbean

## 2.1 Part I: Introduction

The term Offshore Financial Centre (OFC) is synonym with the Caribbean. This is due in part, to the fact that a number of islands in the Caribbean have established themselves as some of the world's most attractive offshore jurisdictions offering prevailing banking confidentiality provisions, strong secrecy and anonymity provisions, and nil or nominal taxes to high net worth international clients (IMF 2017). Islands such as The Bahamas, the Cayman Islands, Bermuda and the British Virgin Islands (BVI) inter alia have developed their economies to such an extent that the offshore financial sector in these jurisdictions has become one of the principal contributors to their gross national product (IMF 2017; Damgaard et al. 2019). This sector overtime has proven successful for these islands as an alternative to agriculture, and as a means to diversify their economies (Saunders 2002 as cited in Butkiewicz and Gordon 2013) away from the tourism industry which traditionally has been the main economic stimulus for these islands for decades (Saunders 2002 as cited in Butkiewicz and Gordon 2013). The development of the offshore financial sector was a means to achieve greater real grow for these islands (Hines 2005 as cited in Butkiewicz and Gordon 2013; Suss et al. 2002). The



A. M. Campbell, *Money Laundering, Terrorist Financing, and Tax Evasion*, https://doi.org/10.1007/978-3-030-68876-9_2

economic benefits range from employment creation, increase spending within the local economy and a rise in government revenues (Suss et al. 2002), to positive growth in other sectors, such as tourism, construction, retail and wholesale trade, resulting in a more favourable climate overall for foreign direct investment (IMF 2017; Butkiewicz and Gordon 2013).

The increase in the offshore finance sector is viewed as having accelerated globalization to a large extent (Christensen and Kapoor 2004). As a result, financial centres located mainly in offshore jurisdictions are said to carry certain costs, which overtime have contributed to concerns raised by the international community. Among them is the role played mainly by these financial centres in increasing global capital mobility, and the perceived risks associated with it, including the exposure of financial systems to sudden shifts in international capital flows. These financial centres are also viewed as being susceptible to exploitation by criminals for their purported use in laundering money (Suss et al. 2002). This is due mainly to their peculiar characteristics, which have helped to define them as offshore financial centres (OFCs) (IMF 2000).Catapulted by the war on drugs, the proceeds generated from drug trafficking led to rampant money laundering, and eventually to terrorist financing through the use of financial institutions, which overtime became a major concern for the international community (Butkiewicz and Gordon 2013).

Another cost that is said to be associated with these OFCs is their attractiveness to wealthy individuals and companies alike from developed and developing countries for their purported use in facilitating tax evasion. The free flow of capital mobility cross-borders is viewed as attributing to increased tax avoidance schemes undertaken by wealthy individuals and transnational businesses to launder their profits (Christensen and Kapoor 2004). These undertakings are regarded as having contributed significantly to an increase in tax competition among developed countries, which consequently led many governments to reduce tax rates on non-residents income, in an effort to entice portfolios and increase foreign direct investments.

Given the magnitude of financial transactions which is reported to pass through mainly offshore jurisdictions, they have been the central focus of the international community in their fight to counter money laundering, terrorist financing and tax evasion. In this *chapter*, we will take a comprehensive look at the four main OFCs in the Caribbean region, namely The Bahamas, the Cayman Islands, Bermuda and the BVI. We will review their general profiles, offshore financial sectors and legislative frameworks implemented prior to 2000, to counter money laundering and tax evasion.

**Overview of Financial System**

## 2.2 The Bahamas

### *2.2.1 Background Information*

The Bahamas is comprised of roughly 700 islands, cays and inlets, located in the north-western part of the Atlantic Ocean. It extends approximately 760 miles from the north-west coast of Florida to the south-east near Haiti (The Government of The Bahamas [GoB] 2021). It has a total area surface of 5,358 square miles distributed across 100,000 square miles of ocean. About thirty of the islands are inhabited. The country's population is estimated at 377,000. Most of whom live on the islands of New providence and Grand Bahama (IMF 2019).

### *2.2.2 Government Structure and Legal System*

The islands became a self-governing nation when it achieved its independence from Great Britain on 10 July 1973. As a former British colony, the legal system in The Bahamas is based on English common law, and its political and legal traditions closely follow the Westminster model in the United Kingdom (IMF 2004). The nations' political system is comprised of a Governor General, Prime Minister, Parliament and Judiciary (GoB 2021). Upon its independence, The Bahamas gained membership as part of the Commonwealth of Nations. As a member, it acknowledges Queen Elizabeth II as its Head of State, who is represented locally by the Governor General.

The power of the government is held by the Cabinet, which is made up of at minimum nine Parliament Members, including the Prime Minister and the Attorney General. The Prime Minister acts as head of Cabinet and retains executive control. The Bahamas has a bicameral Parliament whose principal responsibility is legislative. It is comprised of a Senate which constitutes 16 representatives, and a House of Assembly, which consists of 38 representatives (GoB 2021). Each Parliament Member serves a five-year term.

The Bahamas' judiciary branch acts independent of the executive powers vested in the Prime Minister. It is made up of a Magistracy, a

Supreme Court and a Court of Appeals, whose jurisdiction, authority and powers are conferred by the Constitution. The jurisdiction's highest Court is Her Majesty's Privy Council located in England, where final appeals can be heard for judgements issued by its local Court of Appeals (GoB 2021).

#### 2.2.3 Domestic Economy

The Bahamian economy is highly concentrated on tourism and foreign direct investment (FDI). Tourism contributes approximately 45% to gross domestic product (GDP), whereas FDI represents an estimated 22% of GDP (IMF 2019). In 2018, real GDP was 1.6%, representing a 1.5% increase over 2017. This was supported in part by an increase in tourism and foreign investments in projects, which stimulated activities in the construction sector. Gross national product (GNP) was US$12.425 million, with GDP per capita of US$32,997 (IMF 2019).

There was a notable increase in the consumer price index (CPI) of 2.2%, as a result of a spike in value added tax (VAT) from 7.5 to 12% by the government on 1 July 2018. The country's unemployment rate slightly increased to 10.7% in 2018, which was 0.6% higher than the previous year due to the increase in labour force compared to job gains (Central Bank of The Bahamas [CBB]] 2019). Per the IMF, debt held by the central government increased to 63.3% of the country's GDP during the 2017/2018 fiscal year, up from 54.4% over the prior year. The Bahamas' external reserves decreased by $221.1 million, resulting in $1,196.3 million in reserves as of 31 December 2018 (Central Bank of The Bahamas 2019). The country's local currency remains fixed to the US dollar.

## 2.3 The Offshore Financial Sector in The Bahamas

#### 2.3.1 Market Structure

The Bahamas' offshore financial sector is the fourth largest in the world behind Hong Kong, Singapore and the Cayman Islands, respectively (IMF 2017). Several key factors have been instrumental in its success. The jurisdiction is strategically located near the main business and investment hubs of North America (the US and Canada), and close to those in

Latin America. The country has a stable political and economic climate, and a history of over 280 years of political democracy. Its legal system is established on English common law, which has aided in its stability (IMF 2004). The country adopts a tax-neutral stance, whereby taxes and gains originating within its jurisdiction are not taxed. The jurisdiction also retains a number of financial institutions which offer a wide selection of products and services ranging from private banking and trust services, investment advisory and investment fund administration services, to corporate, insurance, legal and ship registry services. The country also has modern facilities, good infrastructure and a highly educated domestic workforce (The Bahamas Financial Services Board [BFSB] 2019). It also complies with international standards established by the Organization of Economic Cooperation and Development (OECD), Financial Action Task Force (FATF) and Basel Committee on Banking Supervision inter alia.

The jurisdiction's offshore sector originated in the mid-1960s principally due to legislation enacted which provided for the provision of banking and trust services (IMF 2004). Since then, The Bahamas has progressively expanded its offshore legislation to allow for a number of products and services which can be grouped into the following main categories; banking and fiduciary services, corporate services, securities and investment services, and insurance services (IMF 2004).

### 2.3.2 *Banking and Fiduciary Sector*

The banking and fiduciary sector consists of domestic and foreign banks. The jurisdiction has 8 commercial banks which operate domestically. Of these banks, 3 are locally owned, four are Canadian banks and the remaining one is a US bank (CBB 2019). The commercial banking network is extensive with a total of 76 local branches spread throughout the jurisdiction. The Bahamas also has 231 banks and trust companies operating in the jurisdiction whose business activities are concentrated principally on international clients. Among them, 8 have been granted approval to provide fiduciary services to the local market (CBB 2019). The main business services offered to international clients include wealth management, private banking, trading, deposit taking and lending. Licenses granted to banks and trust companies include authorized dealers, authorized agents, residents, non-residents, public licenses, restricted licenses, nominee trust licenses and non-active licenses. Some of the trust products offered in the jurisdiction includes asset protection trusts, purpose trusts, voting trusts, pension trusts and charitable trusts. Additionally, the jurisdiction also offers foundations, executive entities, private trust companies and family offices to manage wealth (The Bahamas Investor 2017).

In 2018, the total number of banks and trusts licensed in the jurisdiction stood at 231 (CBB 2019). Of this segment, those that operated as both banks and trusts entities accounted for 54 licensees, whereas those operating only as banks or trusts accounted for 29 and 148 regulated entities, respectively (CBB 2012). Licensed banks and trusts operating physically in the jurisdiction were 219, and the remaining 12 licensees operated under approved restricted licenses. An estimated 43% of the jurisdiction's licensees originated from G-10 countries. Other entities listed in this segment include private trust companies or PTCs with 136 registered licensees, and licensed corporate service providers. Among those acting as registered representatives were an estimated 23, and those acting as non-licensed registered representatives were approximately 5. Additionally, in the non-bank business category, the total number of non-bank money transfer businesses (MTBs) stood at 5, non-bank money transmission agents (MTAs) 20, cooperative credit unions 10, and one retail payment service provider (CBB 2019).

### 2.3.3 Corporate Sector

Within this category, the jurisdiction offers the International Business Company (IBC) which is governed by the International Business Companies Act, 2000. An IBC provides the means for a corporate vehicle to be tailored to meet the specific demands of clients in asset management, business transactions and estate planning. The Act allows for IBCs to be incorporated as a limited duration company (LDC) which has a limited life of up to 30 years and must serve a specific purpose (The Bahamas Investor 2017). A LDC can also be organized as a partnership to allow profits and losses to be distributed proportionally to its members for tax purposes. IBCs can also be structured as a company limited by shares or guarantee or both, an unlimited company and a segregated account company (SAC), often referred as a protected cell company in other jurisdictions. A SAC establishes separate accounts to hold the assets and liabilities from those of other accounts and those of the company itself. IBCs can undertake legitimate business anywhere in the world and offer a wide range of applications to clients including their use as: a holding company, an investment fund, a shipping company, a captive insurance company, a private trust company, a family office and other applications such as a joint venture, a patent or an e-business (The Bahamas Investor 2017).

As of 31 December 2018, the registered number of financial and corporate service providers was 353 licensees. Of these licensees, 261 provided corporate services, 45 offered financial services and 47 operators provided both corporate and financial services (Securities Commissions of The Bahamas [SCB] 2019).

### *2.3.4 Securities and Investments Sector*

The securities sector in The Bahamas is regulated by the Securities Industry Act, 2011. The type of securities business allowed for under the Act includes: (i) conducting deals in securities, (ii) arranging deals in securities, (iii) management of securities and (iv) securities advising. To conduct specific kinds of securities business, registered firms must be licensed. Individuals are required to be licensed and may only carry out the securities activities that the firm has been granted approval to undertake. Individuals are allowed to register as representative for trading, discretionary management or advising. Investment funds in The Bahamas are governed by the 2003 Investment Funds Act (IFA). The Act provides for the following four classes of funds: (i) the Standard Fund, (ii) the Professional Fund, (iii) the Specific Mandate Alternative Regulatory Test Fund (SMART Fund) and (iv) the Recognized Foreign Fund. The Standard Fund is a modern investment structure created to function as a traditional collective investment vehicle. It is heavily regulated, and its offering is geared towards the general public. The Professional Fund is a different class designed specifically for highly skilled investors that are licensed with the local Securities Commission, and an approved administrator, to allow for a quicker turn-around time to launch. The SMART Fund provides for investment funds to be structured innovatively. The recognized Foreign Fund is one that is incorporated in a prescribed jurisdiction and is in good standing (Bahamas Financial Services Board 2020).

In 2018, the jurisdiction had a total of 157 securities investment firms, of which 32 held joint licenses with the Securities Commission of The Bahamas (SCB) and the Central Bank of The Bahamas (CBB). Investment funds as of the end of 2018 stood at 780. Of this total, Standard Funds accounted for 39 funds, Professional Funds for 230, Recognized Foreign Funds for 33 and SMART Funds for 478 funds (SCB 2019). At the end of 2018, the jurisdiction had a total of 63 fund administrators and 25 authorized representatives (SCB 2019).[1]

### 2.3.5 *Insurance Sector*

The insurance sector in The Bahamas is relatively less developed and has experienced limited success compared to Bermuda, the Cayman Islands and the British Virgin Islands. This sector is governed and regulated by the External Insurance Act, 2009 (The Bahamas Investor 2017). The Insurance Commission of The Bahamas issues licenses to external insurers and captives to operate in the jurisdiction. External insurers are entities domiciled in The Bahamas that are allowed to insure risks located outside of the jurisdiction. Captives are a type of self-insurance that is often used to spread risk within a company or among a group of entities. They provide an alternative means of protection for companies against insurable loss (The Bahamas Investor 2017). Captive insurers are classified as restricted and unrestricted licensees in accordance with the Act. Restricted licensees insure the risks belonging mainly to its members and related entities, whereas unrestricted licensees underwrite the risks of any person or entity. Captives may register as stand-alone insurance companies, segregated accounts companies (SAC) and as captive cells, also known as segregated accounts.

At the end of 2018, there was a total of 172 captive insurers licensees in the jurisdiction. Of these licensees, stand-alone insurance companies accounted for 11, SACs for 6 and segregated accounts stood at 155. On the other hand, unrestricted or non-captive insurer licensees accounted for 5 licensees. External intermediaries operating in this sector comprised of insurances managers and brokers, accounting for 10 and one, respectively (Insurance Commission of The Bahamas [ICB] 2019).

[1] Investment funds that are connected to The Bahamas but do not meet the requirements to be recognized as investment funds based in the jurisdiction are obligated to designate a representative approved by the Securities Commission.

### 2.3.6 Stock Market

Compared to other stock markets launched in Bermuda and the Cayman Islands, The Bahamas' stock exchange has not been very successful. Incorporated in September 1999, the exchange officially launched its services in the domestic market to list and trade local public companies in May 2000. As of 31 December 2018, The Bahamas International Securities Exchange (BISX) had a total of 51 listings, which comprised of 19 common shares with market capitalization of $4.48 billion, 13 preference shares with $327 million in market capitalization, and 19 bonds with a value of $579 million in face value (Securities Commission of The Bahamas 2019). Trading volume was 8.519 million in 2018 which had a market value of $41.832 million, compared to 5.128 million share volume valued at $44.596 million in 2017. The exchange's index closed at 2,109.45 in 2018 in comparison with 2,063.57 in 2017 (Securities Commission of The Bahamas 2019).

## 2.4 The AML/CFT Framework Prior to 2000 in The Bahamas

### 2.4.1 Transparency: Legal Systems and Institutional Measures

The Bahamas' legislative regime to prevent its financial system from being used to launder money comprises of legislations, directives and treaties. Its anti-money laundering regime commenced in 1987 with the enactment of the Tracing and Forfeiture of the Proceeds of Drug Trafficking. This piece of law contained provisions which provided for the proceeds connected to drug trafficking to be confiscated, confiscation orders to be enforced and investigations related to drug trafficking to be undertaken, inter alia (Atkins 1993). This legislation applied to proceeds related to money laundering and drug trafficking committed in the jurisdiction, as well as other jurisdictions. It also criminalized certain conducts committed by a person who entered into or was involved in possessing or retaining on another's behalf, drug trafficking proceeds through specific acts and its use for specific purposes. In order to hold a person legally accountable, one would have to know or suspect that a person conducted or had conducted drug trafficking, or had obtained benefits from such activity. The law also laid out sanction provisions providing for a person who is found guilty of such an offence to be liable for a period of 14 years' confinement or a $25,000 fine or both, for conviction on information, and 5 years of imprisonment or a $10,000 fine or both, for a summary conviction. Under the confiscation order, the recoverable amount was the sum determined by the court to be the value of the proceeds of drug trafficking belonging to the defendant (Atkins 1993).

Another measure implemented by the jurisdiction included becoming the first signatory to ratify the 1988 UN Convention Against the Illicit Trafficking of Narcotic Drugs in 1989 (The Bahamas Financial Services Board [BFSB] 2009), which aimed to improve international cooperation in combating narcotics. It also placed obligations on parties to enact laws to make money laundering a crime and implement forfeiture provisions on illicit drug proceeds and instrumentalities of drug trafficking (Gurule 1998). The Bahamas took steps to implement one of the key objectives of the Convention in 1996, when it introduced the Money Laundering (Proceeds of Crime) Act, which criminalized money laundering. This Act made provisions to: (i) counter the laundering of proceeds originating from illicit activity which included drug trafficking; and (ii) impose regulatory requirements on specific financial institutions. The Act also provided for penalties, corporate offences, the issuance of restraint orders and special warrants, and property forfeitures to be carried out on conviction.

Measures adopted by the jurisdiction to prevent money laundering came by way of the Association of International Banks and Trust Companies. Through its memorandum dated 15 August 1983, banks were mandated to report physical persons or entities that were non-account holders, which attempted to deposit cash above US$5,000, to the local Central Bank whose principal function was to act as licensor and supervisor of banks and trust companies in the jurisdiction.

Through the introduction of the Money Laundering (Proceeds of Crime) Act, 1996, supervisory authority for money laundering was designated to the Central Bank of The Bahamas, the Registrar of Insurance, the Gaming Board, the Securities Board, the Registrar of Companies, and the Treasurer (Statute Law of The Bahamas [SLoB] 1996b). The Money Laundering (Proceeds of Crime) Regulations introduced a number of requirements for business relationships, mandatory obligations for anti-money laundering systems and training, procedures to identify client relationships and transactions, including transactions carried out on behalf of others, as well as procedures for record keeping and internal reporting.

Another measure undertaken by the jurisdiction came by way of the issuance of a "Money Laundering Guidance Notes" by the Central Bank of The Bahamas in 1992. The issuance of this document is noted as the jurisdiction's first initiative to explicitly deal with money laundering, due to the fact that money laundering by itself was only recognized as a crime when it was connected to drug trafficking (Atkins 1993).

### 2.4.2 Preventive Measures

The Bahamas also implemented another measure which dealt with legislation related to suspicious transactions reporting, per Chapter 86 of the Tracing and Forfeiture of Proceeds of Drug Trafficking Act, 1987. Pursuant to the Act, bankers were given permission to inform authorities of transactions considered to be suspicious, without fear of retaliation or legal action brought against them by disgruntled clients due to the breach in confidentiality (Atkins 1993). The Act provided for reporting suspicious transactions to authorities by a banker privy to it. Failure to do so resulted in legal charges being brought against the individual.

### 2.4.3 National and International Cooperation

The jurisdiction also took measures to commence international cooperation in accordance with the 1988 UN Drug Convention, through the introduction of a Mutual Legal Assistance Treaty (MLAT) in conjunction with the US on 12 June 1987. The purpose of this treaty was to provide mutual assistance in relation to criminal matters (SLoB 1990a). The money laundering provision (Article 14) of the Treaty provided for either Party to advise the other of property, including money and vessels, used in committing a crime or obtained due to a crime, that was believed to be held in the other party's territory, to allow them to the extent permissible by law, to assist one another in proceedings related to forfeitures, restitutions, or fine collections (Atkins 1993). Additional measures were also undertaken by the jurisdiction through the signing of a MLAT with the United Kingdom (UK) in connection to investigations involving drug trafficking and confiscating proceeds related to drugs trafficking on 28 June 1988. Another MLAT was signed with Canada to provide mutual assistance in relation to criminal matters on 13 March 1990 (SLoB 1990a). The jurisdiction also became part of the Inter-American Drug Abuse Control Commission (CICAD) and began participation in the Caribbean Financial Action Task Force (CFATF) in 1990 (Atkins 1993). In 1999, the jurisdiction amended the Money Laundering (Proceeds of Crime) Act, 1996, to provide for external orders to be enforced as well.

## 2.5 The Legislative Regime to Counter Tax Evasion Prior to 2000 in The Bahamas

### *2.5.1 Transparency: Legal System and Institutional Measures*

Prior to 2000, measures taken by The Bahamas to counter tax evasion have not been evident. Rather, actions were carried out by the jurisdiction to enhance its confidentiality and anonymity provisions. Confidentiality is considered to be the foundation of The Bahamas' legacy as an offshore financial centre. As an independent country whose legal system is based on English common law, confidentiality was applied on the bases of Tournier v. National Provincial Bank and Union Bank of England (1924). According to the court, a bank was obligated to adhere to confidentiality with respect to the affairs of its customers' subject to the following: (i) where disclosure is required by law; (ii) where there is a public duty to disclose; (iii) where disclosure is required in the interest of the bank; and (iv) where consent (express or implied) is given by the customer for disclosure (Higgs & Johnson Counsel & Attorneys at Law 2013).

The jurisdiction took measures to further enhance its confidentiality provisions through the enactment of the Banks and Trust Companies Regulation Act in 1965. Section 10 of the Act made provisions for executive power to be exercised by the courts to determine the privacy, confidentiality and rights of an individual. It also allowed for the courts to have considerable jurisprudence when applications were presented to it on the basis of Section 10. The ability of the courts to defend the privacy and rights of an individual made the jurisdiction's secrecy rule robust.

Anonymity also played a key role in cementing the jurisdiction as a premier offshore centre. In 1989, the jurisdiction took further measures to strengthen its anonymity stance. This came by way of the passage of the IBC Act. The Act allowed for the issuance of bearer shares, the foregoing of reporting requirements and the maintenance of public records on the identity of officers, directors, shareholders and attorneys-in-fact. It also provided for the director(s) to be either an individual or corporate entity of any nationality. The anonymity element provided under the Act through these aforementioned provisions greatly enhanced the jurisdiction's secrecy rule.

### 2.5.2 *National and International Cooperation*

In terms of international cooperation, the first treaty signed by The Bahamas to provide mutual legal assistance took place during the late 1980s when the jurisdiction adopted a MLAT with US to assist in combating activities related to drugs (Atkins 1993) rather than tax evasion. This treaty came about as a result of pressure exerted by the US on the jurisdiction to sign a tax information exchange agreement (TIEA). Due to fears that such action would result in the diversion of investment from its jurisdiction to other jurisdictions with more stringent tax secrecy laws, The Bahamas was reluctant to do so. To avoid adopting a tax treaty, the jurisdiction took an official stance concluding that the detriment to its local economy that would result from signing a TIEA out weighted the benefits of implementing one. Instead, it channelled its efforts to providing international cooperation in combating the war on drugs.

## 2.6 The Cayman Islands

### 2.6.1 *Background Information*

The Cayman Islands are located in the western Caribbean about 277 miles south of Cuba, 460 miles southwest of Miami, Florida, and 310 miles north-west of Jamaica (Government of the Cayman Islands (GoCI) 2020). It consists of three islands, Grand Cayman, Cayman Brac and Little Cayman. George Town, the capital, is on the western shore of Grand Cayman Island and is the largest of the three islands with total area square miles of 76. It is 22 miles long and four miles in width. Its population is estimated at 65,813 (Government of the Cayman Islands Economics and Statistics Office 2019). Most of whom live on Grand Cayman Island.

### 2.6.2 *Government Structure and Legal System*

The Cayman Islands are an overseas territory of Great Britain with a parliamentary democracy which consists of a judicial branch, an executive branch and a legislative assembly. The judiciary is an independent body comprised of the Summary Court, the Grand Court, the Court of Appeals and the Privy Council. Its role is to carry out the law independent of the executive and legislative branches. Within its hierarchy, the Privy Council is the highest court where appeals coming out of the Court of Appeals are heard (GoCI 2020).

The executive branch or Cabinet assumes responsibility of formulating policy for the entire government, with the exception of special responsibilities retained by the Governor. It is made up of the Premier, 6 Ministers and 2 ex-officio non-voting members. The Premier is appointed by the Governor based on the recommendation made by the majority party's elected members of the Legislative Assembly, whereas the 6 Members are appointed based on the advice given to the Governor by the Premier (GoCI 2020).

The Cayman Islands' Legislative Assembly is unicameral with 21 Members. Two of whom, the Duty Governor is appointed by the Governor (GoCI 2020) based on instructions from Her Majesty and the Attorney General based on the recommendation of the Judicial and Legal Services Commission. Both are ex-officio non-voting members. The remaining 19 Members are elected. Each serves as a representative for one of the 19 constituencies on the islands for a four-year term period. The legal and regulatory system of the Cayman Islands is based on English common law.

### *2.6.3 Domestic Economy*

The largest contributor to the local economy in the Cayman Islands is the services sector which accounted for an estimated 89% of GDP at the end of 2018. Of this percent, the financial and insurance services segments accounted for 31% of GDP, and the business services segment which consists principally of accounting and legal services contributed 16% to GDP. Within the services sector, the hotel and restaurant segment grew by 5.1% as a result of a sharp increase in cruise ship arrivals of 11.1% and stay-overs by 10.7%. The financial and insurance segments increased by 2.0%, and the business services segment expanded by 4.4%.

According to the Economic and Statistics Office of the Government of the Cayman Islands, GDP was CI$4,304.4 million at the end of 2018, which represented a 0.3% increase over the previous year. As a result of this growth, income per capita was CI$66,817, which represented a 4.5% increase over 2017. Inflation expanded by 3.3% in 2018 due mainly to a rise in price on the global market for crude oil inter alia. The unemployment rate stood at 2.8% in 2018, compared to 4.9% in 2017. Unemployment were higher among permanent residents with the rights to work, and in the local Caymanian population compared to the non-Caymanian work force. At the end of 2018, the population had increase by 3.8% to 65,813.

## 2.7 The Offshore Financial Sector in the Cayman Islands

### *2.7.1 Market Structure*

The Cayman Islands is ranked as the third largest offshore financial sector in the world behind Hong Kong and Singapore (IMF 2017). A number of key factors have been instrumental to its success. Among them is the fact that the jurisdiction does not impose any kind of direct taxes. Exempted companies, as well as limited partnerships and unit trusts, can obtain approval from the Cayman Islands government for a preferential tax-free period for a minimum of 20 and 50 years, respectively (Mourant 2017). Another factor is that the Cayman Islands has no restrictions on exchange control, allowing for the free flow of funds in and out of the jurisdiction. The local currency is pegged to the US dollar which is freely accepted and spent locally. Additionally, the jurisdiction is an overseas British territory, with a historically stable government, and a legal system founded on English common law. Another added fact is that the Islands have a very low country risk rating and is home to 47 of the worlds' 50 most leading banks (Mourant 2017). The jurisdiction has a solid network of lawyers and houses all four major international accounting firms. It has many trust professionals and administrators providing specialized skills, and a group of investment professionals which covers its investment funds sector. Additionally, the Cayman Islands are in close proximity to the main business cities in the US and offer direct flights to other major international financial centres. The Islands lie in a central time zone, which allows the jurisdiction to conduct business across all continents. It also has excellent telecommunications and office facilities. Further, the jurisdiction adheres to the international standards established from the OECD, FATF and Basel Committee on Banking Supervision.

In addition to the above, the introduction of the Companies Law of 1960 was a significant piece of legislation which helped to establish the Cayman Islands as an offshore financial centre. The jurisdiction also inherited numerous international business relationships from Jamaica as a result of its independence from Great Britain in 1962, and again in 1967, when

The Bahamas elected its first black premier. Today, the Cayman Islands have evolved into one of the world's leading offshore financial centres and offer a variety of products and services to cater to the needs of high and ultra-net worth clients from around the world. These products and services are grouped into four main sectors. They include banking and fiduciary services, corporate services, securities and investments services, and insurance services.

### 2.7.2 *Banking and Fiduciary Sector*

In the banking and fiduciary sector, two types of bank licenses are permitted in the Cayman Islands pursuant to the Banks and Trust Companies Law (2013 Revision). They include category's A and B. Category A licensees are unrestricted domestic banks which conduct business domestically and internationally, whereas category B licensees are restricted to carrying out international banking and limited domestic business (Cayman Islands Monetary Authority [CIMA] 2017). Category A licensees offer banking and investment services, in addition to mutual funds. Most of the well-known U.S. banks also offer sweep accounts which pay clients higher interest rates through their offshore location. In addition to retail banking and structured finance products for the institutional market, some "A" licensees also provide corporate banking services for their own group. They carry out corporate investment activities for their parent entity, conduct private banking business and administer mutual funds. Category B licensees provide services primarily to clients located outside the Cayman Islands. These licensees are owned by North American, European, Asian and South American banks, including Latin American, the Caribbean and Cayman Island banks. They are either branches, subsidiaries, affiliates or private banks. These banks are allowed to accept deposits, make investments in assets or extend loans to residents of the Cayman Islands with certain exceptions. These banks also facilitate the movement of cash cross-border principally to group entities.

At the end of 2018, there were approximately 133 Banks and Trust Companies registered in the Cayman Islands. Of this number, 11 were licensees in Class A category and 122 in Class B. The regions which accounted for the most banks were Europe with 27, South America with 25, the Caribbean and Central America with 24, the US with 22, followed by Asia and Australia with 20, respectively. Trust companies accounted for 117 licensees in 2018. Among them, those with restricted licenses accounted for 60, compared to those with unrestricted licenses which accounted for 57. Assets held in the jurisdiction were approximately US$670.1 billion, whereas liabilities were US$671.5 billion (GoCI 2019).

### 2.7.3 *Corporate Sector*

The Cayman Islands offers two types of offshore companies. They include an exempted company and an ordinary non-resident company. Exempt companies are exempted from income taxes for a period of 20 years and include immunity of stamp duty on transactions such as the transfer of shares and property. A key feature of an exempted company is that it is restricted from engaging in business activities within the jurisdiction. It can only carry out business for the purpose in which it was licensed. An example of an exempted company is an IBC, which is the most popular entity in the Cayman Islands. It may be incorporated by one person and requires at least a single director and a shareholder. The company may have any number of directors of any nationality. Annual reports are not required by the government and can be kept in any location at the discretion of the company's shareholders. There is also no requirement for an IBC's list of shareholders to be provided to the government. It is required, however, to file an annual declaration confirming that all business activities will be conducted outside of the jurisdiction.

At the end of 2018, the number of registered companies in the Cayman Islands was 107,309. Of this amount, exempted companies accounted for 90,265, followed by resident companies with 6,840 licensees, foreign companies with 5,029, non-resident with 3,465 and limited liability companies with 1,710. New company registrants were approximately 16,326. Among them, exempted licensees accounted for 13,893, limited liability companies 928, foreign company licensees 761, resident companies 729, and non-resident companies 15. Partnerships registration at the end of 2018 was 26,381. Of this number, exempted partnerships accounted for 26,011, foreign partnerships for 349, and limited partnerships for 21 (GoCI 2019).

### 2.7.4 *Securities and Investments Sector*

The Cayman Islands securities sector consists of a stock exchange, investment intermediaries and mutual funds. The sector is governed by the

Securities Investment Business Law (SIBL). Securities range from shares, stocks, debentures, bonds, loan stocks, certificates of deposits, warrants, options, precious metals, futures, forwards, etc. Under the SIBL, regulated activities include dealing in securities, or the arrangement of deals in securities, and managing or advising on securities. Persons conducting securities business are required to be licensed pursuant to the SIBL except for those exempted in accordance with Schedule 3.

In the investment sector, the jurisdiction is known as a domicile for the majority of all hedge funds worldwide (CIMA 2020). Licenses granted in the jurisdiction can be restricted or unrestricted. Restricted licenses allow a licensee the ability to deal with specified funds, whereas unrestricted licenses permit the inclusion of all funds. Fund administrators can provide a variety of services including the provision of director and trustee services, general partner and transfer services, calculation of net asset values, and ensure compliance with regulatory rules. Additionally, fund administrators can provide back office services, including accounts preparation, and investment management services. Most of the funds formed in the Cayman Islands are either hedge fund or a similar type of fund with subscription of US$50,000 minimum. Private equity funds also known as closed-ended funds, and regulated master-feeder investment funds are also popular in the jurisdiction.

At the end of 2017, the number of securities licensees registered in the Cayman Islands was around 34, whereas the registration of excluded persons accounted for 2750. Securities licensees by type of activities included 16 broker/dealers, 20 securities managers, 20 securities advisors, 12 securities arrangers and 4 market makers. In the investment sector, as at the end of 2018, the jurisdiction had a total of 10,992 registered funds. Of this number, the registered category accounted for 7,654 funds, whereas master funds accounted for 2,946 funds (GoCI 2019).

### 2.7.5 *Insurance Sector*

The Cayman Islands is the world's second largest offshore captive domicile. Within this particular sector, the jurisdiction has developed a niche market in healthcare captives, specifically for non-profit agencies in the USA, and houses the largest number of these captives in the world (CIMA 2020). The arrangement is as such where the captive covers a large deductible on medical malpractice insurance. Under the original insurance contract, this reduces the cost of insuring this first layer of loss which may be equivalent to the total expected loss for the insured. The jurisdiction offers the following four types of insurance licenses: Class A, B, C and D. Class A licensees are domestic or external insurers who are permitted to conduct local insurance business or restricted reinsurance business as authorized by the Authority. Class B licensees are exempted insurers who are permitted to undertake insurance business, except for domestic business, with the following stipulations: (i) a minimum of 95% of the net premiums underwritten must derive from businesses related to the insurer's; (ii) more than 50% of the net premiums underwritten must come from businesses related to the insurer's; or (iii) up to 50% of the net premiums underwritten must derive from businesses related to the insurer's. Class C allows exempted insurers to undertake insurance business, including providing reinsurance arrangements in which their insurance obligation options are limited to their funding sources by which they are collateralized, or to the proceeds originating from such funding, including bond issues or those of other instruments, contracts pertaining to the differences, and alternative funding sources authorized by the Authority. However, Class D licensees are permitted to undertake reinsurance business and other business authorized by the Authority under their license.

At the end of 2018, the number of insurance licensees in the jurisdiction stood at 730. Of this number, captive licensees accounted for 703 and domestic licensees 27. North American companies accounted for 632 of all licensees. Among the 703 licensees, companies in the healthcare sector accounted for 227, workers' compensation 152, general liability 80, property 69, professional liability 59, and others 116. Premiums for captives were an estimated US$15.4 billion, while total assets were US$68.7 billion, representing a 24.6% and 12.5% increase respectively over the previous year (GoCI 2019).

### *2.7.6 Stock Market*

The Cayman Stock Exchange (CSX) was established in 1996. The exchange is owned by the government of the Cayman Islands and is regulated and supervised by the Stock Exchange Authority (SXA). The Exchange was initially established to provide a listing facility for specialist products in the jurisdiction, such as mutual funds and specialized debt securities. However, its capability was expanded to include derivatives, warrants, depositary receipts, euro bonds, preferred shares and international equities. The CSX currently lists approximately 4,000 securities with an estimated market capitalization of US$190 billion (Macdonald 2018).

At the end of 2018, the number of stocks listed on the stock exchange was 1,699. Of this number, specialist debt securities accounted for 1,128, sovereign debt securities 293, mutual funds 224, insurance-linked securities 47, and primary equities, retail debt securities, and secondary equities with 4, 2 and 1, respectively. Market capitalization was a record US$310.2 billion, of which specialist debt securities accounted for US$190.4 billion, sovereign debt securities US$100.4 billion, mutual funds US$11.5 billion, and insurance-linked securities US$6.1 billion inter alia (GoCI 2019).

## 2.8 The AML/CFT Framework Prior to 2000 in the Cayman Islands

### *2.8.1 Transparency: Legal System and Institutional Measures*

Commencement of the anti-money laundering framework was observed in the Cayman Islands in 1989 with the introduction of the Misuse of Drugs Law, which dealt with the movement of the proceeds of drugs. The jurisdiction initiated measures to strengthen its anti-money laundering regime through the enactment of the Proceeds of Criminal Conduct Law (PCCL), 1996. This piece of law was essentially an all-crimes law based on the 1993 Criminal Justice Act of the United Kingdom (Mourant 2017). The PCCL was a careful balance between the legitimate privacy rights of a person and adhering to transparency requirements and disclosures in conquering crimes in the interest of the public. It made provisions for local restraint and confiscation orders, which allowed for the freezing of assets during an investigation, and their confiscation on conviction. It also introduced provisions to dissuade local assistance of any kind by a third party, extending liability beyond the individual who conducted the predicate crime, and addressed the enforcement of orders received from other jurisdictions.

The PCCL also made provisions for an application to be presented to the Grand Court for a restraining order to be placed on criminal proceeds during investigation, and inevitably for the confiscation of such property. In addition, it also provided for the registration of confiscation orders originating from certain foreign countries in the Cayman Islands, and the enforcement of such orders by the Grand Court. Additionally, it introduced a dual criminality requirement to its all-crimes provision, whereby a predicate offence committed in a foreign country must be similar to an offence recognized in the Cayman Islands. Pursuant to the PCCL, a criminal conduct was one that constituted an offence applicable by its law or that constituted an offence if it was committed in the Cayman Islands. The purpose of the PCCL was to strengthen the law dealing with the confiscation of crime proceeds in relation to mutual assistance provided in criminal matters. It also aimed to broaden confiscation orders and the power to enforce such orders in foreign jurisdictions.

### 2.8.2 Preventive Measures

Another aspect that the PCCL dealt with was reporting obligations and disclosure practice related to suspicious transactions which formed part of the Criminal Justice Act of the UK. It made failure to report any suspicion that a financial service provider may have had regarding a client which had engaged in or had benefited from criminal activities, a criminal offence.

### 2.8.3 National and International Cooperation

Evidence of the jurisdiction's initial agreement to the provision of mutual legal assistance in international cooperation came by way of the 1984 narcotics treaty with the US, and later in 1986, a similar treaty was signed with Canada and the US. Both agreements were based on the provision of mutual legal assistance in combating the war on drugs and other crimes conducted via the Cayman Islands. On 8 February 1995, the provisions of the 1988 UN Drug Convention became applicable in the Cayman Islands by way of the UK which became signatory to the Convention on 20 December 1988 (UN Treaty Collection 2020). One of the main elements of this Convention obligated parties to implement local legislation to enhance international cooperation to counter narcotic trafficking (Gurule 1998).

## 2.9 The Legislative Framework to Counter Tax Evasion Prior to 2000 in the Cayman Islands

### 2.9.1 *Transparency: Legal System and International Measures*

Similar to The Bahamas, prior to 2000 measures taken by the Cayman Islands to counter tax evasion have not been evident. Rather, actions were carried out by the jurisdiction to enhance its secrecy or confidentiality provisions. Confidentiality laws were the cornerstone of the jurisdiction's regulatory framework which promoted financial crimes such as money laundering and tax evasion in the Cayman Islands. The basis of its confidentiality laws is found in its history as a British colony, and in the 1924 Tournier vs. National Provincial and Union Bank of England case, which established the confidentiality duty of bankers. The jurisdiction took measures to strengthen its confidentiality position through the introduction of the 1960 Companies Law which created a corporate veil between the beneficial owner and the company which owned the assets. This gave way to the legal separation of the assets and the protection of the name of the beneficial owner through the use of a nominee. The Companies Law provided for an exempted company to issue bearer shares whose share certificate did not include the name of the owner, as the owner is considered the holder of the certificate. It also allowed an exempted company to register as a limited duration company and obtain preferential tax treatment in other countries (US Government Accountability Office [GAO] 2008).

The jurisdiction took a number of additional measures to further enhance its confidentiality stance. It based its Trust Law 1967 on the principles of the English Trustee Act 1925, which imposed the common law duty of confidentiality and has been codified into Cayman Island law (Kearns 2011). In the case of a trust, the trustee ("professional person") has a duty to the Settlor ("Principal") not to divulge confidential information obtained during the normal course of conducting business with respect to all property (Lee 1998). The jurisdiction also included confidentiality provisions in its 1966 Banks and Trust Companies Regulations Law. It further strengthened its confidentiality stance through the enactment of the 1976 Confidential Relationships (Preservation) Law (CRPL) which was applicable to business of a professional nature originating in or brought to the jurisdiction, and to any individual obtaining confidential information thereafter whether such individual is within the Cayman Islands or out of the jurisdiction (Lee 1998). The CRPL also introduced civil and criminal penalties for breach of confidentiality. It provided for disclosure of a criminal offence to be punishable by a CI$2000 fine and/or one-year imprisonment. The 1979 Amendment of the CRPL broadened its confidentiality provisions to include people other than the Inspector of Banks and Trust Companies, and increased the punishment for disclosure to CI$5000 and/or 2 years' imprisonment. In certain instances, confidentiality could be breached by specified methods, although the circumstances were narrower when CRPL did not apply (Lee 1998).

### 2.9.2 *National and International Cooperation*

On the international cooperation front, in July 1986, a MLAT was executed between the US and UK governments, including the Cayman Islands Government, for the US and Cayman Islands to render legal assistance to each other in criminal matters. However, the caveat was that the criminal matter had to pertain to activities other than imposing, calculating or collecting taxes, or it had to be punishable by incarceration for at minimum one year. Such alleged activities where assistance could be provided included: (i) obtaining assets, whether wilfully or dishonestly, through fraudulent means with regard to the benefits accessible through tax laws, or (ii) falsifying statements, whether wilfully or dishonestly, pertaining to tax matters regarding the illicit proceeds connected to the criminal offence. Legal assistance included the provision of recording testimony of persons, furnishing documents or evidence, finding and holding persons in custody, carrying out searches and seizures, including freezing assets. Further assistance extended to the proceeds forfeited in relation to the criminal offence, restitution payments made to the victim and the collection of fines, if one party had grounds to believe that the proceeds related to the criminal offence were situated in the jurisdiction of the other party (GAO 2008). Request for assistance had to come from the US Attorney General or his appointed designee, and the Cayman Mutual Legal Assistance Authority. The enactment of the Mutual Legal Assistance (United States of America) Law (1999 Revision) provided for the Cayman Islands to render immediate legal assistance shortly after September 1986.

Another measure taken by the jurisdiction to foster international cooperation took place in 1997, when it enacted what is now known as the Criminal Justice (International Cooperation) Law (2004 Revision). This piece of legislation allowed the jurisdiction to render legal assistance of a similar nature to a large number of countries throughout the world. Under this law, mutual legal assistance was provided if the conduct was a criminal offence pursuant to Cayman Islands law, or if it would had been deemed a criminal offence if it had taken place in the Cayman Islands. Legal assistance provided by the jurisdiction included statement taking, issuing documents, conducting searches and seizures, furnishing documents and evidence, identifying and analysing objects and sites, asset freezing, and assist in forfeiture and restitution proceedings (GAO 2008).

## 2.10 Conclusion

This concludes part I of this chapter. In part II, Bermuda and the British Virgin Islands will be discussed. Specifically, a review of their general profiles, offshore financial sectors and legislative frameworks instituted by each jurisdiction prior to 2000, to counter money laundering and tax evasion will be undertaken. Conclusions will be made at the end of part II.

## 2.11 Part II: Introduction

Similar to The Bahamas and the Cayman Islands, Bermuda and the BVI have also developed their offshore financial sectors over time to the point where they have become main contributors to their GDPs (IMF 2017; Damgaard et al. 2019). These islands have experienced similar economic benefits in terms of job creation, increase government revenues (Suss et al. 2002), and positive spillover effects in other sectors of their economies including tourism, wholesale and retail trade, and enhanced opportunities for foreign direct investment (IMF 2017; Butkiewicz and Gordon 2013). However, the perceived costs associated with OFCs, particularly with respect to the purported role they play in facilitating financial crimes, led to growing concerns in the international community. This resulted in these OFCs becoming the central focus in the international fight to tackle money laundering, terrorist financing and tax evasion. Like the other two jurisdictions, Bermuda and BVI were also impacted by international policy initiatives which eventually came about as a result of these concerns. In this chapter, a review of the general profiles, offshore financial sectors and legislative frameworks implemented prior to 2000, to counter money laundering and tax evasion, is undertaken for Bermuda and the BVI.

## 2.12 Bermuda

### *2.12.1 Background Information*

Bermuda is a group of small islands located in the north-western part of the Atlantic Ocean. It is about 600 miles of the eastern coast of the United States and 900 miles north of the Caribbean. The country consists of 6 main islands connected by bridges and 120 others. It is divided into nine parishes, each of which is around 2.3 square miles. Of its parishes, Pembroke is home to the largest population share, which is estimated at 17%. It is also where the capital Hamilton is located. The islands cover about 21 square miles in total land area and have a population of approximately 63,917 residents (Government of Bermuda Department of Statistics 2016).

### *2.12.2 Government Structure and Legal System*

Bermuda's structure of government is derived from the UK's Westminster Model which is based on parliamentary democracy. Its government is comprised of a legislative branch, a judiciary branch and an executive branch (Government of Bermuda Ministry of Finance 2019). Its legislative branch consists of the House of Assembly and the Senate. The House of Assemble is made up of 36 members who are elected during the general election to represent each of the 36 constituencies. The senate consists of 11 members, all of whom are appointed by the Governor. Of the 11 members, 5 represent the governing party and are recommended by the governing party's Premier, 3 are from the official opposition and are recommended by the official opposition's leader, and the remaining 3 are independent members elected by the Governor. The three principal functions of the legislative branch consist of the passing of laws, the provision of means by way of taxation to carry out the work of the government, and the close monitoring the policies, administration and expenditure proposals of the government (Government of Bermuda Ministry of Finance 2019).

The government is formed by the political party who wins the majority of constituencies during the general election or who garners the support of most of the members who make up the House of Assembly. The political party with the largest minority forms the official opposition.

The Judiciary is an independent branch of the Bermuda Government. It consists of the Magistrates' Court, the Supreme Court and the Court of Appeal. Its main functions include: adjudicate charges related to criminal conduct, determine disputes, protect individual's rights and freedoms, and uphold the rule of law (Government of Bermuda Ministry of Finance 2019).

The executive branch of the government is comprised of the Governor and the Cabinet. The Governor, under the advice of the British Prime Minister, is appointed by the Queen. His primary responsibility is to preserve the Constitution of Bermuda and carry out the duties assigned to him by the Queen or subsequently by her ministers. The Cabinet is made up of the Premier and at minimum 6 elected members of Parliament. The majority leader of the House of Assembly is appointed by the Governor as Premier, and the members of the Cabinet are nominated by the Premier. The Cabinet's main role is to make the principal decisions to run the country. Its functions include making final decisions on policies, ultimate control of the government, and coordinating the various government departments. The decisions made by the Cabinet are acted upon unanimously by its members (Government of Bermuda Ministry of Finance 2019).

### *2.12.3 Domestic Economy*

Bermuda's economy is more diversified compared to The Bahamas, the Cayman Islands and the BVI, with 18 industry groups contributing to its GDP. In 2018, Bermuda's economy experienced a slight increase in real GDP of 0.1%. Nominal GDP was an estimated $6.5 billion, up from $6.269 billion reported in the previous year.[2] GDP per capital was an estimated $95,520 at the end of 2017 (Government of Bermuda Ministry of Finance 2019). Of the 18 industry groups, construction and quarrying division rose by 14.0% ($33.9 million), and International Business contributed the highest to GDP with a growth of 25.2% ($24.7 million) (Government of Bermuda Department of Statistics 2019a). The country's tourism sector also increased by 15.9% in cruise ship arrivals and by 4.6% in air visitors. In the construction and quarrying group, the value added was attributed to an increase in construction activity related to residential improvements, airport expansion and hotel development. In the

[2] Bermuda's GDP was rebased from 2006 to 2013 for the purpose of capturing changes in prices and using current economic data. This exercise was done with the help of the Caribbean Regional Technical Assistance Centre.

international business group,[3] growth was noted in the reinsurance and insurance underwriting services.

In terms of employment, Bermuda's total number of filled jobs rose by 0.4% (151 new jobs) to 33,810 in 2018. Its unemployment rate fell by 1.0% to 6.0% in 2018. Employment income decreased by 0.6% during the first nine months of 2018. The biggest decline was observed in the international business division, which decreased by 3.9% (Government of Bermuda Ministry of Finance 2019). Bermuda's CPI was 1.4% at the end of 2018, representing a decline of 0.5% over the previous year. The country has a credit rating of A+ on long-term sovereign credit, A+ on senior unsecured debt ratings, A–1 on short-term rating, and a AA+ on transfer and convertibility assessment by Standard and Poor (Government of Bermuda Ministry of Finance 2019).[4]

## 2.13 The Offshore Financial Sector in Bermuda

### *2.13.1 Market Structure*

Bermuda is recognized as one of the primer jurisdictions in the world for insurance and reinsurance products. The jurisdiction's location near the eastern boarders of the United States, and its proximity to Canada and Europe, has been advantageous for it. As a result of this, it has been able to build strong economic ties with regulators and business communities in these countries and has attracted many clients to its jurisdiction. Its ties with Britain as an overseas territory also plays a key role in its strong economic relationship with the UK. As a result of this relationship, it has bolstered investors' confidence in the jurisdiction, and in particular, in its legal and judiciary system. Furthermore, thanks to its relationship with the UK, its relationship with other European countries has also flourished.

Additionally, Bermuda's legal system is based on English common law and its courts date back to 1616. Like other British Overseas Territories, it has recourse to the UK's Judicial Committee of the Privy Council. Bermuda is also a politically stable country modelled after the Westminster parliamentary democracy. It is also a tax-neutral jurisdiction where no

[3] The international business group consists of businesses involved in insurance risk-taking and insurance brokerage services.

[4] Ministerial Statement given by the Hon. Curtis Dickinson, JP, MP, Minister of Finance at the House of Assembly on 13 December 2019, in Hamilton, Bermuda.

income taxes, corporate taxes, withholding taxes or capital gains tax are imposed. Bermuda has daily flight connections from the USA, Canada and Great Britain. Its time zone is four hours behind Greenwich mean time and one hour ahead of the US East Coast time, which allows this jurisdiction to easily conduct business to accommodate international clients located in different time zones. Bermuda's specialized concentration in the insurance and reinsurance industry lends itself to a high level of concentrated, professionally skilled workforce, which is very attractive to companies and international clients interested in doing business in the jurisdiction. The country also has modern telecommunication systems, secure broadband, and a very sophisticated electronic stock exchange.

Since its early days after it enacted the American International Company Limited Act in 1947, business in the jurisdiction has grown significantly. Today, Bermuda has an international flare which makes it a very attractive place to conduct business, and it offers a diverse range of products and services which are grouped into the four categories detailed below.

### *2.13.2 Banking and Fiduciary Sector*

Bermuda's banking and fiduciary sector is small compared to that of other jurisdictions such as The Bahamas and the Cayman Islands. The jurisdiction has 4 registered banks, which mainly conducts commercial business. Fiduciary services in Bermuda is governed by the Trusts (Regulation of Trust Business) Act 2001. Trust business is defined under the Act as the services provided by a trustee in the form of a trade, business, vocation or profession (Bermuda Monetary Authority [BMA] 2020). The jurisdiction issues two types of trust licenses, an unlimited license and a limited license. The unlimited license provides for trust business to be conducted by the licensee and for such business to be solicited from the general public. However, with the limited license, the licensee is not permitted to act in the capacity of sole trustee and is restricted to holding up to $30 million in trust assets, unless a higher amount is approved by the Bermuda Monetary Authority (BMA 2020). Unlimited licenses can be issued to exempted companies, companies with permits to operate in and from Bermuda, partnerships, exempted partnerships, overseas partnerships authorized to conduct business in and from Bermuda, and by individuals or unincorporated entities carrying out trust business in or from Bermuda. At the end of 2018, the total number of licensed banks in Bermuda remained at 4, total trust licensees were 27, and new private trust company licenses issued were 11 (BMA 2019).

### 2.13.3 Corporate Sector

In the corporate sector, Bermuda offers two types of companies, exempted and non-exempted companies. Exempted companies are those formed in Bermuda by non-Bermudians to carryout business outside the jurisdiction. They are exempted from specific sections of the Company Act 1982, which requires equity of at minimum 60% to be beneficially owned by its citizens (BMA 2019). They are generally restricted from conducting business within the jurisdiction unless they obtain special authorization from the Minister of Finance to do so, and are also exempted from certain activities. Non-exempted companies are those incorporated in the Jurisdiction by Bermudians for the purpose of trading within Bermuda. A limited company, limited liability company (LLC) and partnership are the most common forms of registered business. With limited companies, the personal finances of the shareholder(s) are separate from that of the business. Such companies can also have a single shareholder. Limited liability companies are similar to limited companies with respect to the separation of personal and business finances, and also to a partnership as an agreement is used by its members to carry out the affairs of the LLC. They can take the form of an exempt or non-exempt company. Partnerships operate pursuant to a partnership agreement. They can be formed as an exempt or non-exempt company, and can take the form of limited or general partnerships. The number of applications approved for companies at the end of 2018 was 745 entities. Overseas companies permitted to conduct business in or from Bermuda were 32, exempted partnerships accounted for 217, and overseas partnership accounted for one (BMA 2019).[5]

### 2.13.4 Securities and Investments Sector

Investment business in Bermuda is defined as "engaging in one or more investment activities by way of business". Investment activity includes dealing in investments, the arrangement of deals in investments,

[5] According to BMA, local company application approvals are included in the data provided. Local limited by Guarantee accounted for 60 and LLCs 40 approvals.

managing investments, providing investment advice, and administering and safeguarding investments. Persons conducting investment business in Bermuda or from the jurisdiction as defined by the Investment Business Act, 2003, are required to be licensed unless an exemption of such license is authorized by the BMA in accordance with the Investment Business (Exemptions) Order 2004.

Investment funds in Bermuda are governed by the Investment Funds Act 2006. Investment funds are investment vehicles which are pooled. They are organized as mutual funds companies, partnership funds, unit trusts or limited liability company funds. Structures that satisfy the investment fund definition must seek approval from the BMA to be authorized or registered. Authorized funds are classified as institutional funds, administered funds, specified jurisdiction funds and standard funds (BMA 2019). Institutional funds are tailored towards sophisticated investors and are limited to qualified participants with a minimum capital investment of $100,000. Administered funds are licensed pursuant to Part III of the Act and require a minimum investment of $50,000 or a listing on a stock exchange endorsed by the BMA per Section 11 of the Act. Specified jurisdiction funds are those which are recognize by Order of the Minister of Finance, the foreign jurisdiction that the fund operates in and its established law or set of laws that apply to the fund. Standard funds are open to retail investors and are subject to meeting more stringent regulatory and supervisory requirements.

Registered funds are categorized as private funds, whereas professional funds are classified as Class A funds and Class B funds. Funds are classified as private pursuant to the Act provided that; (i) there are up to 20 participants at most, and (ii) the fund does not invite or induce the general public by promoting itself. Class A exempt funds are required to complete a self-certification by meeting certain stipulations per subsection 6A(2) of the Act.[6] Class B exempt funds are those that are open to participants who are qualified and can be exempted from stipulations for authorization by meeting the qualification requirements detailed in subsection 7(2) of the Act.

The total number of investment funds in Bermuda at the end of 2018 was 533 (BMA 2019). Institutional funds were the most popular with 264 funds, followed by standard funds with 146, and Class A exempt

[6] Class A exempt funds are required to be open to participants who are qualified, and an investment manager must be appointed by the fund operator within certain stipulations.

funds with 64. Class B exempt funds had a total of 39 funds, and administered funds with 6 funds overall. In terms of insurance-linked securities (ILSs), 125 new ILSs were listed at the end of 2018, which had a nominal value of $11.2 billion. The total number of ILSs was 302 with $30.9 billion in total nominal value. The total international debt listed was 201 securities, which represented a 20% increase over 2017. Nominal value was $7.0 billion compared to $4.6 billion in the previous year. The aggregate total in asset under management of licensees in the jurisdiction was $US172.1 billion (Bermuda Monetary Authority [BMA] 2019). A significant portion of these assets were derived from clients in the European Union (70%) and Bermuda (21%).

### 2.13.5 *Insurance Sector*

Bermuda is considered to be the global leader in the reinsurance market. It is also recognized as a preferred domicile for captive insurance in the world. The jurisdiction offers a number of different classes of captive insures, long-term life insurances and special purpose insurers. A captive is an insurance company that is closely-held, whose principal insurance business is provided and controlled by its shareholders. They are classified into the three following categories: Class 1, 2, 3, 3A and 3B (BMA 2019). Class 1 is a single-captive that insures the risks of its parent or affiliates. Class 2 is a multi-owner captive which insures the risk of its parent or affiliates, or is a single-parent or multi-owner captive which writes up to 20% of unrelated business. Class 3 insures above 20% and below 50% of unrelated business. Class 3A and Class 3B are small and large commercial insurers which insure unrelated business of 50% or more with net premiums of less than $50 million, and in the case of Class 3B, more than $50 million.[7] Class 4 are large commercial type insurers and reinsurers which insure property catastrophe and/or direct excess liability reinsurance risk, with the same capital maintenance requirement as Class 3A and 3B.

[7] Class 3A and Class 3B are required to maintain capital the greater of: (a) a risk-based minimum capital that is calibrated to a grade of 99% Tail Value-at-Risk during a time horizon of one year, (b) $1,000,000, (c) net premiums equivalent to 20% for the initial $6 million written during the financial period and of the excess 15% and (d) net loss provisions equal to 15%.

Bermuda offers Long-Term (Life Insurance) in five different classes: Class A, B, C, D and E. Class A is a long-term single-parent captive insurance firm which insures its parents' and affiliates' long-term business-related risk (BMA 2019). Class B is a long-term multi-owner captive which is owned by unrelated companies, which insures its parents' and affiliates' long-term business-related risks and/or risks associated with or emerging from its parents' and affiliates' businesses or operations (BMA 2019). A long-term captive is a single-parent or multi-owner, which insures up to 20% of unrelated risk. Class C is a long-term insurer or reinsurer with less than $250 million in total assets, and is not registrable as an insurer under Class A or Class B.[8] Class D is a long-term insurer or reinsurer with $250 million or more in total assets and less than $500,000, and is not registrable as an insurer under Class A or Class B.[9] Class E is a long-term insurer or reinsurer with above $500 million in total assets and is not registrable as an insurer under Class A or Class B.[10] In terms of special purpose insurers (SPIs), these insurers underwrite insurance or reinsurance risks, and their risk exposures are fully collateralized. At the end of 2018, the total number of licenses in the jurisdiction was 1,198 (BMA 2019). Class 2, 3, 1 and SPIs were among the most popular with 273, 228, 218, and 133 licenses, respectively. Among the domicile of captive owners, 468 were from North America, 109 from Europe, and 70 from Bermuda. Whereas, among the domicile for commercial insurers and reinsurers owner's licensees, North America accounted for 158, Bermuda 170, and Europe 80 (BMA 2019).

[8] Class C is required to maintain capital the greater of: (a) a risk-based minimum capital that is calibrated to a grade of 99% Tail Value-at-Risk during a time horizon of one year, (b) $500,000 and (c) total assets of 1.5% less the balance(s) of all segregated accounts.

[9] A Class D insurer is required to maintain capital the greater of: (a) a risk-based minimum capital that is calibrated to a grade of 99% Tail Value-at-Risk during a time horizon of one year, (b) $4,000,000 and (c) total assets of 2.0% less the balance(s) of all segregated accounts for initial assets equivalent to $250 million and of 1.5% for total assets above $250 million.

[10] A Class E insurer is required to maintain capital the greater of: (a) a risk-based minimum capital that is calibrated to a grade of 99% Tail Value-at-Risk during a time horizon of one year, (b) $8,000,000 and (c) total assets of 2.0% less the balance(s) of all segregated accounts for initial assets equivalent to $500 million and of 1.5% for total assets above $500 million.

#### *2.13.6 Stock Exchange*

The Bermuda Stock Exchange (BSX) is primarily a domestic equities market. It is an automated exchange that provides trading, settlement and depository services electronically. Its platform is modernized and capable of supporting trades and settlements in the secondary market. The BSX is the world's largest offshore, fully electronic securities market, offering a full range of listing and trading opportunities for international and domestic issuers of equities, debts, depository receipts, insurance securitization and derivative warrants. In 1993, it expanded its offerings to include listings of institutional investment vehicles such as offshore funds, hedge funds, specialist debts and restricted marketing equities. BSX has more than 650 listed issuers, including 300 or more funds, and over 70 insurance-linked securities.

At the end of 2018, the total market capitalization was \$351 billion, of which \$2.4 billion originated from the domestic market (BMA 2019). The total volume of trading was 3.9 million shares which was equivalent in value to \$49.7 million, compared to 3.8 million shares with value of \$40.1 million in the previous year (BMA 2019). The index closed at the end of 2018 at 1,958.99, which represents a decline of 11% over the previous year. The total number of securities listed was 988, in comparison with 867 in the prior year (BMA 2019).

## 2.14 The AML/CFT Framework Prior to 2000 in Bermuda

### *2.14.1 Transparency: Legal System and Institutional Measures*

Similar to the Cayman Islands, commencement of the anti-money laundering framework was observed in Bermuda on 8 February 1995, when provisions of the 1988 UN Drug Convention became applicable in the jurisdiction by way of the United Kingdom, which became signatory to the Convention on 20 December 1988 (UN Treaty Collection 2020). The jurisdiction began implementing measures to enhance its framework to combat money laundering through the introduction of the Proceeds of Crime Act 1997, which came into force on 19 January 1998. This Act made provisions for money laundering to be criminalize (BMA 2020). It also empowered the police and courts to trace and confiscate the proceeds of drug trafficking including other relevant offences. These offences were defined as all indictable offences or all omissions or acts that would be deemed an indictable offence, except for drug trafficking, if it had taken place in Bermuda. The Act also extended seizure and forfeiture powers to the police on the import or export of suspicious proceeds of crime (Faries and Adderley 2012).

In cases where reasonable grounds were suspected for money laundering, the investigative powers of the police provided for production orders and search warrants to be obtained. Orders granting access to customer information could also be issued against certain institutions (Faries and Adderley 2012). Other key provisions provided for the annulment of agreements made for money laundering purposes; the granting of authority to the court for instrumentalities related to a money laundering offence to be forfeited; empowering the police with authority to freeze funds during a seven-day period (Faries and Adderley 2012); broadening the role of the National Anti-Money Laundering Committee (NAMLC); and authorizing the Minister of Justice to set regulations to detect and prevent money laundering after consulting with the NAMLC (BMA 2020).

### *2.14.2 Preventive Measures*

Where risks associated with money laundering were identified, the Proceeds of Crime Act 1997 also empowered the Minister of Justice to obligate regulated licensees to carry out certain actions pertaining to anti-money laundering and anti-terrorist financing. Such actions included undertaking customer's due diligence measures, continual monitoring, and reporting requirements or restricting or ceasing business (Faries and Adderley 2012).

### *2.14.3 National and International Cooperation*

On 8 February 1995, the provisions of the 1988 UN Drug Convention became applicable in Bermuda by way of the United Kingdom which became signatory to the Convention on 20 December 1988 (UN Treaty Collection 2020). One of the main elements of the Convention obligated parties to implement local legislation to enhance international cooperation to counter narcotic trafficking (Gurule 1998). The jurisdiction took measures to foster international cooperation through the enactment of the Criminal Justice (International Co-operation) (Bermuda) Act 1994, the Proceeds of Crime Act 1997 and the Proceeds of Crime (Designated

Countries and Territories) Order 1998, in addition to other relevant mutual legal assistance treaties (GoB 2020). Where no such treaties exist, the jurisdiction assists in international cooperation on a reciprocal basis. It provides legal assistance in criminal matters with regard to requests related to taking evidence, service processes, searches and seizures, enforcement of confiscation orders from foreign jurisdictions, requests related to the attendance of persons and custody of persons in transit, and assistance in securing production orders (GoB 2020).

## 2.15 The Legislative Framework to Counter Tax Evasion Prior to 2000 in Bermuda

### 2.15.1 *Transparency: Legal System and Institutional Measures*

Bermuda's efforts to counter tax evasion began with the enactment of the Taxes Management Act 1976. Although the Act included criminal tax evasion as an offence, its application was constrained to the narrow tax groups detailed in Section 2.[11] These groups excluded taxes based on income/profit, the basis upon which most taxation in a large number of countries outside of Bermuda was based (Bermuda's National Anti-Money Laundering Committee [NAMLC] 2017). Section 37 of the Act was later repealed and replaced with Section 37 of the Taxes Management Amendment Act 1999, mainly to reduce the punitive fines in parts 1 and 2 of Section 31 pertaining the criminal tax evasion (Taxes Management Amendment Act 1999). The Proceeds of Crime Act 1997 did not capture foreign tax crimes as part of the predicate offences for money laundering in the jurisdiction, which created a significant gap in its anti-money laundering regime, as the proceeds of money laundering derived from taxes were considered to be diverted to international offshore financial centres (Bermuda's National Anti-Money Laundering Committee 2017). An implication which the jurisdiction faced due to its scope of predicates for money laundering at that time was that money laundering derived from taxes which originated in another country and brought to Bermuda would not be deemed as money laundering once the proceeds entered the financial system in Bermuda. This therefore made the jurisdiction very

[11] The tax groups listed in Section 2 included employment tax, betting duty, contracts exchange tax, hospital levy, hotel occupancy tax, transport infrastructure tax, passenger departure tax, payroll tax, timesharing occupancy tax and timesharing services tax.

attractive for the purpose of laundering the proceeds deriving from tax crimes which occurred in foreign countries.

Confidentiality played a very important aspect in Bermuda's position as an offshore financial centre. The principles of confidentiality in Bermuda were founded on that of England which was based on the 1924 Tournier vs. National Provincial and Union Bank of England case, which established the confidentiality duty of bankers. Statutory provisions undertaken in Bermuda provided for disclosure requirements where trusts and companies were concerned, by way of the Trusts (Special Provisions) Act 1989, and in the case of purpose trusts, disclosure was possible where a mandatory enforcer was given similar rights to information as those held by the beneficiaries. The Companies Act 1981 also provides for disclosure where company ownership is concerned, requiring the registers of shareholders, officers and directors to be made available in Bermuda at the company's registered office. Additionally, the Trust Companies Act 1991 makes provision for an order issued by the Supreme Court to have effect over any secrecy obligations to give access to the Minister of Finance or the BMA to examine the records and books of trust companies licensed in Bermuda.

### *2.15.2 National and International Cooperation*

Bermuda participates in international cooperation pursuant to the provisions contained in the Criminal Justice (International Co-operation) (Bermuda) Act, 1994,, the Proceeds of Crime Act, 1997, and the Proceeds of Crime (Designated Countries and Territories) Order, 1998,, in addition to other relevant mutual legal assistance treaties (GoB 2020). Where no such treaties exist, the jurisdiction assists in international cooperation on a reciprocal basis. It provides legal assistance in criminal matters with regard to requests related to taking evidence, service processes, searches and seizures, enforcement of confiscation orders from foreign jurisdictions, requests related to the attendance of persons and custody of persons in transit, and assistance in securing production orders (GoB 2020).

Bermuda's efforts to forge international cooperation came by way of the USA—Bermuda Tax Convention Act 1986, enacted on 29 August 1986, which came into force on 2 December 1988 (Conyers Dill & Pearman 2013). The Convention pertained to taxation on insurance companies and the provision of mutual assistance in matters related to tax. The scope of the Convention included US federal income taxes levied by the Code, with the exception of taxes on accumulated earnings and personal holding companies, and excise taxes connected to insurance business. Under the Convention, payment of insurance premiums, including those credited as paid, during the period of 1 January 1986 and 31 December 1989, to a Bermuda qualified insurance company was exempted from excise taxes in the US. This exemption ceased on 31 December 1989 in accordance with the reservation provisions of the Convention (Conyers Dill & Pearman 2013). The Convention also provided for tax exemption on business profits originating from the insurance business of a Bermuda qualified insurance company in the US, provided that such company did not conduct or had not conducted business by way of a permanent establishment in the US. In cases where insurance business is undertaken in the US through a permanent establishment, the profits derived from that insurance company allocated to the permanent establishment were subject to US taxes. The Convention gave effect to profits originating in taxable years commencing on 1 January 1988 or after (Conyers Dill & Pearman 2013).

## 2.16 The British Virgin Island

### *2.16.1 Background Information*

The Virgin Islands, also referred to as the British Virgin Islands (BVI), are a small group of approximately sixty islands, cays and islets. The BVI is located in the eastern Caribbean several miles to the east of the US Virgin Islands, bounded by the North Atlantic Ocean and the Caribbean Sea. Of all the islands, 16 are inhabited. The total land area of the country is 151 kilometres. The main islands are Tortola, Anegada, Virgin Gorda and Jost Van Dyke islands (Pickering 1987). Of these four islands, Tortola is the largest and most populated with around 24,000 people out of the entire population, which is estimated at 30,000 people (Debono et al. 2017). It is home to Road Town the capital, which is the main centre of activities for tourism, trade, financial, administrative and judicial services.

### *2.16.2 Government Structure and Legal System*

The BVI is an overseas territory of the United Kingdom and has a similar system of government to the Westminster model. In accordance with its Constitution Order 2007, the government consists of an executive branch, and a legislative and judicial branch (Government of the Virgin Islands [GoVI] 2020). The Governor acts as head of state and represents the queen. The executive branch consists of the Premier, Ministers and the Attorney General, who together form the Cabinet. The Cabinet is divided into two types of government, the Cabinet and the Executive Council. The Cabinet's principal function is policy making and ensuring the implementation of such policies on the islands. The Cabinet Office is a separate office within the government and is headed by the Cabinet Secretary. The Cabinet grants power to the government which provides for local political power. The Executive Council on the other hand acts in an advisory capacity to the Governor. In this role, Ministers provide the Governor with advice on items to be added to the agenda, and on decisions made by the Executive Council. Sole authority of decision-making is fully vested in the Governor (GoVI 2020).

The legislative branch consists of the House of Assembly elected Ministers and Her Majesty. Jurisdiction over the islands is held by the Eastern Caribbean Supreme Court. The Constitution provides for a number of local commissions designated to public service, teaching service, judicial and legal services, and police service, and for advice regarding appointments to positions in such commissions. The Constitution also provides for the formation of a National Security Council and a Director of Public Prosecutions office (GoVI 2020). Other offices provided for include an office for public finance, a Register of Interests, and a Complaints Commissioner.

The judicial branch is comprised of the Magistrate's Court, the Supreme Court (High Court), the Court of Appeals and the Privy Council. The Magistrate's Court has the lowest jurisdiction on the islands and deals primarily with criminal matters (summary jurisdiction), civil claims (minor), and certain matters related to family law. Decisions made by the Magistrate can be appealed directly to the Court of Appeals. The BVI's Supreme Court is the Eastern Caribbean Supreme Court which has unlimited jurisdiction within the territory. The Eastern Caribbean Supreme Court's Commercial division sits in the BVI and hears cases with a minimum value of US$500,000. Civil procedures are regulated in accordance with the rules of the Supreme Court (GoVI 2020). Appeals from the Magistrate's Court and the Supreme Court are made to the Court of Appeals of the Eastern Caribbean Supreme Court. It rotates through its nine member states and sits in the BVI twice annually. The Privy

Council represents the United Kingdom's highest courts for Commonwealth countries that are independent, crown dependencies or overseas territories of Great Britain, such as the BVI.

### *2.16.3 Domestic Economy*

The BVI's economy is highly concentrated in tourism and financial services, which together accounts for approximately 50% of the country's GDP (Debono et al. 2017). In 2018, the island's GDP increased by 2.3% following the destruction caused by two hurricanes in 2017 (Caribbean Development Bank [CDB] 2018). This growth was driven by increased activity in construction, tourism and financial services. Growth in the construction sector was attributed mainly to recovery efforts related to both hurricanes. Although an increase was observed in the tourism market due to the reopening of several properties and visits by major cruise ships, the total number of stay-overs and passenger arrivals was lower compared to the previous year. In the financial services industry, the increase was attributed mainly to a 16% growth in the number of new incorporations, even though company registrations for limited partnerships were higher. In terms of the country's GDP per capita, the United Nations estimated it at US$48,511 in 2014 (United Nations data 2020).

Inflation increased to 2.1% at the end of 2018, with notable price increases in housing and utilities, food, communications, and transportation (CDB 2018). Overall, the BVI Government improved its fiscal position with an overall surplus equivalent to 1.2% of GDP. Total revenues increased by 27% driven by receipts in the offshore financial segment and increases in taxes on hotel accommodations, fees for work and cruising permits, and taxes related to the environmental/tourism initiative all initiated by the BVI Government in 2017, in addition to an increase fee in financial services in January 2018. In 2018, the BVI's balance in its Reserved Fund increased to US$70 million, due to a contribution of US$13.1 million by the BVI Government derived from fiscal surplus (CDB 2018). On the other hand, at the end of 2018, debt of the Central Government increased from 10.4% in the previous year to 12.5%.

The jurisdiction labour market also exhibited strong growth, with an unemployment rate of 2.8% at the end of 2017.[12] The labour market is

[12] Unemployment data was not available for 2018.

estimated at 20,000 with a high percent of foreign workers (Debono et al. 2017).

## 2.17 The Offshore Financial Sector in the BVI

### *2.17.1 Market Structure*

The BVI is recognized as one of the primer offshore financial centres in the world. Unlike The Bahamas, the Cayman Islands and Bermuda where location has a strong influence in the role these offshore centres play in international business, location does not play an important role for the BVI. Emphasis has been placed on the jurisdiction's strong regulatory structure, the entrepreneurial nature of its business community, and the commitment of the BVI's government to the development of modern legislation have all contributed to building its reputation as a leading offshore financial centre. The jurisdiction has a well-established professional corporate framework. The partnership between the government and private sector is very strong and contributes to an environment conducive for business. The BVI offers efficient service to incorporate and register IBCs, and for the provision of ancillary services such as nominee directors and shareholder services among others.

The jurisdiction is also a politically and economically stable country with a trustworthy, reliable legal system founded on English common law. Although it is an Overseas British Territory, its local legislature is independent from the UK. The territory has very modern statutes dealing with company law, insolvency, banking law, trust law and insurance law. It continually updates its laws through judicial precedent to remain competitive in the offshore financial services industry. The BVI also offers a very attractive tax-neutral environment for international clients. IBCs are exempt from certain duties such as income taxes and stamp duties, as opposed to domestic companies. There are no capital gains taxes, inheritance taxes, gift taxes, sales taxes, including value added taxes and exchange controls.

Although the offshore sector in the BVI dates back to 1976, it was the enactment of its 1984 International Business Companies Act that transformed the jurisdiction's legislative landscape and propelled it to the world's stage to become a preferred jurisdiction for incorporating IBCs. Today, the BVI offers a variety of products and services which are grouped into the four categories noted below.

## 2.18 Banking and Fiduciary Sector

The BVI has a small banking sector which consists of approximately five main commercial banks and one private bank. Commercial banks offer several types of services, including small business financing, project financing and individual consumer mortgages, whereas the private bank offers private and trust services to local and international clients. The BVI is known as one of the premier jurisdictions for trusts in the world due to its unique legislation governing trusts (McKenzie 2014). Its trust products include the Virgin Islands Special Trust Act (VISTA Trust) and Non-Charitable purpose trusts. The VISTA Trust is a special BVI trust provided for through the enactment of the Virgin Islands Special Trusts Act, designed to solve the "prudent man of business rule" with respect to investing and managing the assets of a trust. Non-Charitable purpose trust or a "purpose trust," is a trust created under section 84A of the BVI's Trustee Act for a purpose that is specific, possible and reasonable. It is not immoral, unlawful or goes against public policy. A trustee must meet the "designated person" criteria by definition, and there must be an enforcer and an alternative enforcer to act when necessary, who is appointed by the trust instrument or has consented to act in writing (McKenzie 2014). A non-charitable purpose trust can also benefit an individual and can be perpetual.

In the BVI, there are licensed trustees and private trust companies. Licensed trustees hold an unrestricted trust license and offer a full range of trustee services in the jurisdiction. However, private trust companies, also referred to as "PTCs", are unlicensed and must comply with a number of onerous conditions to conduct business in the territory. The jurisdiction also offers a range of services such as the establishment and administration of trusts, trustee services provisions, and preparation of trust financial accounts.

At the end of 2018, the jurisdiction had a total of 177 fiduciary services licensees. Of these licensees, 60 were Class 1 trust licensees, 54 were restricted Class II trust licensees, 22 were Class II trust licensees, and 18 were Class III trust licensees inter alia. The total number of PTCs registered in the jurisdiction as on 31 December 2018 was 1,115 (BVI FSC Statistical Bulletin 2018b).

### *2.18.1 Corporate Sector*

The BVI has a thriving corporate services sector. It is recognized as the foremost jurisdiction for incorporating companies in the world. The BVI business company is often used in structuring investments and private wealth structures. The International Business Companies Act of 1984, which made provisions for the BVI business company, was amended in 2004 to include additional provisions to allow for the BVI business company to be used more effectively as a transactional vehicle. A BVI Business Company can be incorporated in various forms including a company limited by shares, by guarantee, or as an unlimited company. A company limited by guarantee and an unlimited company both are given the option to be authorized to issue shares or not. A BVI Business Company can also be incorporated as a segregated portfolio company or as a restricted company.

IBCs are mostly used as holding companies for assets such as shares, trust property and other effects. They are exempt from certain duties including inter alia, holding annual shareholder's meetings, publicly maintaining certain records (including a registry of shareholders) and from taxes on income, stamp duties or other taxes. Low registration and license fees, coupled with an exceptionally efficient registration system, and a low reputational risk, all contribute to the significant growth of this sector. At the end of 2017, the total number of BVI business companies incorporated in the BVI was 32,493 (BVI Financial Services Commission 2018a). The total number of business companies registered at the end of December 2018 was 402,907 (BVI FSC Statistical Bulletin 2018b). The total number of other business companies registered for the same period was 1,115 private trust companies, 95 segregated portfolio companies, 60 foreign companies, 31 non-profit organizations, 17 restricted purpose companies, and 2001 continuations.

### *2.18.2 Securities and Investments Sector*

The BVI Financial Commission is responsible for regulating the securities sector in the jurisdiction pursuant to the Securities and Investment Business Act, 2010. In this capacity, the Commission powers include licensing, dealing or arranging deals in investments, providing investment management including the management of mutual funds, segregated portfolios, insurance products, pension schemes, other kinds of investments, etc., providing investment advice, which includes or excludes advice related to mutual funds, acting as custodians for investments, which includes or excludes advice related to mutual funds, and administering investments which includes or excludes advice related to mutual funds (BVI Financial Services Commission 2018a).

The BVI is one of the leading offshore jurisdictions for regulated investment funds in the world. Through the enactment of the Securities and Investment Business Act, and its amendment in 2010, and the introduction of its Mutual Funds Regulations, which was repealed and replaced by the Mutual Funds Act, and its amendment in 1996, the BVI has created the legal framework to conduct investment funds business. The jurisdiction offers professional funds, private funds, public funds, incubator funds and approved funds. Professional funds are mutual funds whose shares are available to professional investors only and require a minimum investment of US$100,000 or in any equivalent currency. Private funds are mutual funds with at most fifty investors, or where the shares issued are purchased or subscribed to privately by invitation per the constitutional documents. A public fund as deemed by the Financial Services Commission (FSC) is one which satisfies the Commission's requirements under the Securities and Investment Business Act, 2010, the Public Funds Code, 2010, and relevant practice of the FSC inter alia and can be a BVI business company or a unit trust based in the jurisdiction and governed by BVI trust laws. Incubator funds are those targeted at managers which may not have access to seed investment capital, require quick set up, minimal costs and less stringent regulatory obligations. They are allowed to operate for a period of two years and do not require functionaries, or an auditor, but must remain within the thresholds of the fund. Approved funds are geared towards managers who want to set up a fund as an offering to private investors on the basis of close connections, for a longer term. They are required to adhere to relevant thresholds and do not need to appoint a manager, auditor or a custodian, other than an administrator.

At the end of 2017, there were 4,099 professional funds, 1,386 private funds, 196 public funds, 24 foreign funds, 134 incubator funds and 193 approved funds licensed in the BVI (BVI Financial Services Commission 2018b). The total number of new funds registered as of 31 December 2018 included 955 professional funds, 329 private funds, 44 public funds, 6 foreign funds, 66 incubator funds, and 98 approved funds.

### 2.18.3 *Insurance Sector*

The BVI has developed a reputation as a recognized domicile for captive insurance. A large majority of captive insurers are established to insure US-based risks and are certified by the Internal Revenue Service in the US under the relevant U.S. tax laws. Captive Insurers are not allowed to underwrite third-party insurance on a direct basis. The insurance premia of a single-parent captive is typically under US$500,000 due to the exemption requirements of the US Risk Retention Act. A small percentage of captives have an in-house business in property casualty with premia that exceeds US$1 million.

The jurisdiction offers two types of licenses for captives: category C and category D. Category C licenses are granted to BVI business companies to conduct non-domestic insurance business, including reinsurance with the exception of open market reinsurance. Category D is also granted to BVI business companies and is entitled to carry out reinsurance business, as well as open market reinsurance. The jurisdiction stipulates a statutory requirement of minimum capitalization to be maintained at all times in cash or its equivalent. For business engaged in long-term insurance, the minimum capitalization is US$200,000, and in all other cases, including captive insurers providing property and casualty services, a minimum capitalization of US$100,000 is required. At the end of 2017, the number of captive licensees in the BVI was 111 (BVI Financial Services Commission 2018b).

### 2.18.4 *Stock Exchange*

In term of a stock exchange, the BVI does not have an established stock market in place. However, it allows for its IBCs to be traded on other international stock exchanges once an international securities identification number (ISIN) is obtained.

## 2.19 The AML/CFT Framework Prior to 2000 in the BVI

### 2.19.1 *Transparency: Legal System and Institutional Measures*

The anti-money laundering framework commenced in the BVI on 8 February 1995, when provisions of the 1988 UN Drug Convention became applicable in the jurisdiction by way of the United Kingdom, which became signatory to the Convention on 20 December 1988 (UN Treaty Collection 2020). The jurisdiction began adopting measures to enhance its anti-money laundering framework through the enactment of the Proceeds of Criminal Conduct Act, 1997, which is considered to be its all-crimes anti-money laundering law (BVI Financial Services Commission 2013). Its purpose was to deter money laundering of all forms in the territory. The Act defined criminal conduct as an act which: (i) comprised an offence that was applicable to the Act, or (ii) would be deemed an offence in the jurisdiction if it had taken place there. The Act applied to all indictable offences with the exception of drug trafficking. It was therefore applicable to the proceeds deriving from any action which constituted, or would have if taken place in the BVI, an indictable offence pursuant to BVI law (Harneys 2000).

### 2.19.2 Preventive Measures

The jurisdiction also introduced a Code of Practice in 1999. The Code sets out the definition for "regulated persons" and stipulated certain rules that must be followed when establishing a business relationship or conducting one-off transactions with a person or on behalf of a person. The Code details the following procedures that should be adhered to: (i) identification process; (ii) record keeping process; (iii) internal reporting process; and (iv) internal controls and adequate procedures for communication aimed at forestalling and suppressing money laundering (Harneys 2000). The Code also requires regulated persons to take requisite measures to make staff aware of the details of the aforementioned procedures, as well as the provisions pertaining to the Act and the Regulations supplemental to it, in addition to the Code and all relevant directives made thereunder from time to time. The Code places obligation on regulated persons to carry out employee training to assist them in: (i) identifying and dealing with transactions performed by or for any person engaged in money laundering or appears to be; and (ii) in handling customers in cases where such transactions were reported to the relevant authorities pursuant to the Act.

The Code places a duty on relevant persons to: (i) submit to the Reporting Authority the procedures related to the identification, recording keeping, internal reporting, internal control and communication processes, copies of which may also be retained by the Reporting Authority; and (ii) appoint an employee as a compliance officer, who will act as a senior officer and has the appropriate qualification and experience, and whose appointment is authorized by the Director of Financial Services. The Code also grants the Director of Financial Services or an individual designed by him in writing, to carry out inspections or relevant persons to assess compliance of such person in accordance with the Code as well as any law or directive pertaining to money laundering. Failure to adhere to the provisions of the Code, or any law and directive pertaining to money laundering, was considered an offence subject to a fine of up to US$5,000 on summary conviction, and on indictment, up to US$10,000 for the initial offence, and up to US$15,000 for the second or successive offence (Harneys 2000).

### *2.19.3 National and International Cooperation*

The BVI initiated measures to commence international cooperation through the enactment of the Evidence (Proceedings in Foreign Jurisdictions) Act, 1988, which brought into effect the terms of the UN Convention on the Taking of Evidence Abroad in Civil or Commercial Matters, 1970. This piece of law gave power to the High Court in the BVI to grant an order for the purposes of obtaining evidence in its jurisdiction for requests made by foreign authorities for assistance to take effect (BVI Financial Services Commission 2013). The extent of assistance provided included witness examinations either in writing or orally, providing documents, inspections, taking photographs, preserving, and taking custody of or detaining property, or the undergoing of a medical examination by a person. Assistance was limited to the steps taken to obtain information having to be equivalent to those the High Court was empowered to take in the same circumstances that the request order related to. Additionally, a person could not be required to give evidence that he would not be able to give in Court during civil proceedings or in the jurisdiction making the request, which involves cases where giving evidence resulted in endangering the BVI's security (BVI Financial Services Commission 2013). The next initiative by the BVI on this front came by way of the Mutual Legal Assistance (United States of America) Act, 1990. This Act represented a treaty between the US, UK and Northern Ireland regarding the Cayman Islands in 1996, and was extended in 1989 to the BVI. The treaty aimed to enhance the effectiveness of the authorities in law enforcement in suppressing and prosecuting crimes in the US and BVI, by providing mutual legal assistance in criminal matters (BVI Financial Services Commission 2013).

Another measure adopted by the jurisdiction included the Drug Trafficking Offences Act, 1992, which provided for the adoption of the 1988 UN Drug Convention. It introduced a legal framework for drug trafficking proceeds to be recovered, and allowed for international cooperation with regard to confiscation orders, in addition to restraints and charging orders related to drug trafficking. This Act was supplemented by the Drug Trafficking Offences (Designated Countries and Territories) Order, 1996, which outlines the assistance to be given to the relevant authorities in certain designated countries in connection with money laundering and drug trafficking (BVI Financial Services Commission 2013). In cases where no relevant authority was specified, the Governor was granted power to issue a certificate which gave effect to the authority listed therein as the relevant authority. The Criminal Justice (International Cooperation) Act, 1993, was another piece of law enacted by the BVI to further enhance its position on international cooperation. It established a legal regime for international cooperation between the BVI and other countries with respect to matters concerning criminal investigations and proceedings. It also regulated substances used to manufacture controlled drugs, apprehension of vessels and individuals in connection with drug offences. The Act was supplemented by the Criminal Justice (International Cooperation) (Enforcement of Overseas Forfeiture Orders) Order, 1996, which allowed for the provision of assistance to any country on matters pertaining to confiscation orders, and orders in relation to restraint and charging (BVI Financial Services Commission 2013).

The Proceeds of Criminal Conduct Act, 1997, completes the jurisdiction's legal framework for international cooperation and introduced provisions for the proceeds of crime to be recovered. It also provided for confiscation orders to be registered and enforced, allowing for applications to be presented to the High Court to secure an order of restraint or charging, to safeguard all specified assets from being depleted. This Act was supplemented by the Proceeds of Criminal Conduct (Designated Countries and Territories) Order, 1999, which made provision for a request to be enforced for the confiscation of assets or for an application to be made for a restraint or charging order (BVI Financial Services Commission 2013).

## 2.20 The Legislative Framework to Counter Tax Evasion Prior to 2000 in the BVI

### *2.20.1 Transparency: Legal System and Institutional Measures*

The jurisdiction's legislative framework to fight tax evasion is found in the Proceeds of Criminal Conduct Act, 1997. Under the Act, tax offences were not applicable as they were only tried summarily (Harneys 2000). Pursuant to BVI law, foreign tax evasion did not constitute an offence, even if such act which amounted to the offence was carried out, or deemed to be committed in the BVI. In accordance with the Act, conspiracy to carry out an offence was considered an offence. Although it is uncertain, current views which point to whether conspiracy to carry out an offence was subjected to a summarily hearing or on indictment was directly dependent upon whether the offence associated with the conspiracy was tried as a summarily hearing or on indictment. A conspiracy to carry out an indictable offence was considered an indictable offence, and as such, the proceeds associated with the conspiracy were relevant to the Act (Harneys 2000). Although it is also uncertain, current views hold that it is not a criminal conduct, which is applicable to the Act, to conspire to defraud the tax authority in a foreign jurisdiction. Although in cases where certain actions constitute conspiracy to defraud a third person, as well as defraud the tax authority in a foreign country, the Act would apply to the proceeds related to the conspiracy (Harneys 2000).

The duty of confidentiality has also been a bedrock principal in the BVI. Derived from English common law and codified in the jurisdiction, the duty of confidentiality has been supplemented by the Trust Companies Act, 1990 and amended in 1995, to strengthen the jurisdiction's stance on banking secrecy. Trust law in the jurisdiction was founded on the English Trustee Act 1925, and supplemented by statutory law. Where trusts are concerned, there is a duty of confidentiality that provides for the trust deed to be handled as a private document, the trustee to abide to keep the information related to the trust confidential, and is granted wide discretion with confidentiality, particularly in its responsibilities as trustee (Kearns 2011).

### *2.20.2 National and International Cooperation*

Evidence of the jurisdiction's provision of mutual legal assistance in international cooperation to counter tax evasion prior to 2000 has not been observed. The 1990 Mutual Legal Assistance treaty which the jurisdiction had in place with the US was limited to criminal matters which excluded matters that directly or indirectly related to regulating, imposing, calculating or collecting taxes (BVI Financial Services Commission 2013).

## 2.21 Conclusion

Similar to the tourism industry, the offshore financial services sector became a main stable for these Caribbean countries, and subsequently a principle contributor to their respective GDPs. This sector has not only been profitable for these countries, but also reportedly for criminals associated with money laundering, and wealthy individuals, as well as transnational companies, capitalizing them to carry out tax avoidance and profit laundering schemes. Over time, these undertakings have resulted in high costs to developed countries, which eventually grew to become principal concerns of the international community. The existence of OFCs and the purported role they play in facilitating financial crimes made them the central focus of international policy initiatives to counter money laundering, terrorist financing and tax evasion. These and other issues such as globalization, which has added to the complexities and dimensions of these three phenomenon, will be discussed in depth in the next two subsequent chapters.

## References

Atkins, Richard D. 1993. *The Alleged Transnational Criminal. The Second Biennial International Criminal Law Seminar*. Hague: Martinus Nijhoff Publishers.

Bermuda Laws. 1999. *Taxes Management Amendment Act 1999*. The Royal Gazette. http://bermudalaws.bm/laws/Annual%20Laws/1999/Acts/Taxes%20Management%20Amendment%20Act%201999.pdf.

Bermuda Monetary Authority. 2019. *Annual Report 2018*. Bermuda Monetary Authority. https://www.bma.bm/publications/annual-reports.

Bermuda Monetary Authority. 2020. *Bermuda Monetary Authority Guidance Notes*. Trust (Regulation of Trust Business) Act 2001. Bermuda Monetary Authority. https://www.bma.bm/.

Bermuda Monetary Authority. *Supervision and Regulation*. Retrieved April 16, 2020. https://www.bma.bm/supervision-regulation

British Virgin Islands Financial Service Commission. 2013. *British Virgin Islands Handbook on International Co-operation and Information Exchange*. The British Virgin Islands Financial Service Commission. https://www.bvifsc.vg/sites/default/files/handbook_on_international_co-operation.pdf.

Butkiewicz, J., and L. Gordon. 2013. The Economic Growth Effect of Offshore Banking in Host Territories: Evidence from the Caribbean. *World Development*, 44: 165–179.

BVI Financial Services Commission. 2018a. *Annual Report 2017*. The BVI Financial Services Commission. https://www.bvifsc.vg/sites/default/files/annual_report_2017.pdf.

BVI Financial Services Commission. 2018b. *Statistical Bulletin*. BVI FSC Statistical Bulletin, 53. https://www.bvifsc.vg/sites/default/files/documents/Statistical%20Bulletins/q4_2018_statistical_bulletin_1.pdf.

Caribbean Development Bank. 2018. *Country Economic Review 2018: British Virgin Islands*. Caribbean Development Bank. https://www.caribank.org/publications-and-resources/resource-library/economic-reviews/country-economic-review-2018-british-virgin-islands.

Cayman Islands Monetary Authority. 2017. *CIMA FACTS: Overview of the Cayman Islands Monetary Authority*. Retrieved September 18, 2020, from https://www.cima.ky/.

Cayman Islands Monetary Authority. 2020. *CIMA FACTS: Overview of the Cayman Islands Monetary Authority*. Retrieved September 18, 2020. https://www.cima.ky/.

Central Bank of The Bahamas. 2012. *Annual Report*. Central bank of The Bahamas. https://www.centralbankbahamas.com/.

Central Bank of The Bahamas. 2019. *Annual Report*. Central bank of The Bahamas. https://www.centralbankbahamas.com/.

Christensen, John, and Sony Kapoor. 2004. Tax Avoidance, Tax Competition and Globalization: Making Tax System Justice a Focus for Global Activism. *Accountancy Business and the Public Interest* 3 (2).

Conyers Dill & Pearman. 2013. *Taxation Convention Between Bermuda and the United States of America*. Conyers Dill & Pearman. https://www.conyers.com/wp-content/uploads/2013/02/Taxation_Convention_Between_Bermuda_and_the_USA-BDA.pdf.

Damgaard, Jannick, Thomas Elkjaer, and Niels Johannesen. 2019. The Rise of Phantom Investments. *Finance & Development* 56 (3). https://www.imf.org/external/pubs/ft/fandd/2019/09/pdf/the-rise-of-phantom-FDI-in-tax-havens-damgaard.pdf.

Debono, Melanie, Alexandra Dreisin, Andrew Evans, and Mark Pragnell. 2017. *Creating Value: The BVI's Global Contribution*. Capital

Economics. https://bviglobalimpact.com/media-centre/creating-value-the-bvis-global-contribution.

Faries, Timothy, and Cameron Adderley. 2012. *Bermuda: Guide to Anti-money Laundering and Anti-terrorist Financing in Bermuda*. Mondaq Limited. https://www.mondaq.com/Government-Public-Sector/207538/Guide-To-Anti-Money-Laundering-And-Anti-Terrorist-Financing-In-Bermuda.

Government of Bermuda. 2020. *Mutual Legal Assistance*. Retreived April 20, 2020. https://www.gov.bm/mutual-legal-assistance.

Government of Bermuda Department of Statistics. 2016. *Population and Housing Census*. Government of Bermuda. https://www.gov.bm/sites/default/files/2016%20Census%20Report.pdf.

Government of Bermuda Department of Statistics. 2019a. *Annual Gross Domestic Product*. Government of Bermuda. https://www.gov.bm/sites/default/files/GDP-2018-annual-publication.pdf.

Government of Bermuda Department of Statistics. 2019b. *The Bermuda Job Market Employment Briefs*. Government of Bermuda. https://www.gov.bm/sites/default/files/9370_EB%20August%202018.pdf.

Government of Bermuda Ministry of Finance. 2019. *2018 National Economic Report of Bermuda*. Government of Bermuda Ministry of Finance. https://www.gov.bm/sites/default/files/NATIONAL-ECONOMIC-REPORT-2018_Web.pdf.

Government of The Bahamas. *About The Bahamas*. Retrieved February 1, 2021. https://www.bahamas.gov.bs.

Government of The Bahamas. *The Government*. Retrieved February 1, 2021. https://www.bahamas.gov.bs.

Government of the Cayman Islands. 2019. *The Cayman Islands Annual Economic Report 2018*. Economics and Statistics Office. https://www.eso.ky/.

Government of the Cayman Islands. 2020. *Cabinet Members*. Retrieved March 26, 2020. https://www.gov.ky/about-us/our-government/the-cabinet.

Government of the Cayman Islands. *About Us*. Retrieved March 26, 2020. https://www.gov.ky/about-us.

Government of the Virgin Islands. *Government*. Retrieved April 20, 2020. https://bvi.gov.vg/.

Gurule, Jimm. 1998. The 1988 U.N. Convention Against Illicit Traffic in Narcotic Drugs and Psychotropic Substances—A Ten-Year Perspective: Is International Cooperation Merely Illusory? *Fordham International Law Journal* 22 (1). https://ir.lawnet.fordham.edu/cgi/viewcontent.cgi?article=1586&context=ilj.

Harneys. 2000. *British Virgin Islands: Proceeds of Criminal Conduct Act 1997*. Mondaq Limited. https://www.mondaq.com/Wealth-Management/8169/Proceeds-of-Criminal-Conduct-Act-1997.

Higgs & Johnson Counsel & Attorneys at Law. 2013. *Bahamas: FATCA as It Related to a Bahamian Law*. Mondaq. https://www.mondaq.com/Wealth-Management/189046/FATCA-As-It-Relates-To-Bahamian-Law.

IMF. 2000. *Offshore Financial Centers IMF Background Paper*. International Monetary Fund. https://www.imf.org/external/np/mae/oshore/2000/eng/back.htm.

IMF. 2004. *The Bahamas: Assessment of the Supervision and Regulation of the Financial Sector—Review of Financial Sector Regulation and Supervision*. Country Report No. 04/318. International Monetary Fund. https://www.imf.org/en/Publications/CR/Issues/2016/12/31/The-Bahamas-Assessment-of-the-Supervision-and-Regulation-of-the-Financial-Sector-Review-of-17773.

IMF. 2017. *The Bahamas: Selected Issues*. IMF Country Report no. 17/315. International Monetary Fund. https://www.imf.org/.

IMF. 2019. *The Bahamas 2019 Article IV Consultation—Press Release and Staff Report*. IMF Country Report no. 19/198. International Monetary Fund. https://www.imf.org/.

Insurance Commission of The Bahamas. 2019. *2018 Annual Report*. Insurance Commission of The Bahamas. https://insurancecommissionbahamas.com/.

Kearns, Lawrie. 2011. *Confidentiality in the BVI and Cayman Islands. Lexology.* https://www.lexology.com/library/detail.aspx?g=931908c7-1fef-4e8d-8fc8-071a7ed58ec7.

Lee, Stacey K. 1998. Piercing Offshore Asset Protection Trusts in the Cayman Islands: The Creditors' View. *Global Business & Development Law Journal* 11 (2): Article 6. https://scholarlycommons.pacific.edu/cgi/viewcontent.cgi?article=1522&context=globe.

Macdonald, Scott. 2018. *The Cayman Islands Stock Exchange: The Impact Of The European Market Abuse*. https://www.mondaq.com/caymanislands/securities/685116/cayman-islands-stock-exchange-the-impact-of-the-european-market-abuse.

Mourant Ozannes. 2017. *The Cayman Islands – Advantages as an Offshore Jurisdiction*. Mourant Ozannes. https://www.mourant.com/.

McKenzie, Christopher. 2014. *An Overview of Trust Law & Trustee Services in the British Virgin Islands*. World Services Group. https://www.worldservicesgroup.com/publications.asp?action=article&artid=6247.

National Anti-Money Laundering Committee. 2017. *Consultation Paper on Proposed Legislative Amendments—Foreign Tax Crimes*. Government of Bermuda. https://www.gov.bm/sites/default/files/Consultation-Paper-on-Foreign-Criminal-Tax.pdf.

Pickering, Vernon W. 1987. *A Concise History of the British Virgin Islands: From the Amerindians to 1986*. New York: Falcon Publications International.

Securities Commission of The Bahamas. 2019. *2018 Annual Report*. Securities Commission of The Bahamas. https://www.scb.gov.bs/.

Statute Law of The Bahamas. 1990a. *Chapter 98, Mutual Legal Assistance (Criminal Matters)*. Extraordinary Official Gazette of The Bahamas. http://laws.bahamas.gov.bs/cms/images/LEGISLATION/PRINCIPAL/1988/1988-0002/MutualLegalAssistanceCriminalMattersAct_1.pdf.

Statute Law of The Bahamas. 1990b. *Tracing and Forfeiture of Proceeds of Drug Trafficking Act. Chapter 93, Proceeds of Crime*. Extraordinary Official Gazette of The Bahamas. http://laws.bahamas.gov.bs/cms/images/LEGISLATION/SUBORDINATE/1990/1990-0055/TracingandForfeitureofProceedsofDrugTraffickingActDesignatedCountriesandTerritoriesOrder1990_1.pdf.

Statute Law of The Bahamas. 1996a. *Money Laundering (Proceeds of Crime) (Designation of Supervisory Authorities) Notice, 1996*. Extraordinary Official Gazette of The Bahamas. http://laws.bahamas.gov.bs/cms/images/LEGISLATION/SUBORDINATE/1996/1996-0078/MoneyLaunderingProceedsofCrimeDesignationofSupervisoryAuthoritiesNotice1996_1.pdf.

Statute Law of The Bahamas. 1996b. Money Laundering (Proceeds of Crime) Act, 1996. *Extraordinary Official Gazette of The Bahamas*. http://laws.bahamas.gov.bs/cms/en/.

Statute Law of The Bahamas. 1996c. *Money Laundering (Proceeds of Crime) Regulations, 1996*. Extraordinary Official Gazette of The Bahamas. http://laws.bahamas.gov.bs/cms/en/.

Suss, Esther C., Oral H. Williams, and Chandima Mendis. 2002. *Caribbean Offshore Financial Centers: Past, Present, and Possibilities for the Future*. IMF Working Paper WP/02/88. International Monetary Fund. https://www.researchgate.net/publication/5124060_Caribbean_Offshore_Financial_Centers_Past_Present_and_Possibilities_for_the_Future.

The Bahamas Financial Services Board. 2009. *The Bahamas: Meeting International Standards*. The Bahamas Financial Services Board. https://bfsb-bahamas.com/.

The Bahamas Financial Services Board. 2019. *The Bahamas: The Clear Choice for International Financial Services*. Clearview Financial Media Ltd. https://bfsb-bahamas.com/.

The Bahamas Financial Services Board. 2020. *Bahamas Investment Funds Guide*. The Bahamas Financial Services Board. https://bfsb-bahamas.com/sectors/assetmanagement/investment-funds-guide/.

The Bahamas Investor. 2017. *Investor's Resource Guide: Wealth Management and Investment in The Bahamas*. Dupuch Publications. http://www.thebahamasinvestor.com/wordpress/wp-content/uploads/2015/01/087-118_IRG_TBIJan17_med.pdf.

UNdata. 2020. *British Virgin Islands: National Accounts Estimate of Main Aggregates*. United Nations Statistics Division. http://www.data.un.org/.

United Nations Treaty Collections. *United Nations Convention Against Illicit Traffic in Narcotic Drugs and Psychotropic Substances, 1998*. Retrieved November 5, 2020. https://treaties.un.org/pages/ViewDetails.aspx?src=TREATY&mtdsg_no=VI-19&chapter=6#3.

U.S. Government Accountability Office. 2008. *Cayman Islands: Review of Cayman Islands and U.S. Laws Applicable to U.S. Persons' Financial Activity in the Cayman Islands*. U.S. Government Accountability Office. https://www.gao.gov/assets/210/203399.pdf.

CHAPTER 3

# The Problems and Dimensions of Money Laundering and Terrorist Financing

## 3.1 Introduction

Money laundering is described as one of the most detrimental issues facing the international financial community.[1] The IMF estimates the scale of transactions associated with money laundering to be between 2% and 5% of global GDP, which is equivalent to approximately $800 billion to $2 trillion US dollars per annum (United Nations Office on Drugs and Crime [UNODC] 2011). Whereas the results of a meta-analysis estimate criminal proceeds to be around 3.6% or between 2.3% and 5.5% of global GDP, approximately US$2.1 trillion (UNODC 2011). Given the scale of money laundering, the potential risks associated with it on a microeconomic level are its ability to corrupt and destabilize markets and small economies. On a macroeconomic level, the impact can result in sudden shifts in the demand for money, a higher level of risk to the soundness of banks, a negative impact on legitimate financial transactions, and a higher degree of volatility in the flow of capital internationally and foreign exchange rates as a result of cross-border asset transfers. The social and political effects of money laundering resonate in the pain victims endure and in the deterioration of the social fabric of society (UNODC 2015).

[1] Michel Camdessus, Managing Director of the IMF, in his address at the Plenary Meeting of the Financial Action Task Force on Money Laundering in 1998.



A. M. Campbell, *Money Laundering, Terrorist Financing, and Tax Evasion*, https://doi.org/10.1007/978-3-030-68876-9_3

The existence of offshore banks in OFCs is perceived as aiding in allowing drug traffickers to establish international networks to launder money. This has resulted in ongoing efforts by international organizations to adopt more stringent measures to curb money laundering (UNODC 2015). At the end of June 1999, cross-border assets on the balance sheets of OFCs accounted for an estimated US$4.6 trillion, which is approximately 50% of cross-border assets worldwide (IMF 2000). This signifies the significant role played by OFCs as an integral component in the global financial marketplace, and as a consequence, this, in addition to their presumed role in facilitating money laundering, placed them in the spotlight of international efforts aimed at combating money laundering.

The UNODC estimated that in 2009, proceeds from criminal activities, with the exception of tax evasion, was approximately 3.6% of global GDP, which is equivalent to US$2.1 trillion. Of this percentage, it attributed 1.5% to criminal activities associated with well-established transnational crime groups, and an estimated 2.7%, which is equivalent to US$1.6 trillion, to money laundering (UNODC 2011). Approximately 70% of these proceeds have passed through the financial system (UNODC 2011). The illicit drug trade is considered to be the most profitable sector, accounting for 50% of transnational crime proceeds, and a fifth of all crime proceeds (UNODC 2011). Of the illicit funds that flow through the global system, less than 1% is seized and frozen. According to Yury Fedotov, the executive director of UNODC, "tracking the flows of illicit funds generated by drug trafficking and other transnational organized crimes and analyzing how they are laundered through the world's financial systems remain daunting tasks".

Money laundering became an urgent matter due to the increased ease and speed to transfer money worldwide. This fuelled with the rise in the use of the US dollar on black markets, the liberalization of financial markets in Europe, and the proliferation of OFCs, have all been reported as contributing to increased difficulty by law enforcement agencies in finding, freezing, and forfeiting assets derived from criminal activities (UNODC 2015). The urgency of developing effective anti-laundering measures became evident, aimed at strengthening the weakest point of infiltration in laundering money, which was considered to be the point of entry into the financial system (UNODC 2015).

## 3.2 The Drug Epidemic

### *3.2.1 US Perspective*

At the turn of the nineteenth century, due to the influx of imported cocoa leaf for production in the US, the use of cocaine grew rapidly, resulting in the first cocaine epidemic in the country (UNODC 2015). Cocaine was not only used as medicine for illnesses such as sinusitis and hay fever, but also as a cure for alcohol, morphine and opium addiction, as an anaesthetic, and for recreational purposes as well (UNODC 2015). Drug control intervention for cocaine came in 1906, by way of the Pure Food and Drug Act which brought about the mandatory inclusion of the word "dangerous" or "addictive" drugs on product labels (Nevius 2016). Later in 1909, opiates were prohibited for recreational use through the enactment of the Smoking Opium Exclusion Act. By 1914, a tax was levied on the manufacturing, importation and sales of drugs deriving from opium and coca leaves through the introduction of the Harrison Narcotics Tax Act (Nevius 2016).

During the period of the Great Depression, an increase in the use of Marihuana in the US was also noted, along with an influx of raw opium from France, Italy and Mexico. Morphine was also imported from Japan, France and Germany, and an increase in the use of heroin due to the inexpensive nature of the drug compared to the cost of morphine was observed (Sacco 2014). These events led to the first session of the newly formed Commission of Narcotic Drugs organized by the Economic and Social Council of the newly established United Nations in 1946. Other significant events which took place post world war, included the excess production of opium and the increase of synthetic drugs such as Demerol, Amidone, Methadone, etc. in the US market, resulting in increased efforts to combat narcotic trafficking in the United States (Sacco 2014). These incidences contributed to US Commission's push to categorize synthetic drugs in the international control class as other narcotics under a U.N. agreement (the 1946 Lake Success Protocol), which was signed by most nations a year later (Sacco 2014).

By the 1960s, the production of licit opiates in Turkey accounted for almost 80% of opiates in the US (UNODC 2015). The use of drugs dramatically increased initially in the United States and later in Europe due to changes both socially and culturally. Eventually, a sharp increase in the illicit production of opiates in nearby South-East Asia, particularly in Myanmar was noted. By the 1970s, Myanmar was recognized as the largest supplier of illicit opiates in the world per the UNODC. The conversion of opium into heroin took place in nearby Thailand, which contributed to the spread of heroin use among US soldiers in South-East Asia during the Vietnam war (UNODC 2015). By 1971, an estimated 24 million Americans had used cannabis and about half a million were heroin addicts compared to 50,000 in 1960, based on a national survey according to the UNODC. By the early 1970s, the abuse of drugs had evolved to the point where it was declared to be the number one enemy in the United States by President Nixon (Sacco 2014).

### 3.2.2 *Europe Perspective*

In Europe, the demand for cocaine rose during the twenty-first century.[2] In fact, over the past decade, the consumption of drugs had doubled in the European market per the UNODC. In 1998 an increased from 2 million cocaine users to 4.1 million users was noted between 2007 and 2008, with the UK and Spain having higher prevalence rates per annum than the US (UNODC 2015). An increase in growth in the cocaine market in Europe of US$20 billion in value over a ten-year period (from US$14B in 1998 to US$34B in 2008) was noted, which was similar in size to the US market (UNODC 2015). To enter Europe, cocaine was transported by sea to two main European hubs; namely to Southern Europe (Spain and Portugal) and Northern Europe (The Netherlands and Belgium), mainly from Columbia, and to a lesser extent, via direct shipments from Peru and the Plurinational State of Bolivia. Certain hubs were also noted in Western Africa, namely in Guinea and Guinea-Bissau, and in the Bight of Benin that stretched from Ghana to Nigeria (UNODC 2015), in addition to large maritime shipments from the Bolivarian Republic of Venezuela.

The UNODC estimated that approximately 124 tons (worth around US$34 billion in market value) of cocaine were distributed throughout Europe. Of this amount, market value of less than 1% go to coca farmers

[2] The UNODC estimated the number or cocaine users worldwide to be approximately 16 to 17 million in 2007/2008, which is similar to the number opiate users globally. Of this amount, North America accounted for at least 40% of worldwide consumption, followed by Europe with more than 25% of consumption globally. Combined, both regions make up 80% or more of the total value of the cocaine market globally, estimated in 2008 at about US$88 billion.

in the Andes, 1% to traffickers in the Andean region, 25% to international traffickers from that region to the main European entry points, 17% for shipping cocaine from such points of entry to wholesalers located in countries of final destination in Europe, and more than 56% are generated between the wholesaler and consumer.

To meet the heroine demand of 87 tons in Europe, approximately 140 tons of heroine departed Afghanistan due to seizures, and travel by land along the "Balkan route", to the Islamic Republic of Iran or via Pakistan to the Islamic Republic of Iran, on to Turkey and then to South-East Europe per the UNODC. Additionally, organized crime groups along this route consisted of nationals that were either from the transit or source countries, in addition to professional transportation workers who were maybe contracted at various stages during the trafficking process that did not necessarily belong to the group who owned the drugs (UNODC 2015). The UNODC noted that opiates that were directed to Western Europe were transported from Afghanistan by groups such as Baluchi and Pashtun that operated on the border regions along Afghanistan, the Islamic Republic of Iran and Pakistan. Other groups with strong regional and international links such as Azeri, Persian, Arab and Kurdish groups were believed to be involved during the trans-shipment to the Islamic Republic of Iran from its eastern to its western border. Once in Turkey, heroine shipments were repackaged into smaller quantities to be distributed throughout Europe. Per the UNODC, the Netherlands served as the second redistribution centre next to Turkey.

The estimated the value of heroin in the global market originating from Afghan was approximately US$55 billion per the UNODC. Of this amount, an estimated US$2.3 billion went to Afghanistan farmers and traders. A larger portion was made by retailers in countries where the drug was destined, but most of the profits were generated by the traffickers that worked along the two main routes. For traffickers on the "Balkan route", an estimated US$20 billion was earned, and for those on the northern route, about US$20 billion was generated annually (UNODC 2015). The increase in the importation of drugs in Europe and in its use among Europeans led to increased concerns in Europe to counter the war on drugs.

## 3.3 Money Laundering

Money laundering attracted international attention in the 1980s due to its association within the context of drug trafficking (Giriraj and Mishra 2001). The substantial gains generated from criminal activities coupled with concern for the drug abuse epidemic in western society, prompted an impetus to enact legislations to deprive drug traffickers of their illicit gains (Giriraj and Mishra 2001).[3] International intervention directed to dealing with the proceeds of crime, which required members to criminalize money laundering (in connection with drug trafficking), came by way of the 1988 United Nations Convention, and the formation of the FATF by the Heads of State of the G-7 countries at its fifteenth annual Economic Summit held in Paris, France in July 1989. The objective of the FATF was to assess the results of existing measures in place to prevent money laundering through the use of banking systems and financial institutions, and to determine other preventative methods, including regulatory and legal measures, to strengthened multilateral judicial efforts to combat money laundering (G-7 Economic Declaration, 1989).

### *3.3.1 Challenges of Money Laundering*

According to the UNODC, money laundering is the principal reason for carrying out criminal activities (UNODC 2015). It is a financial crime that is both a global phenomenon, as well as an international challenge, and concerns a series of complex transactions through the use of multiple financial institutions located in a number of foreign jurisdictions. It is immensely difficult to investigate as it is to prosecute (Buchanan 2003). Globalization has brought about benefits for participants in the legal economy, as well as those in the illegal economy. The evolution of globalization has enabled money launderers to carry out their business with greater ease, tact and profitability per Buchanan. For instance, the development of new financial instruments and opportunities in trading, and the emergence of improvements in financial market liquidity, enable money laundering systems to be created and ceased with greater ease. Increased competition cross-borders has led to a squeeze in transaction costs associated with money laundering (Buchanan 2003).

[3] Per Giriraj and Mishra, huge earnings were also gained by criminal gangsters from prostitution, extortion, bootlegging liquor and gambling.

Additionally, money laundering proportions dirty money throughout the world by bypassing national controls, allowing it to flow to countries that has less rigid controls. Globalization has enhanced the way in which money launderers communicate, thereby enabling them to disperse transactions across more jurisdictions, thus augmenting the number of legal impediments that can hinder investigations per Buchanan. Global money laundering therefore places a considerable cost on the world economy by crippling the effectiveness of national economies' operations and stimulating poorer economic policies. This results in the gradual corruption of financial markets and the erosion of confidence held by the public in the international financial system (Buchanan 2003). This in turn leads to increase risk and instability in financial markets, and a reduction in the world's growth rate.

Money laundering has become increasingly challenging to governments and law enforcement agencies around the world. The advancement of technology, coupled with the ease of communication and obtaining financial information, all contribute to facilitating the transfer of money quickly and easily globally (UNODC 2015). The expansion of free markets and international trade due to globalization also contributes to the challenges of money laundering (Schroeder 2001). Other contributing factors include the intervention of the Internet and the changing habits of money launderers due to the constant changes in regulations (Unger 2007). These, in addition to factors such as corruption and bribery, and globalization among others, all contributed to an increased level of complexity in effectively dealing with money laundering.

## 3.4 Terrorist Financing

The threat of terrorism adds a new perspective to the complexity of money laundering. Terrorist financing was initially recognized by the United Nations General Assembly in its declaration in October 1970, through resolution 2625 (XXV), and was later reinforced through a declaration on 13 August 1998, by its Security Council in its resolution 1189 (1998) (United Nations 2001). However, it was not until the 9/11 terrorist attacks which took place in New York, Washington, DC and Pennsylvania that terrorism was thrusted into the spotlight of the international community. The United Nations Security Council at its 4385th meeting held on 28 September 2001, took a firm stand against terrorism by reaffirming resolutions 1269 (1999) of 19 October 1999, and 1368

(2001) of 12 September 2001 (United Nations 2001). These resolutions, including the United Nations Security Council Resolution 1373 in 2001, resulted in the enhancement of the FATFs mandate to include countering the financing of terrorism.

### 3.4.1 *Challenges of Terrorist Financing*

Like money laundering, terrorism has become increasingly challenging to governments and law enforcement agencies around the world. The use of the Internet poses a unique challenge as it can be used not only to recruit members of a terrorist group and expand its operations, but also to finance terrorist acts and incite terrorism (UNODC 2012). The constant changing landscape of terrorism also poses a challenge to effectively deal with terrorism. Additionally, the increase in terrorist threat by "homegrown" militants also adds another dimension to the complexity of terrorism (FATF 2010). Also, the gradual loss of legitimate funding sources has added to the challenges of effectively managing terrorism, as terrorist groups seeks funding from other sources such as criminal activities (FATF 2010). All these factors added another level of complexity in effectively dealing with terrorism.

## 3.5 Effects of Globalization on Money Laundering and Terrorist Financing

Globalization has contributed further to the complexities and dimensions of money laundering and terrorist financing. The liberalization of trade borders has aided in the movement of physical cash within countries and the smuggling of cash cross-borders for the purposes of moving crime proceeds, as well as carrying out terrorist financing (FATF 2010). Per the FATF, case studies have shown that globally, the same methods used to transfer illicit narcotics have been undertaken to transfer cash and bearer negotiable instruments as well cross-borders. The harms stemming from the illegal physical movement of cash and its smuggling by both criminals and terrorists include: (i) robbery and the risk of incurring violence among criminals; (ii) use of the same mechanisms which facilitate the movement of criminal cash and the transfer of its value to fund further criminal and terrorist activities; (iii) use of unlawful cash which results in the profits of crime being realized; (iv) funds held in the form of cash less likely to be taxed by the relevant authorities; and (v) the removal of currency out of active circulation in the jurisdiction where criminal activity occurs, thereby boosting the demand as well as the cost associated with issuing the currency (FATF 2010).

Globalization has also facilitated international money laundering and terrorist financing as a result of the free movement of cash through the use of financial institutions and businesses with remittance services.[4] This has given rise to the use of third-party accounts by criminals and terrorists. The harms associated with gaining access to the international financial system or using remittance services businesses include: (i) increased risk of robbery for businesses and individuals possessing large volumes of cash; (ii) complicit businesses gaining a competitive advantage where the illicit cash is placed; (iii) substantial costs and resources to governments in mitigating identity fraud which increases with the level of sophistication used in identity fraud as placement usually occurs through the use of stolen or false identities; (iv) placement of cash into the financial system by criminals resulting in profits deriving from crime being realized; and (v) a reduced level of confidence in the data-sets and processes of the public and financial sectors due to the extensive use of stolen and false identities (FATF 2010).

Globalization has also contributed to significant global activity, increased competitive growth, and vulnerability of cash-intensive businesses, particularly in casinos which are frequently used and exploited by criminals based on a survey by the FATF. The harms that result from criminals and terrorists making use of cash-intensive businesses include; (i) a competitive advantage gained by complicit businesses; (ii) the realization of profits originating from crime due to the placement of cash in the financial system by criminals; and (iii) the potential corruption of persons employed in such businesses, either wittingly or by way of coercion, by criminals using such businesses.

The integration of financial markets is another feature of Globalization (BIS 2017). Globalization has aided in the transfer of value by facilitating the movement of millions of transactions across the globe on a daily basis through the use of various integrated networks. These networks include; the financial system, businesses and other systems used to transfer money, the international trade system, business structures of third party, charities, systems of remittance, and new methods of payment (FATF 2010). As

[4] See 2010 FATF Global Threat Analysis related to Cash and Bearer Negotiable Instruments.

most of these transactions are legitimate, distinguishing between the use of legal and illegal transfer of value becomes a challenge. In accordance with the 2009 FATF Strategic Surveillance Survey, the following sub-features are associated with the harms of money laundering and terrorist financing which occur during the transfer of value:

### 3.5.1 *The Banking System*

Wire transfers using cash deposits and withdrawals were the principal means of moving terrorist funds per the survey. It noted the use of financial systems in several countries which were used as part of a series of transactions, where funds linked to terrorism were moved in out of these jurisdictions (FATF 2010). The exploitation of the banking sector by criminals and terrorists to transfer value can erode the public's confidence in the financial system's integrity and tarnish its reputation as well as that of the businesses within it, and could potentially lead to harm caused to businesses, markets, and entire economies (UNODC 2013). This in turn can chase away legitimate business and result in more reliance by institutions on funds that are criminally sourced. Additionally, another potential harm involves the access by such institutions which are tainted to the global financial sector. Identity fraud is another way in which the banking system is abused (O'keefe and Yom 2017). The actions required by governments to mitigate identify fraud call for substantial costs and resources which increases with the level of sophistication used in identity fraud.

### 3.5.2 *Money Transfer Business and Alternative Remittance*

The FATF survey also noted an increase in the exploitation of alternative remittance systems in a number of jurisdictions. It also observed two variations of alternative remittance systems used for terrorist financing. In the first case, the use of an online remittance service by remittance companies using correspondent (nostro) accounts resulted in the existence of limited information regarding the transaction (FATF 2010). In the second case, transactions where bank drafts were obtained by persons on behalf of a money service business were noted. These mechanisms facilitate the movement of cash and the transfer of its value to finance further criminal and terrorist activities (UNODC 2013). They also permit crime profits to be realized (UNODC 2013). The abuse of these remittance services reduced confidence in the integrity of such businesses and harms the system's reputation in addition to the businesses within it (FATF 2010). The use of such alternative services instead of the banking sector, invalidates the controls benefits employed by banks. According to the FATF, it also can allow the use of stolen and false identities. Actions required by governments to mitigate identify fraud call for substantial costs and resources which increases with the level of sophistication used in identity fraud (O'keefe and Yom 2017). Money laundering and terrorist financial through the use of these mechanisms can give rise to the necessity of additional and more rigid controls which can lead to a move underground by some of these remittance operators, close down by others, or additional costs passed on to customers who are usually already at a disadvantage (FATF 2010).

### 3.5.3 *The International Trade System*

The use of the international trade system to move money as well as goods in large quantity with very limited scrutiny by governments to fight its illicit side, allows for it to be exploited for the purpose of tax evasion, tax avoidance, capital flight, and trade-base money laundering (FATF-Egmont Group 2020).[5] Per the FATF, the exploitation of the international trade system, in addition to trade-based money laundering by criminals and terrorists to transfer value, can threaten the credibility and dependability of international trade (FATF 2010). It can also weaken the stability of nations' borders as well as their financial systems (FATF-Egmont Group 2020). Such risks create openings for the evasion of tariffs, duties, and taxes, which leads to losses in government revenue. They also facilitate the flight of capital and/or the bypassing of currency restrictions (FATF-Egmont Group 2020).

[5] Per the FATF, trade-based money laundering is the process of concealing the proceeds of crime and transferring value by using trade transactions in an effort to legitimize their illicit origins or fund their activities. This can be done by falsifying prices, by underpricing or overpricing invoices as well as misrepresenting the quantity or quality of goods.

### 3.5.4 *Third-Party Business Structures, Charities and Other Legal Entities*

The abuse of these structures harms the reputation of lawful businesses and Sectors (FATF 2010). In particular, charities are at risk of their reputation being undermined. In turn, this may result in a negative impact on the amount of charitable donations a charity receives (FATF 2015). For instance, the potential diversion of lawful funds from charitable purposes to fund terrorist acts can dissuade citizens from making donation to charities. Abuse of these types of corporate vehicles can also occur through the use of stolen or false identities per the FATF. Extensive use of stolen or false identities can lead to a lack of confidence in the data-sets and processes of the public sector. Also, the availability of such corporate vehicles for investments can impede the ability for the risk of the investments to be assessed due to the opaque nature of such structures (UNODC 2013). This can thwart integrity, quality of assets, soundness, and stability (FATF 2010).

### 3.5.5 *Retail Payment Systems and the ATM Network*

Non-banks play an increasing role in offering accounts that are transaction-based which provide accessibility to payment systems through the use of cards, mobile phones or computers (FATF 2010). The use of such payment systems and network allows for stolen or false identities to be used (UNODC 2013). Per the FATF, actions required by governments to reduce the negative effect of identity fraud call for substantial costs and resources which increases with the level of sophistication used in identity fraud techniques. The harm caused to the transfer value as a result of the exploitation of retail payment systems such as the ATM network by criminals and terrorists, is the imposition of current and future limits on products due to abuse which can impact innovation, business, as well as economic development (FATF 2010).

Per the FATF, assets and stores of value are the third features that are rampantly abused by money launderers and terrorist financiers. Criminal exploit ways to invest money to obtain profitability or security or continue to hold it in a form that retains its value. Globalization aids in facilitating the investment of funds through a global integrated network of systems (e.g. the global financial systems, etc.) in exchange for assets (e.g. stocks, bonds, etc.) or stores of value (e.g. gold, silver, etc.) for such purposes.

In its 2009 typologies report, the FATF observed that due to the industry's rapid execution of transactions, its adaptability and global reach, the securities sector is very attractive to criminals. The harms associated with abuse of assets/stores of value are described below.

#### *3.5.5.1 Financial Products*

The exploitation of financial products by money launderers and terrorist financiers to invest unlawful funds can weaken the confidence of the financial system's integrity, harm its reputation, as well as that of other businesses within it (UNODC 2013). Interruption in the stock market can result in a negative impact on the confidence of investors and also on market quotations through the manipulation of prices (FATF 2010). Per the FATF, illegal investments in markets can give strength to organized crime groups. Abuse is usually facilitated by identity fraud. Actions required by governments to mitigate identify fraud call for substantial costs and resources which increases with the level of sophistication used in identity fraud techniques. Extensive use of stolen and false identities could give rise to a lack of confidence in the data-sets and processes in the public and financial sectors, and result in financial loss and hindrance to natural persons who are victims of schemes involving fraud due to the use of data obtained illegally (UNODC 2013). The widespread exploitation of certain financial products can weaken social policy geared towards increasing accessibility to the financial system, as actions produce barriers to individuals wanting to establish bank accounts, etc. (FATF 2010).

#### *3.5.5.2 Moveable Goods*

Illegal funds invested in moveable goods[6] of high value allows criminals and terrorists to enjoy their crime proceeds according to the FATF. Displaying the material benefits of the lifestyle of a criminal within communities may drive additional individuals to crime. The ownership by criminals of high value luxury goods, which may not be affordable to honest citizens, is inequitable and may give rise to social classification and feed social tension. Further, complicit businesses selling products to criminals are more profitable than others, thus resulting in economic distortion.

[6] Moveable goods consist of precious stones and gold, vehicles, art, antiques as well as machinery.

#### *3.5.5.3 Real Estate*

The features of the housing market which create opportunities of exploitation by money launderers and terrorist financiers also promote mortgage fraud according to the FATF. Carrying out investment in real estate funds which are illegal allows criminals and terrorists to conceal the beneficial ownership of their investment resulting in the true value not being accessible for tax purposes (European Parliament 2019). The ownership of housing by a criminal that may not be affordable to honest citizens is inequitable (European Parliament 2019). This can gradually lead to the degradation of neighbourhoods as a result of criminal activity, due to the possible increase in criminal ownership of housing in such communities which may cause other types of crime or unlawful behaviour (FATF 2010). The visible display of the benefits gained from a lifestyle of crime within local neighbourhoods may attract additional individuals to crime. Also, the acceptance and integration of criminal behaviour within local communities' result in the corruption of intermediaries. The increased influence of criminals in businesses engaged in real estate can give rise to decision making as well as to the preparation of professional advice that are misleading, bringing about harm to such business sectors (FATF 2010).

### *3.5.6 Jurisdictional/Environmental Aspects*

The jurisdictional and environment aspects are the last features which are rampantly abused by money launderers and terrorist financiers. Money laundering and terrorist financing are principally cross-border activities which are facilitated through the liberalization of trade borders due to globalization (IMF 2021). Weaknesses in the AML/CFT regime established by the international community which all countries are required to follow, result in negative consequences beyond the borders of a jurisdiction, making money laundering and terrorist financing a global issue (IMF 2021). Money laundering and terrorist financing are also global in nature because they can take place anywhere throughout the world, usually involving two jurisdictions or more (IMF 2021). According to the FATF, the harms related to the abuse of jurisdictional and environmental aspects are described below.

#### *3.5.6.1 Variable Standards and Controls*

Money laundering and terrorist financing are problems on a global level which require a collective effort from the international community to combat them (FATF 2010). The strength of the measures of global AML/CFT relies upon the strength of the most vulnerable link. Deficiency in control systems as a result of standards and controls which vary across jurisdictions is a weak link in combating money laundering and terrorist financing globally per the FATF. The harms that result in a jurisdiction from variation in standards and controls can lead to a reduction in the effectiveness of AML/CFT measures in other countries and in a country's inability to cooperate regionally as well as internationally in AML/CFT matters (Yepes 2011). Jurisdictions with weak controls will potentially be susceptible to acceptance, integration or influence of criminal conduct in their jurisdictions (Yepes 2011). Ensuing adverse reactions such as bilateral or multilateral measures taken by the international community can lead to difficulties socio-economically for a population. Such measures can impede accessibility of such jurisdiction to the international financial system and in carrying out international commerce (FATF 2010). Additionally, the countermeasures undertaken by the international community can result in a decline in government aid, as well as in foreign direct investment in the jurisdiction (FATF 2010). The absence of political desire to give power to AML/CFT institutions and enforce the relevant laws can force criminals into collusion with political elites. Further, a jurisdiction is likely to attract more criminal activity to the extent it is seen as a haven for money laundering (FATF 2010).

#### *3.5.6.2 Cash-Intensive Economies*

Such economies facilitate the integration of money easily into the national economy due to the normalcy of large cash transactions (Savona and Riccardi 2017). In such an environment, it can be difficult to detect and prevent cash-based money laundering and terrorist financing activities (Savona and Riccardi 2017). Per the FATF, the exploitation by criminals and terrorists of cash-intensive economies can drive liquidity away from the main financial sector in the jurisdiction where the criminal activity occurs. Funds that usually would stay in a particular jurisdiction are instead shifted to cash-intensive economies to be invested, for example in assets such as properties (FATF 2010). This can be viewed as a distortion in financial flows, and for non-market reasons, investment in economies.

#### 3.5.6.3 *Major Financial Centres, Tax Havens and Offshore Banking Centres*

Major financial centres are recognized as an attractive jurisdiction for laundering of proceeds derived from a range of illicit activities (Sikka 2003; IMF 2017; Butkiewicz and Gordon 2013). In such jurisdictions, many financial institutions are involved in international business transactions of substantial amounts on a frequent basis, resulting in difficulty to detect or identify suspicious or unusual activities (Sikka 2003). In other circumstances, major financial centres are small geographic jurisdictions with a notable financial sector, which are reportedly attractive locations for criminals to deposit, hide and camouflage their proceeds obtained in another jurisdiction (IMF 2017; Butkiewicz and Gordon 2013). The exploitation of such jurisdictions by criminals and terrorists can result in damage to the jurisdiction's reputation (FATF 2010). It can drive liquidity away from other jurisdictions and lead to financial flows as well as investments in such economies that are purportedly not due to the supply and demand of legal markets. Such abuse is viewed as one which leads to the acceptance, integration or influence of criminal conduct in jurisdictions (FATF 2010). This has the potential to undermine the effect of transparency and AML/CFT measures in other jurisdictions. Per the FATF, the transfer of criminal proceeds to tax havens is said to lead to increase difficulty to detect them as well as the possibility to apply taxes to them.

#### 3.5.6.4 *High-Risk and Conflict Zones*

Such countries that are prone to severe social, political, and economic upheaval usually also go through significant crime and terrorism, in addition to money laundering and terrorist financing (OECD 2011). These countries with significant inadequacies in their AML/CFT regimes or regulations or with considerable level of corruption, or those with activities related to criminals or terrorists, may also be susceptible to embargoes, sanctions or similar countermeasures (FATF 2010). The FATF survey observed that in many countries the existence of major criminal and terrorist activities indicates the presence of money laundering and terrorist financing. Per the FATF, the harms which result from high-risk and conflict zones being exploited by money launderers and terrorist financiers include: (i) injury or death, given that their activities can encourage or inflict additional violence or dangerous criminal and terrorist activities; (ii) reputational damage and the implementation of international sanctions resulting in damage to governments as well as social institutions; and (iii) the crippling of legitimate efforts for charitable or humanitarian aids in such regions.

#### *3.5.6.5 Jurisdiction with High Rates of Corruption*

Corruption and money laundering take place together, with the existence of one strengthening the other (FATF 2010). Corrupt persons carry out money laundering in order to earn a profit from their corrupt activity. Per the FATF, money laundering can be conducted with decreased risk if public officers can be coaxed to cooperate. Therefore, to carry out an illegal activity such as bribing PEPs is essential. Thus, the existence of PEPs in a territory indicates that it suffers or is prone to money laundering risks (FATF 2011). According to the FATF, the harms that are associated with money launderers and terrorist financiers exploiting jurisdiction with high levels of corruption include: (i) the facilitation of the movement and realization of profits by corrupt persons deriving from embezzlement and corruption; (ii) the weakening of trust held in governments and institutions where bribery is involved; (iii) the subsequent absence of laundered funds for government spending can lead to an increase in taxes or a decline in services for citizens; and (iv) the higher the level of corruption in a country, the more likely it will have a low index for good governance.

## 3.6 Incentives

Incentives to address the problem of money laundering and terrorist financing came by way of significant detrimental impacts felt by many countries stemming from several fronts. The first of these fronts was the drug epidemic experienced by several nations, which was the root cause for the increased trafficking of illegal drugs orchestrated by organized transnational crime groups (UNODC 2008). The criminal activities carried out by organized transnational crime groups on a global scale is the second front which brought about corruption, bribery, violence, etc. experienced by a significant number of countries (FATF 2010). One of the spillover effects of narcotic trafficking was that the significant profits gained from this illicit activity needed to be laundered into legitimate funds in order to be enjoyed by criminals (Unger 2007). This in turn gave rise to money laundering and an increase need to use of the global financial system to legitimize dirty money. This is the third front which had adverse effects on countries. These effects are discussed in more detail below.

### 3.6.1 *The Drug Epidemic*

The drug epidemic was one of the main impetuses which raised awareness of the need for international intervention. At the turn of the nineteenth century, the end of the opium wars which resulted in the free trade of opium between Britain and China, led to an opium addiction in China in the tens of millions due to the constant importation of opium from India to China per the UNODC. Unable to stop the influx of drugs to its ports, in response, China began to produce opium domestically. The increase in domestic supply of opium in China led to increased consumption from 3 million in the 1830s to 15 million in 1890, to between 21.5 and 25 million by 1906, according to the UNODC. Opium consumption also increased outside China among Chinese adults living in countries in South-East Asia and among Chinese immigrants in the US. Although international intervention came in 1912,[7] as a result of the Chinese drug epidemic, coupled with the US interest to stem the spread of drugs to its shores, due to its awareness of the height of the opium epidemic after taking control of the Philippines, and the UK's economic interest due to the profits it earned from trading opium with China, the consumption of drugs continued to spread.

The 1912 international intervention was followed by a number of other conventions including those introduced under the auspices of the League of Nations in 1925, 1931 and 1936, the 1953 Opium Protocol by the United Nations after World War II, as well as the 1961 Single Convention on Narcotic Drugs. Despite these international measures, due to its use not only for its medicinal properties but also for recreational purposes, drug usage continued to increase in the United States in the 1960s, and eventually in Europe as well (Nevius 2016). The consumption of drugs had escalated to such an extent that an estimated 24 million Americans were reported to have used cannabis and around half a million were heroin addicts by 1970, compared to 50,000 in 1960 (UNODC 2008). Although additional international interventions came by way of

[7] The international conference in Shanghai, China in 1909 did not result in a convention. The 1912 Hague conference that followed resulted in the International Opium Convention, which was the first international drug control treaty.

the 1971 Convention on Psychotropic Substances, and a protocol in 1972, which aimed at managing the social ills which came along with drug abuse,[8] by the early 1970s the drug epidemic had reached such devastating proportions that it was declared to be the number one enemy of the United States by President Richard Nixon (Custodio 2015).

### 3.6.2 *Organized Transnational Crime Groups*

The increased in organized transnational crime groups was another impetus which sparked the need for international intervention. During the 1980s organized crime groups increased in their ability of influence globally (UNODC 2008). The cartels from Medellin and Cali were the most notorious of such organized crime groups which trafficked large volumes of cocaine to North America and Europe. Over time, the activities of organized crime groups became a significant threat to local as well as national governance. Moreover, they used the enormous crime proceeds generated from their cocaine empires to corrupt both local as well as national authorities. In order to curb the drug epidemic problem, further international intervention came through the introduction of the 1981 Drug Abuse Control Strategy, which was aimed at garnering international cooperation to fight drug abuse and drug trafficking. Another came by way of the 1987 Declaration of the International Conference on Drug Abuse and Illicit Trafficking and Comprehensive Multidisciplinary Outline of Future Activities in Drug Abuse Control, to deal with the increased levels of drug production and drug trafficking which contributed to the growing increase in drug abuse into the 1980s (UNODC 2008).

However, despite these interventions, the harms[9] stemming from organized crime and terrorism were significant and were observed at the following three different levels: (i) at an individual and local level; (ii)

[8] Article 20 of the 1971 Convention on Psychotropic Substances included measures for the prevention of psychotropic substances abuse as well as early identification, treatment of abuse and education, in addition to after-care, rehabilitation and also social reintegration. A similar scope of these measures is noted in Article 38 of the 1972 Protocol that amended the 1961 Convention.

[9] The FATF notes that the concepts applied to the harms noted in its GTA may differ among countries. Some harms detailed in the GTA may be applicable globally, while other may be specific to a country, and additional harms may exist that are not included in its report.

the community and regional level; and (iii) at a national and international level (FATF 2010). At the individual and local level, negative impacts on the health, quality of life and personal wealth of individuals who made use of such services and commodities which criminals' control was observed, in addition to direct negative impacts on those engaged in criminal lifestyles given the higher risk they face from physical violence per the FATF. Terrorism had evolved into critically threatening the security of individuals. During the past ten years or more, sponsored kidnappings in addition to the use of violence as well as intimidation to compel innocent individuals to commit crime had been used by criminals and terrorists to accomplish political or military objectives (FATF 2010). At the community and regional level, damage was done to the reputations of areas where illegal activity was rampant and legitimate businesses experienced financial losses as a result of being preyed upon by criminals and terrorists. Per the FATF, local areas which were targeted were also devastated by terrorist attacks. Over time, the long-term effect of criminal and terrorist activities gradually weaken the confidence held by the public in law enforcement and overall in the criminal justice system. At a national and international level, activities carried out by organized crime as well as terrorists, have undermined global economies, corrupted governments and have resulted in or provoked the failure of states. Countries that contain or experience organized crime and terrorism may endure reputational impacts as well as financial impacts on their institutions and economies (FATF 2010). Additionally, the widespread nature of radical views related to terrorism can also destroy the social fabric of countries.

#### *3.6.2.1 Physical Harm*

Organized crime and terrorism also impact the physical, social, environmental, economic, and structural areas of a country (FATF 2010). These harms are associated mostly with predicate criminal actions and terrorism, with money laundering and terrorist financing facilitating such activities (UNODC 2019). Physical harm is recognized as illness, injury or death which can occur as a result of using the services or commodities ran by organized criminals or due to engaging in organized criminal activities (UNODC 2019). At the first level (individual and local), physical harm such as individual illness, injury or death can occur. For example, physical harm as a result of the use of services or commodities can include drug abuse, or as a victim of a terrorist activity, kidnapping or an attack, or due to personal engagement in organized criminal activity, victim of an inter gang violence, or as a terrorist, or a suicide bomber (FATF 2010). At the second level (community and region), incidence of illnesses, injuries or deaths within a specific community or regional area can occur due to the same purposes. Examples include, through the use of services or commodities of organized crime groups, deaths related to drugs, as a result of direct involvement, drug debt, terrorist kidnapping, violence linked to terrorism or via a series of organized crimes (FATF 2010). At the third level (national and international), physical harms and patterns of illnesses, injuries, and deaths can occur within a country. Examples include, through the use of services or commodities owned by organized crime groups, a total number of drug-related deaths annually, and as a result of direct involvement in criminal activities, drug debt, terrorist kidnapping, and violence linked to terrorism or a series of organized crimes can result per the FATF.

#### *3.6.2.2 Social Harm*

Social harm represents the damage which occurs due to criminal and other unacceptable behaviours, and the effect they have on others (UNODC 2019). At the first level (individual and local), damage can occur to individuals due to the behaviour of those engaged in organized crime, or due to the use of their services or commodities (FATF 2010). These damages can stem from the proneness to violence of organized crime groups, prolific breaking of the law stemming from drug addiction and an increase in criminal behaviour. Per the FATF, the influence of organized crime groups on others is negative as young people are lured into crime or terrorism as a result of power, easy money, or a sense of affiliation. Effects on the victims who experience organized crime or terrorism can be in the form of distress or inconvenience or identity fraud (FATF 2010). At the second level, a community or region can experience damage to their sense of well-being in a specific geographical area, or between or within ethnic or other social groups. According to the FATF, a decreased level of confidence in local law enforcement and the overall criminal justice system can result due to the activities undertaken by organized crime groups or terrorists. Given the availability of their services and commodities, acquisitive crimes in high rates occur close to drug markets giving rise to a heightened awareness of crime, as well as community tension due to the prevalence of radical views (UNODC 2019). At the third level (national and international), damage is felt by national society as a result of the weakening of social responsibility and belief in the legal entitlement of others, as well as having less regard for the law (FATF 2010). As a result of the activity of criminals or terrorists, or the availability of their services or commodities, an increased level of criminal or non-compliant conduct occurs, including the recreational use of drugs or the evasion of personal taxes, and the reluctance to give assistance to the criminal justice system due to the prevalence of radical views (UNODC 2019).

#### *3.6.2.3 Environmental Harm*

Environmental harm relates to the damage to locality. At the first level (individual and local), damage occurs to a single property due to the activities of organized crime groups (FATF 2010). For example, physical damage to a residence or premises where drugs are manufactured or sold, or due to a terrorist attack, or the actions of those using their services or commodities per the FATF. At the second level (community and region), damage takes place to an area such as an estate, neighbourhood or city, due to the activity of organized crime or terrorism (FATF 2010). Examples include unforeseen health and safety risks such as chemical waste of drug production which is unsafely disposed of, or the existence of explosive materials; or a site being a target for a terrorist attack, etc. At the third level (national and international), damages happen to the entire nation or to vast areas or other countries as a result of the availability of the services, commodities or activities of organized crime. An example may include the demand for class A drugs in some countries causing deforestation in another region such as South America (FATF 2010).

#### *3.6.2.4 Economic Harm*

Economic harm represents the costs of economic impacts at each level (FATF 2010). At the first level (individual and local), the costs are associated with individuals or families for using the services or commodities of organized crime groups. For example, the loss of one's job and the long-term inability to be employed due to drug addiction. The cost passed on to victims and the greater public has to do with thefts, increased insurance premiums, the cost of security, etc. per the FATF. At the second level (community and region), the costs of economic impact relate to activities by terrorists and organized criminals on businesses, services as well as communities in a specific region, city or town. For example, legitimate businesses can experience losses due to robbery or fraud or trade loss or failed business due to illegitimate activities. According to the FATF, losses due to terrorism can include losses that result by not having the ability to trade due to damages to premises, or discouraged customers, and the costs of repairs to damage property. Losses to domestic, public and social services include costs associated with health services for both criminals as well as the victims of terrorism and crime, and the costs of rebuilding infrastructure and damage property (UNODC 2019). Losses to the local communities include a decline in trade or missed opportunities for inward local investment. At the third level (national and international), the costs of economic impact associated with terrorist or organized criminal activities on the nation is direct and indirect (FATF 2010). For example, direct losses are due to illegal working, job availability and the competitive nature of the national industry, losses of direct and indirect revenue from taxes and duty as a result of smuggling goods, as well as originating from fraud (FATF 2010). Indirect losses stem from public expenditure needed for law enforcement, regulation and controls to combat terrorism and organized crime, and those associated with rebuilding infrastructure and repairing property damage (UNODC 2019).

*3.6.2.5 Structural Harm*

Structural harm is described as damage to the perception of integrity in public and private institutions and systems (FATF 2010). At the first level (individual and local), damage is done to the perception of integrity held by individuals in both public and private institutions as well as systems, due to the activities of organized criminals and terrorists (FATF 2010). For example, as a result of the perceived risks associated with online fraud, individuals are afraid of making use of new technology, or due to the perceived risk of an attack by terrorists or a hesitancy towards them as a result of a previous attack, individuals are afraid of specific locations per the FATF. Also, due to the actions of those making use of the services or commodities of organized crime groups, a decreasing level of confidence is held by individuals in the ability of law enforcement to protect them and their property from the activities of organized crime. At the second level (community and region), damage is done to the commonly shared perception of integrity in private and public institutions, and systems, due to the activities of criminals and terrorists as a result of the actions of those making use of their services and commodities (FATF 2010). For example, local area controlled by criminal elements which were seemingly beyond reach, or local businesses or political leaders who are corrupted by or negatively influenced by organized criminals, or due to terrorist activity, local areas become permeated by radical views (FATF 2010). At the third level (national and international), damage is done to the perception of the country as a whole internationally, due to the activity of organized criminals, or the actions of those making use of their services or commodities, or due to the widespread nature of terrorism (FATF 2010). For example, an attack coordinated on the financial sector, such as subprime mortgage fraud, or illegal immigration which is organized and widespread, weakening the integrity of a country's border.

## 3.7 Responsibility

The main issues coming out of the fight against drugs were centred on the numerous threats to the global financial system as a result of its abuse by criminals to launder the proceeds of crime and finance terrorist acts (FATF 2010). The need to protect the global financial system became evident and of utmost importance to the international community. Another key issue was the role purportedly played by OFCs in facilitating money laundering and terrorist financing, which in part, significantly increased the scale and dimensions of money laundering and terrorist financing globally (OECD 1998; UNODC 1998; IMF 2000). In the wake of these mounting concerns international intervention came by way of the G-7 Ministers in their 1989 Summit which resulted in the establishment of the Financial Action Task Force (FATF). This task force was tasked with the mission to develop and promote policies to combat money laundering and terrorist financing (FATF 2010).

### *3.7.1 Financial Action Task Force*

Established by the G-7 Summit in 1989 due to increasing concerns over money laundering, the FATF was charged with the responsibility to establish and promote policies to counter money laundering and terrorist financing at a national and international level.[10] It is described as a "policy-making body" which labours to garner the political will necessary to bring about reforms in national legislation and regulation in these two areas. According to the FATF, to achieve this objective, it employs the following five principle mechanisms detailed below.

[10] See previous chapter for a more comprehensive review of the role of the FATF.

#### 3.7.1.1 *Setting Standards*

The first of these mechanisms include setting standards. The Forty Recommendations established by the FATF in 1990 are a set of international standards aimed at detecting and preventing money laundering. These Recommendations are periodically updated and detail a broad scope of measures which include the criminal justice system and law enforcement, the financial system and its regulation, and international cooperation (FATF 2010). Although they are non-binding, increasingly countries are pressured to implement them into domestic law with some leeway. After 11 September 2001, the FATF's mandate was also extended to include establishing policies to counter the financing of terrorism. This led to the development of eight Special Recommendations which were later expanded to nine, to supplement the Forty Recommendations. Together these Forty Recommendations and Nine Special Recommendations (FAFT standards) are required to be adopted by countries worldwide (FATF 2020).

#### 3.7.1.2 *Assessing the Progress of the Implementation of Its Standards*

Additional pressure to implement such Recommendations takes place mainly through an exercise designed by the FATF to assess the progress of the implementation of its standard at the national level (FATF 2010). This second mechanism involves the conduct of assessments through a peer review process (also referred to as mutual evaluation) on an ongoing basis. This review details a comprehensive description, as well as an analysis of the anti-money laundering and anti-terrorist financing system in place in countries to prevent the abuse of the financial system by criminals.

#### 3.7.1.3 *Monitoring High-Risk Non-cooperative Jurisdictions*

The third mechanism used by the FATF to achieve its goal is the monitoring of high-risk non-cooperative jurisdictions. Such jurisdictions are those that neglect to adequately put the FATF standard into practice, and as a result are a risk to the global financial system.[11] This mechanism was developed to recognize these systemic weaknesses and advocate for stronger compliance. Through this tool, the FATF is effective at applying pressure on such jurisdictions with the underlying objective of forcing

[11] See FATF's website for more details, http://www.fatf-gafi.org/publications/high-risk-and-other-monitored-jurisdictions/?hf=10&b=0&s=desc(fatf_releasedate).

them to enhance their systems to counter money laundering and terrorist financing (FATF 2010).

#### *3.7.1.4 Sector Studies*

Sector studies often referred to as typology reports, is the forth mechanism used by the FATF to accomplish its objective. These studies are essentially research conducted on specific economic areas and activities to determine current and potential vulnerabilities related to money laundering and terrorist financing (FATF 2010). They also examine the different channels which can potentially be used to illegally transfer funds, and are undertaken by suitable experts in the public and private sectors including financial intelligence units, law enforcement and supervisory authorities, etc. Some of the areas covered in its studies include the securities sector, the real estate industry, trade-base money laundering, and terrorist and proliferation financing among others.

#### *3.7.1.5 High-Risk Jurisdictions*

Global safeguards to fight Anti-Money Laundering and Countering Financing of Terrorism (AML/CFT) are as strong as the country with the weakest standard per FATF. Weak AML/CFT measures can be bypassed by criminals to launder money or transfer assets for the purpose of terrorist financing. Another way in which the FATF monitors threats to the financial system is through a process of identifying countries and jurisdictions with significant weakness in their AML/CFT standards considered to be high-risk or non-cooperative, and recommending specific steps through its International Cooperation Review Group (ICRG), which is the fifth mechanism it uses to accomplish its mission (FATF 2010). Through this undertaking, the FATF issues a number of public warnings bring attention to issues concerning vulnerabilities in the AML/CFT systems of the identified countries (FATF 2010). Due to this added pressure, such jurisdictions are compelled to take measures to enhance their systems in order to retain their standing in the global economy. To avoid being identified publicly or the prospect of it in itself, encourages jurisdictions to act swiftly to make significant enhancements to their AML/CFT systems. As this review process is done on an ongoing basis, the FATF continues to strengthen its method for handling high-risk jurisdictions.

According to the FATF, reviews of jurisdictions are performed on the basis of threats, vulnerabilities or specific risks emanating from countries. More specifically, a review will be conducted when a jurisdiction: (i) does not take part in the FATF-style regional body (FSRB) or does not permit the results of the mutual evaluation to be published in a reasonable time; or (ii) when it is recommended by an FSRB or a FATF member. Such recommendation is based on specific risks or threats related to money laundering, the financing of terrorism or proliferation financing brought to their attention; or (iii) it obtains poor ratings on its mutual evaluation, such as (a) receiving 20 or more non-compliant (NC) or partially compliant (PC) ratings; or (b) it has a rating of NC or PC on 3 or more of the following Recommendations: 3, 5, 6, 10, 11 and 20; or (c) it is rated with a level of effectiveness of low or moderate for 9 or more of the total 11 Immediate Outcomes, having at least two lows; or (d) it has a low rating in the level of effectiveness for 6 or more of the total 11 Immediate Outcomes (FATF 2010).

Per the FATF, jurisdictions that undergo ICRG review due to its mutual evaluation ratings are given an observation period of one year to work in conjunction with the FATF or its FSRB to deal with its deficiencies prior to potential public identification including a formal review conducted by the FATF.[12] During the review process, consideration is taken into account by the FATF of the strategic AML/CFT deficiencies highlighted in relation to technical compliance and the efficacy of measures implemented, in addition to any applicable progress made by the country. If such progress is deemed insufficient by the FATF, it proceeds to develop a plan of action with the jurisdiction to deal with the remaining strategic deficiencies. All jurisdictions which undergo the ICRG review are required to provide a political commitment at a high-level confirming it will put in place the legal, regulatory and operational improvements required by the plan of action.

The process of Public Identification takes place through the publication of two statements by the FATF upon completion of each plenary meeting, which occurs in February, June and October of each year. The statements detail a synopsis of the recent steps taken pursuant to the actions place on each jurisdiction, in addition to a list outlining the remaining strategic deficiencies which required further action. The statements also indicate

[12] See website address for more details on ICRG process, http://www.fatf-gafi.org/publications/high-riskandnon-cooperativejurisdictions/more/moreabouttheinternationalco-operationreviewgroupicrg.html?hf=10&b=0&s=desc(fatf_releasedate).

the various levels of risks present at any given period due to the deficiencies which exist in the jurisdictions that are undergoing reviews (FATF 2010).

The Ongoing Process Statement identifies the jurisdictions determined to have strategic deficiencies within their AML/CFT systems which are subject to review by the FATF pursuant to the milestones and timelines agreed to according to the FATF. Members are encouraged to take into account the risks related to money laundering, the financing of terrorism and proliferation financing emanating from the strategic deficiencies which exist in their jurisdictions. If sufficient progress is not made in a timely manner by the jurisdiction, additional pressure can be placed on the jurisdiction by the FATF to make significant progress in order to protect the global financial system from the risk arising from such jurisdiction, by placing it on its Public Statement.

Two groups of jurisdictions are identified through the FATF's Public Statement. They include: (i) jurisdictions where the FATF requires its members as well as non-members to employ enhance measures of due diligence[13] in proportion to the risks stemming from the deficiencies connected to those jurisdictions; and (ii) jurisdictions with serious, prolonged strategic deficiencies which still have neglected to make further progress after the call for improved due diligence by the FATF. With these jurisdictions, the FATF obliges its members and non-members to implement countermeasures[14] to ensure the protection of the global financial system from the risks related to money laundering, the financing of terrorism and proliferation financing applicable to these jurisdictions, as well as to ensure improved due diligence (FATF 2010).

Jurisdictions are required to substantially address all elements in the plan of action in order to be taken off the FATF monitoring process list according to the FATF. Once a determination has been made by the FATF that the elements have been dealt with, it conducts an o-site visit to confirm that the imperative legal, regulatory and if applicable, operational reforms are in progress and the required political commitment as well as

[13] Per the FATF, these include securing addition information on the customer, information on the origin of funds and customer source of wealth and enhance surveillance of business relationship.

[14] Per the FATF, such measures range from particular elements to improve due diligence as well as systemic reporting of activities associated with the jurisdiction, to a prohibition of financial activities with the jurisdiction.

institutional capacity exists to sustain their implementation. If a positive conclusion is made at the end of the on-site visit, a determination is made by the FATF to remove the jurisdiction at its next plenary from Public Identification. Such jurisdiction is required to continue working with the FATF or the applicable FSRB in accordance with its regular follow-up process to enhance its AML/CFT regime.

### *3.7.2 Basel Committee on Banking Supervision*

To further promote the employment of sound AML/CFT standards, as a follow-up to its 1988 Statement of Principles, the Basel Committee on Banking Supervision reaffirmed its stance in combating money laundering and terrorist financing by publishing an amended version of its core principles for effective banking supervision (Bank of International Settlement 2017). Its purpose was to provide banks with a guide to include the risks related to money laundering and terrorist financing into their entire risk management platform per Bank of International Settlement (BIS). The Committee also endorsed the adoption of the FATF standard on banks and admonished that this standard in addition Basel Core Principles fit into the comprehensive framework of banking supervision (BIS 2017). In addition to adopting its guidelines, banks were also encouraged to carry out the national implementation of the standard set by the FATF. The Committee's pledge to fighting money laundering and terrorist financing is in accordance with its mandate, which is "to strengthen the regulation, supervision and practices of banks worldwide, with the purpose of enhancing financial stability" (BIS 2017). For the purpose of this and subsequent chapters, the Recommendations established by the FATF will be the focus of discussion as it relates to countering money laundering and terrorist financing.

## 3.8 Conclusion

OFCs reportedly attracted money launderers and other types of financial crimes due to their prevailing banking confidentiality provisions (Sikka 2003). The use of intricate corporate structures to form a network of transactions, employing nominees, and non-cooperative regulators, all became part of the investigative process undertaken to trace the ill-gotten gains per Sikka. OFCs allegedly added increase difficulties during investigations and prosecutions, as an ulterior motive to ultimately attract international finance to their shores.

The establishment of the FATF to deal with money laundering, and eventually terrorist financing, and proliferation financing came about as a result of concerns from the international community to address the problems that seemingly emanated from these centres. The implementation of Basel Statement of Principles by the Basel Committee on Banking Supervision essentially supported the work undertaken by the FATF. The overall objective of the FATF was to protect the global financial system from the risks associated with money laundering, terrorist financing and proliferation financing. The strategies implemented by this organization to achieve its objective will be discussed in detail in chapter 5.

## References

BIS. 2017. *Understanding Globalization*. Bank of International Settlements. https://www.bis.org/publ/arpdf/ar2017e6.htm.

Buchanan, Bonnie. 2003. Money Laundering—A Global Obstacle. *Research in International Business and Finance* 18: 115–127. https://isiarticles.com/bundles/Article/pre/pdf/52824.pdf.

Butkiewicz, J., and L. Gordon. 2013. The Economic Growth Effect of Offshore Banking in Host Territories: Evidence from the Caribbean. *World Development* 44: 165–179. https://doi.org/10.1016/j.worlddev.2012.09.017.

Custodio, Rafael. 2015. NGOs and Drug Policy. *Sur Journal* 12 (21). https://sur.conectas.org/wp-content/uploads/2015/09/Sur-21_complete-issue_en.pdf.

European Parliament. 2019. *Understanding Money Laundering Through Real Estate Transactions*. European Parliamentary Research Service. https://www.europarl.europa.eu/cmsdata/161094/7%20-%2001%20EPRS_Understanding%20money%20laundering%20through%20real%20estate%20transactions.pdf.

FATF. 2010. *Money Laundering and Terrorist Financing Threat Assessment*. Financial Action Task Force. http://www.fatf-gafi.org/media/fatf/documents/reports/Global%20Threat%20assessment.pdf.

FATF. 2015. *Combating the Abuse of Non-profit Organisations (Recommendation 8)*. Financial Action Task Force. http://www.fatf-gafi.org/media/fatf/documents/reports/BPP-combating-abuse-non-profit-organisations.pdf.

FATF. 2018. *Annual Report 2017–2018*. Financial Action Task Force. https://www.fatf-gafi.org/publications/fatfgeneral/documents/annual-report-2017-2018.html.

FATF. 2011. *Laundering the Proceeds of Corruption*. Financial Action Task Force. https://www.fatf-gafi.org/media/fatf/documents/reports/Laundering%20the%20Proceeds%20of%20Corruption.pdf.

FATF. 2020. *The FATF Recommendations*. Financial Action Task Force. https://www.fatf-gafi.org/media/fatf/documents/recommendations/pdfs/FATF%20Recommendations%202012.pdf.

FATF-Egmont Group. 2020. *Trade-Based Money Laundering: Trends and Developments*. Financial Action Task Force. www.fatf-gafi.org/publications/methodandtrends/documents/trade-based-money-laundering-trends-anddevelopments.html.

Giriraj, Arvind, and Prashant Kumar Mishra. 2001. Role of Banks in Prevention of Money Laundering in India: An Analytical Study. *Law Mantra* 5 (8). https://journal.lawmantra.co.in/wp-content/uploads/2018/05/%E2%80%9CROLE-OF-BANKS-IN-PREVENTION-OF-MONEY-LAUNDERING-IN-INDIA-AN-ANALYTICAL-STUDY%E2%80%9D-BY-MS.-KARABI-DIHINGIA..pdf.

IMF. 2000. *Offshore Financial Centers IMF Background Paper, the Monetary and Exchange Affairs Department*. International Monetary Fund. https://www.imf.org/external/np/mae/oshore/2000/eng/back.htm.

IMF. 2017. *The Bahamas: Select Issues*. IMF Country Report no. 17/315. International Monetary Fund. https://www.imf.org/.

IMF. 2021. *IMF and the Fight Against Money Laundering and the Financing of Terrorism*. International Monetary Fund. https://www.imf.org/en/About/Factsheets/Sheets/2016/08/01/16/31/Fight-Against-Money-Laundering-the-Financing-of-Terrorism.

Nevius, James. 2016. The Strange History of Opiates in America: From Morphine for Kids to Heroin for Soldiers. *The Guardian*, March 15. https://www.theguardian.com/commentisfree/2016/mar/15/long-opiate-use-history-america-latest-epidemic.

OECD. 1998. *Harmful Tax Competition: An Emerging Global Issue*. Paris: OECD Publishing. https://www.oecd-ilibrary.org/taxation/harmful-tax-competition_9789264162945-en.

OECD. 2011. *OECD Due Diligence Guidance for Responsible Supply Chains of Minerals from Conflict-Affected and High-Risk Areas*. Paris: OECD Publishing. https://doi.org/10.1787/9789264111110-en.

O'keefe, John P., and Chiwon Y. Yom. 2017. *Offsite Detection of Insider Abuse and Bank Fraud Among U.S. Failed Banks 1989–2015*. FDIC CFR, WP 2017-06. https://www.researchgate.net/publication/323328196_Offsite_Detection_of_Insider_Abuse_and_Bank_Fraud_Among_US_Failed_Banks_1989-2015.

Sacco, Lisa N. 2014. *Drug Enforcement in the United States: History, Policy, and Trends*. Congressional Research Service. https://fas.org/sgp/crs/misc/R43749.pdf.

Savona, Ernesto U., and Michele Riccardi, eds. 2017. *Assessing the Risk of Money Laundering in Europe*. Transcrime – Università Cattolica del Sacro Cuore. https://www.transcrime.it/iarm/wp-content/uploads/2017/05/ProjectIARM-FinalReport.pdf.

Schroeder, William. R. 2001. Money Laundering: A Global Threat and the International Community's Response. *FBI Law Enforcement Bulletin* 70 (5). https://www.coursehero.com/file/11601296/cj394laundering/.

Sikka, Prem. 2003. The Role of Offshore Financial Centres in Globalization. *Accounting Forum* 27 (4): 365–399. https://ssn.com/abstract=467682.

Unger, Brigitte. 2007. *The Scale and Impacts of Money Laundering*. Cheltenham: Edward Elgar Publishing Ltd.

United Nations. 2001. *Russian Capitalism and Money Laundering*. United Nations Office of Drug and Crime Prevention. https://www.imolin.org/pdf/imolin/rc84066e.pdf.

UNODC. 2008. *2008 World Drug Report*. United Nations Office of Drugs and Crime. https://www.unodc.org/documents/wdr/WDR_2008/WDR_2008_eng_web.pdf.

UNODC. 2011. *Estimating Illicit Financial Flows Resulting from Drug Trafficking and Other Transnational Organized Crimes*. United Nations Office of Drugs and Crime. https://www.unodc.org/documents/data-and-analysis/Studies/Illicit_financial_flows_2011_web.pdf.

UNODC. 1998. *Financial Havens, Banking Secrecy and Money Laundering*. United Nations Office of Drugs and Crime. https://doi.org/10.1007/s12117-999-1048-8.

UNODC. 2012. *The Use of the Internet for Terrorist Purposes*. United Nations Office of Drugs and Crime. https://www.unodc.org/documents/frontpage/Use_of_Internet_for_Terrorist_Purposes.pdf.

UNODC. 2013. *Risk of Money Laundering Through Financial and Commercial Instruments*. United Nations Office of Drugs and Crime. https://www.imolin.org/pdf/Risk_of_Money_Laundering_Version_2.pdf.

UNODC. 2015. *World Drug Report 2015*. United Nations Office of Drugs and Crime. https://www.unodc.org/documents/wdr2015/World_Drug_Report_2015.pdf.

UNODC. 2019. *Linkages Between Organized Crime and Terrorism*. United Nations Office of Drugs and Crime. https://www.unodc.org/documents/e4j/FINAL_Module_16_Linkages_between_Organized_Crime_andTerrorism_14_Mar_2019.pdf.

Yepes, Verdugo Concepcion. 2011. *Compliance with the AML/CFT International Standard: Lessons from a Cross-Country Analysis*. WP/11/77. International Money Fund. https://www.imf.org/external/pubs/ft/wp/2011/wp11177.pdf.

CHAPTER 4

# The Problems and Dimensions of Tax Evasion

## 4.1 Introduction

The free flow of capital cross-borders represented one of the main driving forces of world globalization since the inception of the Bretton-Woods era (Kraft 2014). This free flow of capital considered to be inviolable by traditional Neoliberal theory, was in essence a force that was unstoppable and should not be interfered with by state actors (Kraft 2014). Offshore financial centres (OFCs) are viewed as being intricately linked to the global flow of capital by reducing market frictions and promoting short-term investments (Naitram 2014). Due to their perceived role in aiding criminal activities such as tax evasion and tax avoidance among others, by residents of welfare states which imposed high taxes, OFCs have faced mounting pressures from the OECD and European Union (Dwyer 2002).

The rise in OFCs is said to be attributed to the significant increase in regulation and taxation by states amid the postwar period (Palan 2002). Heavier regulations and taxation resulted in people seeking more means to avoid them. As banking, insurance and ship registration were the most heavily regulated, it is not by coincidence that they are noted as forming the three core parts of offshore business (Figleton 1989 as cited in Palan 2002). Over the 1960s and 1970s, faced with a growing demand for less regulations, many microstates are reported as becoming providers of zero or nominal regulations as a means to attract business to their



A. M. Campbell, *Money Laundering, Terrorist Financing, and Tax Evasion*, https://doi.org/10.1007/978-3-030-68876-9_4

jurisdictions (Palan 2002). The adoption of so-called permissive regulatory climate in some jurisdictions and a stringent regulatory environment in others resulted in gaps and differentials in the regulations of national systems. These differentials are regarded as giving way to perverse competition, regulatory leniency, and a tendency towards OFCs perceived as least regulated (Johns 1983 as cited in Palan 2002).

While disagreements exist between scholars over the underlying reason for the growth of OFCs, the magnitude of financial transactions which are reported to pass through offshore jurisdictions had increased to such an extent that they could not be considered insignificant any longer to the global economy (Christensen and Kapoor 2004). As a result, it was viewed as a necessity by some authors, if solely on the basis of economic efficiency, that offshore finance be subject to more transparency, effective scrutiny, and regulation. According to Christensen and Kapoor, most schemes associated with tax avoidance and tax evasion are reported to include the use of foundations, offshore trusts, charities, international business corporations, holding companies, special purpose vehicles, and artificial transactions. The growth in tax avoidance schemes is said to have developed along with the use of tax competition as a means to entice inwards investments through the use of tax holidays, export processing zones, fiscal subsidies, accelerated depreciation rates and preferential tax terms. OFCs or tax havens were apparently deeply embedded in and represented a substantial portion of global capitalism although they are not reflected in conventional economic analysis (Hampton 1996 as cited in Christensen and Kapoor 2004). As a result, they were viewed as conduits which facilitated the means by which transnational companies withdrew themselves in part or in whole, from taxes and also from regulatory regimes that are nationally based. OFCs were regarded as providing transnational companies with a considerable tax advantage compared to their competitors which were nationally based. This competitive advantage resulted in what was considered to be an uneven level playing field, which gave rise to market distortions per Christensen and Kapoor.

These distortions purportedly contributed to a significant increase in the accumulated tax burden in OECD member countries during the past three decades averaging from 26% of GDP in 1965 to 37% of GDP in 1997 (Tanzi 2001). This growth was compensated by reforms in the composition of tax revenue due to its decline and even halts in recent years in several countries. Although the portion of personal income tax had fallen and the share of corporate income tax was stable, contributions to social security had increased significantly, meanwhile a move from specific taxes to general sales taxes had occurred (Tanzi 2001). The force of globalization was felt more severely with the liberalization of capital markets and the integration of economies in the 1990s. According to Tanzi, since 2000 to 2001 (more or less), a higher share of tax revenues was collected by most industrialized countries compared to the previous two or three decades. Yet he noted the existence of what he referred to as "fiscal termites" chipping away at the infrastructure of their tax systems.[1] The extent of the damage stemming from these so-called termites remained to be seen per Tanzi.

The need for the development of policy measures to address the distortions which had come about was critical, as transnational companies had left domestic tax regimes struggling (Christensen and Kapoor 2004). According to these authors, the most effective way to counter harmful tax practices was through the use of global initiatives. The need for a multilateral framework which would equalize the need for sovereign states to safeguard their tax revenues against aggressive schemes to avoid tax, and the right to determine the appropriate tax rate by democratic governments for their particular circumstances was critical (Christensen and Kapoor 2004). Equally so, measures were also needed to enable governments to prevent their tax losses and effectively deal with the pressures deriving from transnational companies to weaken their tax regimes (Christensen and Kapoor 2004).

## 4.2 Tax Evasion

Tax evasion was another phenomenon which added an additional layer to the complexity to money laundering. According to the OECD, between 1985 and 1994, the growth of foreign direct investment in low-tax jurisdictions located in the Caribbean and in States of the South Pacific Islands by G7 countries had grown more than fivefold to over $200 billion dollars. This growth rate was dramatically more than the aggregate outbound foreign direct investment of these countries combined (OECD 1998). The authors of the GTZ Sector Programme Public Finance article

[1] Per Tanzi, fiscal termites include; E-commerce and transactions, electronic money, intracompany trade, offshore financial centers, derivatives and hedge funds, inability to tax financial capital, growing foreign activities and foreign shopping. These factors each have adverse effects on the ratio of tax revenue to GDP raised by OECD countries.

noted that an estimated US$285 billion is lost by developing countries to tax evasion in the local domestic economy. They also estimated between US$35 billion to US$160 billion are lost in tax revenues as a result of income shifting by corporations. Among the wealthy, approximately US$15 billion to US$124 billion are lost in tax revenues per year. Overall the article estimated that around US$859 billion to US$1.06 trillion are lost by developing countries in tax revenues annually.

Tax evasion and tax avoidance occur in both developed and developing countries. In fact, in 2007, tax revenues in OECD countries accounted for approximately 36% of the gross national income, whereas in Africa, it was estimated at 23% for the same period, and 17.5% in 2004 in Latin America (GTZ Sector Programme Public Finance, Administrative Reform 2010). The results of these statistics reveal that developing countries were more vulnerable to tax evasion and tax avoidance than developed countries. According to the GTZ Sector Programme Public Finance, Administrative Reform, some of the contributing factors had to do with: (i) tax structures in developing countries not being up to international standards; (ii) inadequate management of tax policy; (iii) low adherence to tax policies; and (iv) inadequacies in tax administration. Other factors related to the economic conditions that differ in each country, and the heavy reliance of developing countries on indirect taxes such as value added taxes (VAT) which accounted for up to two-thirds of tax revenues, compared to the major role that personal income taxes play in tax revenues for OECD countries (GTZ Sector Programme Public Finance, Administrative Reform 2010).

## 4.3 Factors that Facilitate Tax Evasion

Accordance to the GTZ Sector Programme Public Finance Administrative Reform, the factors which facilitate tax evasion and tax avoidance can be divided into two categories: (i) those which negatively impact the tax payer's willingness to pay taxes; and (ii) those which contribute to the difficulties faced by tax administrators and the courts to enforce tax payments.

### 4.3.1 Factors that Negatively Impacts the Tax Payers' Willingness to Pay Taxes

This first category depicts factors which result in a low level of compliance with tax policies. These factors relate to the quality of services provided by governments in return for taxes paid by the tax payer. If the level of service was low or inadequate, tax payers may be unwilling to pay taxes, which could result in tax evasion and tax avoidance. Another factor was the perception of fairness in the tax system (GTZ Sector Programme Public Finance, Administrative Reform 2010). That is, if its tax rates were perceived as high, the tax burden reduced the amount of disposable income available to the tax payer, which in turn encouraged tax evasion and tax avoidance. If the tax structure was such whereby the corporate tax rate was lower compared to the income tax rate for individuals, then tax payers may again be inclined to find alternative means to reduce or avoid tax payments. This concept equally applied to corporate tax payers who in turn would look for alternative means to explore loopholes in the tax system to reduce the amount of taxes owed or evade tax payments (GTZ Sector Programme Public Finance, Administrative Reform 2010).

Equally so, a low level of transparency and the lack of accountability in fiscal spending resulted in public distrust and led to tax evasion and tax avoidance (GTZ Sector Programme Public Finance, Administrative Reform 2010). Similarly, significant levels of corruption, which resulted in uncertainty in the use of tax revenues to pay for public goods and services, could lead to tax evasion and tax avoidance. Similar results applied if there was a lack of rule of law and governance within a jurisdiction. If tax payers were unable to obtain just treatment in the court of law, this encouraged an environment of distrust and increased the lack of transparency in the legal system, which could result in their decision to evade or avoid payment of their tax liabilities. The costs required to adhere to the payment of ones' tax liabilities could be a deterrent factor to individual and corporate tax payers alike and could result in tax evasion and tax avoidance (GTZ Sector Programme Public Finance, Administrative Reform 2010). The average time to prepare and pay taxes in OECD countries is estimated at 210 hours, compared to other countries such as Bolivia at 1080 hours and Brazil at 2600 hours. This greatly increased the administrative cost to comply with tax policies, which could lead to the reduction in the tax payer's willingness to comply.

### 4.3.2 *Difficulties Faced by Tax Administrators and the Courts to Enforce Tax Payments*

This second category relates mainly to the challenges of enforcing tax laws. One of the main difficulties many developing countries face is in the collection of taxes (GTZ Sector Programme Public Finance, Administrative Reform 2010). The principal reason had to do with the challenge of creating and maintaining a proper functioning tax register of all tax payers, especially determining those who were liable for tax payments. One drawback to this challenge was the capacity of tax administrators due to the organizational structure of the tax administration and how it interfaced with the ministry of finance. Whether this relationship was direct, whereby the ministry assumed the tax administration function and was responsible for collecting taxes, or indirect, in that, this function was delegated to another government agency. Another difficulty that developing countries faced was the challenge of detecting and punishing illegal tax practices (GTZ Sector Programme Public Finance, Administrative Reform 2010). The shortage in the capacity of the tax administration to investigate and apply the law to would be offenders influence the tax paper's decision whether to evade or avoid taxes or not. Further, the strength of the legal system also served to enforce the actions of tax payers (GTZ Sector Programme Public Finance, Administrative Reform 2010). If the legal system proved to be effective, it could serve as a deterrent to tax evasion and tax avoidance. If it was ineffective, it could encourage tax payers to commit tax evasion or avoid taxes. Likewise, constant changes to tax laws could result in a higher level of complexity and become confusing to tax administrators and tax payers. This could reduce the level of compliance among tax payers and encourage activities such as tax evasion and tax avoidance, due to the complex or contradictory nature of the tax system.

## 4.4 Challenges of Tax Evasion

In the past, domestic tax systems were primarily focused on economic and social concerns. Although an international element existed which took into consideration the foreign sourced income of residents and income earned by non-residents, domestic tax systems had very minimal spillover effect on other world economies. Today, the liberalization of cross-border trade and investment due to globalization has resulted in the integration of national economies. This integration has provided the ability for domestic tax policies to impact economies of other countries. Considered as one of the main challenges to tax evasion, globalization has also attributed to the ongoing assessment of tax systems in many countries to improve their ability to attract foreign direct investment. These assessment processes have resulted in tax reforms to reduce tax barriers to better facilitate capital inflow. It has not only increased the amount of mobile capital available, but has also contributed to the creation of capital and financial markets, and increased competition among businesses in the global market place. The increase of capital flow across borders and the expansion of capital and financial markets, have ultimately resulted in more efficient management of resources which has led to better welfare and living conditions throughout the world.

### *4.4.1 Globalization and Its Effects*

Although globalization has had positive impacts on improving tax systems overall, it has come at a very high cost to many countries around the world, particularly to G7 countries. The fact that there were individuals and companies which sought ways to avoid or minimize their taxes, and countries that underwent tax reforms to attract capital from these players had become a major concern for G7 countries. This was due mainly to the fact that mobile capital was diverted to countries which offered zero or low tax incentives, adversely affecting countries to which such capital was owed. These negative impacts had the potential to: (1) reduce the pool of money from which taxes were collected; (2) alter the tax structure by shifting the tax burden to other more relevant factors; and (3) restrict the ability to gradually increase tax rates and achieve re-allocative goals.

Another aspect of globalization was that it provided loopholes in which domestic tax legislation could be exploited, particularly by multinational corporations (McClure et al. 2016). According to McClure et al., this occurred due to the fact that the global economy was highly concentrated with multinational companies. The use of integrated financial markets to transfer capital, and digital systems including the Internet to allow connection with customers worldwide, resulted in gaps or mismatches within and among national tax laws. These disparities were exploited by multinational companies with the underlying objective of reducing their overall tax liabilities. Prior to globalization, the main tax concern facing multinational companies was the problem of double taxation, where profits earned by a foreign affiliate were taxed in the country where the operation was located and then taxed again once the after-tax profits were received in the country where the company's headquarters was located (McClure et al. 2016). The implementation of bilateral tax treaties allowed the two countries involved to determine which country would levy taxes. The existence of these tax treaties, however, resulted in another problem referred to as double non-taxation, which essentially was the avoidance of payment of taxes in both countries involved in the bilateral tax treaty (McClure et al. 2016). This process had a negative effect on the corporate tax systems in both countries and allowed multinational companies to have a competitive advantage over domestic companies. Due to the global nature of multinational companies, the problem of double non-taxation affected all countries, particularly developing countries which were faced with other pressing challenges and perhaps were not able to address this issue (McClure et al. 2016).

Globalization also presented opportunities for corporate and individual tax payers to reduce or avoid taxes, and at the same time, it created loopholes that were exploited by countries through the development of tax policies which were reportedly designed primarily to attract financial and other mobile capital from different geographical areas (OECD 1998). The cross-border movement of capital as a result of globalization was viewed as creating a distortion in trade and investment patterns and a reduction of welfare globally according to the OECD. These tax strategies are said to have contributed to the erosion of national tax bases and the alteration of tax structures, thereby shifting a portion of the tax burden from mobile to immobile components, and a movement from income to consumption tax base (OECD 1998). They also were said to prevent the employment of progressive tax rates and the attainment of redistributive goals per the OECD. The inevitable consequences which resulted from the application of such tax strategies included: (i) the reformation of tax structures due to spillover effects, as countries were compelled to make modification to their tax bases despite the fact that better results could have come about through the use of intensified international cooperation; and (ii) the ripple effect of one country's tax policies on that of another country. Both factors were applicable to the corporate income and private investment income of individual tax payers (OECD 1998).

Increased globalization and the interfacing among tax systems also had the potential to cause adverse spillover effects on the spending side per the OECD. Due mainly to financial outlays, countries confronted public spending commitments and constraints. Investors who invested in tax havens with zero or minimal tax, and resided in countries which were non-haven, were viewed as having a competitive edge to take advantage of such jurisdictions to reduce their tax liability at home. These taxpayers were perceived as "free riders" who gained from public spending at home but circumvented contributing their portion to its financing. In a similar light, governments as well as tax haven residents were also viewed as "free riders", benefiting from public goods generated by non-haven countries (OECD 1998). The OECD recognized that mismatches which resulted in harmful effects may exist between tax systems were unintentional in some cases, where a country did not deliberately engage in exploiting the interfacing of tax systems to take from the tax base of another jurisdiction. It also acknowledged the fact that such opportunities could be taken advantage of by taxpayers which could have negative effects on both countries, and could be addressed through measures that were unilateral or bilateral. However, it was reportedly very concerned with mismatching which were said to occur due to the exploitation of the interaction between tax systems through the imposition of special tax policies which were viewed as resulting in the erosion of the tax base of other jurisdictions. The consequences of this process, was perceived as one which allowed such countries to revert capital and financial flows, as well as corresponding revenues, from other countries by what was portrayed as aggressively competing for their tax base, often referred to as "poaching". Per the OECD, this type of practice was considered to be harmful tax competition, as it did assumedly not take into consideration different reasoning regarding the suitable level of taxes and public spending or the right mix of taxes necessary for an economy. Rather, its aim was designed to lure investments or savings which originated in other jurisdictions, or to aid in the avoidance of taxes which belonged to other countries.

### *4.4.2 Tax Havens*

At the centre of the problem of harmful tax competition, namely tax evasion and tax avoidance, were tax havens and harmful preferential tax regimes.[2] Traditionally, the existence of the global financial system

[2] For purposes of this book, tax havens are the focus of this paper. Preferential tax regimes are mentioned here only due to the fact that they have similar adverse factors as tax havens, and to provide a holistic perspective of the complexities of the matter being discussion.

promoted capital flows and enhanced liquidity in financial markets which tax havens for the most part relied on (OECD 1998). The liberalization and deregulation of financial markets in non-haven countries are said to have contributed positively to tax havens due to these factors. However, due to the tax benefits (no or nominal taxes) offered by tax havens, their existence have been perceived as having a significant negative effect on the revenue bases of other jurisdictions as they were viewed as jurisdictions which redirected financial capital from other countries according to the OECD. Due to the incentives offered by tax havens to minimize taxes, coupled with their ability to maintain financial confidentiality, they were reportedly attractive to corporate as well as individual investors. Such jurisdictions were presented by the OECD as carrying out three core functions. They served as a jurisdiction for the purpose of presumably: (i) holding passive investments; (ii) booking "paper" profits; and (iii) providing confidentiality, thereby reportedly safeguarding the bank accounts of taxpayers from examination by tax authorities in other jurisdictions. As a result of these functions, tax havens were positioned as centres which purportedly facilitated income tax evasion and tax avoidance by individuals and corporate taxpayers, which caused potential harm to tax systems in other countries (OECD 1998).

OFCs and tax havens had increased in importance due to their prescribed role as conduits for financial investments. The flow of digital information had spurned their growth and facilitated the movement of money and knowledge more easily and economically in real time (Tanzi 2001). It was estimated that more than US$5 trillion were deposited in legal entities such as international business companies in these jurisdictions. Of this amount, it was not certain how much of the earnings were reported to tax authorities (Tanzi 2001). The growth in derivatives and hedge funds used as agents to channel savings, particularly in OFCs which were viewed as less regulated, was a concern for tax authorities. Per Tanzi, similar to e-commerce, the challenges confronted by tax authorities with these instruments and to a greater degree with hedge funds included: (i) the move from paper transactions which were used by tax authorities to trail evidence, to digital transactions which left little to no identifiable traces; and (ii) the technological shift from the sale of a physical product to a digital one made it increasingly difficult to determine for tax purposes a "permanent establishment", and therefore the tax jurisdiction, thus making it problematic to determine the tax payer who should pay the tax, and the jurisdiction that should collect it. Other challenges per

Tanzi included the fact that earnings derived from derivative instruments presented a significant problem when it came to identifying the transactions, the individual beneficiaries and jurisdictions. Another problem was that such instruments could be used in tax-avoidance strategies, profiting from uncertainties and inconsistencies involved in their tax treatment. Additionally, the differences between capital income and capital losses and gains, as well as between dividends and interests become very fluid. Due to the extensive use of such instruments, the ability to tax income derived from cross-border investments through tax withholding at the source was impossible (Tanzi 2001). Further, there was a growing inability of tax authorities in countries to tax financial capital. This was due to the increasing integration and efficiency of the international capital markets, countries were finding it more difficult to tax mobile capital. The high tax rates imposed in countries served as an incentive to tax payers to transfer capital abroad to countries with lower taxes or take-up residence there (Tanzi 2001).

OFCs and the global mobility of capital also reportedly made possible wealth transfers from citizens to capital, and to the wealthy elites (Sikka 2003). For instance, through the use of approximately 800 subsidiaries registered in well-known offshore tax havens including Bermuda, the Cayman Islands, the British Virgin Islands and the Netherlands Antilles, News Corporation, the business empire of Rupert Murdoch, for a period of 4 years paid only A$325 million in taxes based on the pre-tax profits of A$5.4 billion it generated, which is equivalent to 6% effective tax rate (The Economist, 1999 March 20, 83–84 as cited in Sikka 2003). A principal rationale behind this was the creation of residence in such offshore tax havens with minimal taxes per Sikka. In another case, Newscorp Investments, a British holding company, had accumulated business profits of around £1.4 billion for a period of 11 years but paid minimal or no British corporate tax. At the 30% UK corporate tax rate, more than £350 million should have been paid in taxes, which would be sufficient to put an end to tuition fees for students attending university (The Guardian, 21 July 2001, 1 as cited in Sikka 2003), to fund 7 new hospitals, or construct 50 secondary schools, or 300 elementary schools (The Economist, 20 March 1999, 83–84 as cited in Sikka 2003). Through the use of offshore tax havens, virtually zero corporate tax was paid by Newscorp Investments in Britain. In addition to using OFCs to book their profits, companies also used offshore vehicles to pay employees and thereby accumulated savings on payroll taxes. For example, through the use of a sophisticated offshore structure, Barclays Capital paid staff bonus through a Jersey company, Abacus Corporate Trustee Limited (The Telegraph, 14 November 200,214 as cited in Sikka 2003). In exchange for units at a cost of 1 penny each, employees forewent bonuses, which was over a period of ten years redeemable at £100. This scheme brought in savings of about 12% in payroll taxes for Barclays Capital per Sikka.

## 4.5 Incentives

Incentives to address the problem of tax evasion came about as a result of the significant detrimental impacts aforementioned which were felt to varying degrees by many countries. In addition to these effects, another concern was the increase in tax evasion by organized criminals, wealthy individuals and transnational companies. Another worry was the increasing use of offshore companies to bypass exchange control, and the rise in multinational companies' use of tax avoidance schemes. An emerging issue which eventually rose to the forefront was the concern of harmful tax competition among developed countries, and the pressure placed on governments by lobbyist and business consulting firms to introduce tax incentives to attract inward investments also contributed to the need to address the issue of tax evasion. Further, the issues which came out as a result of the Panama Papers, particularly as they relate to tax havens and their reported use to evade taxes by wealthy citizens of developed countries, and their associated role in tax avoidance schemes by multi-transnational companies, resulted in adverse impacts on developed countries. As a consequence of their reportedly dubious use by select parties, tax havens became the central focus of the international community's fight against tax evasion and tax avoidance.[3]

### *4.5.1 Tax Evasion by Organized Criminals, Wealthy Individuals and Transnational Companies*

The emerging phenomena of tax evasion by organized criminals, wealthy individuals and transnational companies was one of the impetuses which contributed to the urgent need for international intervention. Tax evasion

[3] For purposes of this book, tax evasion is the focus of this chapter. Tax avoidance is mentioned here to provide a holistic perspective of the complexities of the matter being discussion.

was initially viewed as a spillover effect associated with the gains earned from illegal activities through organized crime (Morse 2015). Increasing tax rates in the US and UK during the 1930s in addition to other factors, led to increased tax evasion by wealthy individuals (Morse 2015). The gradual lift of capital controls in European countries and in the UK in the 1980s also increased the demand for OFCs services (Dwyer 2002). The proliferation of OFCs, coupled with the free movement of capital cross borders, has reportedly led to tax regimes searching for ways to protect their tax bases from tax avoidance schemes carried out by wealthy individuals, and from profit laundering activities conducted by transnational businesses (Christensen and Kapoor 2004). The magnitude of tax avoidance schemes was described as a shadow economy functioning in most of the globalized sectors, particularly in extractive industries such as banking and finance, shipping, aviation, communication, media, pharmaceuticals, the weapons industry, and in trading commodities (Christensen and Kapoor 2004). Given the secretive nature of their activities, it was impossible to precisely measure the magnitude of the shadow economy. However, the following estimates gave an idea of its magnitude: (i) at least 50% of the world trade seemingly went through tax havens, although such jurisdictions only made up roughly 3% of global GDP; (ii) the government of the UK observed that 60% of international trade was being conducted through intracompany transactions most of which were said to make use of tax havens which levied zero tax rates on profits (The Economist, 2004 as cited in Christensen and Kapoor 2004); (iii) an estimated US$11 trillion of assets were held offshore in jurisdictions that imposed zero tax rates or minimal tax, which was said to represent more than one-third of global GDP; (iv) tax havens and OFCs had grown considerably, from 25 in the mid-1970s to 60 in 2003 per the IMF, and to as many as 73 per other sources; (v) this growth was purportedly driven by the increase in high net individuals and the rapid growth of multinational companies from 37,000 in the early 1990s per UNCTAD with 175,000 subsidiaries overseas, to an estimated 64,000 multinational companies with 870,000 subsidiaries (The Economist, 2004 as cited in Christensen and Kapoor 2004); (vi) the estimated volume of money passing through tax havens on an annual basis was approximately US$7 trillion, equivalent to the global value of trade in goods and services, which was greater than the sum of the traded value of goods and services through tax havens, with the difference being credited to business dealings financial in nature (Oxfam, 2000 as cited in Christensen and Kapoor

2004); and (vii) the estimated number of offshore companies formed per year was around 150,000 and were now considered to be in the millions (Christensen and Kapoor 2004).

### 4.5.2 *Aggressive Tax Avoidance Schemes*

Aggressive tax avoidance schemes undertaken by transnational companies which could be facilitated through the use of offshore finance centres and tax havens reportedly resulted in the erosion of the equity and integrity of existing tax structures, a rise in the administrative cost to collect tax revenues, and the expansion of income disparities between and within nation states (Christensen and Hampton 2000 as cited in Christensen and Kapoor 2004). Competition of this sort, which was viewed on an uneven level basis, is regarded as unsustainable based on evidence which pointed to a downward trend over the long term in corporate income tax rates noted in OECD countries (Christensen and Kapoor 2004). For example, the average corporate income tax rate in OECD countries was 37.5% in 1996, which decreased to 30.8% by 2003. In Eastern Europe, a substantial reduction in corporate income tax rates between 2003 and 2004 was undertaken by a number of countries including Poland by 29%, Slovakia by 24%, and the Ukraine by 16.7%, leading towards a similar position taken by Estonia, with a zero percent corporate income tax rate.

### 4.5.3 *Tax Competition Among States*

Tax competition among states was also considered to be economically harmful due to the following reasons: (i) it reallocated the tax load between various factors of production and types of economic activities, resulting in an increase in labour costs with regard to capital and promoting short-term speculative activities putting long-term fixed investments at a disadvantage; (ii) it allowed higher mobility of transnational companies and high net individuals to take full advantage of offshore tax structures, thereby diminishing the integrity and fairness of tax structures, thus forming a free-rider economy; (iii) it facilitated the use of tax avoidance structures which were often aggressive and elaborate, and resulted in increased administrative costs in collecting tax revenues; and (iv) it gave way to extensive tax avoidance and tax evasion which increased income disparities between and within nation states, and resulted in the departure of the very wealthy from their social and economic obligations (Christensen and Kapoor 2004).

### 4.5.4 *Pressure by Lobbyist*

Governments of developing countries were under significant pressure by lobbyist, especially business consulting firms, to give tax incentives to attract inward investments. The immense competition between developing countries, most of whom had tax departments that were under-resourced, allowed transnational companies to apply great political pressure to obtain preferential tax treatment (Christensen and Kapoor 2004). Developing countries were reported loosing at least US$50 billion per annum in revenues as a result of tax competition and tax avoidance schemes. This estimate was considered to be conservative and did not take into account losses resulting from transfer pricing and tax evasion (Oxfam 2000 as cited in Christensen and Kapoor 2004).[4] Together, tax avoidance and the issues associated with capital flight and corruption impacted developing countries enormously with approximately US$500 billion in tinted money flowing out of poorer countries (Baker and Nordin 2004 as cited in Christensen and Kapoor 2004). The emanating impact on developing countries as well as transitioning economies were massive, compelling many of them to acquire debt through financial markets to cover revenues and capital expenditures, that if funded using tax revenues, would have otherwise been less expensive (Christensen and Kapoor 2004). Overall, the total impact of capital flight on less developed countries, as well as the proceeds of fraud, tax evasion, corruption, and misappropriation was enormous. Further, most of such countries did not have the resources to pursue tedious investigations in jurisdictions offshore, which provided a nearly impenetrable secrecy veil and were notoriously reluctant to cooperate with other authorities, other than in situations where such authorities provided evidence in advance of a criminal activity taking place in the offshore finance centre (Christensen and Kapoor 2004).

[4] Losses includes; non-taxation on capital gains, tax incentives on inward investment and other techniques, as well as tax holidays. Most have been implemented under pressure stemming from threats to hold back on inward investment from large corporation unless tax incentives are provided.

### 4.5.5 *The Existence of Offshore Financial Centres*

The existence of offshore companies stemmed from their usefulness in bypassing exchange control regulations per the authors. A significant amount of capital which passed through offshore jurisdictions was layered through many offshore finance centres, and was perceived to be for the purposes of money laundering. A significant share of this flight in capital originated from economies in Brazil, Russia, Indonesia, Congo and Nigeria (Christensen and Kapoor 2004). For example, an estimated 60% of the trade transactions going into and leaving Africa were miss-priced through the use of abusive techniques employed in transfer pricing and re-invoicing on average by 11% in the late 1990s, leading to a capital flight component equivalent to 7% of Africa trade accumulating to between US$10 to US$11 billion in prices per annum in 1999. On a similar note, the Financial Times estimated that during the 1990s capital flow going into and out of Russia's economy was to the point that for each dollar flowing into Russia, US$20 flowed out to bank accounts offshore (Christensen and Kapoor 2004). It was also estimated that each year around £16.5 billion left the Russian economy in capital flight (The Times, June 9, 2000 as cited in Sikka 2003), and per the US Treasury, in 1998 approximately $70 billion was moved out of Russia to offshore accounts located in Nauru, a country with a population of 10,000 and 400 banks (Sikka 2003). Further, findings from the Panama papers indicated that an estimated US$2.1 trillion was stashed away overseas by American companies to avoid paying taxes (Bloomberg 2015 as cited in Zaidi et al. 2017).

Due to what was viewed as promoting the capital flight and tax avoidance, offshore tax havens were positioned as jurisdictions which encouraged economic underdevelopment (Sikka 2003). Through the use of offshore vehicles such as tax-exempted companies and International Business Companies (IBCs), company profits were reportedly booked in OFCs even though they conducted little business in such havens. Additionally, due to their adherence to secrecy and so-called lenient regulation, OFCs purportedly facilitated corrupt businessmen and leaders to steal money and impede the economic development of their nations (Sikka 2003). Based on the findings coming out of the Panama Papers by the International Consortium of Investigative Journalists (ICIJ), the majority of the offshore companies which were incorporated by Mossack Fonseca on behalf of their respective clients were presumably for illegal purposes such as financial fraud, money laundering, tax evasion, averting international sanctions, and kleptocracy(Christensen and Kapoor 2004). ICIJ also found that shell companies were used not only by rich individuals, their relatives and associates, but also by public officials including several present and former presidents, their relatives and associates, as well as business tycoons, celebrities, and government bureaucrats from over 40 countries worldwide (Zaidi et al. 2017). The Panama Papers also revealed startling information concerning money laundering and tax evasion on a global scale by a number of the most influential and powerful people in the world, which led to the resignations to many world leaders, including Sigmundur Davíð Gunnlaugsson, former Prime Minister of Iceland, Mauricio Macri, ex-president of Argentina, and Nawaz Sharif, former Prime Minister of Pakistan (Zaidi et al. 2017).

Tax havens were perceived as enabling companies and the very wealthy with a means to avoid their tax obligations, thereby restricting the ability of individual countries to generate tax revenues from their residents, as well as from foreign-owned capital (Oxfam 2000 as cited in Sikka 2003). This reportedly impairs the ability of poor country governments to undertake vital investments in economic infrastructure and social services to sustain economic development and human welfare. This also supposedly gave transnational companies, which took advantage of international tax avoidance loopholes, an unfair competitive edge in comparison with their domestic competitors, in addition to small and medium size companies (Sikka 2003). OFCs also seemingly facilitated a safe haven for proceeds deriving from political corruption, the global drug trade, and illicit arms dealing, thus promoting the spread of global crime and facilitating the looting of public funds by corrupt elites per Sikka. This reportedly contributed to growing criminality and inhibited the transparent development of budget processes in poverty-stricken countries. OFCs have also been said to have contributed to the increasing occurrences of financial crises which ruin livelihoods in impoverished countries, yet they were considered essential to the operation of global financial markets (Sikka 2003). The instability of currency along with the rapid surges and turnaround in capital flows to less developed countries have led to defining characteristics of global financial markets in the past years and have seemingly been partly responsible for the financial crises (Oxfam 2000 as cited in Sikka 2003).

The activities which supposedly took place in OFCs are reported to have left significant social scares. They are said to impair the ability of elected governments to finance healthcare, education, pensions, as well as other social infrastructures needed to eradicate poverty and deal with environmental degradation (Sikka 2003). For example, an estimated US$15 billion per annum is lost in tax revenues in Germany to personal savings that are undeclared and held in bank accounts offshore (Christensen & Hampton, 1999 as cited in Sikka 2003). Due to hidden asset held offshore, approximately $70 billion is reportedly lost in tax revenues in the US per annum, large enough to fund free healthcare for the entire country (Sikka 2003). Per a report published by Deloitte & Touche regarding tax avoidance schemes carried out by wealthy individuals and companies, an estimated £100 billion pounds in tax revenues is lost by Europe per year (Financial Mail, November 25, 2001, p.10 as cited in Sikka 2003), and approximately £85 billion by Britain (Mitchell and Sikka 2002 as cited in Sikka 2003) annually in tax avoidance and tax evasion, which amounts to many schools, hospitals and pensions.

## 4.6 Responsibility

The devastating effects that harmful tax competition had on economies of developed countries became the principal concern of the international community which had to be addressed (Christensen and Kapoor 2004). The billions of dollars lost each year to tax evasion and tax avoidance presumably through the use of OFCs by their very own citizens and transnational companies, which were resident of such offshore countries for tax purposes, as well as their increasing inability to meet their public expenditure requirements due such losses, became a pressing concern (Christensen and Kapoor 2004). Another key issue which became a central concern was the perceived role played by mainly by OFCs in the following: (i) harmful tax competition between developed countries; (ii) competition among tax havens themselves; (iii) their lack of transparency stemming from the bank secrecy provisions which afforded protection to their clients; and (iv) their reluctance to assist in inquiries and investigations (Christensen and Kapoor 2004). To address the growing concerns of harmful tax competition, the OECD was initially delegated with this responsibility, which eventually in turn assigned this duty to the Global Forum (OECD 1998).

### *4.6.1 The OECD*

From its inception, the mission of the OECD was to encourage policies that enhanced the economic and social well-being of people worldwide (Morriss and Moberg 2012). Overtime, its primary focus which was to enhance commerce by finding solutions to double taxation issues gradually shifted to curbing "harmful" tax competition and strengthening automatic exchange of tax information (Morriss and Moberg 2012). From the early 1970s the OECD has been dealings with tax competition stemming from "tax havens", and initiated efforts in the early 1980s to influence tax policies at a national level among member and non-member states on information exchange and tax rates to safeguard member states from harmful tax competition (Morriss and Moberg 2012). At its 1996 ministerial meeting of finance ministers, the OECD was tasked to "analyze and develop measures to counter the distorting effects of 'harmful tax competition' on investment and financing decisions, and the consequences on national tax bases, and report back in 1998" (OECD 1998).

In 1998 the OECD Council adopted the report, "Harmful Tax Competition, An Emerging Global Issue", prepared in response to an appeal from the Ministers to establish measures to combat harmful tax practices. This report laid the groundwork for the OECD's work in this field (OECD 1998). Based upon this report, the OECD's Council established a set of recommendations for all Member countries to follow, in addition to guidelines regarding harmful preferential tax regimes to counteract harmful tax competition. The work originally embarked on three fronts. The first was to identify the harmful features of regimes with preferential taxes in OECD member states and eliminate them. The second was to identify tax havens and encourage their commitments to transparency principles and effective information exchanges. The third front was to encourage other non-OECD countries to partner with the OECD. Over time the approach to the OECD's work has developed into the principles of transparency and effective exchange of information. These two elements as they relate to the work of non-OECD member countries have been increasingly performed jointly with the Global Forum on Exchange of Information for Tax Purposes (the Global Forum), the organization through which the OECD engages in dialogue on issues related to tax matters with non-OECD countries (OECD 2006).

The 1998 Report set forth a number of criteria to identify harmful preferential tax regimes. It also laid out the timeframe set for Member countries of the OECD to identify the harmful features in their respective regimes, report such features and eliminate them (OECD 1998). To encourage the use of these guidelines among non-Member countries, the 1998 Report also provided a forum to identify countries which met the criteria of a tax haven to counter the proliferation of such jurisdictions. It also laid out the general framework for a unified approach to employ defensive strategies to control harmful tax competition (OECD 1998). In 2000, the OECD presented a report which listed 47 potentially harmful preferential regimes based on the factors outlined in the 1998 Report for Member countries, a list of 35 jurisdictions considered to be tax heavens per the criteria set forth in the 1998 Report,[5] and provided an update on the work in progress with non-Member countries. With respect to the list of jurisdictions which met the criteria of a tax haven, the 2000 Report noted that the Committee of Fiscal Affairs would continue ongoing cooperative dialogue with such jurisdictions and would establish a List of Uncooperative Jurisdictions consisting of tax havens, which did not cooperate to eliminate harmful tax practices in their jurisdictions. Such countries would be subject to sanctions which could be applied bilaterally or collectively, should they not cooperate with the initiatives of the OECD or comply with the provisions detailed in the Memorandum of Understanding. Since its initial report, subsequent progress reports were published by the OECD in 2001, 2004, and 2006. Of the 47 jurisdictions identified in its 2000 Report as potentially harmful, only one of such jurisdictions was deemed harmful after further review. Legislation later passed by this jurisdiction led to the abolishment of the regime (OECD 2015).

### 4.6.2 *The Global Forum on Exchange of Information for Tax Purposes (the Global Forum)*

The work conducted by the OECD in the area of transparency and exchange of information for tax purposes on non-OECD economies has been increasingly undertaken by the Global Forum. Since its restructure in 2009, it has become a crucial international body undertaking the enforcement of the internationally agreed standards on tax transparency

[5] See OECD Report to the 2000 Ministerial Council Meeting and Recommendation by the Committee on Fiscal Affairs for both lists.

(OECD 2018). These standards include Exchange of Information on Request (EOIR) and Automatic Exchange of Information (AEOI). EOIR gives tax authority the ability to access specific information from their peers in other jurisdictions. This standard is broad in scope as it allows for any "information foreseeably relevant" to be provided to a tax authority on request for the enforcement or administration of the local tax laws of another country, or for execution of the provisions of an applicable tax agreement (OECD 2018). Information commonly exchanged through EOIR includes beneficial and legal ownership, bank account details and accounting records. According to the OECD, EOIR applies only during the time of an ongoing inquiry or when an investigation is taking place in the requesting jurisdiction (OECD 2018).

The Global Forum tracks the progress of the implementation of its international tax transparency standards through a peer review process (OECD 2016). This process evaluates the compliance with the international standard on transparency and exchange of information on request by jurisdictions in two phases. Phase one analyses the legal and regulatory framework of a jurisdiction taking into consideration the Terms of Reference which consists of ten fundamental elements divided into three main areas: (a) availability of information; (b) access to information; and (c) exchange of information. In order to have an effective exchange of information (EOI), jurisdictions must have the relevant international EOI agreement implemented with the appropriate parties, and also ensure that the availability and accessibility to the information being sought by the relevant competent authority are possible. Each of the ten fundamental elements set out in the Terms of Reference of the standard is assigned a determination which can be one of the following: (i) "the element is in place"; (ii) "the element is in place, but certain aspects of the legal implementation of the element needs improvement"; or (iii) "the element is not in place". Phase two examines the employment of the framework in practice and rates each of the fundamental elements as either "compliant", "largely compliant", "partially compliant", or "non-compliant". Jurisdictions which complete phase one and two reviews are given an overall rating, that assesses the level to which they have complied with the standard (OECD 2016). The first cycle of these peer reviews was conducted for the period 2010 to 2016, using phase one and two, or a combination of both through the use of the EOIR standard based on the Model TIEA of 2002 and Article 26 of the Model Tax Convention and Commentary of 2005 per the OECD. In order to even the playing field and respond to the request by the G20, which called on taking advantage of the work conducted by the FATF on beneficial ownership, the EOIR standard was enhanced and the requirement of information relating to beneficial ownership of legal persons (including companies, Anstalt, foundations and limited liability partnerships) and legal arrangements such as trusts, was included in the 2016 EOIR Terms of Reference (TOR) (OECD 2016). This TOR is based on the Model TIEA of 2002 and Article 26 of the Model Tax Convention and Commentary of 2012, which make clear that requests related to a group of taxpayers which are not individually identified ("group requests") fall within the scope of Article 26 of the Model Tax Convention, so long as the foreseeable relevance is adequately demonstrated (OECD 2016). The second cycle is underway for the period 2016 to 2020 taking into account updates detailed in the 2016 TOR.

A Peer Review Group (PRG), usually consisting of two expert assessors from member jurisdictions, in addition to an administrator from the office of the Secretariat, is established by the Forum to develop the TOR and Methodology to ensure a transparent, robust and quick process (OECD 2016). According to the OECD, the peer review process (PRP) involves several steps. The first step involves setting guidelines which lay out the terms to form assessment, determine the review period and grounds of assessment, and gather input from peers of the jurisdiction, including gathering responses through the EOIR questionnaire. The next step involves the on-site visit which centers on the attention given by high level government on the deficiencies present in the jurisdiction's practices in transparency and exchange of information. This process also provides an opportunity for the jurisdiction undergoing assessment to fully participate in its evaluation and also encourage an open, constructive and efficient dialogue with the assessment team (OECD 2018). The third step includes gathering information for the EOIR review, including taking into consideration the overall legal and regulatory structure of the assess jurisdiction to determine its adequacy in satisfying the transparency standard and exchange of information. The fourth step includes preparing the draft report in four to six weeks after the on-site visit for the PRG. The draft report is then circulated to members of the PRG several weeks prior to the PRG meeting, providing them with four weeks to give their comments (OECD 2018). A delegate for all PRG member jurisdiction is required to attend the meeting, including representatives from the jurisdiction still undergoing reviews to attend as an observer (step five).

The next step involves circulation of the report, once it has been accepted by the PRG, along with Annex 1, which details the weaknesses identified in the assessed jurisdiction and the plans laid out to address them (OECD 2016). The following step involves publication of the EOIR report, once it has been approved by the Secretariat of the Global Forum, on it's website. The underlying objective of this step is to ensure transparency by providing the public with regular information on the work of the Global Forum and the enforcement of its Standard, including the overall ratings of EOIR report, and findings on the individual elements. It is also a method used to inform all parties of the results of the report and to increase awareness of the practice of EOI within a particular jurisdiction (OECD 2016). Such jurisdictions are also urged to circulate the reports among the relevant groups in their specific administration. The last step involves follow-up by the Global Forum on the advancement made by the jurisdiction in satisfying with the recommendations outlined in the EOIR report from the prior reviews (first and second), and also assess and publish substantial improvements through the process of an EOIR supplementary review at the jurisdiction's request.

The PRG can also conduct an EOIR supplementary review on its own if: (i) it becomes aware that the jurisdiction has neglected to enforce its legal and regulatory framework, or has implemented practices which may adversely impact the application of international standards; and (ii) a risk exists for a jurisdiction to overestimate the degree to which it has dealt with the Global Forum's recommendations (OECD 2018). Where it has addressed all recommendations, it should request an EOIR supplementary review to be performed, and in cases where it fails to do so, it should provide a written report to the PRG detailing the improvements it has completed per the OECD.

A process is also laid out for an assessed jurisdiction, which, after the first round of peer review, may have been blocked from proceeding to phase two of the review process due to the lack of implementation of crucial elements required to achieve an effective exchange of information (OECD 2016). Jurisdiction included in the schedule for the 2016–2020 period will eventually go on to an EOIR review and be rated based on the normal procedure. Under the methodology for 2010, a blocked jurisdiction can request an EOIR supplementary review to assess the reforms made to its legal and regulatory structure, and be moved to phase two review, if it is successful. Under the methodology for 2016, a blocked jurisdiction may, after six months from the publication of phase one report, demonstrate that it has carried out the actions necessary to deal with the recommendations detailed in phase one report, that pursuant to the 2010 TOR, allowance for it to be moved to phase two review would be granted (OECD 2016). If a request is not submitted by the blocked jurisdiction for an EOIR review to be undertaken, then it will be invited to make such a request within a period of six months. If a determination has been made by the PRG that sufficient progress has been achieved, an acceleration of the jurisdiction's EOIR review will be carried out. If on the other hand, such progress has not been made, the jurisdiction will be deemed non-compliant based on the results of phase one under the first round of reviews (OECD 2016). Procedures for EOIR reviews conducted on non-members of the Global Forum are done in a similar manner to those of its members to the largest extent possible.

To strengthen the use of the EOIR, the automatic exchange of standardized financial account information, as well as country-by-country reports, provided additional means by which tax evasion and tax avoidance can be detected by tax authorities (OECD 2016). Automatic exchange of information (AEOI) was developed in 2014 by the OECD while working with G20 countries and was later adopted by the Global Forum due to its ability to enhance the EOIR standard. AEOI subjects' financial institutions to disclose information automatically on financial accounts they hold on behalf of non-residents to tax authorities in their jurisdictions in accordance with common reporting standards (CRS) (OECD 2018). These tax authorities will in turn provide this information to the tax authorities in the country of residence of the account holders. Information exchanged under AEOI includes information held at banks on assets and accounts, certain insurers, as well as investment entities (e.g. funds and certain types of trusts).

According to the OECD, this process calls for rules surrounding the collection and reporting of the information obtained by financial institution. It also requires administrative capabilities, as well as information technology to receive and exchange such information. Additionally, the existence of a legal instrument allows information to be exchanged between the relevant jurisdictions and also measures to guarantee confidentiality of the highest standards and protection of data (OECD 2018). The Standard for automatic exchange consists of four key elements per the OECD. They include: (i) CRS, which includes due diligence rules which require adherence by financial institutions to collect, as well as report, financial information for AEOI; (ii) the Model Competent

Authority Agreement ("CAA") which details the financial information to be exchanged and connects CRS to the legal grounds for the exchange; (iii) the Commentaries which provide illustrations and interpretation for CRS and CAA; and (iv) technical solutions guidance, as well as an XML schema, to be used when exchanging information and standards on data protection and confidentiality, transmission, and encryption.

In order to implement this Standard, four main requirements must be carried out by jurisdictions, which can be implemented in any order (OECD 2018). Requirement one obligates jurisdictions to translate the reporting, as well as the due diligence rules into domestic law, and also include rules to ensure their effective implementation. The Standard comes with a set of detailed rules for due diligence and reporting which are standardized for financial institutions to follow to ensure the scope and the quality of information exchanged is consistent (OECD 2018). These due diligence and reporting rules together make up the CRS. To ensure that due diligence and reporting rules are carried out by financial institutions, it is necessary for jurisdictions to enact new legislation, which may need to be accompanied in some cases, with detailed guidance per the OECD. In some areas, the Standard allows optional approaches to be adopted by jurisdictions applicable to their particular circumstances. Most of these approaches provide financial institutions with greater flexibility and reduce their costs. The use of these optional provisions by jurisdictions depends on the particular context in which the CRS is implemented domestically (OECD 2018).

Requirement two deals with selecting the legal basis for AEOI (OECD 2018). The enactment of an international framework which allows jurisdictions to automatically exchange information is a key element of the effective application of the Standard. A multilateral approach seems to be the most practical and preferred way to establish an international framework with all relevant partners according to the OECD. Exchange relationships between jurisdictions for CRS information are commonly based on Article 6 of the Convention on Mutual Administrative Assistance in Tax Matters, which is a multilateral agreement that provides AEOI between tax administrations in more than 110 jurisdictions that are parties to the Convention (OECD 2018). Another means to allow the legal basis for the automatic exchange of information under the Standard is by way of the Multilateral Competent Authority Agreement on Automatic Exchange of Financial Account Information ("MCAA"), drafted specifically for this purpose in accordance with the Standard and is established on the Model CAA included in the Standard. Other means include, by way of Double Tax Treaties ("DTTs"), and Tax Information Exchange Agreements ("TIEAs"), provided that they allow for the automatic exchange of information per the OECD. In addition to the existence of a legal instrument to exchange tax information, relationships for automatic exchange usually require an administrative agreement which lays out the specifics of the information to be exchanged between Competent Authorities, and also the timing, as well as the operational process for the automatic exchanges. The Standard includes a Model CAA containing three options to suit different scenarios of exchange relationships. The first option of Model CAA is a bilateral and reciprocal model created to be used along with Article 26 of the OECD Model Tax Convention. The second option is non-reciprocal for use where applicable, such as for jurisdictions without income tax, whereas the third option is created as an umbrella agreement aimed at facilitating the operation of a multilateral legal instrument like the Convention. This option has facilitated the use of the MCAA as the most popular by far, as it reduces the time as well as the resources required to bring about multiple bilateral agreements (OECD 2018).

Requirement three obliges jurisdictions to put adequate IT and administrative infrastructure and resources in place (OECD 2018). To properly handle the information which is sent or received, tax administrations require the technical as well as the administrative capacity to do so. These requirements should be taken into consideration at an early stage of the implementation process to ensure sufficient resources are in place at the time of exchange. For collecting and reporting information, jurisdictions must determine the deadlines for financial institutions to report information to the tax authority, the format in which such information is to be reported, and the submission process for reporting the information. Prior to receiving information from financial institutions, jurisdictions should ensure that they have adequate operational security to maintain the data (OECD 2018). This entails having adequate procedures in place to manage, organize and operate the data, and also technical measures, as well as hardware and software tools. The data should be validated by checking the format to ensure it is relevant to the receiving jurisdiction. Transmitting and receiving the CRS information is required to be done through the Common Transition System ("CTS"), which is a secure and encrypted "Pipe", which allows for such information to be reported in an IT-based and standardized format. All the necessary steps should be carried out to ensure that files are properly prepared, and the data is encrypted in order to transmit it via CTS (OECD 2018).

Requirement four calls for jurisdictions to protect confidentiality and safeguard data (OECD 2018). The confidentiality of information on taxpayers is the foundation for all exchanges of tax information. In order for automatic exchange of information to be successfully implemented under CRS, it is critical for committed jurisdictions to be confident and comfortable upfront in sending financial information annually on an automatic basis to their exchange partners. Confidentiality and safeguarding information involve both the legal framework and systems, and procedures to make certain that the legal framework is upheld in operational practice. Monitoring compliance on an ongoing basis and ensuring sanctions are in place to deal with breaches of confidentiality are important elements to ensure that CRS information is exchanged in an efficient, reliable and secure manner (OECD 2018). The systems as well as procedures should contain relevant policies with regard to employees (e.g. training and background checks), limiting access to sensitive information, processes to safeguard data (e.g. identifying personnel with access, audit trails that monitor access), restrictions on data transmission, and suitable policies to dispose of information. Jurisdictions are to ensure prior to sending information that their exchange partners satisfy the required standards for confidentiality and data safeguard. The questionnaire included in the Standard maybe used by jurisdiction to make such assessment. A preliminary confidential assessment process is carried out by the Global Forum as part of its mandate to implement AEOI to facilitate the decision of each jurisdiction on partners for the automatic exchange of financial information, as well as to ensure that the required standard for confidentiality and data safeguard is met by all committed jurisdictions before receiving financial information. If weaknesses are identified during this process, specific recommendations are provided to the assessed jurisdictions to address such issues (OECD 2018). Such jurisdictions are required to develop an action plan outlining steps that will be taken to resolve these issues to become fully compliant with the Standard. Upon the execution of the action plan, a reassessment is made by the Global Forum on the measures carried out to improve confidentiality and safeguard data. In the interim until the required Standard is met, such jurisdictions will transmit information to all exchange partners on a non-reciprocal temporary basis (OECD 2018). A provision related to breached is contained in the MCAA, which obligates a competent authority to promptly notify the other relevant competent authority of the failure or breach in the confidentiality requirements. Non-compliance with the provisions of confidentiality and data safeguard is grounds for swift suspension of the MCAA. The suspension is lifted once the breach is investigated, concluded and polices implemented to avoid further breach from occurring in the future per the OECD.

Soon after its adoption, the Global Forum called upon all members, with the exception of those which do not have financial centres, to begin exchanges by 2018, and for such exchanges to be carried out with "all interested appropriate partners", which essentially meant with all interested parties which satisfied the standard requirements of confidentiality and the proper use of information (OECD 2018). This approach facilitates the delivery of a level playing field, and also prevents the movement of assets by taxpayers to other jurisdictions which are not committed, in an attempt to circumvent information from being shared with their tax resident jurisdiction.

By facilitating the implementation of information sharing through global cooperation, the Global Forum helps jurisdictions worldwide in combating tax evasion and tax avoidance, addressing illegal financial flows and dealing with the mobilization of local tax revenues. To ensure its Standards are effectively implemented worldwide, and provide for countries to enforce their own domestic laws, the Global Forum established a monitoring and peer review process (OECD 2018). Designed to encourage commitments to the delivery of a level playing field, this process provides pre-assessment assistance, it conducts peer reviews and ongoing monitoring, and it provides post-review assistance and assesses impact.

## 4.7 Conclusion

Globalization and the adoption of economic policies by nations-states to reduce capital restrictions resulted in capital becoming mobile beyond national territorial boundaries (Sikka 2003). Due to their unique characteristics such as prevailing confidentiality provisions, minimal or no tax, and so-called lenient regulation, OFCs played a critical role in facilitating global capital mobility. Used by professionals such as bankers, accountants, and lawyers to create sophisticated tax avoidance schemes, OFCs reportedly contributed to the loss of billions in tax revenues by countries (Sikka 2003). They also purportedly deprived less developed countries of tax revenues, and allowed transnational companies to select between jurisdictions based on preferential tax conditions, thereby cutting their tax bills, and increasing their profits and dividends, as well as stockholders returns (Boskin et al. 1987 as cited in Christensen and Kapoor 2004).

Tax competition eventually led to the erosion of the potential tax base of countries, particularly developing ones, resulting in the reallocation of the tax load to labor and consumption, which were both socially regressive, or alternatively, resulted in a net reduction of available revenues to the state for investment in physical and social infrastructure (Christensen and Kapoor 2004). The Panama papers further highlighted the use of manipulative tax schemes and consequential damages to developing countries and their domestic resources. The result of the leak led to mounting pressure mainly surrounding OFCs, and the need to enhance transparency and due diligence were brought to the forefront (Zaidi et al. 2017). These issues combined with the accelerated integration of global financial services heightened the need for the international community to address concerns regarding the provision of services by sovereign states and their dependent territories, to non-residents and corporate entities to avoid tax and regulatory requirements in their own countries. The most effective way to counter harmful tax practices was through the use of global policy initiatives.

Global intervention came by way of the OECD, but real measures to effectively assess tax transparency and exchange of information for tax purpose came about as a result of the reorganization of the Global Forum in 2009, which eventually took over this work from the OECD. The underlying objective of the Global Forum was to enforce internationally agreed standards of tax transparency and exchange of information set by the OECD and itself. The ultimate goal was to make certain that taxpayers at an individual and corporate level do not use tax havens to shelter their income and assets, and that the correct taxes are paid in the relevant country (OECD, 2016). The strategies used to enforce these standards to ensure compliance by jurisdictions globally will be discussed in chapter 6.

## References

Alldridge, Peter. 2008. Money laundering and globalization. *Journal of Law and Society* 35 (4): 437–463. https://doi.org/10.1111/j.1467-6478.2008.00446.x.

Basle Committee on Bank Supervision. 2017. Sound management of risks related to money laundering and financing of terrorism. *Bank of International Settlements*. https://www.bis.org/bcbs/publ/d405.pdf

Christensen, John, and Kapoor, Sony. 2004. Tax avoidance, tax competition and globalization: Making tax system justice a focus for global activism. *Accountancy Business and the Public Interest* 3(2). http://visar.csustan.edu/aaba/Christensen&Kapoor2004.pdf

Dwyer, Terry. 2002. 'Harmful' tax competition and the future of offshore financial centres. *Journal of Money Laundering Control* 5 (4): 302–317. https://doi.org/10.1108/eb027311.

FATF. 2010a. Global money laundering & terrorist financing threat assessment. *Financial Action Task Force*. http://www.fatf-gafi.org/media/fatf/documents/reports/Global%20Threat%20assessment.pdf

FATF. 2010b. 20 years of the FATF recommendations 1990–2010. *Financial Action Task Force*. http://www.fatf-gafi.org/media/fatf/documents/brochuresannualreports/20%20Years%20of%20the%20FATF%20Recommendations.pdf

FATF. 2018. Annual report 2017–2018. *Financial Action Task Force*. https://www.fatf-gafi.org/publications/fatfgeneral/documents/annual-report-2017-2018.html

GIZ Sector Programme Public Finance, Administrative Reform. 2010. Addressing tax evasion and tax avoidance in developing countries. *Deutsche Gesellschaft fur*. https://www.taxcompact.net/sites/default/files/resources/2010-12-ITC-Addressing-Tax-Evasion-and-Avoidance.pdf

Kraft, Jeffrey. 2014. Changing tides: Tax haven reform and the changing views of transnational capital flow regulation and the role of states in a globalized world. *The Indiana Journal of Global Legal Studies* 21(2), Article 8. https://www.repository.law.indiana.edu/ijgls/vol21/iss2/8/

McClure, Ross, Lanis, Roman, and Govendir, Brett. 2016. Analysis of tax avoidance strategies of top foreign multinationals operating in Australia: An expose. *University of Technology Sydney*.

Morriss, Andrew P., and Moberg, Lotta. 2012. Cartelizing taxes: Understanding the OECD's campaign against "harmful tax competition." *Columbia Journal of Tax Law* 4. https://scholarship.law.tamu.edu/facscholar/53

Naitram, Simon M. 2014. Offshore financial centers in the global capital network. *Global Economy Journal* 14(03n04): 435–445. https://doi.org/10.1515/gej-2013-0059

OECD. 1998. Harmful tax competition, an emerging global issue. *OECD Publishing*. https://www.oecd.org/tax/harmful/1904176.pdf

OECD. 2000. Report to the 2000 ministerial council meeting and recommendations by the committee on fiscal affairs. *OECD Publishing*. https://www.oecd.org/tax/harmful/2090192.pdf

OECD. 2001. The OECD's project on harmful tax practices: The 2001 progress report. *OECD Publishing*. https://www.oecd-ilibrary.org/taxation/the-oecd-s-project-on-harmful-tax-practices_9789264033993-en

OECD. 2005. OECD economic outlook: Preliminary edition. *OECD Publishing*. https://www.oecd-ilibrary.org/economics/oecd-economic-outlook-volume-2005-issue-1_eco_outlook-v2005-1-en

OECD. 2006. The OECD's project on harmful tax practices: 2006 update on progress in member countries. *OECD Publishing*. https://www.oecd.org/ctp/harmful/37446434.pdf

OECD. 2010. Measuring globalization: OECD economic globalisation indicators. *OECD Publishing*. https://www.oecd.org/sti/ind/measuringglobalisationoecdeconomicglobalisationindicators2010.htm

OECD. 2013. Economic globalisation: Origins and consequences. *OECD Publishing*. https://doi.org/10.1787/19936753.

OECD. 2015. G20/OECD principles of corporate governance. *OECD Publishing*. https://doi.org/10.1787/9789264236882-en.

OECD. 2015b. Exchange of information on request: Handbook for peer reviews 2016–2020. *OECD Publishing*. http://www.oecd.org/tax/transparency/global-forum-handbook-2016.pdf

OECD. 2018a. Tax transparency 2018, report on progress. *OECD Publishing*. https://www.oecd.org/tax/transparency/global-forum-annual-report-2018.pdf

OECD. 2018b. Standard for automatic exchange of financial information the tax matters. *OECD Publishing*. https://www.oecd.org/tax/exchange-of-tax-information/implementation-handbook-standard-for-automatic-exchange-of-financial-information-in-tax-matters.pdf

OECD. 2018c. Automatic exchange of information implementation report 2018. *OECD Publishing*. https://www.oecd.org/tax/transparency/AEOI-Implementation-Report-2018.pdf

Palan, Ronen. 2002. Tax havens and the commercialization of state sovereignty. *Cambridge University Press* 56(1): 151–176. https://www.cambridge.org/core/journals/international-organization/article/tax-havens-and-the-commercialization-of-state-sovereignty/EA2015432154579711CD97E6126911D1

Sikka, Prem. 2003. The role of offshore financial centres in globalization. *Accounting Forum* 27(4): 365–399. https://ssn.com/abstract=467682

Tanzi, Vito. 2001. Globalization and the work of fiscal termites. *Finance & Development* 38(1). https://www.imf.org/external/pubs/ft/fandd/2001/03/tanzi.htm

UNODC. 2010. The globalization of crime: A transnational organized crime threat assessment. *United Nations Office on Drugs and Crime*. https://www.unodc.org/unodc/data-and-analysis/TOC-threat-assessments.html

UNODC. 2011. Estimating illicit financial flows resulting from drug trafficking and other transnational organized crimes. *United Nations Office on Drugs and Crime*. https://www.unodc.org/documents/data-and-analysis/Studies/Illicit_financial_flows_2011_web.pdf

Zaidi, Syed H.A., Wang, Xin-Yu., Ahmad, Sardar, Ping, Tan-Xue, and Qi, Meng. 2017. Panama papers and the dilemma of global financial transparency. *International Journal of Modern Research in Management* 1(2): 18–35. http://www.ijournalmrm.com/article/12/panama-papers-and-the-dilemma-of-global-financial-transparency

CHAPTER 5

# The International Solution to Money Laundering and Terrorist Financing

## 5.1 Introduction

International organizations and bodies have played a critical role in establishing international rules in the area of money laundering, terrorist financing and tax evasion. The international body that has been key to the development of global standards recognized for anti-money laundering (AML) and countering the financing of terrorism (CFT) is the Financial Action Task Force (FATF 2018). Formed by the Ministers of the G-7 Summit in 1989, its objectives have been twofold, to establish standards and to promote the implementation of regulatory, legal and operational measures which are effective for countering money laundering, the financing of terrorism, and other relevant threats posed to the integrity of the global financial system (IMF 2017). In this regard, the FATF Recommendations set forth a comprehensive framework of measures which are consistent for countries to adopt in order to counter money laundering and terrorist financing, in addition to financing the proliferation of weapons of mass destruction (FATF 2018). Per the FATF, publications of these Recommendations including revisions which took place in 1990, 1996, 2001, 2003, and 2012, are to ensure that they are current and relevant to allow for universal application. In this chapter, an examination is conducted of the functions in which this international standard is used to shape the legal systems and governing institutions of countries globally.



A. M. Campbell, *Money Laundering, Terrorist Financing, and Tax Evasion*, https://doi.org/10.1007/978-3-030-68876-9_5

## 5.2 The FATF's Recommendations

### 5.2.1 *Compel National Action to Increase Transparency*

The FATF's Recommendations consist of six essential components. They include: (i) prevention of money laundering and the financing of terrorism and proliferation; (ii) identification of risks, and the development of policies and national coordination; (iii) application of preventative measures in the financial segment and relevant designated segments; (iv) establishment of powers and responsibilities for relevant competent authorities; (v) improvement in transparency and the availability of information on beneficial ownership of legal persons and arrangements; and (vi) enhancement in international cooperation (FATF 2018).

Section i applies the international standard established by the FATF to compel national governments to act to increase transparency in their AML/CFT regimes (Burke-White and Slaughter 2006). This objective is accomplished by placing an obligation on all countries to push them to take the necessary actions to criminalize money laundering based on the Vienna and Palermo Conventions, and see to it that the offence of money laundering is applied to all serious crimes to the broadest extent possible of predicate offences.[1] The FATF also compels countries to adopt confiscation and provisional measures as those outlined in the Vienna, Palermo, and the Terrorist Financing Conventions, including enacting legislations, to empower competent authorities to expropriate and confiscate the following, without causing harm to bona fide third parties: (i) property involved in; (ii) proceeds deriving from, instrumentalities intended for use in or used in committing money laundering or its predicate offences; (iii) property involved in, or proceeds deriving from, or intended for use in or used in financing terrorism, terrorist acts or terrorist organizations; or (iv) property of equivalent value.[2] The FATF also binds countries to include in their confiscation provisions the granting of powers to competent authorities to: (i) identify, trace and assess the property subject to confiscation; (ii) freeze, seize and prevent the transfer or disposition of such property; (iii) take action to prevent the country from not being able to freeze, seize or recuperate the confiscated property; and (iv) conduct any relevant investigative measures. Countries are also pushed to provide

[1] See Recommendation 3 of the FATF Recommendations.

[2] See Recommendation 4 of the FATF Recommendations.

for the confiscation of such proceeds or instrumentalities on the basis of non-conviction, or as a requirement for the offender to prove the alleged property's lawful origin to the extent permissible under domestic law.[3]

Similar obligations are placed on countries to criminalize terrorist financing, including the financing of terrorist organizations and terrorists acting alone, despite not having any connection to specific terrorist act(s), on the grounds of the Terrorist Financing Convention.[4] They are to ensure that these offences are included as predicate offences for money laundering.[5] Countries are also required to implement financial sanctions pursuant to the United Nations Security Council resolutions regarding the prevention and suppression of terrorism and terrorist financing, which require the immediate freezing of funds or other assets.[6] They are to make certain that no funds or other assets are directly or indirectly made available to or on behalf of any individual or entity either: (a) delegated by, or within the powers of the United Nations Security Council per Chapter VII of its Charter, including per resolutions 1267 (1999) and previous resolutions; or (b) identified by that country in accordance with 1373 (2001).[7] In the same vein, countries are also obliged to implement financial sanctions pursuant to the United Nations Security Council resolutions regarding the prevention, suppression and disruption of proliferation of weapons of mass destruction, including their financing.[8] This resolution imposes the same freezing stipulation detailed in Chapter VII of the United Nations Charter.[9] Additionally, countries are urged to use a risk-based methodology and ensure that adequate legislation, which are proportionate to mitigate the identified vulnerabilities, are implemented to prevent non-profit organizations from being abused for terrorist financing by terrorist organizations which front as legitimate entities or use legitimate entities as a means to finance terrorism, avoid

[3] See Recommendation 4 of the FATF Recommendations.

[4] See Recommendation 5 of the FATF Recommendations.

[5] See Recommendation 5 of the FATF Recommendations.

[6] See Recommendation 6 of the FATF Recommendations.

[7] See Recommendation 6 of the FATF Recommendations.

[8] See Recommendation 7 of the FATF Recommendations.

[9] See Recommendation 7 of the FATF Recommendations.

asset-freezing measures, or conceal the secret diversion of funds destined for legitimate use to terrorist organizations.[10]

### 5.2.2 *Backstop/Reinforce National Governance to Prevent Money Laundering and Terrorist Financing*

Sections ii, iii, iv and v apply international standard to function as a backstopping mechanism to provide support and reinforcement for national institutions (Burke-White and Slaughter 2006). The underlying objective is to strengthen the national capacity of governments by implementing preventive measures to effectively deal with money laundering and terrorist financing. This objective is accomplished by obligating countries to undertake a process to identify risks, develop policies to manage such risks, use national coordination to mitigate these risk, and provide support to domestic institutions (FATF 2018). First, countries are obligated to establish and implement a national risk assessment program.[11] The aim of this program is to get countries to undertake a risk assessment process on an ongoing basis to identify and assess the potential changes in their AML/CFT framework, and take the necessary actions, including delegating competent authorities to assign and prioritize AML/CFT resources accordingly, to mitigate such risks. This also includes obligating financial institutions and designated non-financial businesses and professions (DNFBPs) to undertake similar measures to mitigate these risks. Second, countries are obliged to develop and implement AML/CFT policies at a national level based on the identified risks, review such policies continually and assign the management of these policies to an authority.[12] A key aspect of this backstopping measure is requiring countries to ensure that the relevant competent authorities at the policy setting and operational levels have implemented effective mechanisms to enable them to collaborate together, and where necessary, coordinate local information exchange with each other, regarding the creation and employment of policies and measures to counter money laundering, and the financing of terrorism and proliferation. This mechanism helps to build a country's capacity to effectively deal with AML/CFT risks at a national level and

[10] See Recommendation 8 of the FATF Recommendations.

[11] See Recommendation 1 of the FATF Recommendations.

[12] See Recommendation 2 of the FATF Recommendations.

fosters a cooperative network among competent authorities at a policy making and operative level, to ensure measures are in place to facilitate collaboration and coordination between them.

The FATF Recommendations also established a number of additional preventative measures as backstopping mechanisms to further strengthen the capacity of financial institutions at the supervisory and private sector levels (FATF 2018). The first of these measures required countries to see to it that the secrecy laws adhered to by financial institutions do not impede the implementation of the Recommendations in any way.[13] Customer due diligence and record-keeping provisions are the second of these preventative measures.[14] The provisions for customer due diligence achieved the backstopping mechanism objective in various ways. First, they prohibited financial institutions from maintaining anonymous accounts or fictitious named accounts. Second, they obligated financial institutions to carry out customer due diligence (CDD) when: (i) establishing business relationships; (ii) conducting occasional transactions above the threshold of (USD/EUR 15,000); or (iii) when wire transferring funds[15]; (iv) when suspicion exists for money laundering or terrorist financing; or (v) when doubts exist regarding the accuracy or adequacy related to the identification of customer data.[16] The provisions require countries to enact laws or implement an alternative enforcement means to make the conduct of CDD mandatory for financial institutions. The CDD requirements outlined in the Recommendations obligate financial institutions to carry out the following steps using a risk-based methodology: (i) use valid documents, information or data to identify the customer and verify his/her identity; and (ii) identify the beneficial owner and carry out practicable steps to verify the beneficial owner's identity with certainty.[17]

[13] See Recommendation 9 of the FATF Recommendations.

[14] See Recommendation 10 of the FATF Recommendations.

[15] Per Interpretive Note to Rec. 16.

[16] See Recommendation 10 of the FATF Recommendations.

[17] See Recommendation 10 of the FATF Recommendations. The verification process for the customer and beneficial owner is required per Recommendation 10 to be carried out before or while establishing the business relationship or while performing transactions for infrequent customers. In cases where the risks for money laundering and terrorist financing are managed effectively, and it is essential not to disrupt the normal course of business, financial institutions are permitted to perform the verification process within a reasonable time upon establishing the relationship.

Where legal entities and arrangements are concerned, financial institutions are required to understand the customer's ownership and control make-up; (iii) understand and obtain information regarding the purpose and intent of the business relationship; (iv) conduct due diligence reviews of business relationships on an ongoing basis to verify that the transactions are consistent with the institution's customer profile, their business and risk-profile, including the source of funds.[18] In circumstances, where the financial institutions are not able to adhere to requirements i–iv, having modified their measures using a risk-based methodology, countries are required to obligate such institutions to: (a) not establish the account, nor initiate the business relationship or carry out the transaction; (b) conclude the business relationship; and (c) give consideration to filing a suspicious transaction report pertaining to the customer.[19] Financial institutions are required to apply steps i–iv to new customers, including existing customers based on materiality and risk, and perform due diligence on such relationships as needed.

The record-keeping provisions also served to achieve the backstopping mechanism objectives of the FATF Recommendations (FATF 2018). Countries are obligated to pass legislation to require financial institutions to keep records for a period of five years minimum, of local and international transactions, to allow them to comply promptly with information request from their competent authorities.[20] Such records should be adequate enough to replicate individual transactions, taking into account the amounts and currency types, for use as evidence in prosecuting crimes as necessary.[21] Customer identification records collected through the CDD process, customer files and business correspondence, inclusive of the outcomes of any analysis conducted, are also required to be kept by financial institutions for five years upon account closure, or after the occasional transaction date. All records are required to be made available to local competent authorities upon proper authority.[22]

The FATF Recommendations also includes additional provisions to deal with specific customers and activities, such as: (a) politically exposed

[18] See Recommendation 10 of the FATF Recommendations.

[19] See Recommendation 10 of the FATF Recommendations.

[20] See Recommendation 11, for examples, of CDD and analysis documents.

[21] See Recommendation 11 of the FATF Recommendations.

[22] See Recommendation 11 of the FATF Recommendations.

persons (PEPs); (b) correspondent banking; (c) money or value transfer services; (d) new technologies; and (e) wire transfers (FATF 2018). These provisions are also designed as a backstopping mechanism to increase countries capacity to stem the threat of money laundering and financing terrorism within their territories, and inevitably within the global financial system (FATF 2018). Where foreign PEPs are concerned, obligations are placed on financial institutions to carry out the following measures, in addition to conducting normal CDD: (a) implement a proper risk-management process to ascertain whether a beneficial owner or customer is a PEP; (b) obtain approval from senior management to establish or continue such relationship; (c) take practical steps to determine the source of funds and wealth; and (d) perform ongoing enhanced reviews of the business relationship.[23] Countries are mandated to also require financial institutions to take reasonable steps to ascertain whether a beneficial owner or customer is a domestic PEP, or an individual employed in a prominent position with an international organization.[24] For these higher-risk relationships, financial institutions should be obligated to perform steps b, c and d. These requirements are also applicable to family members of all PEPs, including their close associates.

In cases where correspondent banking and other like relationships are used, obligations are placed on countries to oblige financial institutions to perform the following measures, in addition to conducting normal CDD: (a) obtain adequate information on the respondent institution to: (i) fully understand the nature of its business; and (ii) determine its reputation based on information publicly available and the quality of its supervision inclusive of any regulatory action brought against it for money laundering and terrorist financing; (b) evaluate its AML/CFT controls; (c) secure senior management's approval prior to initiating a new correspondent relationship; (d) clearly understand each institution's responsibilities; and (e) for "payable-through accounts", satisfy itself that CDD has been performed by the respondent bank on customers with direct access to the correspondent bank accounts, and that the respondent bank, upon its request, furnish appropriate CDD information.[25] This

[23] See Recommendation 12 of the FATF Recommendations.

[24] See Recommendation 12 of the FATF Recommendations.

[25] See Recommendation 13 of the FATF Recommendations.

backstopping mechanism also requires countries to ban financial institutions from commencing or continuing relationships with correspondent banks that are shell banks and require such institutions to ensure that respondent institutions also prohibit the use of their accounts by such banks.[26]

In countries where money or value transfer services (MVTS) are used, countries are compelled to make certain that persons or legal entities which provide such services are registered or licensed and are subjected to implementing effective monitoring systems to ensure adherence with the relevant measures required by the FATF Recommendations.[27] They are also impelled to take steps to identify unregistered or non-licensed persons or legal entities that conduct MVTS and apply the relevant sanctions. In cases were persons or legal entities work in an agent capacity, countries are to ensure that they are registered with or licensed by the relevant competent authority, or an up to date list of agents is kept by the MVTS provider and is available to competent authorities in the territories where the provider and its agents conduct business.[28] Additionally, such agents are to be subjected to the provider's AML/CFT program and monitored accordingly for compliance with such program.[29]

Where new technologies are involved, countries, as well as financial institutions, are bind to identify and evaluate the risks that may originate from money laundering and terrorist financing in relation to: (a) the establishment of new products, as well as new business practices, including new methods of delivery; and (b) the employment of new or evolving technologies for new and existing products.[30] Financial institutions are required to ensure that the risk assessment is performed prior to steps (a) and (b) and are obligated to take the necessary actions to manage and prevent such risks.[31] In cases where virtual assets are implicated, countries are required to ensure that the relevant service providers are governed pursuant to the Recommendations.

[26] See Recommendation 13 of the FATF Recommendations.

[27] See Recommendation 14 of the FATF Recommendations.

[28] See Recommendation 14 of the FATF Recommendations.

[29] See Recommendation 14 of the FATF Recommendations.

[30] See Recommendation 15 of the FATF Recommendations.

[31] See Recommendation 15 of the FATF Recommendations.

Where wire transfers are concerned, countries are bind to make certain that the required originator and beneficiary information are accurate and are included by financial institutions on all wire transfers and corresponding messages, and that such information is kept with the wire transfer or corresponding message during the entire payment chain.[32] Countries are also to ensure that wire transfers are monitored by financial institutions, and where the originator information and/or beneficiary information is lacking, appropriate action is taken by such institutions.[33] They are also required to make certain that financial institutions apply freezing measures when performing wire transfers and refrain from carrying out such activities with designated persons and entities pursuant to the relevant UN Security Council resolutions including resolutions 1267 (1999) and 1373 (2001).[34]

The backstopping element is also used to establish standard measures for financial institutions to follow when relying on third parties (FATF 2018). Countries are allowed to permit financial institutions to depend on third parties to carry out steps (a) to (c) of the CDD process outline in Recommendation 10, or for the purpose of introducing business, subject to the certain criteria, with the understanding that the ultimate responsibility for CDD remains with such institutions.[35] These criteria require financial institutions to: (a) obtain the required information regarding steps (a) to (c) of the CDD process; (b) take reasonable measures to satisfy themselves that identification data records and other related documents pertaining to CDD requirements will be furnished by the third party immediately upon request; (c) make certain that the third party is governed, supervised, and employs measures to comply with CDD and record-keeping rules in accordance with Recommendations 10 and 11; and (d) use available information on the risk level of a country, when making a decision on the countries in which third parties meeting these conditions can be located. In cases where third parties are of the same financial group, and: (i) such group employs CDD and record-keeping rules per Recommendations 10, 11 and 12, and processes to counter money laundering and terrorist financing per Recommendation 18; and

[32] See Recommendation 16 of the FATF Recommendations.

[33] See Recommendation 16 of the FATF Recommendations.

[34] See Recommendation 16 of the FATF Recommendations.

[35] See Recommendation 17 of the FATF Recommendations.

(ii) where such CDD and record-keeping rules and AML/CFT programs are effectively implemented and overseen by a competent authority at the group level, the relevant competent authorities can take into account that such financial institution employs measures per steps (b) and (c) above via its group program, and can determine that step (d) is not a necessary stipulation for reliance where higher country risk is sufficiently managed through the AML/CFT polices of the group.[36]

Backstopping is also used as a mechanism to strengthen internal controls in financial institutions including foreign branches and subsidiaries, and within financial groups (FATF 2018). This is done by compelling financial institutions to adopt programs to combat money laundering and terrorist financing. The same principal applies where financial groups are concerned, as programs to combat money laundering and terrorist financing are to be adopted group-wide, as well as policies and procedures that allow for information sharing within the financial group for AML/CFT purposes.[37] Where financial institutions have foreign branches and subsidiaries that are majority owned, they are required to see to it that the same AML/CFT measures that are applied in the home country, are also complied with by their subsidiaries.[38] Backstopping is also used to enhance the capacity of financial institutions in their dealings with higher-risk countries (FATF 2018). This goal is achieved by requiring financial institutions to employ increased due diligence measures when handling transactions and business relationships with legal and natural persons, as well as with financial institutions in countries where this stipulation is required by the FATF.[39] Countries are obliged to employ appropriate countermeasures as required by the FATF, and also be able to apply them independent of the FATF. All enhanced measures applied to higher-risk countries are to be effective and commensurate with the risks identified.[40]

Backstopping is also used in other Recommendations as an element to strengthen institutional reporting measures for filing suspicious transactions reports, to prevent tipping off and encourage adherence to

[36] See Recommendation 17 of the FATF Recommendations.

[37] See Recommendation 18 of the FATF Recommendations.

[38] See Recommendation 18 of the FATF Recommendations.

[39] See Recommendation 19 of the FATF Recommendations.

[40] See Recommendation 19 of the FATF Recommendations.

confidentiality (FATF 2018). This backstopping measure places a duty on countries to ensure that where financial institutions have suspicion or a reasonable basis to believe that funds held in their possession are proceeds connected to criminal activity or terrorist financing, they are obligated by law to file a suspicions report immediately with the financial intelligence unit (FIU).[41] In circumstances where such reports are submitted, financial institutions are mandated to ensure their employees, officers, and directors are protected from both civil and criminal liability for the breach of any legal provisions imposed on disclosing information, provided such act is done in good faith, even in circumstances where precise knowledge of the criminal activity was not known, regardless whether such activity actually took place.[42] This backstopping function also entails the prohibition of employees, officers, and directors from informing concerned customers of such reporting.[43]

Another method in which backstopping is used, is to increase institutional support in DNFBPs, by subjecting them to apply the same CDD and record-keeping measures outlined in Recommendations 10, 11, 12, 15 and 17 (FATF 2018). These measures are to be employed in circumstances where: (a) casino customers deal in financial transactions equivalent to or greater than the designated threshold; (b) realtors engaged in client transactions related to the purchase and sale of real estate; (c) precious metals and stone dealers involved in client cash transactions equal to or greater than the designated threshold; (d) legal professionals and accountants when preparing or conducting client transactions including: (i) real estate purchases and sales; (ii) managing money; securities or assets on behalf of clients; (iii) managing accounts such as bank, savings or securities; (iii) organizing contributions to establish, operate or manage companies; (iv) creating, operating or managing legal entities or arrangements, and purchasing or selling business structures; and (v) providers of trust and company services when preparing for or conducting transactions on behalf of a client related to the following activities: (i) acting as an agent to incorporate legal persons; (ii) acting as or providing for another person to act as, or making provisions for

[41] See Recommendation 20 of the FATF Recommendations.

[42] See Recommendation 21 (a) of the FATF Recommendations.

[43] See Recommendation 22 (b) of the FATF Recommendations.

another to act as, a company secretary or director, a partner in a partnership, or an other similar position with regard to legal persons; (iii) providing the services of registered office, accommodation or business address, including address for administrative or correspondence purposes for companies, partnerships, other legal persons or arrangements; (iv) acting or providing for a person to act as, trustee of an express trust, or carrying out the equivalent role for another legal arrangement; and (v) acting as or providing for another person to act as a nominee shareholder on behalf of another person.[44] Another stipulation that countries are required to comply with is placed on legal professionals and accountants, to file suspicious transaction reports when performing the services outlined in step (d) above, for a client or on behalf of such client.[45] They are also highly encouraged to place such reporting requirement on the remaining activities of professional accountants.[46] Additionally, they are required to extend such reporting requirements to: (i) precious metal and stones dealers to file such reports when dealing with client cash transactions equal to or greater than the designated threshold[47]; and (ii) providers of trust and company services when engaging in activities noted in step (e) above for a client or on behalf of such client.[48]

Backstopping measures are also used to remove the secrecy element in countries that adhere to them by increasing transparency in the control and beneficial ownership of legal persons and arrangements (FATF 2018). This is done by mandating countries to take action to ensure effective measures are in place to prevent legal persons from being misused for money laundering or terrorist financing.[49] They are also to make certain that sufficient, correct and timely information regarding the control and beneficial ownership of legal persons is made available to competent authorities in a timely manner. In cases where bearer share warrants, and bearer shares are issued through legal persons, or the provision of nominee directors or nominee shareholders are offered by such entities, countries are to ensure that effective measures are in place to protect

[44] See Recommendation 23 of the FATF Recommendations.

[45] See Recommendation 23 (a) of the FATF Recommendations.

[46] See Recommendation 23 (a) of the FATF Recommendations.

[47] See Recommendation 23 (b) of the FATF Recommendations.

[48] See Recommendation 23 (c) of the FATF Recommendations.

[49] See Recommendation 24 of the FATF Recommendations.

them from being misused for terrorist financing and money laundering.[50] Countries are also obligated to see to it that financial institutions and DNFBPs provide access to information related to the control and beneficial ownership of legal persons when carrying out the steps outlined in Recommendations 10 and 22.[51] The same provisions apply to countries where express trusts are concerned, including information related to the beneficiary, settlor, and trustee.[52]

Backstopping is used to further strengthen national capacity by implementing measures to regulate and supervise financial institutions, empower supervisors, and provide regulatory and supervisory measures for DNFBPs (FATF 2018). This is done by obligating countries to make certain that financial institutions are sufficiently regulated and supervised, and the FATF Recommendations are applied effectively.[53] The necessary measures, whether legal or regulatory, should be taken by competent authorities to prohibit criminals or persons connected to them from holding, or beneficially owning a significant or controlling interest, or having a management position in a financial institution.[54] They are also to prohibit the formation of or continuation of shell banks. For financial institutions which must adhere to the Core Principles, the same supervisory and regulatory provisions that are applicable for prudential purposes and are related to money laundering and terrorist financing, should be urged to employ such measures in a similar way for the purposes of AML/CFT, and apply them in cases where consolidated group oversight is concerned.[55] Countries are also obligated to require other financial institutions to be either registered or licensed, and adequately regulated and supervised for the purposes of AML/CFT, taking into account the risk associated in that sector with money laundering and terrorist financing. At minimum, money or value transfer businesses, or those engaged in money or currency changing, are to be registered or licensed

[50] See Recommendation 24 of the FATF Recommendations.

[51] See Recommendation 24 of the FATF Recommendations.

[52] See Recommendation 25 of the FATF Recommendations.

[53] See Recommendation 26 of the FATF Recommendations.

[54] See Recommendation 26 of the FATF Recommendations.

[55] See Recommendation 26 of the FATF Recommendations.

and should be monitored effectively to ensure adherence with the national AML/CFT rules.[56]

Countries must be certain that supervisors are empowered with adequate authority to oversee and ensure the adherence of financial institutions with AML/CFT requirements and are granted power to carry out inspections (FATF 2018). Supervisors should also be empowered to access from financial institutions, any information relevant to overseeing the compliance and imposition of sanctions in accordance to Recommendation 35, for the lack of adherence to such requirements.[57] Further, supervisors should also be granted with powers to apply a number of financial and disciplinary sanctions, including the ability to cancel, restrict or suspend the license of financial institutions, as necessary.[58]

Where DNFBPs are concerned, countries are required to ensure that they adhere to the following supervisory and regulatory measures[59]: (a) casinos should be regularized and supervised by a regime that guarantees the following minimum requisite measures for AML/CFT to be effectively implemented: (i) casinos should be required to be licensed; (ii) the necessary measures, whether legal or regulatory, should be taken by competent authorities to prohibit criminals or persons connected to them from holding, legally owning a controlling interest, or having a management position in a casino, or operating a casino; and (iii) competent authorities are required to see to it that casinos are managed effectively to ensure adherence with AML/CFT rules; and (b) countries are required to see to it that DNFBPs are monitored effectively to ensure adherence with AML/CFT rules. Performance of which should be done on the basis of risk sensitivity, by a supervisor or by a relevant self-regulatory group, provided its members adhere to their AML/CFT rules. Such supervisor or group is also required to employ measures to: (i) prevent criminals or persons connected to them from holding, legally owning a controlling interest, or having a management position; and (ii) apply effective sanctions commensurate to Recommendation 35 to handle matters due to failure to adhere to AML/CFT rules.[60]

[56] See Recommendation 26 of the FATF Recommendations.

[57] See Recommendation 27 of the FATF Recommendations.

[58] See Recommendation 27 of the FATF Recommendations.

[59] See Recommendation 28 of the FATF Recommendations.

[60] See Recommendation 28 of the FATF Recommendations.

Backstopping measures are also used to strengthen the operational and law enforcement infrastructure of countries (FATF 2018). This is achieved by urging countries to form a Financial Intelligent Unit to act as a national agency for receiving and analysing: (a) suspicious transaction reports (STR); and (b) other information relevant to money laundering, as well as its predicate offences, and the financing of terrorism, including sharing the outcome of such analysis.[61] The FIU should also have access to other information from reporting entities, in addition to financial, administrative and law enforcement information, in a reasonable timeframe to allow it to carry out its function properly.[62]

Countries are also obligated to ensure that the responsibility for investigations related to money laundering and terrorist financing are designated to law enforcement authority within the national AML/CFT policies.[63] They are also required to develop proactive investigations for money laundering, its related predicate offences, and financing terrorism, at least in circumstances in connection to offences that generate major proceeds.[64] This includes situations where the related predicate offence takes place in other jurisdictions. Countries are also to make certain that competent authorities are responsible for immediately detecting, tracing and taking measures to freeze and seize such property that is or subsequently become susceptible to confiscation, or is believed to be the proceeds of crime. They are required to make use of multi-disciplinary groups with expertise in asset or financial investigation, as necessary, and conduct cooperative investigations with the relevant overseas competent authorities when necessary.[65]

Backstopping mechanism has also been used to empower law enforcement and investigative authorities (FATF 2018). Countries are obligated to provide for competent authorities to have access to all required information and documents for use in investigations, prosecutions and other related actions.[66] They are also to empower competent authorities to

[61] See Recommendation 29 of the FATF Recommendations.

[62] See Recommendation 29 of the FATF Recommendations.

[63] See Recommendation 30 of the FATF Recommendations.

[64] See Recommendation 30 of the FATF Recommendations.

[65] See Recommendation 30 of the FATF Recommendations.

[66] See Recommendation 31 of the FATF Recommendations.

impose mandatory measures on financial institutions, DNFBPs, in addition to natural or legal person to produce records to undertake searches involving persons and property, take statements from witnesses, carry out seizures and gather evidence. Countries are also required under this Recommendation to allow competent authorities that carry out investigations to use a broad variety of investigative techniques appropriate for investigations involving money laundering and its related predicate offences and terrorist financing.[67] Such techniques include, intercepting communications, undercover operations, control delivery and gaining access to computer systems. Countries are also required to implement mechanisms to: (i) determine whether legal or natural persons own or control accounts in a timely manner; (ii) allow competent authorities to identify assets without the need to provide the owner with prior notice; and (iii) allow for competent authorities to be able to request any relevant information from the FIU.[68]

Backstopping is also used to put measures in place to regulate the movement of currency cross-border, bearer negotiable instruments, and declaration systems used by cash couriers (FATF 2018). Countries are compelled to empower competent authorities with the legal authority to prevent or restrain the transport of currency or bearer negotiable instruments suspected of being related to money laundering, its predicate offences, or terrorist financing, or those that are declared or disclosed falsely.[69] Countries are to see to it that commensurate and dissuasive sanctions are implemented to deal with culprits who submit false disclosure(s) or declaration(s).[70] In cases where bearer negotiable instruments or currency are connected to the financing of terrorist, money laundering, and its predicate offences, relevant measures should be adopted by countries, including legislative measures, in accordance with Recommendation 4, to enable such instruments or currency to be confiscated.[71]

The backstopping function is also used to further strengthen national capacity through the creation of a comprehensive statistical database on information to determine the efficiency and effectiveness of national

[67] See Recommendation 31 of the FATF Recommendations.

[68] See Recommendation 31 of the FATF Recommendations.

[69] See Recommendation 32 of the FATF Recommendations.

[70] See Recommendation 32 of the FATF Recommendations.

[71] See Recommendation 32 of the FATF Recommendations.

AML/CFT systems (FATF 2018). This is done by obliging countries to: (i) keep statistics on the receipt and circulation of STRs, investigations, prosecutions and convictions related to money laundering and terrorist financing, (ii) freeze, seize and confiscate property; and (iii) cooperate in international requests for mutual legal support.[72] It is also used to establish measures for the provision of guidance and feedback among competent authorities, self regulatory bodies (SRBs), and supervisors.[73] Countries are to make certain that competent authorities establish guidelines, and give feedback to assist financial institutions and DNFBPs, in implementing national measures to counter terrorist financing and money laundering, and in identifying and reporting suspicious transactions.[74] Lastly, it is used to establish administrative, civil and criminal sanctions to deal with specific Recommendations. This is accomplished by urging countries to ensure that sanctions are effective, proportionate and dissuasive in administrative, civil or criminal cases, and are applicable to deal with legal or natural persons in accordance with Recommendations 6, and 8 to 23, when AML/CFT requirements are not adhered to. These sanctions are to be applied to financial institutions, DNFBPs, in addition to senior management and directors.[75]

### 5.2.3 *Strengthen National Institutions to Increase International Cooperation*

Section vi applies international standard to enhance international cooperation. This objective is achieved by implementing measures to increase national and international cooperation among countries (FATF 2018). International cooperation is provided in the following five principal areas: (i) implementation of key international instruments; (ii) provision of mutual legal assistance; (iii) mutual legal assistance in relations to freezing and confiscation; (iv) extradition; and (v) other forms of international cooperation (FATF 2018).

First, international standard is used as a mechanism to create a network among national administrations, competent authorities, and central banks

[72] See Recommendation 33 of the FATF Recommendations.

[73] See Recommendation 33 of the FATF Recommendations.

[74] See Recommendation 34 of the FATF Recommendations.

[75] See Recommendation 35 of the FATF Recommendations.

in different countries (FATF 2018). These networks are used to support the efforts of domestic officials and their governments to improve international cooperation. The basis on which this network is formed is through the implementation of key international instruments. Countries are required to fully adopt the following conventions: (a) the Vienna Convention, 1988; (b) the Palermo Convention, 2000; (c) the United Nations International Convention for the Suppression of the Financing of Terrorism, 1999; and where applicable, the following should be ratified and implemented: (a) the Council of Europe Convention on Cybercrime, 2001; (b) the Inter-American Convention against Terrorism, 2002; and (c) The Council of Europe Convention on Laundering, Search, Seizure and Confiscation of the Proceeds from Crime and on Financing of Terrorism, 2005.[76]

This network function places obligations on countries to provide the broadest range of mutual legal support possible in investigations, prosecutions and legal proceedings related not only to money laundering and terrorist financing, but also to the predicate offences associated with money laundering, in a quick, constructive and effective manner.[77] It also requires countries to have sufficient legal grounds for rendering assistance, in addition to treaties, arrangements and other tools, to enhance collaboration. Countries are required to: (a) not impede or apply unreasonable limiting conditions on the terms of the mutual legal support[78]; (b) ensure that processes which are efficient and clear are in place to carry out requests for mutual legal support, a central authority is responsible for the transmitting and executing such requests, and a case management system be kept to monitor the progress of all requests[79]; (c) not decline to proceed with a request for mutual legal support on the sole basis that the offence is related to fiscal matters[80]; (d) not decline to carry out a request for mutual legal support on the sole basis of secrecy laws and confidentiality that financial institutions and DNFBPs are required to maintain.[81] An exception is made when such information sought relates

[76] See Recommendation 36 of the FATF Recommendations.

[77] See Recommendation 37 of the FATF Recommendations.

[78] See Recommendation 37a of the FATF Recommendations.

[79] See Recommendation 37b of the FATF Recommendations.

[80] See Recommendation 37c of the FATF Recommendations.

[81] See Recommendation 37d of the FATF Recommendations.

to cases where professional legal privilege or secrecy applies; and (e) to keep the request for mutual legal help confidential, including the information enclosed in the request to protect the validity of the investigation subject to domestic law.[82] In cases where confidentiality is not possible, the requesting country should be informed immediately.

This function of international standard also places additional stipulation on countries by obligating them to provide mutual legal support, despite the lack of dual criminality, provided that coercive actions are not involved.[83] Countries are required to adopt the necessary measures to allow for a wide range of assistance in cases where dual criminality is absent. Where there is a requirement for dual criminality in order to render mutual legal support, such requirement should be accepted as satisfied despite the offence not being placed within the same offence category, or the use of the same terminology to describe the offence, provided that the conduct of the offence is criminalized by both countries.[84] Further, countries are to see to it that the investigative techniques and powers pursuant to Recommendation 31 and others, including: (a) those pertaining to information, evidence, documents, as well as financial records that are searched, produced or seized from financial institutions, other persons or through taking statements from witnesses; and (b) a wide range of other investigative techniques and powers are accessible for use in petitions for mutual legal support, and if permissible by domestic law, are available to judicial authority or law enforcement agency of the requesting country.[85] Where there are cases that are to be prosecuted in both jurisdictions, countries should devise and employ mechanism to decide in the interests of justice, which jurisdiction would be best to prosecute the defendants to prevent conflict of jurisdiction.[86] Countries are obliged to make their best efforts to give thorough, factual, legal information to allow for the execution of requests in a timely and efficient manner, and obtain the legal protocols to seek assistance prior to sending requests.[87] Such requests are required to be sent by express means. Finally, countries

[82] See Recommendation 37e of the FATF Recommendations.

[83] See Recommendation 37 of the FATF Recommendations.

[84] See Recommendation 37 of the FATF Recommendations.

[85] See Recommendation 37 of the FATF Recommendations.

[86] See Recommendation 37 of the FATF Recommendations.

[87] See Recommendation 37 of the FATF Recommendations.

are also required to see to it that sufficient human, financial and technical resources are provided to the relevant authorities that are responsible for providing mutual legal help.[88] They are also required to see to it that the employees of such authorities uphold professional standards that are high, particularly with regard to confidentiality and integrity, and that they are adequately skilled.

The network function of international standard is also used to form an alliance among countries to further strengthen international cooperation through the provision of mutual legal assistance with regard to freezing and confiscation (FATF 2018). This is achieved by obligating countries to make certain where the proceeds from terrorist financing and money laundering, including its underlying offences are concerned, that an authority is delegated to undertake expeditious action in accordance with requests received from foreign jurisdictions to identify, seize, freeze and confiscate property that has been laundered, including the aforementioned proceeds, and instrumentalities that are used in or is allotted to be used in perpetrating these offences, or property of equivalent value.[89] Countries are also to ensure that the relevant authority is allowed to respond to requests received on the grounds of confiscation proceedings which are based on non-conviction and relevant provisional measures, provided that it is in accordance with domestic law.[90] It also calls for countries to establish measures that are effective to manage such property, property of equivalent value and instrumentalities, as well as arrangements, to coordinate proceedings for seizures, confiscations and proportioning confiscated assets.[91]

The network mechanism is also used to form a coalition among countries for the purpose of further enhancing international cooperation through the provision of mutual legal assistance with regard to extradition in matters relating to money laundering and terrorist financing (FATF 2018). Countries are mandated to immediately execute extraditions in a constructive and effective manner.[92] They are required to take the necessary measures to see to it that safe havens are not provided to persons who

[88] See Recommendation 38 of the FATF Recommendations.

[89] See Recommendation 38 of the FATF Recommendations.

[90] See Recommendation 38 of the FATF Recommendations.

[91] See Recommendation 38 of the FATF Recommendations.

[92] See Recommendation 39 of the FATF Recommendations.

finance terrorism, acts of terrorism or terrorist organizations.[93] Countries are particularly obliged to: (a) deem money laundering and terrorist financing extraditable offences[94]; (b) implement processes that are clear and efficient to execute requests for extradition in a timely manner, and prioritize where necessary, as well as maintain a system to manage cases in order to monitor the progress of such requests[95]; (c) not impose condition that is unreasonable or restrictive on executing requests[96]; and (d) ensure a sufficient legal framework is in place for extradition.[97]

Countries are obliged to extradite their respective nationals, or in cases where extradition by a country is not carried out solely on the basis of nationality, countries are to immediately provide the extradition request received from the foreign country, to their relevant competent authorities to allow for the offences outlined in the request to be prosecuted.[98] Competent authorities are required to make their decision and carry out their proceedings in a similar manner for other serious offences under their domestic law. Countries are required to work together, particularly on the procedural and evidentiary elements, to provide for efficiency during the prosecution process.[99] In extradition cases where a requirement of dual criminality exists, such requirement is to be regarded as satisfied regardless if the offence is not placed in the same offence category by both countries, or the same terminology is not used to describe the offence, subject to the conduct of the predicate offence being criminalized by both countries.[100]

Countries are also required to see to it that their domestic laws reflect simplified extradition processes such as: (i) those that permit provisional arrest requests directly to the relevant authorities; (ii) extraditing persons through the use of arrest warrants or judgements; or (iii) the implementation of a simplified extradition process whereby formal proceedings for extradition is waived by the consenting person. Countries are also

[93] See Recommendation 39 of the FATF Recommendations.

[94] See Recommendation 39a of the FATF Recommendations.

[95] See Recommendation 39b of the FATF Recommendations.

[96] See Recommendation 39c of the FATF Recommendations.

[97] See Recommendation 39d of the FATF Recommendations.

[98] See Recommendation 39 of the FATF Recommendations.

[99] See Recommendation 39 of the FATF Recommendations.

[100] See Recommendation 39 of the FATF Recommendations.

to ensure that sufficient human, financial and technical resources be provided to authorities who are responsible for extradition.[101] Countries are also required to see to it that employees of such authorities uphold high professional standards, particularly with regard to confidentiality and integrity, and that they are adequately skilled.[102]

The final networking function in which international standard is used, is to establish measures to provide other forms of international cooperation between countries (FATF 2018). This mechanism requires countries to allow their competent authorities to provide the broadest possible range of international assistance to their foreign counterparts with regard to the exchange of information related to money laundering and its underlying predicate offences, and terrorist financing.[103] Countries are obliged to facilitate such information automatically or upon request, and to have lawful grounds on which to do so. They are also required to ensure that competent authorities be empowered to use the most efficient way to cooperate. Where agreements, bilateral or multilateral, or arrangements, including Memorandum of Understanding are needed by competent authorities, they should be negotiated and executed in a timely fashion to allow for the broadest range of cooperation with foreign counterparts, if necessary.[104] Countries are also required to make certain that competent authorities utilize clear mechanisms for request of information or additional assistance to be transmitted and executed effectively.[105] Finally, competent authorities are also to use established processes that are clear and efficient to ensure request for information is prioritized and executed in a timely manner, and to protect information received.[106]

## 5.3 Conclusion

According to the FATF, the international standard established to counter money laundering and terrorist financing is only as effective as the jurisdictions which adhere to such measures contained therein. In this regard,

[101] See Recommendation 39 of the FATF Recommendations.

[102] See Recommendation 39 of the FATF Recommendations.

[103] See Recommendation 40 of the FATF Recommendations.

[104] See Recommendation 40 of the FATF Recommendations.

[105] See Recommendation 40 of the FATF Recommendations.

[106] See Recommendation 40 of the FATF Recommendations.

a critical goal of the FATF is the ongoing monitoring of jurisdictions to identify those with substantial deficiencies in their AML/CFT framework, and working closely with them to effectively deal with such deficiencies. For jurisdictions which are identified, a public warning is issued by the FATF regarding the risks emerging from them. This in turn is meant by putting pressure on such jurisdictions to swiftly and effectively deal with their deficiencies to maintain their position in the global economy, as well as to assist in safeguarding the integrity of the global financial system. How this Standard has impacted the legal systems and institutions of offshore jurisdictions in the Caribbean region will be discussed in detail in Chapter 7.

## References

Bank of International Settlement. 2016. *Sound Management of Risks Related to Money Laundering and Financing of Terrorism.* Bank of International Settlement. https://www.fsa.go.jp/inter/bis/20140121-1/02.pdf.

Burke-White, William W. & Anne-Marie Slaughter. 2006. *The Future of International Law Is Domestic (or, the European Way of Law).* Faculty Scholarship at Penn Law, 962. https://scholarship.law.upenn.edu/faculty_scholarship/962.

FATF. 2018. *International Standards on Combating Money Laundering and the Financing of Terrorism & Proliferation: The FAFT Recommendations.* Financial Action Task Force. https://rm.coe.int/fatf-recommendations-2012-updated-october-2018-/168093829b.

IMF. 2017. *The IMF and the Fight Against Money Laundering and the Financing of Terrorism.* International Monetary Fund. http://www.imf.org/external/np/exr/facts/aml.htm.

CHAPTER 6

# International Solutions to Tax Evasion

## 6.1 Introduction

The OECD has played a critical role in the development of international standards to counter tax evasion. Established in 1961, its mission is to "promote policies that will improve the economic and social well-being of people around the world".[1] The OECD developed the standard of transparency and exchange of information which comprises of Article 26 in its Model Tax Convention, and its 2002 Model Agreement on Exchange of Information in Tax Matters (The Global Forum on Transparency and Exchange on Information for Tax Purposes, 2017). It is also responsible for developing the standard on Automatic Exchange of Financial Account Information in Tax Matters which consists of the Model Competent Authority Agreement (the Model CAA) and the Common Reporting Standard (CRS) (OECD 2016, 2017). Through the work carried out by its special task force, the Global Forum on Transparency and Exchange of Information for Tax Purposes (the Global Forum), the OECD has advanced the work related to transparency, as well as information exchange for tax purposes among members and non-member countries alike (OECD 2012). The Global Forum has played a key role in establishing international standards for the Exchange of Information on Request (EOIR), and Automatic Exchange of Information (AEOI) by

[1] See OECD's website: http://www.oecd.org/about/.



A. M. Campbell, *Money Laundering, Terrorist Financing, and Tax Evasion*, https://doi.org/10.1007/978-3-030-68876-9_6

way of Common Reporting Standards (CRS), and has been instrumental in implementing these Standards globally (OECD 2012).

Other works pertaining to tax evasion have been carried out by the US and EU in their very own push to combat this phenomenon in their respective countries. Domestic policies initiated by each country have had global reach, impacting countries around the world. The introduction of Foreign Accounts Tax Compliance Act (FATCA) by the US has also significantly influenced and shaped international policies instituted by the OECD and EU (US Senate and House of Representatives (US Congress, 2010). FATCA has been the basis upon which CRS was established, and has also been used by the UK, which implemented its very own version. FATCA's approach in obligating countries to report directly to its competent tax authority has been employed by the EU through its Code of Conduct Group on Business Tax (CCG), (Council of the EU 2016). The EU CCG advocated for tax transparency, fair play in taxation, and the application of anti-base erosion profit shifting (BEPS) among members and non-member states. Similar to the US, it also placed an obligation on countries worldwide to establish a bilateral or multilateral agreement for information exchange with its member countries or satisfy another requisite which endorsed the OECD's EOIR Standard.

In this chapter, we will review these Standards to see how they have been carefully crafted to achieve their set objectives to counter tax evasion. We will begin with EOIR, followed by AEOI, CRS, FATCA, and the EU Code of Conduct.

## 6.2 Exchange of Information on Request (EOIR)

Similar to the strategy used by the FATF to compel nations to take action, reinforce national governance, and strengthen national institutions to counter money laundering, terrorist financing and proliferation, the OECD through the Global Forum adopted an identical approach to counter tax evasion. The 2010 Protocol to the Multilateral Convention on Mutual Administrative Assistance in Tax Matters (MCAA) was introduced by the OECD to amend the 1988 Multilateral Convention on Mutual Administrative Assistance in Tax Matters (OECD 2018). This was done to bring the Convention in line with the Standard for the exchange of information on request (EOIR) for tax purposes. To apply, the Standard countries were required to implement EOIR into their domestic law (OECD 2018). To achieve this objective, the OECD employed measures to: (i) compel countries to act; (ii) reinforce national governance; and (iii) increase international cooperation (Burke-White and Slaughter 2006).

### 6.2.1 *Compel National Action to Increase Transparency*

To compel countries to take action, the OECD used coercion by placing countries on its blacklist for non-compliance with EOIR. It obligated countries to sign twelve agreements which would enable tax information to be exchanged with OECD Member States by 31 March 2010 (OECD 2018). Failure to comply resulted in placement on its blacklist and possible sanctions from OECD Member States. To implement EOIR, obligations are also placed on countries to become a party to the Protocol by either accepting, ratifying or approving the Protocol and agreeing to simultaneously accept, ratify or approve the Convention.[2] Further, countries were required to deposit at a Depository, the instrument of acceptance, ratification or approval. The Protocol would then take effect on the first day of the month after the expiration of a three-month period following the date consent is received from five Signatories to the Convention agreeing to be bind by the Protocol, pursuant to the provisions of paragraph 1. Countries are also obligated to comply with the type of information to be exchanged. Parties were required to exchange any specified information deemed as foreseeably relevant to administer or enforce their national laws with respect to the taxes which fall within the scope of the Convention.[3] Parties were also obliged to address a declaration to a Depositary, stating that, pursuant to its domestic law, its authorities may advise its citizen or resident prior to sending information related to that person, in accordance with Articles 5 and 7.[4] These provisions instituted by the Protocol, required countries to undergo relevant reforms in their domestic laws in order to conform with it.

[2] See Paragraph 1, Article IX, Protocol to Multilateral Convention on Mutual Administrative Assistance in Tax Matters (Protocol MCMAA).

[3] See Article 4, Chapter III, Protocol MCMAA.

[4] See Paragraph 1, Article 4, Chapter III, Protocol MCMAA.

### 6.2.2 *Backstop/Reinforce National Governance to Prevent Tax Evasion*

The Protocol employed a number of backstopping measures to reinforce national governance to counter tax evasion. The aim is to strengthen a country's national capacity by implementing preventive measures to effectively address tax evasion. In this regard, backstopping measures are used to protect the rights of persons, given that none of the provisions detailed in the Convention would have an effect on the rights and protection afforded to persons under the domestic laws of the requested State or of its administrative practices.[5] Backstopping measures are also used to ensure that countries receiving a request are not obligated to undertake the following: (a) pursue measures that are contradictory to their own laws or administrative practices or of those belonging to the requesting State; (b) conduct measures that would be at variance to public policy; (c) provide information that cannot be obtained within their own laws or administrative practices or of those belonging to the requesting State; (d) provide information that would reveal any business, trade, commercial, industrial, or professional trade process or secret, or information which upon disclosure would be at variance to public policy; (e) render administrative assistance when they determine the taxation in the requesting State is in contradiction to taxation principles that are generally accepted, or to the provisions contained in the Convention for the Avoidance of Double Taxation, or any other related convention that the requested State has in place with the requesting State; (f) give administrative assistance for the objective of administrating or applying a provision contained in the tax law of the requesting State, or any obligation related to it, which is biased against a citizen of the requested State as opposed to a citizen of the requesting State in the same situation; (g) give administrative assistance in a case where the requesting State has not explored all reasonable avenues available within its laws or administration, with the exception when pursuing such measures will result in significant difficulty; and (h) give assistance in recovery where the burden administrative wise for that State is not in proportion to the benefit to be obtained by the requesting State.[6]

[5] See Paragraph 1, Article 21, Protocol MCMAA.

[6] See Paragraph 2, Article 21, Protocol MCMAA.

Backstopping measures have also been implemented to encourage privacy. For instance, any information that is obtained under the Convention by a Party is required to be handled as confidenctial and safeguarded in a similar manner as information gathered in accordance with the national law of that Party, and to ensure an adequate level of protection with regard to personal data to the extent necessary, in accordance with measures detailed by the Party supplying such information pursuant to its domestic law.[7] Such information is required to only be shared with authorities such as supervisory or administrative bodies and courts, or with persons associated with the assessment, as well as the collection, recovery of, prosecution with respect to or enforcement, or the decision of the appeals regarding that Party's taxes, or the supervision of the above. The information is only to be used by the aforementioned authorities or persons, and only for the purposes mentioned. Regardless of the provisions detailed in paragraph 1, they may disclose the information in judicial decisions or in court proceedings which are public and connected to such taxes.[8]

### *6.2.3 Strengthen National Institutions to Increase International Cooperation*

The Protocol also included backstopping measures to ensure legal mutual assistance is provided upon request. For example, if a request for information is made pursuant to the Convention by the requesting Country, the requested Country is required to pursue measures to obtain the requested information, although it may not require such information for its own needs. Although this obligation is subject to restrictions within the Convention, such restrictions, particularly those detailed in paragraphs 1 and 2, should in no case be understood to allow the requested State to refuse to provide information solely due to the fact that it has no local interest in the information.[9] Backstopping measure is also used to remove the veil of secrecy by requiring that the provisions contained in the Convention do not in any way allow a requested Country to refuse to provide information solely due to the fact that it is in the possession of

[7] See Paragraph 1, Article 22, Protocol MCMAA.

[8] See Paragraph 2, Article 22, Protocol MCMAA.

[9] See Paragraph 3, Article 22, Protocol MCMAA.

either a bank, another banking institution, or a person or nominee acting in a fiduciary or agency capacity, or because it is in relation to a person's ownership interests.[10]

To increase international cooperation, the Protocol contains provisions to facilitate the exchange of information. It allows for any non-member State of the OECD or the Council of Europe to make a request to become a signatory to the Convention, after the 2010 Protocol enters into force.[11] Such request is to be directed to a Depositary, who in turn will submit it to the Parties and inform the OECD Council and the Committee of Ministers of the Council of Europe. The decision to invite a State to become a signatory to the Convention is done by consensus among the Parties to the Convention by the coordinating arm. For States ratifying the Convention as modified by the 2010 Protocol pursuant to this paragraph, the Convention becomes effective on the first day of the month after the expiration of the three-month period following the date that the instrument of ratification is deposited with a Depository. Further, parties of two or more may agree mutually for the Convention as modified by the 2010 Protocol, to take effect for administrative assistance in relation to charges of tax or earlier taxable periods.[12]

## 6.3 Common Reporting Standard (CRS)

The introduction of Common Reporting Standards (CRS) by the OECD is aimed at doing away with secrecy by increasing transparency through the use of automatic exchange of financial account information in tax matters between countries worldwide (OECD 2014). To achieve this objective, CRS employs the following three steps: (i) compel countries to act; (ii) use of backstopping measures to strengthen national institutions and reinforce national governance; and (iii) the use of measures to increase international cooperation.

[10] See Paragraph 4, Article 22, Protocol MCMAA.

[11] See Paragraph 5, Article 22, Protocol MCMAA.

[12] See Paragraph 6, Article 22, Protocol MCMAA.

### *6.3.1 Compel National Action to Increase Transparency*

To compel countries to take action, jurisdictions were urged to commit to satisfying at least two of the following set criteria: (i) adopt EOIR and attain a "Largely Compliant" rating from the Global Forum; (ii) implement AEOI to allow for the first exchange to occur by 2018 the latest, based on information pertaining to 2017; and (iii) execute the Multilateral Tax Convention on Administrative Assistance, or another similar exchange mechanism, which would provide for information exchange under both AEOI and EOIR (Council of the EU 2016), and more recently, activate agreements with the majority of interested and relevant partners by the end of 2019 (Knobel 2018). Countries which failed to satisfy this set of criterion were blacklisted and faced possible sanctions (Knobel 2018). Further, to push countries to adopt AEOI, obligations were placed on them to implement rules for reporting and due diligence into domestic law (OECD 2014). They were also required to determine a legal basis on which to adopt AEOI, implement an IT system and administrative infrastructure, which served to collect and exchange the information received, and adopt confidentially and data protection requirements (OECD 2014). Some of the salient points as they relate to reporting, due diligence, and confidentiality and data protection rules are discussed below.

CRS places a reporting obligation on all jurisdictions to implement rules which obligate financial institutions within their jurisdiction to report all information (OECD 2017). All Reporting Financial Institutions are required to report specific information regarding all Reportable Accounts which are held at the Reporting Financial Institution.[13] This information includes the following: (1) for Account Holders who are individuals, the name, address, country(ies) of residence, place and date of birth and tax identification numbers (TIN)for all Reportable Person of an account.[14] For Account Holders which are Entities per Sections V, VI and VII, having more than one Controlling Persons identified as Reportable Persons, information such as name, address, country(ies) of residence, and the Entity's TIN(s) is required. Whereas for all Reportable Persons, the information required includes the name, address, country(ies) or residence, place and date of birth, and TIN(s) (Paragraph 1 of Section IA of

[13] See Section IA of Common Reporting Standard (CRS).

[14] See Paragraph 1 of Section IA of CRS.

CRS). In addition to the above, countries are also to report the following information: (i) the account number or its equivalent[15]; (2) the name of the Reporting Financial Institution, and its identifying number, if available[16]; (3) the value of the account or its balance as at end of the relevant calendar year or reporting period, or as of account closure, if applicable[17]; (4) for Custodial Accounts: (a) the total gross amount of interest, dividends, and other income earned on assets within the account, that are credited or paid to the account during the calendar year or reporting period[18]; and (b) the total gross proceeds credited or paid to the account from the redemption or sale of Financial Assets during the calendar year or reporting period where the Reporting Financial Institution served as the broker, custodian, nominee or as the Account Holder's agent[19]; (5) for a Depository Account, the total gross amount of interest credited or paid during the calendar year or the relevant reporting period to the account[20]; and (6) for any other account not mentioned in subparagraph A(5) or (6), the total gross amount credited or paid during the calendar year or reporting period to the Account Holder where the Reporting Financial Institution acts as debtor, or obligor, in addition to the total amount of redemption payments made during the calendar year or reporting period to the Account Holder.[21] The reported information must state the currency in which each amount is denominated.[22]

Detailed reporting obligations are also set forth for Preexisting Accounts that are Reportable Accounts.[23] Information such as date of birth or the TIN(s) does not need to be reported if such information is not included in the Reporting Financial Institution's records and is not obligated to be collected pursuant to the domestic laws of the Reporting Financial Institution.[24] However, the Reporting Financial Institution is

[15] See Paragraph 2 of Section IA of CRS.

[16] See Paragraph 3 of Section IA of CRS.

[17] See Paragraph 4 of Section IA of CRS.

[18] See Paragraph 5a of Section IA of CRS.

[19] See Paragraph 5b of Section IA of CRS.

[20] See Paragraph 6 of Section IA of CRS.

[21] See Paragraph 7 of Section IA of CRS.

[22] See Paragraph B of Section IA of CRS.

[23] See Paragraph C of Section IA of CRS.

[24] See Paragraph C of Section IA of CRS.

required to take reasonable measures to obtain such information as at the end of the second calendar year after the year such Account was deemed a Reportable Account.[25] Also, the TIN does not need to be reported if: (i) a TIN is not supplied by the applicable Reporting Jurisdiction; or (ii) the national law of the applicable Reportable Jurisdiction does not stipulate the need to include the TIN furnished by the Reportable Jurisdiction.[26] Additionally, there is no need to report the place of birth except when the Reporting Financial Institution is obligated to secure and report it pursuant to its domestic law and it is accessible in a searchable electronic database kept by the Reporting Financial Institution.[27] Domestic laws enacted by countries are required to provide the necessary provisions to obligate financial institutions within their respective territories to report such information to the relevant authority within the jurisdiction, and in turn, grant the jurisdiction powers to report the same in accordance with its reporting obligations under CRS.

### *6.3.2 Backstop/Reinforce National Governance to Prevent Tax Evasion*

CRS also uses backstopping measures to reinforce national governance to prevent tax evasion. This objective is attained by obligating jurisdictions to put rules and administrative policies in place to ensure the effective establishment of, and adherence to, reporting requirements and due diligence procedures detailed in Sections II–VII. They include: (1) rules to prohibit Financial Institutions, intermediaries or person from supporting practices designed to bypass reporting and due diligence procedures[28]; (2) rules obligating Reporting Financial Institutions to maintain records of the processes undertaken and information used to conduct the above procedures and appropriate measures to collect such records[29]; (3) administrative procedures to confirm the adherence of the Reporting Financial Institution to the reporting and due diligence procedures; (4) administrative steps to make inquiries with a Reporting

[25] See Paragraph C of Section IA of CRS.

[26] See Paragraph D of Section IA of CRS.

[27] See Paragraph E of Section IA of CRS.

[28] See Paragraph A1 of Section IX of CRS.

[29] See Paragraph A2 of Section IX of CRS.

Financial Institution in cases where accounts which are undocumented are reported[30]; (5) administrative procedures to confirm that accounts and Entities as described in national law as Excluded Accounts and Non-Reporting Financial Institutions maintain a low risk for their use in tax evasion cases[31]; and (6) enforcement provisions that are effective to deal with non-compliance.[32]

Backstopping measures are also used to obligate countries to adhere to due diligence procedures. This objective is achieved by establishing a number of due diligence provisions to be implemented in specific circumstances by financial institutions. The first of these provisions are noted in Section II which pertains to the requirements for general due diligence. As of the date an account is determined to be a Reportable Account in accordance with the due diligence process set out in Sections II–VII it is treated as such, and information on such account is required to be reported on an annual basis of the ensuing calendar year.[33] The account value or balance is calculated as at the end of the calendar year or the relevant reporting period.[34] Where the value threshold or balance is required to be calculated as of the end of the calendar year, the appropriate value or balance is to be calculated as at the end of the relevant reporting period ending with or that ends within such calendar year.[35] Jurisdictions are allowed to permit Reporting Financial Institutions to utilize the service of service providers to meet their obligations for reporting due diligence placed upon them, as taken into account by domestic law, but such obligations remain those of the Reporting Financial Institution.[36] Jurisdictions are also allowed to permit Reporting Financial Institutions to use the due diligence procedures for New Accounts in Preexisting Accounts, and the due diligence procedures for High Value Accounts in Lower Value

[30] See Paragraph A3 of Section IX of CRS.

[31] See Paragraph A4 of Section IX of CRS.

[32] See Paragraph A5 of Section IX of CRS.

[33] See Paragraph A of Section IIA of CRS.

[34] See Paragraph B of Section IIA of CRS.

[35] See Paragraph C of Section IIA of CRS.

[36] See Paragraph D of Section IIA of CRS.

Accounts.[37] Where Jurisdictions permit the use of due diligence procedures for New Account in Preexisting Accounts, the rules that otherwise apply in Preexisting Account remained applicable.[38]

The second set of due diligence provisions are noted in Section III which deals with Preexisting Individual Accounts. This section outlines certain procedures to be applied to determine which accounts out of the Preexisting Individual Accounts are Reportable Accounts. Paragraph A details the accounts not required to be identified, reviewed or reported. There is no requirement for an Annuity Contract or a Cash Value Insurance Contract which is a Preexisting Individual Account to be identified, reviewed or reported, under the condition that the Reporting Financial Institution is legally prohibited from the sale of such Contract to persons residing in a Reportable Jurisdiction.[39] Specific procedures regarding Lower Value Accounts are detailed in Paragraph B and must be adhered to when dealing with such accounts.[40] Likewise, for High Value Accounts, procedures for enhanced review are set out in paragraph C.[41] Compliance with such rules is obligatory on the part of Reporting Financial Institutions.

The third set of due diligence provisions are detailed in Section IV which deals with New Individual Accounts. This section outlines certain procedures that are to be applied to determine which accounts out of the New Individual Accounts are Reportable Accounts. The Reporting Financial Institution is required to obtain at account opening, a self-certification which can be included in the account opening documents, that permits the Reporting Financial Institution to conclude for tax purposes the residence(s) of the Account Holder, and confirm the integrity of the self-certification using the information collected by the Reporting Financial Institution in relation to the account opening, in addition to the documentation obtained in accordance with anti-money laundering and know your customer (AML/KYC) Procedures.[42] If the Account Holder

[37] See Paragraph E of Section IIA of CRS.

[38] See Paragraph E of Section IIA.

[39] See Paragraph A of Section III of CRS.

[40] See Paragraph B of Section III of CRS.

[41] See Paragraph C of Section III of CRS.

[42] See Paragraph A of Section IV of CRS.

is determined to be a resident in a Reportable Jurisdiction by self-certification for tax purposes, the account is required to be regarded by the Reporting Financial Institution as a Reportable Account and the date of birth and the Account Holder's TIN with regard to that Reportable Jurisdiction, conditional upon Section I paragraph D, is required to be included on the self-certification.[43] If circumstances change with regard to a New Individual Account that results in the Reporting Financial Institution having cause to know or knowledge that the initial self-certification is inaccurate or is not trustworthy, the Reporting Financial Institution is not able to rely on that self-certification and is required to attain for tax purposes a valid self-certification confirming the residence(s) of the Account Holder.[44]

The fourth set of due diligence provisions are set out in Section V which deals with Preexisting Entity Accounts. This section details the procedures to be applied when identifying which accounts among Preexisting Entity Accounts are Reportable Accounts. Paragraph A refers to entity accounts not required to be reviewed, identified or reported. An exception applies when a Reporting Financial Institution chooses otherwise, with regard to all Preexisting Entity Accounts or independently with regard to any group of accounts clearly identified. In this case, a Preexisting Entity Account having an accumulated account value or balance as of 31 December of a particular year of not more than USD250,000, is not obligated to proceed to review, identify or report such account as a Reportable Account until the accumulated account value or balance is greater than USD250,000 as at 31 December of the following calendar year.[45] Paragraph B looks at an entity account subject to a review. A review is required to be conducted pursuant to procedures as detailed in paragraph D for a Preexisting Entity Account having an accumulated account value or balance as of 31 December of a particular year greater than USD250,000, and a Preexisting Entity Account as of 31 December of a particular year having an accumulated account value or balance less than USD250,000, but having an accumulated account value or balance greater than USD250,000 as at 31 December of any ensuing

[43] See Paragraph B of Section IV of CRS.

[44] See Paragraph C of Section IV of CRS.

[45] See Paragraph A of Section V of CRS.

calendar year.[46] Paragraph C deals with entity accounts where reporting is required. With regards to Preexisting Entity Accounts as detailed in paragraph B, only accounts belonging to one Entity or more regarded as Reportable Persons or held by Passive Non-Financial Entities (NFE) having one Controlling Persons or more which are Reportable Persons, are required to be regarded as Reportable Accounts.[47]

Paragraph D looks at review procedures for identifying entity accounts where reporting is required. As they pertain to Preexisting Entity Accounts detailed in paragraph B, a Reporting Financial Institution is required to employ the review procedures outlined in paragraph D to decide if an account belongs to one or more Reportable Persons, or held by Passive NFEs with one or more Controlling Persons that are Reportable Persons.[48] A Reporting Financial Institution is also required to determine whether the entity is a Passive NFE with one or more controlling person who are Reportable Persons. With regard to a Preexisting Entity Account, and an Entity that is identified as a Reportable Person of an Account Holder, the Reporting Financial Institution is required to decide if the Account Holder is considered a Passive NFE with one or more Controlling Persons deemed as Reportable Persons. If a Passive NFE has a Controlling Person who is determined to be a Reportable Person, the account is required to be regarded as a Reportable Account. The Reporting Financial Institution is required to follow the procedures noted in subparagraphs D(2)(a) to (c) in the most appropriate order in making such determinations. Details related to the timing of a review and additional procedures applicable to Preexisting Entity Accounts are set out in paragraph E. If circumstances change with regard to a Preexisting Entity Account that results in the Reporting Financial Institution having reason to know or knowledge that the self-certification is inaccurate or not trustworthy or other documents connected to the account, the Reporting Financial Institution is required to make another determination of the account status pursuant to the procedures detailed in paragraph D.[49]

[46] See Paragraph B of Section V of CRS.

[47] See Paragraph C of Section V of CRS.

[48] See Paragraph D of Section V of CRS.

[49] See Paragraph E of Section V of CRS.

The fifth set of due diligence provisions are set forth in Section VI which deals with New Entity Accounts. This section details the procedures to be applied when identifying which accounts among New Entity Accounts are Reportable Accounts. Paragraph A outlines the procedures detailed below which must be performed by a Reporting Financial Institution to determine if an account belongs to one Reportable Person or more, or by a Passive NFE having one Controlling Person or more who is a Reportable Person.[50] To determine whether the entity is a Reportable Person, it must attain a self-certification, which can be included in the account opening documents, that permits the Reporting Financial Institution to make a determination for tax purposes the residence(s) of the Account Holder, and confirm the integrity of the self-certification using the information collected by the Reporting Financial Institution in relation to the account opening or documents obtained in accordance with AML/KYC Procedures.[51] The Reporting Financial Institution can depend on the Entity's principal office address to decide the Account Holder's residence.[52] If for tax purposes the Entity confirms that it has no residence, the Reporting Financial Institution is required to regard the account as a Reportable Account if the self-certification implies that the Account Holder is a Reportable Jurisdiction resident, except when it determines, using the information maintained or publicly available with regard to such Reportable Jurisdiction, that the Account Holder is regarded not as a Reportable Person.[53]

Step 2 of the procedures requires a determination to be made whether the Entity is a Passive NFE with one of more controlling persons who are Reportable Persons. With regard to an Account Holder who owns a New Entity Account, inclusive of an Entity identified as a Reportable Person, it is required for the Reporting Financial Institution to decide if the Account Holder is considered a Passive NFE with one Controlling Person or more who are Reportable Persons.[54] If the Passive NFE has Controlling Persons who are Reportable Persons, the account is required

[50] See Paragraph A of Section VI of CRS.

[51] See Paragraph 1a of Section VI of CRS.

[52] See Paragraph 1a of Section V.

[53] See Paragraph 1b of Section VI of CRS.

[54] See Paragraph 2 of Section VI of CRS.

to be regarded as a Reportable Account.[55] The Reporting Financial Institutions are obligated to adhere to the specific procedures outlined in step 2 in the most appropriate order in making such determination.[56] Overall, a Reporting Financial Institution can depend on an Account Holder's self-certification or that of such Controlling Person to determine if a Controlling Person is a Reportable Person of a Passive NFE.

The final set of due diligence provisions are noted in Section VII which deals with special due diligence rules. This section details additional rules which are applicable in carrying out due diligence procedures. For reliance on self-certifications and documentary evidence, if a Reporting Financial Institution has reason to know or knowledge that the self-certification or the Documentary Evidence is inaccurate or not trust worthy, the Reporting Financial Institution cannot depend on the self-certification or such Documentary Evidence.[57] In circumstances, when alternative procedures for financial accounts held by individual beneficiaries of a cash value insurance contract or an annuity contract, it can be presumed by a Reporting Financial Institution that an individual beneficiary who is not the owner of an Annuity Contract or a Cash Value Insurance Contract which obtains a death benefit is not considered a Reportable Person and may regard the Financial Account as such, except when the Reporting Financial Institution holds information or has reason to believe, that the beneficiary is determined to a Reportable Person.[58] A Reporting Financial Institution has grounds to believe that a beneficiary of an Annuity Contract or a Cash Value Insurance Contract is a Reportable Person if the Reporting Financial Institution obtains information that is connected to the beneficiary with an indicium as detailed in Section III paragraph B.[59] The Reporting Financial Institution is required to adhere to the procedures set out in Section III paragraph B in such case.[60]

CRS also employs backstopping measures by setting out compulsory disclosure rules for specific types of offshore structures. These rules are designed to gather information to strengthen the integrity of CRS by

[55] See Paragraph 2 of Section V.

[56] See Paragraph 2a, b and c of Section VI of CRS.

[57] See Paragraph A of Section VII of CRS.

[58] See Paragraph B of Section VII of CRS.

[59] See Paragraph B of Section VII.

[60] See Paragraph B of Section VII.

discouraging Intermediaries and advisors from marketing such schemes. The purpose behind establishing these rules of mandatory disclosure is to supply tax authorities with information on avoidance arrangements and non-transparent offshore structures, including users and providers of such structures (OECD 2017). This objective is accomplished by obligating the provider or user of an Opaque Offshore Structure or CRS Avoidance Arrangement to reveal specific information to tax authorities per the OECD. In cases where the information concerns a user which resides in another jurisdiction, such information is to be exchanged with the relevant tax authorities of that jurisdiction pursuant to the applicable provisions set out in the international legal agreement (OECD 2018).

Rule 1 sets forth the definition of the terms used in the mandatory disclosure rules. Rule 2 pertains to the obligation to disclose CRS Avoidance Arrangements as well as Opaque Offshore Structures. Rule 2.1 deals with the obligation placed on an Intermediary to disclose. With regard to CRS Avoidance Arrangements or Opaque Offshore Structures, this rule requires a person acting as an Intermediary to disclose a Structure or Arrangement to tax authorities located in [Jurisdiction Name], if such person: (a) makes available for implementation such CRS Avoidance Arrangement or Opaque Offshore Structure or supplies Relevant Services with regard to such CRS Avoidance Arrangement of Opaque Offshore Structure using a branch situated in [Jurisdiction Name]; (b) has an office of management or is resident in [jurisdiction Name]; or (c) is organized within the laws of or is incorporated in [Jurisdiction Name].[61] Rule 2.2 refers to when information is obligated to be disclosed. The requirement to disclose per Rule 2.1 is to be done by the Intermediary thirty days after: (a) making available the CRS Avoidance Arrangement or Opaque Offshore Structure for implementation; or (b) rendering Relevant Services related to a CRS Avoidance Arrangement or an Opaque Offshore Structure.[62]

Rule 2.3 concerns information which must be disclosed by an Intermediary. In accordance with Rule 2.1, with regard to a CRS Avoidance Arrangement or an Opaque Offshore Structure, an Intermediary is obligated to disclose the following information: (a) the name, in addition to

[61] See Rule 2.1a of Model Mandatory Disclosure Rules for CRS Avoidance Arrangements and Opaque Offshore Structures (Mandatory Disclosure Rule for CRS).

[62] See Rule 2.2 of Mandatory Disclosure Rule for CRS.

the address, jurisdiction(s), as well as the TIN(s) related to the tax residence of such persons: (i) the individual who makes the disclosure; (ii) any Client of such individual with respect to such Structure or Arrangement (identifying apart any Client considered to be a Reportable Taxpayer, in addition to the date of birth of such individuals); (iii) any Beneficial Owner of an Opaque Offshore Structure or existing user of a CRS Avoidance Arrangement; and (iv) any individual who is an Intermediary with regard to such Structure or Arrangement (that is not the person carrying out the disclosure); (b) details of the CRS Avoidance Arrangement or Opaque Offshore Structure such as: (i) regarding a CRS Avoidance Arrange, a description which is factual containing the characteristics of the Arrangement that is aimed to have or promoted as having or have the ability of, bypassing CRS legislation; and (ii) regarding an Opaque Offshore Structure, a description which is factual containing the characteristics that have the ability of not permitting an accurate conclusion on the Beneficial Ownership of the Reportable Taxpayer or giving the appearance that a Passive Offshore Vehicle's Beneficial Owner is not a Reportable Taxpayer; and (c) the jurisdiction(s) in which CRS Avoidance Arrangement or Opaque Offshore Structure was made available for implementation, to the degree that the information is within the possession, knowledge or control of the individual that provides the disclosure.[63]

Rule 2.4 pertains to circumstances where an Intermediary is not obligated to disclose. They include the following: (a) pursuant to Rule 2.3 where such information is safeguarded from disclosure in accordance with secrecy rules under domestic law, only to the degree that such disclosure would divulge professional confidential information which is in the possession of a solicitor, attorney or other admitted legal official with regard to a Client, per the definition noted in Article 26 Commentary of the OECD Model Tax Convention; (b) pursuant to Rule 2.4 where it is required to give the Client written notice of the Client's disclosure responsibilities set forth by these rules within the time noted per Rule 2.2.[64] Rule 2.5 deals with the obligation of an Intermediary not to disclose to the extent to which information has been disclosed already. An Intermediary is not obligated to divulge any information as detailed in

[63] See Rule 2.3 of Mandatory Disclosure Rule for CRS.

[64] See Rule 2.4 of Mandatory Disclosure Rule for CRS.

Rule 2.3, to the degree that it holds evidence proving that: (a) such information had already been disclosed to the tax authority in [Jurisdiction Name]; (b) the information is related to the Relevant Services rendered, or to an Opaque Offshore Structure or a CRS Avoidance Arrangement which were made accessible for implementation, via a branch related to the Intermediary located in a Partner Jurisdiction, and the disclosure of such information to the tax authority located in the Partner Jurisdiction has been made; or (c) pursuant to Rule 2.1(c), the Intermediary is obligated to reveal such information and the same has been revealed to the tax authority located in a Partner Jurisdiction where such Intermediary has its office of management or is resident.[65]

Rule 2.6 pertains to the requirements of a Reportable Taxpayer to disclose under certain circumstances. They include: (a) disclosure is to be made to the tax authority located in [Jurisdiction Name] by any Reportable Taxpayer residing in [jurisdiction Name] and uses a CRS Avoidance Arrangement or is a Beneficial Owner of an Opaque Offshore Structure, of any information on the Arrangement or the Structure not revealed by an Intermediary due to the Intermediary not being bound to any disclosure requirements per Rule 2.1 or is not obligated to disclose such information in accordance with Rule 2.4; (b) the Reportable Taxpayer is not obligated to reveal any information per Rule 2.6(a) to the degree that the Reportable Taxpayer has evidence from the Intermediary proving that the information had already been disclosed by it to the tax authority located in the Partner Jurisdiction pursuant to mandatory disclosure rules that are very similar to those detailed in this legislation; (c) in accordance to Rule 2.6(a) above, the disclosure should contain all information obligated per Rule 2.3 to be disclosed and done within thirty days following the first step of the implementation of CRS Avoidance Arrangement or Opaque Offshore Structure.[66] Rule 2.7 concerns disclosure of Arrangements which are entered into following 29 October 2014, and prior to the effective date of these mandatory disclosure rules. Under this rule; (a) a Promoter is required to disclose a CRS Avoidance Arrangement by the end of 180 days of the date effective of such rules where: (i) that Arrangement was established on or following 29 October 2014, but

[65] See Rule 2.5 of Mandatory Disclosure Rule for CRS.

[66] See Rule 2.6 of Mandatory Disclosure Rule for CRS.

prior to the effective date of these disclosure rules; and (ii) such individual was a Promoter with regard to that Arrangement; despite whether the individual renders Relevant Services with regard to the Arrangement following the effective date; (b) per paragraph (a), a disclosure is not required where the Promoter has evidence to prove that the total value or balance of the Financial Account per CRS Avoidance Arrangement just after its implementation was lower than USD1,000,000; (c) regardless of Rule 1.4(e), and per Rule 2.7 for the motive of articulating the defined terms, CRS Legislation refers to the Standard set by the OECD for Automatic Exchange of Financial Account Information in Tax Matters, published on 15 July 2014.[67]

### *6.3.3 Strengthen National Institutions to Increase International Cooperation*

CRS also employs measures to strengthen national institutions to increase their capacity for international cooperation. It does this through the implementation of the model competent authority arrangement (the Model CAA). The Model CAA and CRS, together form the Standard for reporting all due diligence and the exchange of information related to financial account (OECD 2017). Its purpose is to provide the legal basis for information to be exchanged between countries. On this basis, CRS uses the Model CAA to create government networks between jurisdictions to strengthen international cooperation. It also increases national capacity by enhancing local regulatory systems to achieve common international objectives. The Model CAA binds both parties to provide mutual legal assistance in tax matters based on the terms agreed to (OECD 2017). CRS allows flexibility for other similar instruments to be used to facilitate information exchange (OECD 2017). The main provisions of the agreement allow for Competent Authorities to agree on several key elements.

The first of these elements is the exchange of information with regard to reportable accounts. Subject to the provisions contained in the legal instrument agreed to, the reporting requirement and due diligence rules pursuant to CRS, each Competent Authority is permitted to automatically

[67] See Rule 2.8 of Mandatory Disclosure Rule for CRS.

exchange information obtained on an annual basis with other Competent Authorities[68] in accordance with the following: (a) for an Account Holder who is an individual, the name, address, place and date of birth and TIN(s) for all Reportable Persons, and for an Account Holder which is an Entity identified as having more than one Controlling Person as a Reportable Person, the name, address, TIN(s), place and date of birth of all Reportable Persons, and for the Entity, the name, address and TIN(s); (b) the account number or its equivalent; (c) the name of the Reporting Financial Institution and its identifying number, if available; (d) the value of the account or its balance as at end of the relevant calendar year, or period, or as at account closure, if applicable; (e) for Custodial Accounts: (i) the total gross amount of interest, dividends and other income earned on assets within the account, which are credited or paid to the account during the calendar year or reporting period; and (ii) the total gross proceeds credited to or paid to the account from the redemption or sale of Financial Assets during the calendar year or reporting period where the Reporting Financial Institution served as the broker, custodian, nominee or as the Account Holder's agent; (f) for a Depository Account: (i) the total gross amount of interest credited or paid during the calendar year or reporting period to the account; and (g) for any other account, the total gross amount credited or paid during the calendar year or reporting period to the Account Holder where the Reporting Financial Institution acts as debtor, or obligor, in addition to the total amount of redemption payments made during the calendar year or reporting period to the Account Holder.[69]

The second element is the time and manner in which exchange of information takes place. For the objective of exchanging information in accordance with the above (Sect. 6.3), the payment amounts and characterization made to a Reportable Account may be decided upon by the jurisdiction involved in information exchange pursuant to their tax laws.[70] It is also required to: (i) note the currency each amount is dominated in[71]; (ii) exchange such information within a nine-month period

[68] See Section 2, paragraph 1 of Model Competent Authority Agreement.

[69] See Section 2, paragraph 2 of Model Competent Authority Agreement.

[70] See Section 3, paragraph 1 of Model Competent Authority Agreement.

[71] See Section 3, paragraph 2 of Model Competent Authority Agreement.

following the calendar year end which the information relates to[72]; and (iii) regardless of the aforementioned sentence, such information should only be exchanged with regard to a calendar year, if each respective jurisdiction has legislations in effect which provides for reporting with regard to such calendar year that falls within the scope of Section 2 as it relates to the exchange, reporting and procedures of due diligence which falls within Common Reporting Standard. Regardless of the aforementioned paragraph, the information to be exchanged with regard to what is agreed to, is the information detailed in Section 2 paragraph 2, with the exception of gross proceeds mentioned in Section 2, subparagraph 2(e)(2) of the agreement.[73] Competent Authorities are permitted to exchange the information automatically as noted in Section 2 in Extensible Markup Language in a common reporting standard schema.[74] The method to transmit data including encryption standards are to be agreed to by the Competent Authorities.[75]

The third element is collaboration with regards to compliance and enforcement. This section requires Competent Authority to give notice to a Competent Authority when the former Competent Authority has basis to assume that a mistake may have resulted in inaccurate or insufficient information reporting or the existence of non-adherence to reporting obligations and due diligence procedures in accordance with CRS by a Reporting Financial Institution. The Competent Authority which is notified is required to pursue all relevant measures allowed pursuant to its domestic law to deal with the mistakes or non-adherence detailed in the notice.[76]

The forth element refers to confidentiality and the safeguard of data. All information which is exchanged is subjected to the rules of confidentiality and other safeguards allowed for in accordance with the legal instrument agreed to, as well as the provisions restricting the use for which the information is exchanged, and an adequate degree of protection

[72] See Section 3, paragraph 3 of Model Competent Authority Agreement.

[73] See Section 3, paragraph 4 of Model Competent Authority Agreement.

[74] See Section 3, paragraph 5 of Model Competent Authority Agreement.

[75] See Section 3, paragraph 6 of Model Competent Authority Agreement.

[76] See Section 4 of Model Competent Authority Agreement.

necessary for personal data pursuant to the requirement of the Competent Authority which supplied the information within its domestic law.[77] Immediate notice is required to be given by each Competent Authority to the other Competent Authority for any violation of confidentiality or neglect of safeguards and any penalties or remedial actions imposed.[78]

The fifth element deals with consultations and amendments. All difficulties related to the interpretation or the application of the Agreement can be dealt with by either of the Competent Authority through requesting consultations to establish proper measures to see to it that the Agreement is executed.[79] The Agreement can be modified by written agreement between the Competent Authorities, with the effective date as agreed or on the first day of the month after the expiration of a one-month period following the date of the latest signature of the written agreement or the date the later notification has been exchanged regarding the written agreement.[80]

The last element pertains to the terms of the agreement. It allows for the decision on the effective date the Agreement is to take effect, to be decided on by the Competent Authorities, or for the date of the later notification given by the respective Competent Authorities advising that the proper laws are in place in their jurisdictions to be used to establish the Agreement.[81] It also provides for a Competent Authority to suspend information to be exchanged pursuant to the Agreement, by providing written notice to the other Competent Authority of its conclusion that the other Competent Authority has not or is significantly non-adherent to the Agreement. The suspension's effect is to be immediate.[82] Finally, it permits the Agreement to be terminated by each respective Competent Authority. The effective date of termination is the first day of the month after a 12-month period expires following the date of the termination notice. Should termination occur, the information which was received

[77] See Section 5, paragraph 1 of Model Competent Authority Agreement.

[78] See Section 5, paragraph 2 of Model Competent Authority Agreement.

[79] See Section 6, paragraph 1 of Model Competent Authority Agreement.

[80] See Section 6, paragraph 2 of Model Competent Authority Agreement.

[81] See Section 7, paragraph 1 of Model Competent Authority Agreement.

[82] See Section 7, paragraph 2 of Model Competent Authority Agreement.

under the Agreement is to remain confidential in accordance with the terms of the legal instrument agreed to.[83]

## 6.4 Policy Initiatives Instituted by the US and EU

### *6.4.1 US Foreign Account Tax Compliance Act (FATCA)*

The US took a similar approach to the FATF in 2001 and OECD in 2002 in their use of coercion to compel countries to act. This is evident through the imposition of a 30% withholding tax on US source income on financial institutions which failed to implement FATCA (IRS 2020). The adoption of FATCA by the US, in accordance with the Hiring Incentives to Restore Employment (HIRE) Act 2010, was also instituted in a way as to establish a legal framework to enable jurisdiction to implement the Standard (US Congress 2010). To do so, countries were required to incorporate FATCA into their domestic legal system by putting the requisite legislation or legal measures in place. FATCA placed a reporting obligation on foreign financial institutions to report to the IRS-specified information related to foreign assets held in the accounts of US persons, or by various types of non-financial foreign entities in which a substantial ownership interest is held by US taxpayers (IRS 2020). FATCA also functions in a way to create an institutional structure to facilitate the reporting obligations of countries. Jurisdictions were given two options. The first allowed Foreign financial institutions (FFI) to register directly with the competent tax authority (IRS) in the US, to satisfy the FATCA regulations if applicable, with the FFI agreement. The second option provided for countries to sign an Intergovernmental Agreement (IGA) with the US Government and adhere to the provisions contained therein (IRS 2020). These two options also served to establish a system to facilitate the effective exchange of information through national and international cooperation.

### *6.4.2 European Union Code of Conduct Group*

Like the US, the EU took a similar stance in introducing its Standard to push countries to act. Jurisdictions were obligated to commit at a high political level and put measures in place by 31 December 2018 to tackle

[83] See Section 7, paragraph 3 of Model Competent Authority Agreement.

harmful tax practices, tax evasion and base erosion profit shifting. Failure to do so resulted in placement on the EU's List of non-cooperative jurisdictions for tax purposes. To be removed from the List, a jurisdiction had to become tax compliant in accordance with the criteria set by the European Union (Council of the EU 2017). The EU also used its Standard to establish a legal framework to enable countries to implement it. This required countries to employ the legal measures to incorporate the Standard into their domestic legislation. These measures had to satisfy two of the following three requirements: (i) establish exchange agreements with all EU States by September 2018; (ii) obtain a largely compliant rating on the EOIR Standard introduced by the Global Forum; and (iii) become party to the Multilateral Convention on Mutual Administrative Assistance in Tax Matters (Council of the EU 2017). These legal measures also established an institutional structure in which the Standard was to function in each of these three scenarios. They also each served as mechanisms to implement effective exchange of information by way of bilateral and multilateral agreements to enhance a jurisdiction's capacity to provide assistance in international cooperation.

## 6.5 Conclusion

International policy initiative established by the OECD and its special task force, the Global Forum, have evolved over time in a strategic way to shape the domestic legal systems of countries globally. Similar to the OECD and the Global Forum, the US and EU have also had long reaching effects in moulding the legal frameworks of countries worldwide, although the US to a lesser extent, compared to the other three in its role of reforming their legislative landscape. These Standards contained a common element which was aimed at enhancing transparency to effectively counter tax evasion. To achieve this objective, each Standard was designed in a way to obligate countries to reform their legal systems and implement measures to establish the institutional structure required to apply and operate them Standards. To compel countries to participate in the EOIR, AEOI, FATCA and the EU Code of Conduct Standards, coercion was used to varying degrees, to get countries to undertake the necessary legal measures to apply the Standards for each of these players to achieve their underlying objectives.

The Standards were also crafted to function as backstopping mechanisms to strengthen domestic institutions and reinforce national governance, particularly in the areas of reporting, due diligence and confidentiality, and data protection rules. These measures served as preventative mechanisms to counter the risks associated with tax evasion.

The Standards were also designed to function as a mechanism to facilitate the effective exchange of information between countries, and increase their propensity to assist in international cooperation. Whether by establishing bilateral or multilateral accords with other countries, these exchange mechanisms which came about as a result of set Standards, effectively increased the capacities of countries to participate in information exchanges, and significantly enhanced tax transparency among participating jurisdictions globally.

These Standards have revolutionized the idea of tax evasion from one associated with jurisdictions which based their business on strict secrecy provisions and lack of cooperation in tax matters, thereby encouraging opacity, to one linked to countries that have gradually opened up to actively participate in information exchange, which has resulted in increased transparency. The exchange Standards introduced have also evolved over time, from exchange of tax information upon request, to automatic and spontaneous information exchange, to automatic exchange of information through common reporting standards. Along with this evolution, the obligations placed on jurisdictions worldwide have also increased, in addition to the power ceased by the OECD, the Global Forum, the US and EU over the years. Whereas, countries on the other hand have increasingly lost internal power to implement their very own legal measures independently, within their sovereign rights. The effects of these international policy initiatives have been far reaching and have had significant impact on countries globally, particularly on The Bahamas, the Cayman Islands, Bermuda and the BVI. How these countries address the criteria established to satisfy these Standards and that of the FATF, will be the focus of the next two subsequent chapters.

## References

Burke-White, William W., and Anne-Marie Slaughter. 2006. *The Future of International Law Is Domestic (or, the European Way of Law)*. Faculty Scholarship at Penn Law, 962. https://scholarship.law.upenn.edu/cgi/viewcontent.cgi?article=1958&context=faculty_scholarship.

Council of the European Union. 2017. *The EU List of Non-cooperative Jurisdictions for Tax Purposes*. European Commission, 15429/17. https://data.consilium.europa.eu/doc/document/ST-15429-2017-INIT/en/pdf.
Council of the European Union. 2016. *Communication on Further Measures to Enhance Transparency and the Fight Against Tax Evasion and Avoidance*. European Commission, 10977/16. https://data.consilium.europa.eu/doc/document/ST-10977-2016-INIT/en/pdf.
Internal Revenue Service. 2020. *FATCA User Guide*. Internal Revenue Service. https://www.irs.gov/pub/irs-pdf/p5118.pdf.
Knobel, Andres. 2018. *Blacklist, Whitewashed: How the OECD Bent Its Rules to Help Tax Haven USA*. Tax Justice Network. https://www.taxjustice.net/2018/07/27/blacklist-whitewashed-how-the-oecd-bent-its-rules-to-help-tax-haven-usa/.
OECD. 2012. *The Global Forum on Transparency and Exchange of Information for Tax Purposes Information Brief*. OECD Publishing. https://www.oecd.org/ctp/harmful/43757434.pdf.
OECD. 2014. *Standard for Automatic Exchange of Financial Account Information in Tax Matters*. OECD Publishing. https://read.oecd-ilibrary.org/taxation/standard-for-automatic-exchange-of-financial-account-information-for-tax-matters_9789264216525-en#page1.
OECD. 2016. *Exchange of Information on Request: Handbook for Peer Reviews 2016–2020*. OECD Publishing. http://www.oecd.org/tax/transparency/global-forum-handbook-2016.pdf.
OECD. 2017. *Standard for Automatic Exchange of Financial Account Information in Tax Matters*. OECD Publishing. http://www.oecd.org/tax/automatic-exchange/common-reporting-standard/common-reporting-standard-and-related-commentaries/#d.en.345314.
OECD. 2018. *Inclusive Framework on BEPS*. OECD Publishing. https://www.oecd.org/tax/flyer-inclusive-framework-on-beps.pdf.
US Senate and House of Representatives. 2010. *Hiring Incentives to Restore Employment Act. Public Law 111–147*. US Government. https://www.govinfo.gov/content/pkg/PLAW-111publ147/pdf/PLAW-111publ147.pdf.

CHAPTER 7

# The Impact of International Policy Initiatives Against Money Laundering and Terrorist Financing on the Legislative Systems and Institutions of Offshore Financial Centres in the Caribbean

## 7.1 Introduction

Prior to 2000, The Bahamas, the Cayman Islands, Bermuda and the BVI addressed money laundering in accordance with what each jurisdiction had deemed adequate to counter this phenomenon. Through the publication of its Forty Recommendations in 1990, amended in 1996, the FATF sort to encourage countries around the world, including these four jurisdictions to enhance their legal systems to strengthen their legal capacity to fight money laundering (FATF 1991, 1997). With the introduction of the 2000 FATF blacklist, the FATF took a firm stance to enforce its standard by compelling countries worldwide to implement its Recommendations (FATF 2000).

With the introduction of its mutual evaluation report (MER), which involved an onsite review of the legislative system of jurisdictions to determine if adequate measures were undertaken to enforce its Recommendations, the FATF continued to strengthen its Recommendations and reinforce its influence over countries globally (Sansonetti 2000). Between 2012 and 2013, additional enhancements were incorporated into the FATF's Recommendations and methodology, with which it conducts its



A. M. Campbell, *Money Laundering, Terrorist Financing, and Tax Evasion*, https://doi.org/10.1007/978-3-030-68876-9_7

assessment of jurisdictions to produce its MER (FATF 2021). These enhancements have increased the obligations placed on jurisdictions, and have in part, impacted their legal systems and institutions in many ways. As a result of the actions taken by the FATF, jurisdictions were forced to implement required measures to effectively mitigate all risks financial system.

Measures introduced by the Basel Committee on Bank Supervision through its Statement of Principles mainly serve to support the work of the FATF. These measures included setting policies and procedures for bank management to implement at their respective institutions to suppress money laundering within the national and international banking systems (FATF 2021).

In this chapter, we will examine the impact of the Forty Recommendations on the legal systems of The Bahamas, the Cayman Islands, Bermuda and the BVI. The period used for this analysis will be from 2007 to 2012. This period has been chosen because it coincides with the timeframe in which each jurisdiction underwent their third MER. The information used for this analysis includes the mutual evaluation reports (MERs) published by the Caribbean Financial Action Task Force (CFATF), literature produced by the FATF, along with the annual financial reports and special reviews published by the central banks and government institutions in each country. The MERs used in this analysis are the most recently available ones for each jurisdiction.

## 7.2 International Policy Initiative

### *7.2.1 Forty Recommendations*

The publication of its Non-Cooperative Countries and Territories (NCCT) list on 22 June 2000, was its first push by the FATF to compel jurisdictions to act. Jurisdictions were obligated to implement specific legal measures to satisfy the rules set by the FATF outlined in its Forty Recommendations (FATF 2000). In 2007, the FATF increased its powers through the introduction of guidance notes focused on a risk-based approach to counter money laundering and terrorist financing (FATF 2007). It also eliminated its NCCT list and replaced it with a High-Risk

Jurisdiction list.[1] These measures, in addition to its MER process which required jurisdictions to agree to an in-country onsite visit by expert representatives of the FATF, placed increased obligations on countries globally (FATF 2021). The purpose of the onsite visit was to review the legal, regulatory and operational aspects of the anti-money laundering and anti-terrorist financing regimes of jurisdictions, to ensure adequate measures were taken to properly implement its Recommendations. Countries were also obligated to commit at a high political level and employ measures to address all deficiencies which came about as a result of the onsite inspection (FATF 2021). Failure to satisfy the Recommendations resulted in placement on its High-Risk Jurisdiction list and potential defensive measures brought against such jurisdictions by OECD countries (FATF 2021).

## 7.3 The Bahamas

### *7.3.1 Transparency*

To increase transparency and strengthen its institutional framework, The Bahamas implemented a number of measures between 2007 and 2012. These measures were undertaken by the jurisdiction in response to the results of the third MER published by the CFATF on 3 November 2007 (FATF 2021). The MER revealed a rating of partially compliant in four core Recommendations (R.1, R.5, R.10, and R.13), partially compliant in four key Recommendations (R.23, R.35, SR.1 and SR.III), partially compliant in 15 Recommendations (R.6, R.8, R.9, R.11, R.12, R.15, R.16, R.17, R.21, R.22, R.24, R.29, R.30, and R.32), and non-compliant in three Recommendations (R.7, R.19 and SR.VII) (CFATF 2007). The MER results also highlighted a number of deficiencies in various areas of the jurisdictions' AML/CFT regime.

To address the concerns raised by the CFATF, the Government of The Bahamas underwent reforms to several key Acts aimed at strengthening its institutional framework, and supervisory powers. These measures also allowed for information sharing and collaboration between local regulators. The first of these amendments included the Banks and Trust

[1] See FATF website http://www.fatf-gafi.org/publications/high-riskandnon-cooperativejurisdictions/more/moreabouttheinternationalco-operationreviewgroupicrg.html?hf=10&b=0&s=desc(fatf_releasedate).

Companies Regulations Act, which was amended in 2006 to make provisions for the supervisory authority of stand-alone money transmission businesses to be subjected to the supervision and regulation of the Central Bank of The Bahamas (CFATF 2009b). It also allowed for the Central Bank to share information pertaining to such businesses with local regulators (CFATF 2009b). The next amendment introduced the Financial and Corporate Service Providers (Amendment) Act, 2008, which granted increased authority to the Inspector in carrying out its duties including setting rules, guidelines, directives and enforcing sanctions (CFATF 2012b).[2] Another amendment carried out by the jurisdiction was the passage of the Securities Industry (Amendment) Act, 2007, which empowered the Securities Commission to impose an obligation on its licensees to provide information to it. This amendment also granted it with powers to share such information with other regulatory bodies in the jurisdiction (CFATF 2009b). Through the Securities Industry (Amendment) Regulations, 2009, provisions were introduced for all requests made by the Commission to licensees to be carried out by court order (CFATF 2009b). Finally, on 10 January 2007, the jurisdiction amended the Investments Fund Act, which empowered the Commission to collaborate with other financial regulators (CFATF 2009b).

Additional measures were undertaken by the jurisdiction to strengthened its supervisory oversite in the various key segments of the industry. For example, The Bahamas introduced the Insurance Act, 2005, which gave AML/CFT powers to the Registrar of Insurance, and allowed for supervisory intervention at various levels (CFATF 2010c). It also enacted the External Insurance Act, 2009 (EIA), which empowered the Registrar of Insurance to carry out inspections at any time and demand documentation. Both Acts were brought into force in 2009 (CFATF 2010c). The EIA was later amended to allow for the accounts of policyholders to be accessed by the Insurance Commission (CFATF 2013). In 2011, the jurisdiction revoked and replaced the Securities Industry Act, 1999 and the Securities Industry Regulations, 2000, with the enactment of the Securities Industry Act, 2011 (SIA) and the Securities Industry Regulations, Act, 2012 (SIR), which became effective 30 December 2011 and on 9 January 2012, respectively (CFATF 2012b). The SIA provided for supervisory powers to be extended to the Securities Commission over

[2] This Act was brought into force on February 12, 2009.

the securities and capital market in the jurisdiction, including investment funds in addition to others. It also granted powers to the Securities Commission to impose sanctions on registrants or licensees for failure to adhere to its directive (CFATF 2012b). Additionally, it contained a broad range of powers aimed at protecting the interest of the public. Both the SIA and SIR provided for information and records including documents to be accessed by the Commission and shared with local as well as foreign authorities (CFATF 2012b). To further improve its institutional framework, the Securities Commission adopted the AML/CFT Guidelines of the Central Bank of The Bahamas (CFATF 2011a). On 1 January 2008, the Securities Commission Board was designated as Inspector of the Financial and Corporate Service Providers and took on administrative responsibility of the Financial and Corporate Service Providers Act (FCSPA) (CFATF 2012b). Finally, on 7 August 2007, the jurisdiction also established a Special Anti-Terrorism Unit to deal with terrorist financing matters (CFATF 2009b).

### *7.3.2 Preventative measures*

To enhance its anti-money laundering and countering the financing of terrorism (AML/CFT) framework to prevent financial institutions and DNFBPs from being used by money launderers and terrorists, the jurisdiction implemented a number of backstopping measures. The first of these measures was the passage of the Financial Transactions Reporting (Amendment) Act, 2009 (CFATF 2009b). Through this Act, The Bahamas imposed penalties for failure to adhere to AML/CFT guidelines and the Code of Practice by the Compliance Commission. It also provided for certain DNFBPs, such as precious metals and precious stones dealers to be deemed financial institutions, per the Financial Transaction Reporting (Amendment) Act, 2014 (FTRA), for the purpose of subjecting them to AML/CFT rules pursuant to the principal Act (CFATF 2009b). The jurisdiction also stipulated a mandatory requirement to conduct a full customer due diligence (CDD) for transactions below B$15,000, where suspicion exists for money laundering and terrorist financing by way of the Financial Transactions Reporting Regulations (Amendment) Act, 2009 (CFATF 2009b). It also instituted penalties for failure to adhere to AML/CFT guidelines and the Codes of Practice by the Compliance Commission, through the Financial Intelligence (Transactions Reporting) Regulations, 2009 (CFATF 2009b). The jurisdiction also obligated financial institutions to carry out minimum requirements to verify the identity of persons conducting business on behalf of corporate entities under (Regulation 4(1)(b) and (c)), partnerships or other businesses that were not incorporated per (Regulation 5(1)(c) and (d), as well as settlors and power holders of trusts (Regulation 6(2)), with the passing of the Financial Transaction Reporting (Wire Transfer) Regulations 2009 (CFATF 2009b). It also placed responsibility on financial institutions to carry out reasonable steps to verify the identity of ultimate beneficial owners of corporate vehicles per (Regulations 4(1)(e)), partnerships or ultimate beneficial owners of unincorporated businesses or partnerships under (Regulation 5(1)(a)), and identify the natural persons who control or own legal persons and legal arrangements (CFATF 2009b). The final measure undertaken by the jurisdiction was the imposition of penalties for failure to adhere to AML/CFT guidelines and the Codes of Practice by the Compliance Commission through the enactment of the Financial Intelligence Unit (Amendment) Act, 2009 (CFATF 2009b).

Other measures taken by the jurisdiction included the revision of the Central Bank of The Bahamas AML/CFT Guidelines to include the requirement of senior management's approval in order to begin or continue a business relationship with PEPs, or with customers who become PEPs pursuant to Paragraph 161 (iii) (CFATF 2009b). The revisions also included provisions which placed the onus of due diligence obligations on licensees in determining the AML/CFT controls to be adhered to by respondent businesses, and in commencing new correspondent relationships, particularly in handling transactions and business relationships with persons from or located in countries known to contain deficiencies in AML/CFT measures (CFATF 2009b). Another measure taken by the jurisdiction took place in 2010, with the reorganization of the Bank Supervision Department at the Central Bank of The Bahamas to adopt an improved Risk-Based Supervision Framework (CFATF 2011a). This newly adopted methodology placed attention on material risk issues related to licensees. Another measure included the adoption of the AML/CFT Guidelines of the Central Bank of The Bahamas by the Securities Commission (CFATF 2011a). Additionally, the jurisdiction also developed a Codes of Practice for accountants, which allowed for enhanced provisions for effective CDD procedures when conducting business with non-face-to-face customers. Similar provisions were also noted in the Codes of Practice for legal and real estate professions and for financial and corporate service providers (CFATF 2009b). The last measure adopted by the jurisdiction was the subjection of Credit Unions to the supervisory authority of the Compliance Commission, and the introduction of a Code of Practice to improve CDD measures among Credit Unions (CFATF 2009b).

### *7.3.3 National and International Cooperation*

To increase its capacity to assist in international cooperation, The Bahamas amended two key pieces of legislations. The first, allowed for Bahamian evidence to be used abroad through the amendment of the Mutual Legal Assistance (Criminal Matters) Act (CFATF 2013). The second included an amendment to the Extradition Act to incorporate the jurisdiction's international obligations pursuant to the Palermo Convention, and also Section 5(2) of the principal Act, to increase the extraditable offence categories (CFATF 2013). The jurisdiction also passed the Criminal Procedure Plea Discussion and Plea Agreement Act, 2008, which made provisions for a statutory basis to determine judgement in criminal matters without the need for full trail to increase the speed to conclude criminal cases (CFATF 2009b).

Other measures carried out by the jurisdiction included: (i) the ratification of the United Nations Convention against Transnational Organized Crime on 26 September 2008; and (ii) bring into force the Palermo Convention and its Protocols on 25 December 2008 (CFATF 2009b). Additionally, the Trafficking in Persons (Prevention and Suppression) Act, 2008 was also assented to on 9 December 2008 and commenced the following day (CFATF 2009b). To round out its capacity to assist in international cooperation, the Anti-Terrorism (Amendment to First Schedule) Order, 2008 modified the Anti-Terrorism Act (ATA) to include all of the Conventions noted on the Annex of the Terrorist Financing Convention (CFATF 2009b). Further, in 2009 the jurisdiction became a B signatory to the International Organization of Securities Commissions Multilateral Memorandum of Understanding (IOSCO MMOU), and an A signatory in 2013.

## 7.4 The Cayman Islands

### *7.4.1 Transparency*

The third MER by the FATF of the Cayman Islands was adopted on 23 November 2007 (CFATF 2007a). The results revealed a rating of largely compliant in 24 Recommendations (R.1, R.3, R.6, R.8, R.10, R.11, R.13, R.14, R.21, R.22, R.23, R.24, R.25, R.26, R.29, R.35, R.36, SR I, SR II, SR III, SR IV, SR V and SR VI), partially compliant in 10 Recommendations (R.5, R.9, R.12, R.5, R.6, 8-11, R.15, R.16, R.18, R.30, SR VII, SR VIII and SR IX), and non-compliant in R.7 (CFATF 2007a).

To address the deficiencies raised in each of these areas, the Cayman Islands Government undertook a number of measures aimed at enhancing transparency and strengthening its legal system and institutions. Among the key measures adopted, was the enactment of the Proceeds of Crime Law (POCL) on 30 June 2008, which went into effect on 21 August 2008. The POCL revoked and replaced the Proceeds of Criminal Conduct Law (CFATF 2009a). Under Section 133 of POCL, the money laundering definition was broadened to include, "concealing, disguising, converting, transferring or removing of criminal property from the Cayman Islands", to comply with the Vienna Convention, removing the former requirement for "intent to avoid prosecution or the making of a confiscation order (CFATF 2009a)".

Additionally, Sections 88 and 118 of Part IV were incorporated to provide for asset-tracing and civil forfeiture provisions (CFATF 2009a). Section 88 allowed for the Attorney-General to make application to the Grand Court for a recovery order against any individual it considers holds property acquired through unlawful means, whereas, Section 118 provides for the Attorney-General to apply to a summary court for cash detained by a constable or customer officer to be forfeited (CFATF 2009a). Further, Section 166 subject's financial institutions to hand over information on the individual stated in the order, related to a money laundering or confiscation investigation, and also specific account information for the time period noted on the order per Section 173 (CFATF 2010a). Furthermore, Section 139 introduced a tipping off offence for the disclosure of information which could bias a potential or current investigation (CFATF 2009a). Finally, to satisfy the requirement for SR. VIII, the jurisdiction introduced the Charities Bill, 2010, which provided for the supervision of non-profit organizations (NPOs) (CFATF 2009a).

### 7.4.2 *Preventative measures*

Other initiatives undertaken by the jurisdiction were backstopping measures aimed at preventing money laundering and terrorist financing within different segments of the jurisdiction to address deficiencies observed in the MER. The first of these was the passage of the Money Laundering (Amendment) Regulations, 2008, which revised the Money Laundering Regulations (2008 Revision) (MLRs), and became effective 24 October 2008 (CFATF 2009a). This amendment made provisions for enhanced CDD measures related to conducting identity procedures on the following: (a) a business applicant (Reg. 11 of the MLRs); (b) a person carrying out business on behalf of or having the power of, the business applicant, who is a legal person or arrangement, holding evidence of such power (Reg. 7 of MLRs); and (c) a natural person who controls or ultimately owns the business applicants who are legal persons or arrangements (Reg. 7 of MLRs). Additional enhancements to CDD measures included: (a) the implementation of ongoing monitoring procedures for business relationships or transactions considered to be one-off undertakings; (b) the disapproval of simplified CDD measures (Reg. 11 of the MLRs); (c) requirements when dealing with introducers (Reg. 10 of the MLRs); (d) the imposition of record-keeping requirements (Regs. 12 & 8 of MLRS); (e) applying procedures for internal reporting (Reg. 14 of the MLRs); and (e) the prohibition of conducting business with shell banks (CFATF 2010a).

The next backstopping measure employed by the jurisdiction was the revision to the Guidance Notes on the Prevention and Detection of Money Laundering and Terrorist Financing (GN), which was published in September 2008 (CFATF 2009a). As the GN was considered as other enforceable means under MER, it was accepted as meeting the compliance criteria under the FATF Recommendations (CFATF 2009a). The CDD process was the principal area covered by the GN to enhance measures to prevent money laundering and terrorist financing. Some of the salient points included: (a) the development and implementation of policies and procedures to make certain documents and information collected are reviewed regularly and kept current (Para 4.2); (b) the obtainment of senior management approval to continue or begin a business relationship with a PEP (Para. 3.47); (c) requirements for dealing with cross-border relationships with correspondent banks (Para. 3.7); (d) specifications for eligible introducers (Chpt. 3); (e) retaining evidence on file related to unusual transactions (Para 5.13); (f) provisions dealing with DNFBPs (Para. 1.4 & 2.16); (g) reporting of suspicious transactions (Para. 5.34); (h) establishing and applying internal controls, compliance and audit for screening new hires (Para. 6.2), appointing an MLRO (Para 5.2) and conducting an AML/CFT audit (Chpt. 6); (i) obligating financial services providers to ensure that their foreign counterparts do not make use of shell banks (Chpt. 3); (j) inclusion of terrorist financing (Section I, Para. 1.10–1.15) and precious metal and precious stones dealers (Para. 1.4); and (h) reporting to the FRA, attempted transactions which result in suspicion or knowledge of money laundering or terrorist financing (Para. 5.34) (CFATF 2010a).

The GN was used by the jurisdiction to implement additional back-stopping measures to address deficiencies in dealing with cross-border relationships with correspondent banks, to include precious metals and precious stones dealers, and to incorporate other recommended actions (CFATF 2009a). Whereas, the MLRs was used to address the weaknesses in SR. VII providing for prosecutions for failure to comply, and the MLRs and GN both addressed the inadequacies in R.5, and R.15, by incorporating the recommended actions (CFATF 2009a). The deficiencies in R.16 were also addressed through the GN Para. 5.34 regarding the treatment of a transaction that leads to knowledge or suspicion of money laundering or terrorist financing, and Section 201 (3) of POCL, 2008 which imposed stipulations in dealing with higher risk countries (CFATF 2009a). SR. VIII remained under public consultation, while SR. IX was satisfied through the implementation of an obligatory declaration system (CFATF2009a). Further, as a result of an additional revision to its GN in March 2010, which further enhanced its CDD procedures, the jurisdiction met an acceptable level of compliance for R.5 (CFATF 2010a).

Finally, to satisfy the requirement for SR. VIII, the jurisdiction introduced the Charities Bill, 2010 (CFATF 2010a). In addition to making provision for the supervision of NPOs, the Bill also provided for the identification of NPOs which failed to comply with regulatory measures, allowance for information regarding NPOs to be accessible to the public, and the provision of a central unit to assist with international queries related to terrorist financing (CFATF 2009a). Together, the POCL, the passage of the Money Laundering Regulations (2008 Revision) (MLRs) and the revision to the Guidance Notes addressed a significant amount of the deficiencies highlighted by the CFATF.

### 7.4.3 *National and International Cooperation*

To enhance its capacity to assist in international cooperation, the jurisdiction carried out additional measures. To facilitate the appearance of persons voluntarily who are not held in lawful custody, to provide information or give testimony to a requesting jurisdiction, the Criminal Justice (International Cooperation) Act was amended on 24 February 2010 to satisfy this requirement (CFATF 2010a). An additional measure was undertaken by the jurisdiction in 2010, when it signed a multi-lateral agreement, referred to as the US Securities & Exchange Commission which became effective on 09 March 2012. This agreement provided for information exchange and cooperation in relation to the oversite of cross-border regulated entities (CIMA 2012). Further, the jurisdiction became a party to the UN Convention against Transnational Organized Crime (The Palermo Convention) by extension on 17 May 2012, as a result of the UK's ratification of the Convention, due to its status as a British Overseas Territory (CFATF 2012a). However, it is still pending an extension to the International Convention for the Suppression of Financing of Terrorism, as the UK had not yet ratified it as of the end of 2012.

## 7.5 Bermuda

### 7.5.1 *Transparency*

In November 2007, the CFATF Council of Ministers adopted its third detailed assessment report (DAR) of Bermuda and required the jurisdiction to address the deficiencies based on its recommendations and report back to it. The recommendations were based on ratings the jurisdictions received upon being assessed. Of the core and key Recommendations, the jurisdiction received a rating of partially compliant in six Recommendations (Rec. 3, 13, 35, SR. I, SR. II and SR. IV) and a rating of non-compliant in two Recommendation (Rec. 5 and 23) (CFATF 2008a). In other Recommendations, the jurisdiction obtained a rating of partially compliant in ten Recommendations (Rec. 14, 15, 17, 25, 29, 30, 31, 32 SR. VI and SR. VIII), and a rating of non-compliant in 12 Recommendations (Rec. 6, 7, 8, 9, 11, 12, 16, 21, 22, 24, SR.VII and SR. IX) (CFATF 2008a).

In an effort to increase transparency and strengthen its legal system and institutions, Bermuda enacted a number of legislations to satisfy the deficiencies highlighted by the CFATF. Among them, the jurisdiction introduced the Proceeds of Crime (Anti-Money Laundering and Anti-Terrorist Financing Supervision and Enforcement) Act, 2008, which came into force on 1 January 2009 (CFATF 2008a). This Act provided for powers to be granted to the Bermuda Monetary Authority (BMA) to vigilante financial institutions to ensure compliance in accordance with the provisions contained in the Regulations. The powers granted under the Act, empowered the BMA to impose significant penalties for non-compliance with a number of its provisions (Section 20 (20A–20I)) (CFATF 2014a). The jurisdiction also passed the Corporate Service Provider Business Act, 2012 (CSPBA), which made provisions to regulate businesses operating as corporate service providers (CSPs) and safeguard the interests of clients, including potential clients engaging in such businesses (CFATF 2014a). The CSPBA also empowered the BMA with supervisory and licensor powers, which applies the AML/CFT framework to CSPs. Another measure taken by the jurisdiction was the enactment of the Financial Intelligence Agency Act 2007, which took effect on 15 November 2008. This Act made provision for the establishment of the Financial Intelligence Agency (FIA). Subsequent to its formation, the Financial Investigation Unit, which was under the Bermuda Police Service, was transferred to the FIA (CFATF 2014a).

### 7.5.2 *Preventative measures*

Other initiatives undertaken by Bermuda to address the concerns raised in the third DAR were essentially backstopping measures designed to enhance its AML/CFT regime to prevent money laundering and terrorist financing. The first of these measures included the passage of the Proceeds of Crime (Anti-Money Laundering and Anti-Terrorist Financing) Regulations, 2008, which became effective on 1 January 2009 (CFATF 2014a). These Regulations replaced the Proceeds of Crime (Money Laundering) Regulations. Additionally, they expanded the types of entities regulated in the jurisdiction, and obligated financial institutions regulated in Bermuda to implement a risk-based approach in their AML/CFT framework and controls (CFATF 2014a). Another backstopping measure undertaken by the jurisdiction was the incorporation of the legal and accounting professions under "relevant persons" in accordance with 2(1) and 4(b) of the AML/ATF Regulations (CFATF 2014a). This was accomplished through the creation of the Anti-Money Laundering and Anti-Terrorist Financing

Board, through the passage of the Proceeds of Crime (Anti-Money Laundering and Anti-Terrorist Financing Supervision and Enforcement) Designation Order, 2012 (CFATF 2014a). This Order granted the Board with supervisory authority over the legal and accountancy business. The jurisdiction also enacted the Anti-Terrorism Order which established the classes of business which pertained to the regulated sector, and set forth regulations for wire transfers by way of the Proceeds of Crime (Anti-Money Laundering & Anti-Terrorist Financing) Regulations, 2008 (CFATF 2011b).

Further backstopping measures undertaken by the jurisdiction included the issuance of Guidance Notes on 27 March 2009, to assist regulated entities to ensure compliance in accordance with Proceeds of Crime (Anti-Money Laundering and Anti-Terrorist Financing Supervision and Enforcement) Act 2008 (CFATF 2014a). The jurisdiction also issued Guidance Notes in 2012, to assist persons working in the accounting and legal sectors to ensure adherence to the provisions contained in the Proceeds of Crime (Anti-Money Laundering and Anti-Terrorist Financing Supervision and Enforcement) Designation Order, 2012 (CFATF 2014a).

### 7.5.3 *National and International Cooperation*

To further enhance its capacity to facilitate international cooperation, the jurisdiction passed the Proceeds of Crime and Related Measures Amendment Act, 2013, and the Transnational Organised Crime Act, 2013 (CFATF 2014a). These legislations strengthened the AML/CFT regime by modifying inter alia, the POCA, the Anti-Terrorism (Financial and Other Measures) Act, 2004 (ATFA), and other relevant laws (CFATF 2014a). The legislation enacted also made provisions for the Palermo and the Suppression of Financing of Terrorism Conventions to be adopted into local laws to address the necessary deficiencies to allow these Conventions to be extended by the UK to Bermuda (CFATF 2014a). Additional enhancements to further strengthened the jurisdiction's ability to assist in international cooperation came by way of the enactment of the Proceeds of Crime Amendment (No.2) Act, 2013, which introduced a recovery regime for civil assets to the jurisdiction (CFATF 2014a). Bermuda also implemented further reforms during the following year to improve synergies between agencies in law enforcement.

## 7.6 The BVI

### 7.6.1 Transparency

The third round MER on the BVI was adopted by the CFATF at its Plenary on 23 November 2008 (CFATF 2008a). The Report revealed a rating of partially compliant in two core and key Recommendations (Rec. 5 and 23), and in other Recommendations, a partially compliant rating in thirteen Recommendations (Rec. 8, 9, 11, 12, 15, 16, 17, 21, 22, 24, 30, 33, and SR. VIII), and a non-compliant rating in SR. VI (CFATF 2008a). To address the deficiencies concluded by the CFATF, the BVI undertook a number of measures. These included changes to its AML/CFT laws, regulations and guidelines to incorporate the majority of the actions recommended. To enhance transparency and strengthen its AML/CFT legal framework and institutional measures, the BVI introduced the Securities and Investment Business Act 2010 (CFATF 2008a). This Act made provisions for insider trading and market manipulations to be criminalized as indictable offences, and deemed predicate offences under money laundering (CFATF 2011b). Another measure implemented by the BVI was the enactment of the Proceeds of Criminal Conduct (Amendment) Act, 2010, which became effective in February 2010. This amendment provided for a tipping off offence which pertained to the disclosure of knowledge that a suspicious transaction report (STR) or information related to it has been submitted to the FIA (CFATF 2011b). The jurisdiction also passed the Financing and Money Services Act (FMSA), which took effect in May 2009 (CFATF 2011b). The FMSA subjected operators providing money value transfer services to licensing and supervisory oversight by the Financial Services Commission (FSC), which included off-site monitoring, onsite inspections, and adherence to provisions contained in the Anti-Money Laundering and Terrorist Financing Code of Practice, 2009 (AMLTFCOP), and the Anti-Money Laundering Regulations (2008) (AMLR). The FMSA also established a framework to provide registered and licensed money value transfer operators to keep an up to date list of licensed and registered operators including their names and addresses (CFATF 2011b).

The jurisdiction also introduced the Proliferation Financing (Prohibition) Act, 2009 (CFATF 2011b). This Act granted powers to the BVI Financial Investigation Agency (FIA) to deal with individuals and activities connected to money laundering, terrorist financing and proliferation financing. The FIA was given the responsibility for issuing directives on individuals or any class of individuals conducting business in the financial sector in a country where it had reasonable grounds to believe that such business activities undertaken in such country or by such government, or any individual resident or formed in such country, represented a high risk of money laundering, terrorist financing or financing weapons used for mass destruction, which presented a threat to the interests of the BVI or UK (British Virgin Islands Financial Services Commission [BVI FSC 2013). Information gathered during the course of carrying out its duties, was subject to information exchange once a request was made pursuant to the terms of the relevant legislation (BVI FSC 2013).

### *7.6.2 Preventative measures*

Other measures were implemented by the jurisdiction as backstopping measures to prevent money laundering and terrorist financing. The first of these was the enactment of the Anti-Money Laundering and Terrorist Financing Code of Practice, 2009 (AMLTFCOP), and the Anti-Money Laundering Regulations, 2008 (AMLR) (CFATF 2011b). Both the AMLTFCOP and the AMLR subjected "relevant businesses", including financing institutions, credit unions and professional firms to increased AML requirements (CFATF 2011b). The AMLTFCOP obligated financial institutions to make certain that persons acting on behalf of clients, including legal persons or legal entities, were authorized and their identity certified (Section 19(3)) (CFATF 2011b). The AMLTFCOP was also amended to provide for simplified or less rigid CDD measures to be applied in certain circumstances (Section 19(6)) (CFATF 2011b). It also established the legal framework for recognized jurisdictions to be listed, which adhered to the FATF Recommendations and applied or adequately applied such Recommendations, and whose AML/CFT laws were equivalent to the provisions contained in the AMLR of the AMLTFCOP (Section 52(2)) (CFATF 2011b). Section 23(2) was also amended to allow for the verification process to be completed by a professional or an entity after commencing business relations under certain circumstances (CFATF 2011b).

Additional amendments were incorporated into the AMLTFCOP to prevent technological developments from being misused to launder money and finance terrorism (Section 11A), and to impose obligations on financial institutions to implement policies and procedures to deal with specific risks related to business relationships and transactions that were not in person (Section 13) (CFATF 2011b). Section 13 was also amended to require financial institutions to examine and document the background and intent of transactions that were complex, unusual or had unusual patterns or that did not show any apparent or obvious economic or legal purpose (CFATF 2011b). Its amendment also included the maintenance of such findings for a period of five years minimum and to make such information available to the relevant authority. Section 45 was later amended to allow for files to be retained, including business correspondence, for at minimum five years once the business relationship terminated (CFATF 2011b). Additionally, the Anti-Money Laundering (Amendment) Regulations, 2010, provided for records to be maintained for a five-year period from the date of the last transaction (CFATF 2011b).

Further amendments to the AMLTFCOP included placing a requirement on financial institutions to maintain an audit function with sufficient resources to test adherence to AML/CFT policies, procedures and controls (Section 11) (CFATF 2011b). Financial institutions were also to ensure that they pay close attention to transactions and business relationships dealing with individuals from countries which did not apply adequately the FATF Recommendations, and provide for a list of such jurisdictions to be established for the purpose of AMLTFCOP and the AMLR (CFATF 2011b). Section 13(2) was also amended to include a requirement for transactions that had no obvious economic or apparent lawful purpose originating from jurisdictions which applied inadequately the FATF Recommendations, to be examined and made accessible to aid auditors and competent authorities (CFATF 2011b). Section 53 was also modified to provide for financial institutions to advise their head office supervisor in cases where a foreign branch was not able to carry out relevant AML/CFT rules due to legal, regulatory or other measures (CFATF 2011b). An additional amendment was also done to the AMLTFCOP to incorporate provisions to obligate charities or other non-profit entities to put internal control systems in place for CDD rules, maintain requirements for record-keeping and carry out employee training (CFATF 2011b).

### *7.6.3 National and International Cooperation*

The jurisdiction also undertook measures to enhance its ability to provide assistance in international cooperation through the adoption of the Palmero Convention and the Terrorist Financing Convention (CFATF

2011b). Both Conventions were given effect within the BVI under its domestic laws, even though they have not yet been extended to the jurisdiction through ratification by the UK (CFATF 2011b). Other measures carried out by the BVI included the use of domestic legislation to implement resolutions SRES/1267(1999) and SRES/1373(2001) by the UN Security Council (CFATF 2008a). The last measures adopted by the jurisdiction was the publication by the BVI FSC of an international cooperation handbook to strengthen its efforts with foreign competent authorities in international cooperation (CFATF 2008a).

## 7.7 Comparative Analysis

The impact of international policy initiatives against money laundering and terrorist financing on the legal systems and institutions of offshore financial centres in the Caribbean is observed in the following three principal areas: (i) transparency; (ii) preventative measures; and (iii) national and international cooperation.

### 7.7.1 *Transparency*

The purpose of transparency was to strengthen the legislative systems and institutional measures within countries to increase their legal and supervisory capacity to counter money laundering and terrorist financing. As the deficiencies highlighted in the third MER varied among jurisdictions, the impact of the FATF standard on each jurisdiction and the actions taken by each have also varied. For example, in The Bahamas, measures implemented by the jurisdiction were centred on strengthening institutional measures, in particular, building supervisory powers among institutions within the jurisdiction. This was done through the introduction of a supervisory framework within the money transmission businesses sector, the financial and corporate service providers sector, and the securities and investment sector (CFATF 2009b).[3] Measures taken by the jurisdiction were also aimed at improving the supervisory oversight of licensees in the insurance sector, securities sector, and the financial and corporate services

[3] See the Banks and Trust Companies Regulations (Amendment) Act, 2006; the Financial and Corporate Service Providers (Amendment) Act, 2008; the Securities Industry (Amendment) Act, 2007; the Securities Industry (Amendment) Regulations, 2009 and the Investments Fund (Amendment) Act, 2007.

providers sector (CFATF 2010c; CFATF 2013).[4] The last measure undertaken by The Bahamas in the area of transparency was the establishment of a special anti-terrorism unit to deal with terrorist financing matters.

In the Cayman Islands, on the other hand, the impact on the FATF standard was centred on strengthening the capacity of its domestic legal system. For example, legislation was enacted to broaden the scope of the definition of money laundering to include criminal property concealed, disguised, converted, transferred or removed from the jurisdiction.[5] The Act was also amended to incorporate asset-tracing and civil forfeiture provisions, and to empower the Attorney-General with specific powers related to recovery orders and cash forfeitures under certain circumstances. The Act also made provisions for tipping off to be an offence, which involved the disclosure of information that could potentially bias a current or future investigation. The other measure undertaken by the jurisdiction brought about supervisory oversight to NPOs (CFATF 2010b; CFATF 2013).[6]

In Bermuda, the impact on the FATF standard was aimed at satisfying the deficiencies in the jurisdictions' institutional framework and supervisory oversight. To this end, the jurisdiction established an institutional framework to regulate corporate service providers and granted supervisory and licensing powers to the BMA (CFATF 2014a).[7] Additionally, through the Proceeds of Crime (Money Laundering) Regulations 1998, the jurisdiction broadened the scope of entities regulated within its territory. It also enacted legislation to establish a legal framework to regulate the legal and accounting professions and granted supervisory authority to the newly created Anti-Money Laundering and Anti-Terrorist Financing Board (CFATF 2014a).[8] The jurisdiction also created the Financial Intelligence Agency, and subsequently transferred the Financial Investigation Unit to the newly formed agency (CFATF 2014a).[9] Further, it enacted

[4] See the Insurance Act, 2005; the External Insurance Act, 2009; the Securities Industry Act, 2011 and the Securities Industry Regulations Act, 2012.

[5] See the Proceeds of Crime Law, 2008.

[6] See the Charities Bill, 2010.

[7] See the Corporate Service Provider Business Act, 2012.

[8] See the Proceeds of Crime (Anti-Money Laundering and Anti-Terrorist Financing Supervision and Enforcement) Designation Order, 2012.

[9] See the Financial Intelligence Agency Act, 2007.

legislation to empower the BMA with supervisory powers to ensure that financial institutions adhere to the provisions of its anti-money laundering and anti-terrorism Act (CFATF 2014a).[10]

Unlike the other three jurisdictions however, the impact on the FATF standard on the BVI was focused on enhancing both its legal system and institutional framework. To satisfy the deficiencies highlighted in the MER, the BVI undertook measures to strengthen its legal system by criminalizing insider trading and market manipulations as indictable offences. It also broadening the predicate offences under money laundering to include insider trading and market manipulations.[11] Further, it introduced legislation to provide for a tipping off offence in certain cases (CFATF 2011c).[12] Furthermore, to reinforce its institutional measures, the BVI established a legal framework to regulate money value transfer services and subjected them to the licensing and supervisory oversight of the Financial Services Commission.[13] It also granted powers to the BVI FIA to deal with individuals and activities connected to money laundering, terrorist financing and proliferation financing (CFATF 2011c).[14]

In the area of transparency, the impact of the FATF standard against money laundering and terrorist financing on the legislative systems and institutional measures on offshore financial centres in the Caribbean varied among the four jurisdictions. In The Bahamas, the main focus was on the strengthening institutional measures specifically in the area of supervisory oversite for institutions in the jurisdiction (CFATF 2011a). Whereas, in the Cayman Islands the impact was aimed at increasing the capacity of the legislative system in the territory (CFATF 2009b). In Bermuda, the impact of the FATF standard was focused on building the institutional framework and supervisory structure in the jurisdiction (CFATF 2014a). Whereas in the BVI, the impact was on enhancing both the legal system and institutional framework in the territory (CFATF 2011b). The extent of the impact of the FATF standard depended on the legislative system and institutional measures each jurisdiction had in place

[10] See the Proceeds of Crime (Anti-Money Laundering and Anti-Terrorist Financing Supervision and Enforcement) Act, 2008.

[11] See the Securities and Investment Business Act, 2010.

[12] See the Proceeds of Criminal Conduct (Amendment) Act, 2010.

[13] See the Financing and Money Services Act.

[14] See the Proliferation Financing (Prohibition) Act, 2009.

prior to 2007. In this regard, the impact of the FATF standard was more significant in the BVI, followed by the Cayman Islands,[15] Bermuda and The Bahamas, which was the least impacted in the area of transparency of all the jurisdictions.

### 7.7.2 *Preventative measures*

Preventative measures were aimed at strengthening the capacity of the AML/CFT regime in jurisdictions to ensure their effectiveness in responding to money laundering and terrorist financing threats. As the measures undertaken by each jurisdiction however varied based on the deficiencies highlighted in their respective MERs, the impact of the FATF standard on each jurisdiction and the actions taken by each have also varied. In the Bahamas, backstopping measures implemented by the jurisdiction were focused on employing AML/CFT rules, particularly within financial institutions and among designated non-financial businesses and professions, and on strengthening customer due to diligence rules. This objective was achieved by imposing sanctions on financial institutions for failure to comply with AML/CFT guidelines and the Codes of Practice through legislation (CFATF 2011a). The jurisdiction also regulated DNFBPs and subjected them to AML/CFT rules (CFATF 2009b).[16] In terms of CDD procedures, the jurisdiction introduced mandatory CDD procedures for certain transactions under B$15,000 (CFATF 2009b),[17] and increased obligations to verify the identity of persons under certain circumstances (CFATF 2009b).[18]

In the Cayman Islands on the other hand, backstopping measures were aimed at applying AML/CFT rules in a number of areas and implementing CDD procedures under certain circumstances. Through the revision of its Guidance Notes the jurisdiction applied AML/CFT measures when dealing with PEPs, correspondent banking relationships, eligible introducers, record-keeping for unusual transactions, DNFBPs, STRs, internal controls and audits, shell banks, precious metal and

[15] Weighting more heavily legislative system over institutional measures.

[16] See the Financial Transaction Reporting (Amendment) Act, 2014.

[17] See the Financial Transactions Reporting Regulations (Amendment) Act, 2009.

[18] See the Financial Transaction Reporting (Wire Transfer) Regulations, 2009.

precious stones dealers, NPOs, etc. (CFATF 2009a). Whereas, backstopping measures were undertaken by the jurisdiction to improve CDD rules related to identity procedures in specific circumstances, and increased ongoing monitoring with regard to one-off transactions, handling introducers, record-keeping, simplified CDD procedures, internal reporting and shell banks (CFAFT 2009a).[19]

In Bermuda, backstopping measures instituted by the jurisdiction were centred on enhancing the AML/CFT framework in financial institutions. This was accomplished through the implementation of a risk-based approach in the AML/CFT systems and controls of financial institutions (CFATF 2011b).[20] It also introduced an anti-terrorism order to determine the business classes of the regulated sector,[21] and to established anti-money laundering and anti-terrorist financing regulations for wire transfers.[22] The jurisdiction also issued guidance notes for regulated entities as well as the accounting and legal professions, to assist them in complying with such legislation.

Backstopping measures implemented in the BVI, on the other hand, were aimed at enhancing AML/CFT rules in relation to "relevant businesses", and strengthening CDD procedures in a number of areas. To accomplish this, the jurisdiction enacted legislations to impose increased AML requirements on "relevant businesses" including financing institutions, credit unions and professional firms (CFATF 2011c).[23] It also placed obligations on financial institutions to adhere to CDD rules when dealing with persons acting on behalf of clients, including legal persons or legal entities. Further, the jurisdiction provided for the application of less rigid CDD measures in certain circumstances, recognition of jurisdictions with sound AML/CFT systems, completion of a verification process after commencing business relations, mitigation of risks in certain circumstances and transactions, and the adoption of record-keeping requirements inter alia.

[19] See the Money Laundering (Amendment) Regulations, 2008.

[20] See the Proceeds of Crime (Anti-Money Laundering & Anti-Terrorist Financing) Regulations, 2008.

[21] See the Anti-Terrorism Order.

[22] See the Proceeds of crime (Anti-Money Laundering & Anti-Terrorist Financing) Regulations, 2008.

[23] See the Anti-Money Laundering and Terrorist Financing Code of Practice, 2009 (AMLTFCOP) and the Anti-Money Laundering Regulations, 2008.

In the area of preventative measures, although the impact of the FATF standard varied among the four jurisdictions, the underlying objective was to improve the AML/CFT regimes including CDD procedures of each jurisdiction. In the Bahamas backstopping measures were aimed at employing AML/CFT rules in financial institutions, including DNFBPs. They were also centred on strengthening CDD rules for transactions under B$15,000, and on increasing requirements to verify the identity of persons in certain cases (CFATF 2009b). In the Cayman Islands, on the other hand, backstopping measures were aimed at broadly applying AML/CFT rules in multiple areas, and CDD rules on identity procedures in a number of specific circumstances (CFATF 2009b). Whereas in Bermuda, backstopping measures were centred on enhancing the AML/CFT framework in financial institutions (CFATF 2014a), and in the BVI, on enhancing AML/CFT rules in relation to "relevant businesses", and strengthening CDD procedures in a number of areas (CFATF 2011c). Overall, the impact of the FATF standard on these four jurisdictions was more significant in the Cayman Islands, followed by the BVI, The Bahamas, and Bermuda, which was the least affected of these four jurisdictions in the area of preventative measures.

### *7.7.3 National and International Cooperation*

National and international cooperation was aimed at increasing cooperation among domestic institutions and mutual legal assistance with counterparties in foreign jurisdictions. The impact of the FATF standard on the four jurisdictions varied based on the measures implemented in each jurisdiction prior to 2007. To increase their domestic capacity to actively participate in international cooperation, each of the jurisdiction implemented legal measures to satisfy the recommendations detailed in their respective MERs. For instance, in The Bahamas legal measures instituted were aimed at broadening its legal capacity to provide for more flexibility in international cooperation. To accomplish this goal, the jurisdiction allowed for the use of Bahamian evidence in foreign jurisdictions (CFATF 2013),[24] and an increase in the categories of extraditable offences.[25] It also allowed for judgement to be determined in criminal

[24] See the Mutual Legal Assistance (Criminal Matters) Act.

[25] See the Extradition Act.

matters foregoing a full trial (CFATF 2009b).[26] The Bahamas also ratified the United Nations Convention against Transnational Organized Crime, assented to the Trafficking in Persons (Prevention and Suppression) Act, 2008, and amended the ATA to include all of the Conventions noted in the Annex of the Terrorist Financing Convention (CFATF 2009b).

In the Cayman Islands measures undertaken by the jurisdiction was centred on increasing information exchange among domestic parties and also at an international level. For example, through the enactment of the Proceeds of Crime Law, 2008, the jurisdiction provided for financial institutions to share information upon presentation of an order related to a money laundering or confiscation investigation (CFATF 2009a). It also allowed for information regarding NPOs to be accessible to the public, and for a central unit to assist with international queries related to terrorist financing. Through the amendment of the Criminal Justice (International Cooperation) Act, the jurisdiction provided for a person to voluntary appear to give testimony or provide information (CFATF 2009a). To provide for information exchange and cooperation on the oversite of cross-border regulated entities, the jurisdiction executed a multi-lateral agreement.[27] It also became a party to the UN Convention against Transnational Organized Crime (The Palermo Convention) by extension of the UK (CFATF 2012a).

Measures implemented by Bermuda to enhanced international cooperation were aimed at broadening domestic legislation and adopting international conventions. Among the initiatives undertaken by the jurisdiction was the enactment of legislation which introduced a recovery regime for civil assets.[28] Another measure taken by Bermuda was the adoption of the Palermo and the Suppression of Financing of Terrorism Conventions (CFATF 2014a).[29]

In the BVI, on the other hand, measures carried out by the jurisdiction were mainly centred on complying with international conventions. For example, the Palmero Convention and the Terrorist Financing Convention were both given effect in the jurisdiction. Additionally, resolutions

[26] See the Criminal Procedure Plea Discussion and Plea Agreement Act, 2008.

[27] See the US Securities & Exchange Commission, 2012.

[28] See the Proceeds of Crime Amendment (No.2) Act, 2013.

[29] See the Proceeds of Crime and Related Measures Amendment Act, 2013 and the Transnational Organised Crime Act, 2013.

SRES/1267(1999) and SRES/1373(2001) by the UN Security Council were adopted by the jurisdiction (CFATF 2011c). Further, the jurisdiction published an international cooperation handbook to assist foreign competent authorities in international cooperation.

The impact of the FATF standard in the area of national and international cooperation varied among the four jurisdictions. For example, in The Bahamas the impact was aimed at broadening the jurisdiction's legal capacity to increase its participation in international cooperation and in adopting the requisite Conventions. In the Cayman Islands measures were centred on increasing information exchange at a domestic and international levels. In Bermuda, on the other hand, measures undertaken were aimed at broadening domestic legislation and adopting international conventions. Whereas in the BVI, measures were centred mainly on complying with international conventions. Overall, the impact of the FATF standard in the area of national and international cooperation was most significant in The Bahamas, followed by Bermuda, the Cayman Islands and the BVI, which was the least affected of the four jurisdictions.

## 7.8 Comparative Analysis by Period

The impact of the FATF standard on the four offshore financial centres in the Caribbean is more evident when comparing the previous period (2000–2006) to the current period (2007–2012). For example, during the periods 2000–2006 and 2007–2012, The Bahamas underwent extensive legislative changes to satisfy the recommendations by the CFATF. Between 2000 and 2006, the jurisdiction implemented nine pieces of legislations which laid the foundation of its AML/CFT framework mainly in the areas of legal systems and institutional measures, and in establishing preventative measures centred on employing DDR policies and procedures, and KYC rules.[30] Between 2007 and 2012, the jurisdiction underwent another significant legislative reform, which essentially were equivalent to the prior period (see Table 7.1). These measures were designed to complete the construction of its AML/CFT framework by further enhancing its legal system and institutional structure, employing additional backstopping measures through enhancing DDR

[30] See Table 7.1.

**Table 7.1** The Bahamas: legislation implemented to counter money laundering and terrorist financing

| *Prior to 2000* | *2000–2006* | *2007–2012* |
|---|---|---|
| *Transparency the Bahamas* | | |
| Tracing and Forfeiture of the Proceeds of Drug Trafficking, 1987 | The Proceeds of Crime Act, 2000 | The Insurance Act, 2005 |
| UN Convention Against the Illicit Trafficking of Narcotic Drugs, 1989 | The Proceeds of crime (Money Laundering) Regulations, 2001 | The Banks and Trust Companies Regulations (Amendment) Act, 2006 |
| Money Laundering (Proceeds of Crime) Act, 1996 | Anti-Terrorist Act, 2004 | Investments Fund (Amendment) Act, 2007 |
| Money Laundering (Proceeds of Crime) Regulation Act, 1996 | United Nations Convention Respecting the Suppression of the Financing of Terrorism | The Securities Industry (Amendment) Act, 2007 |
| The Securities Industry Act, 1999 | Resolution 1373 of the United Nations Security Council | The Financial and Corporate Service Providers (Amendment) Act, 2008 |
| | The Central Bank of The Bahamas Act, 2000 | The External Insurance Act, 2009 |
| | Banks and Trust Companies Regulation Act, 2000 | The Securities Industry (Amendment) Regulations, 2009 |
| | The Financial and Corporate Service Providers Act, 2000 | The Securities Industry Act, 2011 |
| | The International Business Companies Act, 2000 | The Securities Industry Regulations, Act, 2012 |
| | The Securities Industry Regulations, 2000 | |
| *Preventative Measures* | | |
| The Money Laundering (Proceeds of Crime) Act, 1996 | | The Financial Transactions Reporting (Amendment) Act, 2009 |
| The Money Laundering (Proceeds of Crime) Regulation Act, 1996 | The Financial Transactions Reporting Act, 2000 | The Financial Transactions Reporting Regulations (Amendment) Act, 2009 |

(continued)

**Table 7.1** (continued)

| *Prior to 2000* | *2000–2006* | *2007–2012* |
|---|---|---|
| Money Laundering Guidance Notes | The Financial Transactions Reporting (Amendment) Act, 2001 | The Financial Intelligence (Transactions Reporting) Regulations, 2009 |
| The Tracing and Forfeiture of Proceeds of Drug Trafficking Act, 1987 | The Financial Transactions Reporting Regulations, 2000 | The Financial Transaction Reporting (Wire Transfer) Regulations, 2009 |
| | The Financial Transactions Reporting (Amendment) Regulations, 2001 | The Financial Intelligence Unit (Amendment) Act, 2009 |
| | The Financial Intelligence Unit Act, 2000 | AML/CFT Guidelines |
| | The Financial Intelligence Unit (Amendment) Act, 2001 | Compliance Commission Code of Conduct |
| | The Financial Intelligence (Transactions Reporting) Regulations, 2001 | |
| | The Bank and Trust Companies Regulation Act, 2000 | |
| | The Financial and Corporate Service Providers Act, 2000 | |
| | The International Business Companies Act, 2000 | |
| *National and International Cooperation* | | |
| 1988 UN Drug Convention | The Evidence (Proceedings in other Jurisdictions) Act, 2000 | The Mutual Legal Assistance (Criminal Matters) Act |
| Mutual Legal Assistance Treaty (MLAT) with the US, 12 June 1987 | The Criminal Justice (International Cooperation) Act, 2000 | The Extradition Act |
| MLAT with the UK, 28 June 1988 | | The Criminal Procedure Plea Discussion and Plea Agreement Act, 2008 |

| *Prior to 2000* | *2000–2006* | *2007–2012* |
|---|---|---|
| MLAT with Canada, 13 March 1990 | | Ratified the United Nations Convention against Transnational Organized Crime |
| Money Laundering (Proceeds of Crime) Amendment Act, 1999 | | Assented to the Trafficking in Persons (Prevention and Suppression) Act, 2008 |
| Member of the Inter-American Drug Abuse Control Commission | | Amended the Anti-Terrorism Act |
| Participant in the Caribbean Financial Action Task Force | | A signatory to IOSCO MMOU |

*Source* Central Bank of The Bahamas Annual Reports 2000–2013; The Bahamas Competent Authority, 2020 and The Bahamas Financial Services Board, 2020 and KYC measures, and increasing its capacity to assist in international cooperation.[31]

Similar to The Bahamas, the Cayman Islands also underwent significant changes to its legislative framework, particularly during the period 2000–2006. During this period, the jurisdiction implemented approximately ten legal measures (enactments and amendments) aimed at establishing its AML/CFT regime in the area of legal system and institutional structure. The jurisdiction also implemented a number of preventative measures aimed at enhancing CDD and KYC rules, through the enactment of the Proceeds of Criminal Conduct Law Regulations, 2000, and the guidance notes which accompanied it.[32] Between 2007 and 2012, less legislative measures were undertaken by the jurisdiction compared to The Bahamas, as its guidance notes served to satisfy a number of deficiencies highlighted in the third MER (see Table 7.2). These measures were aimed at strengthening its institutional structure and supervisory oversight of licensees in the jurisdiction. Other measures introduced in the jurisdiction's guidance notes were aimed at implementing backstopping measures mainly in applying CDD, KYC and internal policies and procedures in certain areas to enhance the jurisdiction's ability to prevent money laundering and terrorist financing. The remaining measures served to increase the jurisdiction's ability to provide international assistance (see Table 7.2).

In Bermuda on the other hand, only two legislative measures were implemented during the period 2000–2006. Both were aimed at strengthening its AML/CFT framework, specifically in its legal system to enhance transparency to counter money laundering and terrorist financing.[33] Between 2007 and 2012, the impact of international policy initiatives is more evident in the jurisdiction with the enactment of eight pieces of legislation (see Table 7.3). Half of these measures were aimed at building its institutional framework for financial institutions, CSPs, and the accounting and legal professions. While other measures were geared towards implementing preventative measures through the adoption of a risk-based approach, and the subjection of AML/CFT rules on the accounting and legal professions. The remaining measures were employed

[31] See Table 7.1.

[32] See Table 7.2.

[33] See Table 7.3.

**Table 7.2** The Cayman Islands: legislation implemented to counter money laundering and terrorist financing

| *Prior to 2000* | *2000–2006* | *2007–2012* |
|---|---|---|
| *Transparency Cayman Islands* | | |
| The Misuse of Drugs Law, 1989 | Proceeds of Criminal Conduct (Amendment) (Money Laundering Regulations) Law, 2000 | The Proceeds of Crime Law, 2008 |
| The Proceeds of Criminal Conduct Law, 1996 | The Building Societies (Amendment) (Regulation by Monetary Authority) Law, 2000 | The Charities Bill, 2010 |
| | The Cooperative Societies (Amendment), Law 2000 | |
| | The Money Services Law, 2000 | |
| | The Monetary Authority (Amendment) (Regulations of Non-Bank Financial Institution) Law, 2000 | |
| | The Proceeds of Criminal Conduct Law (2001 Revision) The Money Laundering (Amendment) Regulations, 2002 | |
| *Preventative Measures* | | |
| The Proceeds of Criminal Conduct Law, 1996 | The Proceeds of Criminal Conduct (Amendment) (Money Laundering Regulations) Law, 2000 | The Money Laundering (Amendment) Regulations, 2008 |
| | The Monetary Authority Law, 2000 | The Charities Bill, 2010 |
| | The Banks and Trust Companies Law, 2000 | |
| | The Companies Management Law, 2000 | |
| | The Money Laundering (Amendment) (Client Identification) Regulations, 2001 | |

(continued)

Table 7.2 (continued)

| *Prior to 2000* | *2000–2006* | *2007–2012* |
|---|---|---|
| | The Money Laundering (Amendment) (Electronic Payments) Regulations, 2001 | |
| | The Banks and Trust Companies (Amendment) (Prudent Management) Law, 2001 | |
| | The Insurance (Forms) (Amendment) (Licence Applications), 2001 | |
| | The Mutual Funds (Amendment) (Prudent Administration) Law, detailed in the Mutual Funds Law (2001 Revision) | |
| | The Companies Management (Amendment) Law, detailed in The Companies Management Law (2001 Revision) | |
| | The Monetary Authority (Amendment) (International Cooperation) Law detailed in the Monetary Authority Law (2001 Revision) | |
| | Money Laundering (Client Identification) (Extension of Period) Order 2002 | |
| | Monetary Authority Law (2002 Revision) | |
| | The Cayman Islands Registered Stock Law, 2002 | |
| | The Companies (Amendment) (Segregated Portfolio Companies) Law, 2001 | |

| *Prior to 2000* | *2000–2006* | *2007–2012* |
|---|---|---|
| | The Money Laundering Regulations issued under the Monetary Authority Law (2003 Revision) | |
| *National and International Cooperation* | | |
| Narcotics treaty with the US, 1984 | The Proceeds of Criminal Conduct (Amendment) (Financial Intelligence Units) Law, 2001 | The Proceeds of Crime Law, 2008 |
| Narcotics treaty with the US and Canada, 1986 | The Proceeds of Criminal Conduct (Designated Countries) (Further Designation of Countries) Order, 2001 | The Charities Bill, 2010 |
| Adoption of the 1988 UN Drug Convention in 1988 | The Afghanistan (United Nations Sanctions) Order 2001 adopted. | Amended the Criminal Justice (International Cooperation) Act |
| | The Al Qa'ida and the Taliban (United Nations Measures) Order 2002 adopted 25 January 2002. | US Securities & Exchange Commission, 2012 |
| | The New Consolidated List per the Security Council Resolution 1267 (1999), 1333 (2000) and 1390 (2002) was updated. | Party to the UN Convention against Transnational Organized Crime |
| | The Money Laundering (Amendment) (No.2) Regulations 2002 issued under the Proceeds of Criminal Conduct Law (2001 Revision) | |
| | The Money Laundering (Amendment) Regulations, 2003 | |

*Source* The Cayman Islands Monetary Authority Annual Reports 2000–2013 and the Cayman Islands Department of International Tax Cooperation, 2020

**Table 7.3** Bermuda: legislation implemented to counter money laundering and terrorist financing

| *Prior to 2000* | *2000–2006* | *2007–2012* |
|---|---|---|
| *Transparency Bermuda* | | |
| 1988 UN Drug Convention | The Proceeds of Crime Amendment Act 2000 | The Proceeds of Crime (Anti-Money Laundering and Anti-Terrorist Financing Supervision and Enforcement) Act 2008 |
| The Proceeds of Crime Act 1997 | The Anti-Terrorism (Financial and Other Measures) Act 2004 | The Financial Intelligence Agency Act, 2007 |
| | | The Corporate Service Provider Business Act, 2012 |
| *Preventative Measures* | | |
| | | The Proceeds of Crime (Anti-Money Laundering & Anti-Terrorist Financing) Regulations, 2008 |
| | | The Proceeds of Crime (Anti-Money Laundering and Anti-Terrorist Financing Supervision and Enforcement) Designation Order, 2012 |
| | | The Anti-Terrorism Order |
| *Effective Exchange of Information* | | |
| The Criminal Justice (International Cooperation) (Bermuda) Act 1994 | | |
| The Proceeds of Crime Act 1997 | | |
| The Proceeds of Crime (Designated Countries and Territories) Order 1998 | | |
| Mutual Legal Assistance (Criminal Matters) 1998 | | |

*Source* Bermuda Monetary Authority Annual Reports 2000–2013 and Government of Bermuda Ministry of Finance, 2020

to increase the jurisdiction's ability to provide mutual legal assistance to foreign jurisdictions (see Table 7.3).

Like the other jurisdictions, the BVI also undertook measures to enhance its legal system and institutional measures. Between 2000 and 2006, two legislative measures were implemented by the jurisdiction aimed at strengthening its institutional structure. The jurisdiction adopted two backstopping measures which were focused on restricting the provisions of funds and financial services to terrorists,[34] and on transactions dealing with terrorist property.[35] Further, several measures were undertaken to increase the jurisdiction's participation in international cooperation.[36] Between 2007 and 2012, an increase in legislative measures was undertaken by the jurisdiction (see Table 7.4). For example, four pieces of legislations were implemented to enhance its legal framework and strengthen its institutional structure. Two other measures were enacted by the jurisdiction as backstopping measures aimed at subjecting "relevant businesses" to increased AML/CFT requirements. Finally, several additional measures were adopted by the jurisdiction to enhance its capacity to provide international assistance (see Table 7.4).

The impact of the FATF standard has been significant during the periods 2000–2006 and from 2007 to 2012 on offshore centres in the Caribbean. The jurisdictions that have been affected most during the period 2000–2006 have been The Bahamas, followed by the Cayman Islands. Both jurisdictions were blacklisted by the FATF in 2000, and as a result underwent major reforms in their legal systems, compared to Bermuda and the BVI which were not blacklisted, and as a result underwent minor changes in their legislative systems. Between 2007 and 2012, similar results are observed, with The Bahamas and the Cayman Islands undergoing significant reforms in their legislative systems in order to satisfy the deficiencies highlighted in their respective MERs. Of the two jurisdictions, The Bahamas has been most impacted in terms of legislative changes undertaken by the jurisdiction, as the Cayman Islands resorted to satisfying a number of deficiencies through its guidance notes, which met the criteria set by the FATF. Of the two remaining jurisdictions, the BVI implemented more legislative measures compared to Bermuda and

[34] See the Terrorism (United Nations Measures) (Overseas Territories) Order 2001.

[35] Weighting more heavily legislative system over institutional measures.

[36] See Table 7.4.

**Table 7.4** The BVI: legislation implemented to counter money laundering and terrorist financing

| *Prior to 2000* | *2000–2006* | *2007–2012* |
|---|---|---|
| *Transparency the BVI* | | |
| 1988 UN Drug Convention | The Financial Services Commission Act, 2001 | The Securities and Investment Business Act 2010 |
| The Proceeds of Criminal Conduct Act, 1997 | The Financial Investigation Agency Act, 2003 | The Proceeds of Criminal Conduct (Amendment) Act, 2010 |
| | | The Financing and Money Services Act |
| | | The Proliferation Financing (Prohibition) Act, 2009 |
| *Preventative Measures* | | |
| Code of Practice, 1999 | The Terrorism (United Nations Measures) (Overseas Territories) Order 2001 | The Anti-Money Laundering and Terrorist Financing Code of Practice, 2009 (AMLTFCOP) |
| | The Anti-terrorism (Financial and Other Measures) (Overseas Territories) Order 2002 | The Anti-Money Laundering Regulations, 2008 |
| *National and International Cooperation* | | |
| The Evidence (Proceedings in Foreign Jurisdictions) Act, 1988 | The Financial Services Commission Act, 2001 | Palmero Convention |
| The UN Convention on the Taking of Evidence Abroad in Civil or Commercial Matters, 1970 | The Financial Investigation Agency Act, 2003 | The Terrorist Financing Convention |
| The Mutual Legal Assistance (United States of America) Act, 1990 | The Anti-terrorism (Financial and Other Measures) (Overseas Territories) Order 2002 | UN Security Council resolution SRES/1267(1999) |
| The Drug Trafficking Offences Act 1992 | The Extradition Act | UN Security Council S/RES/1373(2001) |

(continued)

**Table 7.4** (continued)

| *Prior to 2000* | *2000–2006* | *2007–2012* |
|---|---|---|
| The Drug Trafficking Offences (Designated Countries and Territories) Order, 1996 | The Extradition (Overseas Territories) Order 2002 | International Cooperation Handbook |
| The Criminal Justice (International Cooperation) Act, 1993 | Criminal Justice (International Cooperation) (Amendment) Act, 2004 | |
| The Criminal Justice (International Cooperation) (Enforcement of Overseas Forfeiture Orders) Order, 1996 | The Al-Qaida and Taliban (United Nations Measures) (Overseas Territories) Order 2002 | |
| The Proceeds of Criminal Conduct Act, 1997 | The North Korea (United Nations Measures) (Overseas Territories) Order 2006 | |
| The Proceeds of Criminal Conduct (Designated Countries and Territories) Order, 1999 | The Iran (United Nations Measures) (Overseas Territories) Order 2007 | |

*Source* BVI Financial Services Commission Annual Reports 2000–2013 and BVI International Tax Authority, 2020

as a result, is placed as the third jurisdiction most affected by the FATF standard, followed by Bermuda, which was the least affected of the four jurisdictions.

## 7.9 Conclusion

Prior to 2000, anti-money legislation adopted by The Bahamas, the Cayman Islands, Bermuda and the BVI were carried out independently in accordance with the measures each jurisdiction had deemed appropriate. By the late 1990s, this legislative role was still performed independently to a large degree, taking into consideration the recommended anti-money laundering guidelines introduced by the FATF through its Forty Recommendations in 1990. By 2000 a marked shift was noted in the approached used by the FATF to get countries to participate in adopting its Forty Recommendations in their domestic legal systems. The publication of its blacklist in 2000, backed by the threat of defensive measures by OECD members against countries that failed to comply, forced countries such as these four Caribbean jurisdictions to take action. Significant legislative measures were undertaken by The Bahamas and the Cayman Islands as result of being placed on the blacklist, compared to Bermuda and the BVI, which were not placed on the list.

Between 2007 and 2012, of the four jurisdictions, The Bahamas underwent a second round of legislative changes, followed by the Cayman Islands, the BVI, and Bermuda to a lesser degree. These changes were in response to recommendations made by the CFATF upon completion of its third MER of each jurisdiction. The legislative changes implemented by these jurisdictions were all aimed at: (i) increasing transparency in the legislative systems and institutional structures of each jurisdiction; (ii) implementing backstopping measures to prevent money laundering and terrorist financing; and (iii) enhancing the capacity of each jurisdiction in providing mutual legal assistance in international cooperation.

As a result of the international policy initiative imposed by the FATF, the legislative systems and institutional structures of each jurisdiction have been strengthened, backstopping measures have been implemented, and national governance has been reinforced. Additionally, the adoption of exchange mechanisms significantly increased, which has resulted in greater participation in international cooperation on the part of all jurisdictions.

Another notable outcome of the impact of the FATF standard on these OFCs is a shift by these jurisdictions away from the use of the term "offshore financial centre" to a more adequate term "financial centre", as they were now deemed to be compliant with international standards like other financial centres located in onshore jurisdictions. This move was aimed at removing themselves away from the stigma of being associated with money laundering and terrorist financing inter alia.

Despite these measures of success however, it is unknown to what extent, if at all, the FATF standard has been effective in countering money laundering and terrorist financing. What is certain is that its international policy initiative has had a significant impact on the legal systems and institutions in The Bahamas to a greater degree, followed by the Cayman Islands, and to a lesser degree, on the BVI, followed by Bermuda, which was the least impacted of the four jurisdictions.

## References


Bank of International Settlement. 2016. *Sound Management of Risks Related to Money Laundering and Financing of Terrorism*. Bank of International Settlement. https://www.fsa.go.jp/inter/bis/20140121-1/02.pdf.

BVI Financial Services Commission. 2008. *Annual Report 2007*. BVI Financial Services Commission. https://www.bvifsc.vg/library/bvifsc-annual-reports.

BVI Financial Services Commission. 2013. *Annual Report 2012*. BVI Financial Services Commission. https://www.bvifsc.vg/library/bvifsc-annual-reports.

CFATF. 2007a. *Mutual Evaluation/Detailed Assessment Report Cayman Islands*. Financial Action Task Force. https://www.cima.ky/upimages/commonfiles/1499854071CaymanIslandsCFATFMEVFinalNov2007.pdf.

CFATF. 2007b. *The Bahamas Ministerial Report*. Caribbean Financial Action Task Force. https://www.cfatf-gafic.org/member-countries/the-bahamas.

CFATF. 2008a. *Detailed Assessment Report*. Caribbean Financial Action Task Force. https://www.cfatf-gafic.org/member-countries/bermuda.

CFATF. 2008b. *Mutual Evaluation Report*. Caribbean Financial Action Task Force. https://www.cfatf-gafic.org/member-countries/virgin-islands.

CFATF. 2009a. *Cayman Islands, First Follow-Up Report: Anti-Money Laundering and Combating the Financing of Terrorism*. Caribbean Financial Action Task Force. https://www.cfatf-gafic.org/cfatf-documents/follow-up-reports-2/cayman-islands/188-cayman-islands-1st-follow-up-report/file.

CFATF. 2009b. *The Bahamas Follow-Up Report*. Caribbean Financial Action Task Force. https://www.cfatf-gafic.org/member-countries/the-bahamas.

CFATF. 2010a. *Cayman Islands, Second Follow-Up Report: Anti-money Laundering and Combating the Financing of Terrorism*. Caribbean Financial Action Task Force. https://www.fatf-gafi.org/media/fatf/documents/reports/fur/CFATF-2nd-Follow-Up-Report-Cayman-Islands.pdf.

CFATF. 2010b. *Cayman Islands, Third Follow-Up Report: Anti-money Laundering and Combating the Financing of Terrorism*. Caribbean Financial Action Task Force. https://www.fatf-gafi.org/media/fatf/documents/reports/fur/CFATF-2nd-Follow-Up-Report-Cayman-Islands.pdf.

CFATF. 2010c. *The Bahamas Third Follow-Up Report*. Caribbean Financial Action Task Force. https://www.cfatf-gafic.org/member-countries/the-bahamas.

CFATF. 2011a. *The Bahamas Fourth Follow-Up Report*. Caribbean Financial Action Task Force. https://www.cfatf-gafic.org/member-countries/the-bahamas.

CFATF. 2011b. *Second Follow-Up Report: Bermuda*. Caribbean Financial Action Task Force. https://www.cfatf-gafic.org/documents/follow-up-reports-2/bermuda/52-bermuda-2nd-follow-up-report?format=html.

CFATF. 2011c. *Third Follow-Up Report: Virgin Islands*. Caribbean Financial Action Task Force. https://www.cfatf-gafic.org/documents/follow-up-reports-2/virgin-islands/139-virgin-islands-3rd-follow-up-report.

CFATF. 2012a. *Cayman Islands, First Biennial Report*. Caribbean Financial Action Task Force. https://www.cfatf-gafic.org/documents/follow-up-reports-2/cayman-islands/4142-cayman-islands-1st-biennial-report-1?format=html.

CFATF. 2012b. *The Bahamas Fifth Follow-Up Report*. Caribbean Financial Action Task Force. https://www.cfatf-gafic.org/member-countries/the-bahamas.

CFATF. 2013. *The Bahamas, Sixth Follow-Up Report*. Caribbean Financial Action Task Force. https://www.cfatf-gafic.org/member-countries/the-bahamas.

CFATF. 2014a. *Fifth Follow-Up Report: Bermuda*. Caribbean Financial Action Task Force. https://cfatf-gafic.org/index.php/documents/follow-up-reports-2/bermuda/3556-bermuda-5th-follow-up-report-1.

CFATF. 2014b. *Cayman Islands, Second Biennial Report*. Caribbean Financial Action Task Force. https://www.cfatf-gafic.org/documents/cfatf-follow-up-reports/cayman-islands/4637-cayman-islands-2nd-biannual-report/file.

CIMA. 2012. *Annual Report 2012*. Cayman Islands Monetary Authority. https://www.cima.ky/upimages/publicationdoc/AnnualReportandAu_1499163437.pdf.

FATF. 1991. *Financial Action Task Force on Money Laundering Report 1990–1991*. Financial Action Task Force. https://www.fatf-gafi.org/media/fatf/documents/reports/1990%201991%20ENG.pdf.

FATF. 1997. *The forty Recommendations*. Financial Action Task Force. https://www.fatf-gafi.org/media/fatf/documents/recommendations/pdfs/FATF%20Recommendations%201996.pdf.

FATF. 2000. *Review to Identify Non-cooperative Countries or Territories: Increasing the Worldwide Effective of Anti-Money Laundering Measures*. Financial Action Task Force. https://www.fatf-gafi.org/media/fatf/documents/reports/1999%202000%20NCCT%20ENG.pdf.

FATF. 2007. *FATF Guidance on the Risk-Based Approach to Combating Money Laundering and Terrorist Financing—High Level Principles and Procedures*. Financial Action Task Force. https://www.fatf-gafi.org/publications/fatfrecommendations/documents/fatfguidanceontherisk-basedapproachtocombatingmoneylaunderingandterroristfinancing-highlevelprinciplesandprocedures.html.

FATF. 2021. *Procedures for the FATF Fourth Round on AML/CFT Mutual Evaluations*. Financial Action Task Force. https://www.fatf-gafi.org/publications/mutualevaluations/documents/4th-round-procedures.html.

Sansonetti, R. 2000. The Mutual Evaluation Process: A Methodology of Increasing Importance at International Level. *Journal of Financial Crime* 7 (3): 218–226. https://doi.org/10.1108/eb025942.

CHAPTER 8

# The Impact of International Policy Initiatives Against Tax Evasion on the Legislative Systems and Institutions of Offshore Financial Centers in the Caribbean

## 8.1 Introduction

The OECD took similar measures to those implemented by the FATF to counter tax evasion. Through its 1998 Report, the organization highlighted the need to enhance the legislative frameworks of countries worldwide considered to be "tax heavens" and "preferential tax regimes" (OECD 1998). Both according to the OECD, undertook harmful tax practices which were detrimental to OECD countries. The publication of its 2002 blacklist was the first step taken by the OECD to urge such countries to take action.[1] Between 2002 and 2010, the OECD further strengthened its position through the formation of the Global Forum on Transparency and Exchange of Information for Tax Purposes (the Global Forum), dedicated to deal with tax evasion, particularly among tax heavens (OECD 2012).

Over time, the OECD via the Global Forum also seized the opportunity to enhance its powers through the imposition of increased obligations it placed on jurisdictions. Similar to the mutual evaluation reports (MER) used by the FATF, the Global Forum introduced its very own peer

[1] See OECD's website: https://www.oecd.org/ctp/harmful/list-of-unco-operative-tax-havens.htm.



A. M. Campbell, *Money Laundering, Terrorist Financing, and Tax Evasion*, https://doi.org/10.1007/978-3-030-68876-9_8

review process (PRP), which also entailed an onsite examination of the legal systems of jurisdictions to ensure compliance with satisfying the criteria it deemed necessary to eliminate harmful tax practices (OECD 2003). The Global Forum continued to place additional obligations on countries over time through the establishment of two standards which included, exchange of information upon request (EOIR) in 2009 (OECD 2016), and automatic exchange of information (AEOI) based on common reporting standards (CRS) in 2014 (OECD 2017). These standards were both designed to increase tax transparency through facilitating the exchange of financial account information between countries, aimed at mitigating tax evasion.

The Global Forum and OECD's efforts to fight tax evasion were complimented by measures undertaken by the US and EU in their very own battle to counter this phenomenon. The US introduced Foreign Account Tax Compliance Act (FATCA) in 2010, which eventually formed the model on which AEOI was based (US Senate and House of Representatives (US Congress) 2010). The underlying objective of FATCA was to increase tax transparency through the reporting of specified information by foreign countries to the Internal Revenue Service (IRS) in the US (US Congress 2010). The EU in its efforts to foster tax transparency and fairness of taxation, established its own standard to counter tax evasion and the effects it had on countries within its borders.

In this chapter, these key initiatives are reviewed to determine the impact of international policy initiatives against tax evasion on the legal systems and institutions in The Bahamas, the Cayman Islands, Bermuda and the BVI. To perform this analysis, we will look at the period 2010 to 2016 which coincides with the introduction of the EOIR and CRS by the Global Forum, FATCA by the US, and the standard implemented by the EU Code of Conduct Group on Business Taxation (EU CCG). The information used for this analysis includes the peer review reports prepared by the OECD, literature published by the OECD, along with the annual financial reports and special reviews published by the central banks and government institutions in each country. We will examine the response of each jurisdiction to these policy initiatives and analyse the trends observed in a comparative analysis to conclude our findings.

## 8.2 International Policy Initiatives

### *8.2.1 Exchange of Information on Request*

Shortly after its formation in 2009, EOIR was initiated by the Global Forum. Its objective was to increase international cooperation by giving tax authority the ability to access specific information from their peers in another jurisdiction. EOIR is broad in scope as it allows for any information that is "foreseeably relevant" to be provided to a tax authority upon request for the enforcement or administration of its local tax laws or for the execution of the provisions of an applicable tax agreement (OECD 2018). Information commonly exchanged through EOIR includes, beneficial and legal ownership, bank account details and accounting records (OECD 2018). EOIR applies only during the time an ongoing inquiry or investigation is taking place in the requesting jurisdiction (OECD 2018). Jurisdictions are obligated to adopt the new standard which consist in the Principles of Transparency and Exchange of Information on Request in Tax Matters, otherwise they are placed on the OECDs blacklist (OECD 2010).[2] To be removed from the list, countries were obligated to sign at least twelve (12) agreements or unilateral mechanisms to facilitate information exchange with OECD countries by March 31, 2010. Failure to do so would result in sanctions imposed by OECD countries (OECD 2018).

### *8.2.2 Foreign Account Tax Compliance Act*

The implementation of FATCA in 2010 by the US took a similar approach. FATCA obligated foreign financial institutions (FFIs) to report foreign assets held in the accounts of US persons, or held by various types of non-financial foreign entities, in which a substantial ownership interest is held by US taxpayers, to the IRS (IRS, 2020). FFIs could opt to register directly with the IRS to satisfy FATCA regulations by way of

[2] The Standard consisted of Article 26 of the OECD Model Tax Convention, the 2002 Model Agreement on Exchange of Information on Tax Matters and the implementation of the 2006 standards established by the Joint Ad Hoc Group on Accounts on the availability and reliability of accounting records. The Standard required for information to be exchanged upon request: (i) it is considered to be "foreseeable relevant" to administer and enforce local laws of the contracting partner; (ii) no stipulations on exchange due to bank secrecy or requirements for domestic/local tax interest; (iii) reliable information being available and powers to access it; (iv) the rights of taxpayers respected; and (v) information exchanged in strict confidence.

the FFI agreement if applicable, or adhere to the FATCA Intergovernmental Agreements (IGA) in effect in their respective jurisdictions (IRS 2020). Failure to do so resulted in a 30% withholding tax on US source income for that particular financial institution. To avoid withholding on payments, foreign financial institutions were obligated to undergo registration with the IRS and consent to report specific information to the agency on accounts held by US persons, including certain foreign entities accounts with substantial US owners (IRS 2020). The UK also adopted a similar strategy to address tax evasion by its citizens referred to as UK "FATCA", which imposed reporting requirements for equivalent information on its Overseas Territories and Crown Dependencies (UK Statury Instruments 2014).

### *8.2.3 Common Reporting Standard*

Similar to FACTA, in 2014 the Global Forum introduced CRS. CRS facilitated AEOI, which obliged jurisdictions to collect specified information on financial accounts belonging to non-residents from financial institutions operating in their territories, and exchange such information automatically on an annual basis with jurisdictions in which the account holders are residence (OECD 2014). This process facilitated what the Global Forum refers to as the effective automatic exchange of information without having to request it (OECD 2014). CRS outlined specific information required to be exchanged on financial accounts, reporting duties for certain financial institutions including the types of accounts and taxpayers implicated, and due diligence rules financial institutions are obligated to comply with (OECD 2014).

### *8.2.4 EU Code of Conduct on Business Taxation*

Like the US, the EU also imposed its very own standard to counter tax evasion. In November 2016, the EU CCG established a set of criteria to promote tax transparency, fairness of taxation and the employment of anti-base erosion profit shifting (BEPS) standards. Jurisdictions were required to meet two of the following three criteria: (i) implement agreements with all EU Member Countries to exchange information automatically by September 2018; (ii) maintain a largely compliant rating on the Global Forum's EOIR standard; and (iii) adopt the Multilateral Convention on Mutual Administrative Assistance in Tax Matters (OECD

2014). Jurisdictions were also compelled to commit at a high political level and put measures in place by 31 December 2018, to tackle harmful tax practices, tax evasion and BEPS. Failure to do so resulted in placement on the EU's list of Non-Cooperative Jurisdictions for Tax Purposes. To be removed from the list, a jurisdiction had to become tax compliant pursuant to the EU CCG's set criteria (Council of the EU 2016).

## 8.3 The Bahamas

### *8.3.1 Transparency*

To increase transparency in its legal system and strengthen institutional measures, The Bahamas enacted a number of laws to satisfy the requirements of EOIR introduced by the Global Forum. The first of these measures carried out by the jurisdiction was the enactment of the International Tax Cooperation Act, 2010. This Act provided the legal framework to enabled the jurisdiction to exchange information based on the Tax Information Exchange Agreements (TIEAs) signed with other countries, including the two recently signed TIEAs with the US.[3] It also laid out required procedures to be followed when making a request for tax information.[4] The Act was accompanied by the International Tax Cooperation Act, 2010 (Regulations), which set forth the procedures in detail, for the obtainment of information by document, examination, and on-side interview, including the forms required to be used when making such requests.[5] To satisfy the criteria for US FATCA, the jurisdiction enacted The Bahamas and The United States of America Foreign Account Tax Compliance Agreement Act, 2015. This Act made provisions to implement the Agreement to Improve International Tax Compliance.[6] Its purpose was to establish and empower the Competent Authority to obtain the information necessary to properly enforce and administer the Act and

[3] See The Bahamas and the United States Tax Information Exchange Agreement (Amendment) Act, 2010 and The Bahamas and the United States Tax Information Exchange Agreement (Amendment) Regulations, 2010.

[4] See the International Tax Cooperation Act, 2010.

[5] See the International Tax Cooperation Act, 2010 (Regulations).

[6] See The Bahamas and The United States of America Foreign Account Tax Compliance Agreement Act, 2015.

ensure the obligations agreed to were carried out by the jurisdiction.[7] To this end, a Competent Authority Agreement was later signed by the jurisdiction in accordance with the IGA executed in November 2014.[8]

To comply with the demands of CRS, The Bahamas enacted three pieces of legislation to put the necessary mechanisms in place. The first of these was the Automatic Exchange of Financial Account Information Act, 2016, which made CRS effective in the jurisdiction, and empowered the Competent Authority to implement agreements to engage in automatic exchange of financial account information in tax matters with other jurisdictions.[9] This piece of legislation also provided for the appropriate administration of the Act, its enforcement, as well as ensured that the jurisdiction complies with the obligations set forth in each Agreement it executes pursuant to the Act. The second piece of legislation passed by the jurisdiction was the Automatic Exchange of Financial Account Information Regulations, 2017, which required all reporting financial institutions to create, maintain and document due diligence procedures. It also imposed reporting obligations on reporting financial institutions, introduced cash value insurance procedures, and record keeping requirements.[10] The last piece of legislation enacted was the International Tax Cooperation (Amendment) Act, 2017, which provided for previous Agreements noted in the First Schedule to be revised to include the automatic exchange of financial account information for tax purposes through the adoption of the Articles as set forth in the Protocol on the Second Schedule of the amendment.[11] Together these three Acts facilitated the implementation of CRS.

To satisfy the requirements of the EU Code of Conduct, The Bahamas became signatory to the Multilateral Convention on Mutual Administrative Assistance in Tax Matters on 15 December 2017, which came into force on 1 August 2018. The jurisdiction also became party to the Inclusive Framework on BEPS making it the 116th country to participate in the project. The Convention made provisions for the jurisdiction to

[7] See The Bahamas and The United States of America Foreign Account Tax Compliance Agreement Act, 2015.

[8] Per announcement by the Bahamas Ministry of Finance on 7 March 2017.

[9] See the Automatic Exchange of Financial Account Information Act, 2016.

[10] See the Automatic Exchange of Financial Account Information Regulations, 2017.

[11] See the International Tax Cooperation (Amendment) Act, 2017.

undertake measures to comply with the OECD/G20 BEPS Project inter alia.[12]

### 8.3.2 Preventative Measures

The jurisdiction also implemented a number of backstopping measures to address areas of deficiencies brought to its attention by the Global Forum. To comply with the demands placed on it by the Global Forums EOIR standard, The Bahamas sought to make improvements in the maintenance of accounting records among certain types of legal entities and arrangements. To do so, the jurisdiction amended a number of laws to include express obligations to provide for entities and arrangements including companies, partnerships, trusts, foundations etc., to keep reliable accounting records, in addition to underlying documents for at least five years (OECD 2013). The laws amended included, the Exempted Limited Partnership (Amendment) Act, 2011; the Foundations (Amendment) Act, 2011; the International Business Companies (Amendment) Act, 2011; the Investment Funds (Amendment) Act, 2011; the Purpose Trusts (Amendment) (No. 2) Act, 2011; and the Segregated Accounts Companies (Amendment) Act, 2011 (OECD 2013).

In January 2013, additional amendments were passed by the jurisdiction for the same purpose with respect to general and limited partnerships, general and foreign companies, and resident trustees (OECD 2013). These Acts included: The Companies (Amendment) Act, 2013; the Business License (Amendment) Act, 2013; the Partnerships (Amendment) Act, 2013; and the Trustee (Amendment) Act, 2013. To address issues highlighted in the peer review report regarding notification requirement rights, and safeguards and compulsory powers, in December 2011, the jurisdiction implemented the International Tax Cooperation (Amendment) Act, 2011, and also The Bahamas and the United States of America Tax Information Exchange Agreement (Amendment) Act, 2011 (OECD 2013). Given the number legal reforms undertaken by the jurisdiction, at the end of Phase 2 of the first found of peer reviews the overall rating of The Bahamas was largely compliant (OECD 2013).

[12] See the Multilateral Convention on Mutual Administrative Assistance in Tax Matters, 2017.

### 8.3.3 National and International Cooperation

To enhance its stance on national and international cooperation, the jurisdiction enacted the International Tax Cooperation Act, 2010, which enabled it to implement EOIR (OECD 2013). On 20 March 2010, the jurisdiction obtained the standard on Transparency and Cooperation in Tax Matters in accordance with the EOIR requirements set by the Global Forum. By March 2013, the jurisdiction had also signed 29 TIEAs with other jurisdictions, 26 of these agreements were in force at the time of the OECD's 2013 report. Twenty-two of which were with OECD member countries (OECD 2013). The jurisdiction also began exchanging information in accordance with EOIR.

To satisfy the stipulations imposed by US FATCA, on 3 November 2014, The Bahamas Government signed an Agreement referred to as the Agreement to Improve International Tax Compliance with the US Government, which came into force 18 August 2015 (Bahamas Ministry of Finance 2015). Based on Model I of the IGA,[13] the agreement was aimed at improving international tax compliance, in addition to providing for the adoption of FATCA in the jurisdiction.[14] The provisions of the agreement provided for financial institutions based in the Bahamas to provide required information to the Bahamas Competent Authority who in turn was responsible for forwarding such information to the US Competent Authority (Bahamas Ministry of Finance 2015). The Agreement also provided for confidentiality and protection with respect to the use of information exchanged.

With regard to CRS, The Bahamas made a commitment to exchange information automatically in 2018, by way of a declaration to the Secretary General of the OECD on the effective date for information to be exchange in accordance with the Multilateral Competent Authority Agreement on Automatic Exchange of Financial Information. Prior to this, the jurisdiction had executed a declaration on 13 December 2017, to join the Multilateral Competent Authority Agreement on Automatic Exchange of Financial Account Information. The jurisdiction successfully completed the first exchange under Automatic Exchange of Information (AEOI) by way of CRS in September 2018.

[13] See the IGA Model is non-reciprocal (Model 1B).

[14] The IGA came into force 17 September 2015 and was treated as having an IGA effect from 30 June 2014 per the IRS.

With respect to complying with the EU CCG set criteria, as signatory to the Multilateral Convention on Mutual Administrative Assistance in Tax Matters, on 15 December 2017 (OECD 2020) The Bahamas undertook measures to comply with the OECD/G20 BEPS Project. As at 31 December 2016, The Bahamas had approximately 34 exchange agreements in place.

## 8.4 The Cayman Islands

### *8.4.1 Transparency*

Similar to the Bahamas, the Cayman Islands also introduced new legislation to increase transparency in its legal system and strengthen institutional measures to address the concerns stemming from EOIR, FATCA, CRS and the EU Code of Conduct Group. The first of these measures was the enactment of the Tax Information Authority Law (TIA Law), which made provisions for the formation of the Tax Information Authority in the Cayman Islands and provided the legal framework which enabled the jurisdiction to share tax information. Further amendments to the TIA Law in 2005 provided for the Cayman Islands Tax Information Authority (CITIA) to preside over the exchange of information for tax purposes and obtain relevant information to respond to exchange of information (EOI) requests. The CITIA is supervised by the Cayman Islands Monetary Authority (CIMA), which carries out this role through the enactment of statutes, regulations and rules, in addition to the issuance of statements of guidance and principals (OECD 2013).

The second measure undertaken by the jurisdiction was in response to US FATCA. On 15 March 2013, the Government announced its commitment to execute Model I IGA (CIMA 2013). This was followed by the introduction of the Tax Information Authority Law (2013 Revision) to make provisions for Model I IGA to be entered into between the jurisdiction and the United States. This led to US FATCA taking effect in the Cayman Islands on 1 July 2014 (Cayman Islands Tax Information Authority 2015). The third measure undertaken by the jurisdiction was the shifting of responsibility of the Tax Information Authority from the Financial Secretary to the Minister for Financial Services by way of the Tax Information Authority (Amendment) Bill, 2014. This bill was further amended to provide for the Tax Information

Authority (TIA) to expedite automatic exchange of information in accordance with the Agreement listed on the schedule included in the Tax Information Authority Law (Cayman Islands Tax Information Authority 2015). The fourth measure initiated by the jurisdiction was the enactment of the Tax Information Authority (International Tax Compliance) (United States of America) Regulations, 2014 for US FATCA, and for UK FATCA, the Tax Information Authority (International Tax Compliance) (United Kingdom) Regulations, 2014. Both Agreements were based on the United States Model 1 IGA, providing for financial institutions to provide specified information to the Competent Authority in the Cayman Islands, for onward forwarding to its counterpart in the relevant jurisdiction. The objective of these Agreements was to enhance compliance with international tax rules between the respective countries involved.

The jurisdiction later passed the Tax Information Authority (International Tax Compliance) (United States of America) (Amendment) Regulations, 2015, which modified the calendar years 2014 to 2016, and changed the date of notification from 31 March to 30 April to the Competent Authority. In another amendment (The Tax Information Authority (International Tax Compliance) (United States of America) (Amendment) (No.2) Regulations, 2015), the jurisdiction removed the reporting obligation for Reporting Financial Institutions with no Reportable Accounts. Under both Agreements, the jurisdiction issued guidance notes to provide advice to businesses and advisers, as well as the competent authority, in applying the terms of the Agreements (Cayman Islands Tax Information Authority 2015).

The fifth measure undertaken by the Cayman Islands was the passage of the Tax Information Authority Law (TIA Law) to implement common reporting standards (CRS). The TIA Law made provisions for the exchange of information for tax purpose of all forms (via the Bilateral Competent Authority Agreements (CAA) and the Multilateral Competent Authority Agreement (MCAA)).[15] Another measure implemented by the jurisdiction was the enactment of the Tax Information Authority (International Tax Compliance) (Common Reporting Standard) Regulations, 2015, which became effective on 1 January 2016. These Regulations required financial institutions in the Cayman Islands to submit the required information for CRS to the relevant competent authority.

[15] See the Tax Information Authority Law, 2005.

Another measure initiated by the jurisdiction was the issuance of guidance notes by the Tax Information Authority, in accordance with the legislation to assist in the consistency of its application and interpretation by financial institutions (Cayman Islands Tax Information Authority 2015). The Regulations were further amended in 2016 to provide for the jurisdiction to implement CRS and meet its obligations for the "effective implementation" of reporting and compliance rules under CRS. This criterion set by the EU was one of the determinants to be deemed compliant for tax transparency within its screening guidelines of non-EU jurisdictions for its intended Non-Cooperative Jurisdictions for Tax Purposes list (Council of the EU 2016). Financial institutions were required to report specified financial account information for the first reporting year of 2016 by 31 May 2017, to the Department of International Tax Co-operation (DITC), for accounts opened on 1 January 2016 or after (Cayman Islands TIA 2016). The TIA completed the jurisdictions first exchange of information with partner jurisdictions in September 2017 (Cayman Islands Tax Information Authority 2015).

### 8.4.2 Preventative Measures

To address the concerns raised by the Global Forum in its PRP report with respect to the EOIR standard, the jurisdiction implemented a number of backstopping measures aimed at preventing tax evasion. In 2012, to make changes to entities such as companies, exempted partnerships, and partnerships, the Cayman Islands Monetary Authority (CIMA) introduced the Companies Amendment Bill, 2012, the Exempted Partnership Amendment Bill, 2012, and the Partnership Amendment Bill, 2012 (OECD 2013). These amendments increased the penalties for exempted companies and exempted partnerships, including limited partnerships, for failure to comply with the requirements for maintaining ownership and identity information. They also imposed new obligations on exempted companies and partnerships to provide upon request by the CITIA, ownership and accounting information (OECD 2013). Under the Banks and Trust Companies Amendment Bill, 2012, the jurisdiction amended the Bank and Trust Companies Law, (2009) to enforce sanctions for non-compliance with the Private Trust Companies Regulations on Private Trust Companies including for breach of requirements for information keeping (OECD 2013). The same sanctions were also imposed through the introduction of the Private Trust

Company (Amendment) Regulations, 2013, which modified the Private Trust Companies Regulations, (2011), in addition to increased requirements for information keeping for Private Trust Companies, as well as the trusts structures managed by them (OECD 2013).

Another measure taken by the jurisdiction was the introduction of the Private Trust Companies (Amendment) Regulations, 2013. This amendment made provisions for beneficial information to be kept at the private trust company's registered office. Failure to comply resulted in the imposition of a fine equivalent to $5,000 (Sections 3(2) and 4(2) of the amendment) (OECD 2013). To address the concerns raised in the 2013 Report regarding legal and beneficial ownership and identity information, the jurisdiction made a number of amendments to abolish all bearer shares in May 2016 and required that such shares be registered by 13 July 2016.[16]

### *8.4.3 National and International Cooperation*

Measures implemented by the jurisdiction to increase international cooperation included the passage of the Monetary Authority Law (MAL) and the signing of a number of exchange of information mechanisms. The MAL made provision for the CIMA to render assistance to regulatory authorities in other jurisdictions as one of its main functions.[17] During the course of 2010, the CIMA signed several bilateral memoranda of understandings (MOU) and a multilateral agreement which became effective in 2011. These TIEAs detailed when consultation was required and the type of information to be exchanged. By January 2013, the jurisdiction had in place 29 TIEAs and 1 DTC (OECD 2013).

To comply with US FATCA, the Cayman Islands enacted the Tax Information Authority (International Tax Compliance) (United States of America) Regulations, 2014, and for UK FACTA, the Tax Information Authority (International Tax Compliance) (United Kingdom) Regulations, 2014. Under US FATCA, the first transmissions of data to the

[16] See the Companies (Amendment) Law, 2016 and the Companies Management (Amendment) Law, 2016.

[17] See the Monetary Authority Law, 2010.

IRS was completed in September 2015,[18] whereas UK FATCA reporting took place on 31 May 2015 (Cayman Islands Tax Information Authority 2015). With regard to CRS, the jurisdiction executed a declaration on 29 October 2014 to join the Multilateral Competent Authority Agreement on Automatic Exchange of Financial Account Information (Council of Europe 2017). As of 1 January 2014, the jurisdiction had participated in the Convention on Mutual Administrative Assistance in Tax Matters by way of extension through the UK. For assistance in tax administration matters, the Cayman Islands have in place 36 bilateral agreements and arrangements under the Convention on Mutual Administrative Assistance in Tax Matters.[19]

With respect to complying with the EU CCG requirements, the Multilateral Convention on Mutual Administrative Assistance in Tax Matters was extended to the Cayman Islands by the UK and became effective in the jurisdiction on 1 January 2014 (OECD 2020). On 13 April, the jurisdiction joined the Inclusive Framework for the implementation of the OECD/G20 BEPS Project (OECD 2021). As of 31 December 2016, the Cayman Islands had around 35 information exchange mechanisms in place with other jurisdictions.

## 8.5 Bermuda

### *8.5.1 Transparency*

Similar to The Bahamas and the Cayman Island, Bermuda also introduced new legislation to increase transparency in its legal system and strengthen institutional measures to address the concerns stemming from EOIR, FATCA, CRS and the EU Code of Conduct Group. To implement EOIR, the jurisdiction had already enacted legislation in 2005 by way of the International Cooperation (Tax Information Exchange Agreements) Act 2005. This Act provided the necessary provisions for the implementation of EOIR. Other measures implemented by the jurisdiction to deal with concerns raised by the Global Forum related to EOIR were aimed

[18] See the Agreement between the Government of the Cayman Islands and the Government of the United States of America to Improve International Tax Compliance and to Implement FATCA 2013.

[19] See the Cayman Islands Department for International Tax Cooperation website, https://www.ditc.ky/wp-content/uploads/2020/06/International_Exchange_of_Information_Instruments.pdf.

at strengthening institutional measures. The first measure was the passing of the Corporate Service Provider Business Act 2012 (CSPBA), which subjected corporate services providers (CSPs) to the licensing obligations and AML/CFT framework of the jurisdiction (OECD 2013). CSPs were also given until 1 October 2016 to make application for a license (OECD 2013). The jurisdiction also enacted legislation to incorporate the limited liability company (LLC), which represented a separate legal entity with a similar membership makeup and governance structure to a partnership (OECD 2013).

To facilitate FATCA with the US, Bermuda undertook more measures. The first of these was the signing of Model 2 IGA with the US on 19 December 2013.[20] Under this arrangement, the jurisdiction committed to enacting the requisite legislation to instruct and allow FFIs within its jurisdiction to gather and report information required under FATCA (including Specified U.S. Persons) to the IRS. The jurisdiction elected the Model 2 option principally because there were no conflicts in its local laws to prevent FFIs from reporting directly to the IRS. As domestic law had already existed to provide for reporting to the IRS,[21] the jurisdiction amended its law to be able to instruct FFIs within its territory to adhere to US FATCA Regulations. The jurisdiction also passed the USA-Bermuda Tax Convention Amendment Act, 2015, to require FFIs to comply with the conditions contained in the agreement between the Governments of Bermuda and the US on 19 December 2013. The underlying objective was to improve compliance in international tax and implement FATCA.[22] Similar to US FATCA, on 26 November 2013, an IGA was executed between the governments of the UK and Bermuda to provide for the jurisdiction to exchange information on an automatic basis with the UK.[23] The agreement was modelled after US FATCA agreement and placed a reporting requirement on financial institutions in Bermuda to

[20] See the Agreement between the Government of the United States of America and the Government of Bermuda for Cooperation to Facilitate the Implementation of FATCA 2013.

[21] See the International Cooperation (Tax Information Exchange Agreements) Act, 2005.

[22] See the USA-Bermuda Tax Convention Amendment Act, 2015.

[23] See the Agreement between the Government of the United Kingdom of Great Britain and Northern Ireland and the Government of Bermuda to Improve International Tax Compliance, 2013.

identify account holders which were UK tax resident, and submit specified account information to the tax authorities in the UK. Financial accounts implicated were those that existed on or after the reporting date of 30 June 2014. The jurisdiction had up to 30 September 2016 to report specified information for the calendar year 2014, to the UK tax authorities.

To implement CRS, additional measures were carried out by Bermuda. The jurisdiction executed a Multilateral Competent Authority Agreement (MCAA) in October 2014 to commence exchanging information via CRS in 2017. This MCAA along with the International Cooperation (Tax Information Exchange Agreements) Act, 2005, the International Cooperation Act, and the International Cooperation (Tax Information Exchange Agreements) Common Reporting Standard Regulations, 2017, referred to as the CRS Regulations, provided the legal framework for financial institutions in Bermuda to gather, maintain and submit specified information for exchange with participating jurisdictions (Government of Bermuda 2019). The jurisdiction also issued guidance notes on CRS to provide assistance to financial institutions in its jurisdiction on how to apply and interpret CRS under Bermuda law (Government of Bermuda 2019).

### 8.5.2 *Preventative Measures*

With regard to preventative measures undertaken by the jurisdiction, due to the implementation of recent measures to establish a legal framework to regulate corporate services providers in the jurisdiction, Bermuda received no recommendations on its PRP report conducted by the Global Forum (OECD 2017).

### 8.5.3 *National and International Cooperation*

To increase its capacity to assist in international cooperation, the jurisdiction undertook several additional measures. Since 2005, Bermuda had legislation in place which made provisions for it to implement EOIR.[24] The International Cooperation (Tax Information Exchange Agreements) Act, 2005, also allowed the jurisdiction to satisfy the requirements under

[24] See the International Cooperation (Tax Information Exchange Agreements) Act, 2005.

EOIR. To satisfy US FATCA requirements, Bermuda signed an intergovernmental agreement with the United States to facilitate information exchange on financial accounts in accordance with the FATCA (OECD 2017). To facilitate UK FATCA, the International Cooperation Act made provisions for the jurisdiction to comply with UK FATCA requirements (OECD 2017). To comply with the requirements to implement CRS, the Government of the Bermuda executed a declaration on 29 October 2014 to join the Multilateral Competent Authority Agreement on Automatic Exchange of Financial Account Information (Council of Europe 2017).

To meet the criterion of the EU Code of Conduct Group, the jurisdiction became party to the Multilateral Convention on Mutual Administrative Assistance in Tax Matters by extension from the UK on 1 March 2014 (OECD 2020). On 6 January 2017, it joined the Inclusive Framework for the implementation of the OECD/G20 Base Erosion and Profit Shifting (BEPS) Project (OECD 2021). As of 31 December 2016, Bermuda had about 45 information exchange mechanisms (bilateral TIEAs and DTAs) in place with other jurisdictions.

## 8.6 The BVI

### *8.6.1 Transparency*

Similar to The Bahamas, the Cayman Island and Bermuda, the BVI also introduced new legislation to increase transparency in its legal system and strengthen institutional measures to address the concerns stemming from EOIR, FATCA, CRS and the EU Code of Conduct Group. With regard to EOIR, the Mutual Legal Assistance (Tax Matters) Act, 2003, made the necessary provisions for the jurisdiction to adopt EOIR. Other measures undertaken by the BVI to deal with deficiencies highlighted by the Global Forum were aimed at strengthening institutional measures within the jurisdiction. The first of these measures was the enactment of the Securities and Investment Business Act. This Act created a regulatory framework for the investment business and provided updates on requirements to license public, private, and professional mutual funds. The Act also subjected all funds to designate an authorized local representative, an individual or a BVI entity, certified by the Financial Service Commission (FSC) for such purpose. This authorized representative is required to keep records pursuant to the Mutual Funds Regulations, and liaise between the two parties (the FSC and the Fund) (OECD 2011a). Other measures taken by the jurisdiction was the establishment of the International Tax Authority (ITA) within the BVIs Ministry of Finance, for the purpose of handling cross border tax issues. The ITA took over authority from the Commission of Inland Revenue to act as Competent Authority for information exchange (OECD 2013).

To comply with US FATCA, on 30 June 2014, the Government of the BVI signed the Agreement to Improve International Tax Compliance with the US to implement FATCA.[25] In response to UK FATCA, the Government of the BVI signed the Agreement to Improve International Tax Compliance with the UK on 28 November 2013.[26] Both Agreements were based on the non-reciprocal Model I B intergovernmental agreement, which required BVI financial institutions to provide the ITA with specified information, which the ITA would forward to the Competent Authority in the UK and US (BVI Ministry of Finance 2015). The jurisdiction provided the legal framework to implement both US FATCA and UK FATCA by way of amendment to the Mutual Legal Assistance (Tax Matters) Act, 2003 (MLAT), which broadened the scope of information exchange. In addition to being triggered upon request, information could now be exchanged automatically or spontaneously, allowing for FATCA agreements to be implemented with the US and UK governments.[27] The jurisdiction also introduced the Mutual Legal Assistance (Tax Matters) (No. 4) Order, 2014, which made Part I of the MLAT applicable to both IGAs. Under the MLAT, tax information is exchanged upon request by way of the Tax Information Exchange Agreement executed by the BVI, whereas, under the IGAs, such information is exchanged automatically, as provided for under Section 3A of the MLAT. The MLAT also makes provision for further orders to be made by the Minister, including the information required to be submitted to the ITA, and the latest date in which to do so. The ITA also issued guidance notes with respect to each agreement, with the aim of providing a practical guide to directors,

[25] See the Agreement between the Government of the United States of America and the Government of the British Virgin Islands to Improve Tax Compliance and to Implement FATCA, 2014.

[26] See the Agreement between the Government of the United Kingdom of Great Britain and Northern Ireland and the Government of British Virgin Islands to Improve International Tax Compliance, 2013.

[27] See the Virgin Islands Mutual Legal Assistance (Tax Matters) (Amendment) Act, 2014.

advisors and officers of entities as well as to the ITA (BVI Ministry of Finance 2015).

Measures carried out by the BVI to implement CRS were initiated on 4 November 2013, by way of extension of the Convention on Mutual Administrative Assistance in Tax Matters to the jurisdiction by the UK (OECD 2020). This Convention went into force in the BVI on 1 March 2014. To incorporate CRS, the jurisdiction became a signatory to the Multilateral Competent Authorities Agreement, the legal basis of which was provided for in Article 6. Another measure undertaken by the BVI, was the decision of the jurisdiction along with the UK and its Crown Dependencies and Overseas Territories, to enter into a Bilateral Competent Authority Agreement rather than implement information exchange agreements.[28] Additional measures carried out by the jurisdiction included, the amendment to the Mutual Legal Assistance (Tax Matters) Act, 2003, to incorporate the CRS Commentary text into Schedule 4 of the Mutual Legal Assistance (Tax Matters) (Amendment) Act, 2015. This Act was later amended in 2018, to revise certain requirements under CRS which could impose increase responsibilities on certain financial institutions (International Tax Authority, 2019). The jurisdiction later issued guidance notes on 12 October 2016, to provide a practical guide to BVI financial institutions on CRS and on legislation requirements to implement CRS in the BVI (International Tax Authority 2019).

### *8.6.2 Preventative Measures*

In an effort to deal with the deficiencies highlighted in the Global Forums PRP report, the BVI introduced a number of backstopping measures to prevent tax evasion. The first of these measures included an amendment to the Anti-Money Laundering and Terrorist Financing Code of Practice (CoP) in 2012, to expand the obligations placed on providers of trust services to require the collection of information pertaining to the identity of trust beneficiaries with a normal level of risk, in addition to high risk trust beneficiaries (OECD 2013). It also amended the Business Companies Act in July 2012, to impose obligations on registered agents to maintain the current identity information on bearer share owners, in

[28] See the Convention on Mutual Administrative Assistance in Tax Matters, 2013.

addition to the custodian holder of such shares (OECD 2013). The jurisdiction also introduced record keeping requirements for a period of five years minimum, on companies and limited partnership by way of amendments passed in November 2012 to the Partnership Act and the Mutual Legal Assistance Act (OECD 2013).

#### *8.6.3 National and International Cooperation*

To increase its capacity to participate in international cooperation, the jurisdiction undertook several additional measures. EOIR was implemented by the jurisdiction through the use of existing domestic law.[29] To implement FATCA, the BVI became party to the Agreement to Improve International Tax Compliance with the US. For UK FATCA, it executed the Agreement to Improve International Tax Compliance with the UK (OECD 2013). Both Agreements were implemented by way of amendment to the Mutual Legal Assistance (Tax Matters) Act, 2003, the Mutual Legal Assistance (Tax Matters) (No. 4) Order, 2014, and the Mutual Legal Assistance (Tax Matters) Order (OECD 2013). To incorporate CRS, the jurisdiction became party to the Convention on Mutual Administrative Assistance in Tax Matters by way of extension through the UK on 1 March 2014 (OECD 2020). The BVI also became a signatory to the Multilateral Competent Authorities Agreement, to complete the requisite requirements for CRS. To satisfy the EU Code of Conduct, the jurisdiction became Party to the Multilateral Convention on Mutual Administrative Assistance in Tax Matters by extension from the UK. The jurisdiction also joined the Inclusive Framework to satisfy the OECD/G20 BEPS Project (OECD 2021). As of 31 December 2016, the jurisdiction had approximately 84 information exchange mechanisms (MAAC and TIEAs) in place, three of which had not yet entered into force with other jurisdictions.

## 8.7 Comparative Analysis

### *8.7.1 Tax Evasion*

The objective of the EOIR, AEOI by way of CRS, FATCA and the EUs Code of Conduct standard is to counter tax evasion (and tax avoidance).

[29] See the Mutual Legal Assistance (Tax Matters) Act, 2003.

The OECDs approach through the use of its special task force (the Global Forum), to tackling tax evasion is aimed at enhancing tax transparency by facilitating information exchange between countries worldwide, through the use of the EOIR and AEOI standards. To compel countries worldwide to adopt its standards, the OECD used coercive action by placing countries which failed to comply with its standards on its blacklist (OECD 2010). Placement on its blacklist meant that these countries would face defensive actions taken against them by OECD member states (OECD 2010). This strategy served effective to compel countries worldwide to establish the required measures to implement EOIR and AEOI. The US took a similar approach to increase tax transparency and information reporting on the assets held by US account holders at foreign banks located outside the US (IRS 2020). To force financial institutions globally to take action, the US threat to withhold 30% on payments also proved successful (IRS 2020). The EU also followed suit to get rid of harmful tax practices, particularly among tax havens, with the establishment of its very own blacklist. Countries placed on its list faced counter measures by EU member countries for failure to meet its set standard (Council of the EU 2016). Each of these stance taken by the OECD, US and EU proved successful in compelling countries globally to take action, including The Bahamas, the Cayman Islands, Bermuda and the BVI. These coercive actions forced each jurisdiction to implement the necessary measures to increase tax information exchange with other countries, particularly with US and EU members, to effectively deal with the global threat of tax evasion. The degree to which these standards have been effective in countering tax evasion, largely depended on the active participation of national governments.

### *8.7.2 Transparency*

To increase transparency in their legal systems, the actions taken by the four Caribbean jurisdictions were broadly the same. For example, The Bahamas enacted specific legislation, namely the International Tax Cooperation Act, 2010, and the International Tax Cooperation Act, 2010 (Regulations), which made provisions for the establishment of the legal framework to enable it to carry out the necessary duties under EOIR (OECD 2013). To comply with US FATCA, the jurisdiction passed The Bahamas and The United States of America Foreign Account Tax Compliance Agreement Act, 2015, which provided for the implementation of the Agreement to Improve International Tax Compliance. It also signed a Competent Authority Agreement with the US in accordance with the Model 1 IGA it had in place with the US (OECD 2013). To meet the requirements to implement CRS, the jurisdiction enacted the Automatic Exchange of Financial Account Information Act, 2016, the Automatic Exchange of Financial Account Information Regulations, 2017, and the International Tax Cooperation (Amendment) Act, 2017 (OECD 2013). Together these three Acts facilitated the implementation of CRS. These pieces of legislation enhanced the jurisdictions regulatory framework and also brought about benefits such as enhanced transparency in its legal system overall.

This trend is also observed in other jurisdictions such as the Cayman Islands, Bermuda and the BVI. In the Cayman Islands, for example, the enactment of the Tax Information Authority Law (TIA Law), established the legal framework to empower the jurisdiction to participate in the provision of assistance in tax matters.[30] To implement Model 1 IGA to facilitate FATCA, the Cayman Islands amended its Tax Information Authority Law in 2013 (Cayman Islands Tax Information Authority 2015). It also enacted additional legislation, including the Tax Information Authority (International Tax Compliance) (United States of America) Regulations, 2014 to incorporate US FATCA in its jurisdiction, and the Tax Information Authority (International Tax Compliance) (United Kingdom) Regulations, 2014 to adopt UK FATCA (Cayman Islands Tax Information Authority 2015). To provide for CRS, in addition to the provisions set forth in the TIA Law to facilitate information exchange bilaterally and multilaterally, the Cayman Islands also enacted the Tax Information Authority (International Tax Compliance) (Common Reporting Standard) Regulations, 2015, to place reporting obligations on financial institutions to comply with CRS.[31]

Bermuda also implemented similar measures. The International Cooperation (Tax Information Exchange Agreements) Act, 2005 (ICA), made the necessary provisions for the adoption of EOIR (OECD 2010). This Act, along with the passage of the Multilateral Competent Authority Agreement in 2014, paved the way for the jurisdiction to adopt CRS.

[30] See the Tax Information Authority Law, 2005.

[31] See the Tax Information Authority Law, 2005.

To implement US FATCA, the jurisdiction selected the Model 2 intergovernmental agreement option, and further amended the ICA 2005, to allow it to instruct FFIs to comply with US FATCA Regulations. It also enacted the USA-Bermuda Tax Convention Amendment Act, 2015, to instruct FFIs to comply with the provisions contained in its December 2013 agreement with the US.[32] Bermuda also signed a similar IGA with the UK to facilitate UK FATCA.[33]

The BVI also took a similar approach to implementing EOIR. The legislation used to effect EOIR in the jurisdiction was the Mutual Legal Assistance (Tax Matters) Act, 2003. To implement US FATCA and UK FATCA, the BVI signed a Model 1 IGA with each country.[34] In addition, it amended the Mutual Legal Assistance (Tax Matters) Act, 2003, to make provisions for information exchange automatically or spontaneously under US FATCA and UK FATCA. The BVI also passed the Mutual Legal Assistance (Tax Matters) (No. 4) Order, 2014, to provide for tax information to be exchanged under both IGAs. To implement CRS, the BVI further amended the Mutual Legal Assistance (Tax Matters) Act, 2003, to make provisions for CRS. Additionally, it became a signatory to the Convention on Mutual Administrative Assistance in Tax Matter through an extension by the UK (OECD 2020), which provided the legal basis for the jurisdiction to adopt CRS.

Measures undertaken by offshore centres in the Caribbean to enhance transparency were essentially the same to satisfy the requirements for EOIR, US FATCA, UK FATCA,[35] CRS, and the EU Code of Conduct standard, which were centered on enhancing their legal systems. Exceptions were noted in Bermuda and the BVI, which both used existing laws to adopt the EOIR standard, US FATCA and UK FATCA. Although additional legislations were undertaken by both, more legal measures were

[32] See the USA-Bermuda Tax Convention Amendment Act, 2015.

[33] See the International Cooperation (Tax Information Exchange Agreements) Act, 2005 and the International Cooperation (Tax Information Exchange Agreements) Common Reporting Standard Regulations, 2017.

[34] See the Agreement between the Government of the United States of America and the Government of the British Virgin Islands to Improve Tax Compliance and to Implement FATCA, 2014 and the Agreement between the Government of the United Kingdom of Great Britain and Northern Ireland and the Government of British Virgin Islands to Improve International Tax Compliance, 2013.

[35] UK FATCA was imposed on Overseas Territories and Crown Dependencies of the UK.

implemented by the BVI compared to Bermuda. In the area of transparency, equal legal measures were undertaken by The Bahamas and the Cayman Islands, followed by the BVI and Bermuda to a lesser degree.

### *8.7.3 Preventative Measures*

As part of the implementation of EOIR, the provision of technical assistance to countries came as part of the package to promote a more effective national governance among domestic institutions within jurisdictions. The purpose for backstopping domestic institutions was to strengthen their capacity to ensure the effectiveness of national governments in responding to transnational threats such as tax evasion. Where necessary, recommendations were given by the Global Forum and follow-ups were conducted through a peer review process (PRP), to ensure that appropriate backstopping measures were implemented in required jurisdictions to mitigate the risks associated with tax evasion. As a result, the PRP impacted the legal systems and institutional measures of jurisdictions worldwide, particularly, those in the Caribbean.

In the case of The Bahamas, for example, preventative measures were aimed a placing obligation on entities and other types of legal arrangements to maintain accounting records and hold such records for a minimum period of 5 years (OECD 2013). To implement these requirements, the jurisdiction amended a number of laws including, the Exempted Limited Partnership (Amendment) Act, 2011; the Foundations (Amendment) Act, 2011; the International Business Companies (Amendment) Act, 2011; the Investment Funds (Amendment) Act, 2011; the Purpose Trusts (Amendment) (No. 2) Act, 2011; and the Segregated Accounts Companies (Amendment) Act, 2011 (OECD 2013). The jurisdiction also amended other laws to incorporate these accounting requirements and record maintenance rules for general and limited partnerships, general and foreign companies, and resident trustees. These amendments included: The Companies (Amendment) Act, 2013; the Business License (Amendment) Act, 2013; the Partnerships (Amendment) Act, 2013; and the Trustee (Amendment) Act, 2013 (OECD 2013).

In the case of the Cayman Islands, preventative measures for tax evasion were focused on increasing penalties for failure to comply with maintaining ownership and identity information as it relates to exempted companies, exempted partnerships, and limited partnerships. To effect these amendments, the CIMA introduced the Companies Amendment

Bill, 2012, the Exempted Partnership Amendment Bill, 2012 and the Partnership Amendment Bill, 2012 (OECD 2013). These amendments also impose obligations on exempted companies and partnerships to share ownership and accounting information upon request with the CITIA. Similar amendments were made to the Bank and Trust Companies Law, (2009) to impose sanctions for non-compliance with the Private Trust Companies Regulations on private trust companies, and to the Private Trust Companies Regulations, (2011) for failure to maintain records (OECD 2013).

Bermuda on the other hand received no recommendation from its PRP report. This was due to the recent establishment of institutional measures for corporate service providers in the jurisdiction, which were not previously regulated (OECD 2017).

In the case of the BVI, the area of focus for the prevention of tax evasion was on CDD, specifically, on obtaining the identity of normal and high risk beneficiaries of trusts. To implement this requirement, the BVI amended the Anti-Money Laundering and Terrorist Financing Code of Practice (OECD 2013). Another area of focus was obtaining the identity information on the owners of bearer shares and on the custodian of such shares. These issues were addressed through the Business Companies Act, 2012 (OECD 2013). The last area of concern was the imposition of record keeping requirements for a 5-year period on companies and limited partnerships. This was done by way of an amendment to the Partnership Act and the Mutual Legal Assistance Act (OECD 2013).

With respect to preventative measures related to CRS, such measures are not applicable due to the fact that the peer review process for CRS had not yet been implemented for the period (2010–2016), this analysis takes into consideration. Regarding preventative measures for FATCA and the EU Code of Conduct standard, the method used by the US and EU was mainly coercion to compel countries to act. This method also served as a backstopping mechanism to prevent non-compliance of each standard by countries.

In the area of preventative measures, the initiatives carried out by each jurisdiction to prevent tax evasion were mainly centered on improving CDD measures based on the deficiencies outlined in their respective PRP reports. In the Bahamas, for example, such measures were centered on maintaining accounting records and employing record keeping requirement rules (OECD 2013). Similar to The Bahamas, in the Cayman Islands, preventative measures were focused on maintaining accounting information and also that on the ownership and identity of certain entities, and on sharing such information with the relevant authority (CITIA) upon request. Like the Cayman Islands, backstopping initiatives in the BVI were also aimed at maintaining information, however, such information pertained to the identity of normal and high risk trust beneficiaries, and to the owners and custodians of bearer shares (OECD 2013). Additionally, similar to The Bahamas, measures to adhere to record keeping requirements were also implemented in the BVI (OECD 2013). Unlike the three jurisdictions, however, no deficiencies were highlighted in the Global Forums PRP report for Bermuda, as it had recently implemented a legal framework to regulate entities in its jurisdiction (OECD 2017). As a result, more legal actions were undertaken by The Bahamas, followed by the Cayman Islands, the BVI and Bermuda, which had no deficiencies in this area.

### *8.7.4 National and International Cooperation*

Further to compelling countries to take action to strengthen their legislative systems, and obligating them through the PRP to implement additional measures to mitigate the risks related to tax evasion, countries were also subjected to implement other mechanisms aimed at blending national policies to create a system of “government networks” (Burke-White and Slaughter 2006). This network was aimed at bringing together local government officials within the same country to increase domestic capacity by making effective use of local regulatory systems to achieve common international objectives. In the case of tax evasion, these governmental networks serve as a basis for facilitating the exchange of information with other jurisdictions with whom an agreement was in place, to increase national and international cooperation (Burke-White and Slaughter 2006).

For example, The Bahamas increased its capacity for international cooperation by enacting the International Tax Cooperation Act, 2010, which made provisions for the jurisdiction to implement EOIR (OECD 2013). To satisfy the requirements of US FATCA, the Bahamas Government passed the Agreement to Improve International Tax Compliance with the US Government, which allowed it to exchange information in accordance with the criteria set out in the Model 1 IGA it signed with the US (Bahamas Ministry of Finance 2015). To make provisions to implement CRS, the Bahamas joined the Multilateral Competent Authority

Agreement on Automatic Exchange of Financial Account Information on 13 December 2017, and on 15 December 2017, the jurisdiction became a signatory to the Multilateral Convention on Mutual Administrative Assistance in Tax Matters to comply with the OECD/G20 Base Erosion and Profit Shifting Project (OECD 2020). As of 31 December 2016, The Bahamas had approximately 35 exchange agreements in place with respect to BEPS and 29 TIEAs as of March 2013 with respect to EOIR (Bahamas Ministry of Finance 2015).

In the case of the Cayman Islands, the Monetary Authority Law was passed to allow the jurisdiction to implement EOIR. As of January 2013, the Cayman Islands had 29 TIEAs and one double tax convention in place to conform with the Global Forums requirements. The jurisdiction also passed the Tax Information Authority (International Tax Compliance) (United States of America) Regulations, 2014, for US FATCA, and the Tax Information Authority (International Tax Compliance) (United Kingdom) Regulations, 2014, for UK FATCA (Cayman Islands Tax Information Authority 2015). Both agreements were based on Model 1 IGA. To comply with CRS, the Cayman Islands joined the Multilateral Competent Authority Agreement on Automatic Exchange of Financial Account Information on 29 October 2014. Additionally, the jurisdiction began participating in the Convention on Mutual Administrative Assistance in Tax Matters by extension through the UK on 1 January 2014, which also allowed it to comply with the OECD/G20 Base Erosion and Profit Shifting (BEPS) Project (OECD 2020). As of 31 December 2016, the Cayman Islands had around 35 information exchange mechanisms in place with other jurisdictions. With regard to EOIR, the jurisdiction had approximately 29 TIEAs and one DTC in place, and for CRS, it had about 36 bilateral agreements and arrangements in place under the Convention on Mutual Administrative Assistance in Tax Matters (Cayman Islands Department of International Tax Cooperation 2020).

Bermuda on the other hand, already had the necessary legislation in place to implement and satisfy the requirements under EOIR, through the International Cooperation (Tax Information Exchange Agreements) Act, 2005. This Act, also allowed for the jurisdiction to meet the requirements set out under the US FATCA and UK FATCA. The jurisdiction also signed Model 1 IGA to complete the implementation of US FATCA (OECD 2017). To comply with CRS, the jurisdiction joined the Multilateral Competent Authority Agreement on Automatic Exchange of Financial Account Information on 29 October 2014 (Council of Europe

2017). Bermuda also became party to the Multilateral Convention on Mutual Administrative Assistance in Tax Matters on 1 March 2014, by extension from the UK, which allowed it to comply with the OECD/G20 Base Erosion and Profit Shifting (BEPS) Project (OECD 2020). As of 31 December 2016, the Bermuda had an estimated 45 information exchange mechanisms (bilateral TIEAs and DTAs) in place with other jurisdictions (Government of Bermuda 2020).

The BVI also undertook similar measures. The jurisdiction passed the Mutual Legal Assistance (Tax matters) (Automatic Exchange Information) Order, 2011, which went into force on 1 January 2012. This Order made provisions for the BVI to exchange information with EU members and comply with the criteria for the EOIR standard. To satisfy the requirements for US FATCA, the jurisdiction signed the Agreement to Improve International Tax Compliance with the US on 30 June 2014, and to comply with UK FATCA, it executed the Agreement to Improve International Tax Compliance with the UK on 28 November 2013 (OECD 2013). To meet the criteria for CRS, the jurisdiction became party to the Convention on Mutual Administrative Assistance in Tax Matters on 1 March 2014, and the Multilateral Competent Authorities Agreement (OECD 2020). The Multilateral Convention on Mutual Administrative Assistance in Tax Matters also made provisions for the jurisdiction to meet the OECD/G20 BEPS Project criteria to become party to the Inclusive Framework.

In the area of national and international cooperation, each of the jurisdictions carried out similar measures with the exception of Bermuda. For example, in The Bahamas, the Cayman Islands and the BVI, local legislation was enacted to provide for compliance with the EOIR standard, US FATCA and UK FATCA, in addition to signing agreements with the US and UK. Whereas in Bermuda, existing legislation allowed for each of these standards to be implemented, other than the signing of agreements with the US and UK by the jurisdiction. Although the BVI used an existing piece of law to allow for the EOIR, it still had to enact another piece of legislation to make provisions for its investment business sector to comply with EOIR,[36] and an order[37] to provide for both US FATCA and UK FATCA, in addition to signing an IGA with both jurisdictions.

[36] See the Securities and Investment Business Act, 2010.

[37] See the Mutual Legal Assistance (Tax Matters) (No. 4) Order, 2014.

In terms of satisfying the requirements under CRS and the EU Code of Conduct standard, each jurisdiction took the same approach. To comply with CRS, each implemented the Multilateral Competent Authority Agreement (MCAA), and to meet the requirements under the EU Code of Conduct standard, they all signed the Multilateral Convention on Mutual Administrative Assistance in Tax Matter. The only exception observed was the BVIs application of both the MCAA and the Multilateral Convention to satisfy CRS requirements. In doing so, it also met the requirements for the EU Code of Conduct standard. In the area of national and international cooperation, more legal measures were carried out by the Cayman Islands, followed by The Bahamas, the BVI and Bermuda, which was the least impacted jurisdiction.

## 8.8 Comparative Analysis by Period

The extent to which international standards against tax evasion have impacted the legal systems and institutions in The Bahamas, the Cayman Islands, Bermuda and the BVI, are more evident conducting a comparative review of the legal measures implemented by each jurisdiction at different periods to counter tax evasion. For this analysis, the following periods used are: (i) prior to 2000; (ii) between 2000 and 2009; and (iii) from 2010 to 2016. For example, in The Bahamas, legislation enacted prior to 2000 were very few and were aimed principally at strengthening the jurisdictions confidentiality stance, which in turn encouraged secrecy and opacity.[38] Between 2000 and 2009, due to its placement on the blacklist instituted by the OECD in 2002, the jurisdiction undertook measures to counter tax evasion by signing a commitment letter with the OECD on 15 March 2002. Prior to this act, the jurisdiction had introduced the International Business Companies Act, 2000, which abolished bearer shares. It recalled all bearer shares which were formally issued as of 30 June 2001, and obligated licensees and registered agents to maintain beneficial ownership records for the shares of all IBCs incorporated within its territory, pursuant to the Banks and Trust Companies Regulation Act, and the Financial and Corporate Service Providers Act. However, the impact of international standard has been more evident during the period 2010–2016 with the enactment of a number of legislations. The first of

[38] See the Banks and Trust Companies Regulation Act 1965 and the International Business Companies (IBC) Act, 1989.

these initiated by the jurisdiction was aimed at establishing the legislative framework required to comply with the EOIR standard imposed by the Global Forum. To this effect, The Bahamas enacted two pieces of legislation.[39] It also amended ten existing laws to place obligations on entities and other legal arrangements to keep reliable accounting records and maintain records for a five-year period. The jurisdiction also carried out three amendments and passed three new pieces of laws to establish the framework to initiate international cooperation by way of an effective exchange of information under EOIR, FATCA and CRS. It also signed a number of agreements to effect information exchange under each.

A similar trend is observed in the Cayman Islands. Prior to 2000, legislation enacted by the jurisdiction were principally focused on enhancing confidentiality, which strengthened the jurisdiction stance on secrecy.[40] Between 2000 and 2009, the jurisdiction undertook measures to counter tax evasion by signing a commitment letter with the OECD on 18 March 2000, agreeing to abstain from practicing and introducing any new initiatives that were deemed harmful tax practice in accordance with the OECD Report inter alia.[41] Since then the impact of international standards on the jurisdiction is more clearly observed between 2010 to 2016, in the number of legal measures undertaken by the jurisdiction in response to satisfying the standards set by the Global Forum, the US and EU (see Table 8.2). For example, although legislation existed[42] to provide for the implementation of EOIR, the jurisdiction further amended the TIA law to create an institutional structure by establishing a Competent Authority to provide supervisory oversight and facilitate the exchange of information on request.[43] To facilitate US FATCA and UK FATCA, to make provisions for financial institutions to provide specified information to the Competent Authority in the jurisdiction in accordance with Model I Intergovernmental Agreement, the Cayman Islands enacted two pieces

[39] See Table 8.2.

[40] See Table 8.1. Refer to the 1960 Companies Law, 1960 the Banks and Trust Companies Regulations 1966, the Trust Law 1967, the 1976 Confidential Relationships (Preservation) Law 1976 and its subsequent amendment in 1979.

[41] Refer to Harmful Tax Competition: An Emerging Global Issue.

[42] See the Tax Information Authority Law 2003 (the TIA Law).

[43] See the Tax Information Authority Law (2013 Revision) and the Tax Information Authority (Amendment) Bill, 2014.

of legislation,[44] in addition to two amendments to make the necessary administrative changes to better facilitate US FATCA.[45] The jurisdiction also made a further amendment to the TIA Law to make provisions to implement CRS, allowing for both bilateral and multilateral agreements to be signed with other jurisdictions (OECD 2020). It also enacted legislation imposing CRS reporting obligations on financial institutions in its jurisdiction.[46] To institute preventative measures, the jurisdiction amended numerous existing laws to increase the penalties for failure to comply with maintaining ownership and identity information for entities and other types of legal arrangements.[47] It also imposed new obligations on exempted companies to provide information upon request to the CITIA inter alia.[48] To facilitate international cooperation, the Cayman Islands executed five agreements, two to implement US FATCA and UK FATCA,[49] and the reminder to comply with CRS,[50] one of which allowed for the EU Code of Conduct criteria to be satisfied, whereas an existing law with the jurisdiction provided for EOIR to take place to facilitate international cooperation.

In Bermuda, the same tendency is observed. Prior to 2000, legislation enacted by the jurisdiction were principally focused on confidentiality

[44] See the Tax Information Authority (International Tax Compliance) (United States of America) Regulations, 2014 and the Tax Information Authority (International Tax Compliance) (United Kingdom) Regulations, 2014.

[45] See the Tax Information Authority (International Tax Compliance) (United States of America) (Amendment) Regulations, 2015 and the Tax Information Authority (International Tax Compliance) (United States of America) (Amendment) (No.2) Regulations, 2015.

[46] See the Tax Information Authority (International Tax Compliance) (Common Reporting Standard) Regulations, 2015.

[47] See the Companies Amendment Bill, 2012; the Exempted Partnership Amendment Bill, 2012 and the Partnership Amendment Bill, 2012.

[48] See the Banks and Trust Companies Amendment Bill, 2012; the Private Trust Companies (Amendment) Regulations, 2013; the Private Trust Companies Regulations, 2011 and the Private Trust Companies (Amendment) Regulations, 2013.

[49] See the Tax Information Authority (International Tax Compliance) (United States of America) Regulations, 2014, and The Tax Information Authority (International Tax Compliance) (United Kingdom) Regulations, 2014.

[50] See the Multilateral Competent Authority Agreement on Automatic exchange of Financial Account Information, the Multilateral Competent Authority Agreement on Automatic Exchange of Financial Account Information and the Convention on Mutual Administrative Assistance in Tax Matters by way of extension through the UK, 2014.

**Table 8.1** Bahamas: Legislation implemented to counter tax evasion

| *Prior to 2000* | *Standard* | *2000–2009* | *Standard* | *2010–2016* |
|---|---|---|---|---|
| *Transparency the Bahamas* | | | | |
| Banks and Trust Companies Regulation Act, 1965 | OECD 2002 Blacklist | Commitment letter on 15 March 2002 | OECD EOIR | The International Tax Cooperation Act, 2010 |
| International Business Companies (IBC) Act, 1989 | OECD 2002 Blacklist | The International Business Companies Act, 2000 | OECD EOIR | The International Tax Cooperation Act, 2010 (Regulations) |
| *Preventative measures* | | | | |
| | | | OECD EOIR | The Exempted Limited Partnership (Amendment) Act, 2011 |
| | | | OECD EOIR | The Foundations (Amendment) Act, 2011 |
| | | | OECD EOIR | The International Business Companies (Amendment) Act, 2011 |
| | | | OECD EOIR | The Investment Funds (Amendment) Act, 2011 |
| | | | OECD EOIR | The Purpose Trusts (Amendment) (No. 2) Act, 2011 |
| | | | OECD EOIR | The Segregated Accounts Companies (Amendment) Act, 2011 |
| | | | OECD EOIR | The Companies (Amendment) Act, 2013 |
| | | | OECD EOIR | The Business License (Amendment) Act, 2013 |

(continued)

**Table 8.1** (continued)

| *Prior to 2000* | *Standard* | *2000–2009* | *Standard* | *2010–2016* |
|---|---|---|---|---|
| | | | OECD EOIR | The Partnerships (Amendment) Act, 2013 |
| | | | OECD EOIR | The Trustee (Amendment) Act, 2013 |
| *Effective exchange of information* | | | | |
| | | | OECD EOIR | The International Tax Cooperation (Amendment) Act, 2011 |
| | | | OECD EOIR | 34 EOIR Mechanisms |
| | | | FATCA | The Bahamas and the United States of America Tax Information Exchange Agreement (Amendment) Act, 2011 |
| | | | FATCA | Agreement to Improve International Tax Compliance with the US Government (18 August 2015) |
| | | | FATCA | Competent Authority Agreement (November 2014) |
| | | | FATCA | The Bahamas and The United States of America Foreign Account Tax Compliance Agreement Act, 2015 |

| *Prior to 2000* | *Standard* | *2000–2009* | *Standard* | *2010–2016* |
|---|---|---|---|---|
| | | | CRS | The Automatic Exchange of Financial Account Information Act, 2016 |
| | | | CRS | The Automatic Exchange of Financial Account Information Regulations, 2017 |
| | | | CRS | The International Tax Cooperation (Amendment) Act, 2017 |

*Source* Central Bank of The Bahamas Annual Report, 2001–2017

**Table 8.2** The Cayman Islands: Legislation implemented to counter tax evasion

| *Prior to 2000* | | *2000–2009* | | *2010–2016* |
|---|---|---|---|---|
| *Transparency Cayman Islands* | | | | |
| The 1960 Companies Law | EOIR | TIA Law in 2005 | FATCA | The Tax Information Authority Law (2013 Revision) |
| The Banks and Trust Companies Regulations, 1966 | | | FATCA | The Tax Information Authority (Amendment) Bill, 2014 |
| The Trust Law, 1967 | | | FATCA | Model I Intergovernmental Agreement |
| The Confidential Relationships (Preservation) Law 1976 and its subsequent amendment in 1979 | | | UK FATCA | The Tax Information Authority (International Tax Compliance) (United Kingdom) Regulations, 2014 |
| | | | US FATCA | The Tax Information Authority (International Tax Compliance) (United States of America) Regulations, 2014 |
| The Monetary Authority Law, 1996 | | | US FATCA | The Tax Information Authority (International Tax Compliance) (United States of America) (Amendment) Regulations, 2015 |
| | | | US FATCA | The Tax Information Authority (International Tax Compliance) (United States of America) (Amendment) (No.2) Regulations, 2015 |
| | | | CRS | Tax Information Authority, 2015 |
| | | | CRS | The Tax Information Authority (International Tax Compliance) (Common Reporting Standard) Regulations, 2015 |
| *Prevention* | | | | |

| *Prior to 2000* | *2000–2009* | | *2010–2016* |
|---|---|---|---|
| | | EOIR | The Companies Amendment Bill, 2012 |
| | | EOIR | The Exempted Partnership Amendment Bill, 2012 |
| | | EOIR | The Partnership Amendment Bill, 2012 |
| | | EOIR | The Banks and Trust Companies Amendment Bill ,2012 |
| | | EOIR | The Private Trust Companies Regulations |
| | | EOIR | The Private Trust Companies (Amendment) Regulations, 2013 |
| | | EOIR | The Private Trust Companies Regulations, (2011) |
| | | EOIR | The Private Trust Companies (Amendment) Regulations, 2013 |
| *Effective exchange of information* | | | |
| | | US FATCA | The Tax Information Authority (International Tax Compliance) (United States of America) Regulations, 2014 |
| | | UK FATCA | The Tax Information Authority (International Tax Compliance) (United Kingdom) Regulations, 2014 |
| | | CRS | The Multilateral Competent Authority Agreement on Automatic exchange of Financial Account Information |

(continued)

**Table 8.2** (continued)

| *Prior to 2000* | *2000–2009* | | *2010–2016* |
|---|---|---|---|
| | | CRS | The Multilateral Competent Authority Agreement on Automatic Exchange of Financial Account Information |
| | | CRS | The Convention on Mutual Administrative Assistance in Tax Matters by way of extension through the UK, 2014 |

*Source* Cayman Islands Monetary Authority Annual Report, 2001–2017 to supplement the confidentiality law of the UK, which the jurisdiction followed.[51] Between 2000 and 2009, Bermuda carried out measures to counter tax evasion through the signing of a commitment letter with the OECD on 15 May 2000. In the letter, the jurisdiction agreed to refrain from practicing or introducing any new measures that were deemed harmful tax practice in accordance with the OECD Report inter alia. However, the impact of the standards to counter tax evasion has been more evident between 2010 and 2016.[52] For example, Bermuda used its existing legislation to implement EOIR,[53] and introduced an addition piece of legislation to establish the institutional framework to facilitate EOIR for certain entities.[54] To satisfy the criteria established for US FATCA, the jurisdiction enacted another piece of law to obligate foreign financial institutions to comply with the terms of Model 2 IGA.[55] Bermuda also executed a similar agreement with the UK to provide for information to be exchanged on an automatic basis through UK FATCA. To implement CRS, the jurisdiction passed regulations and executed the Multilateral Competent Authority Agreement, which together with existing legislations, made provisions to facilitate CRS.[56] These measures undertaken by Bermuda allowed for the effective exchange of information by way of EOIR, US FATCA, UK FATCA, CRS and the EU Code of Conduct, with the jurisdiction becoming party to the Multilateral Convention on Mutual Administrative Assistance in Tax Matters by extension from the UK (OECD 2020).

A similar pattern is also evident in the BVI. Prior to 2000, legislation enacted by the jurisdiction limited tax offences to summarily trials. Foreign tax evasion was not recognized in the BVI, even if committed in the jurisdiction.[57] Between 2000 and 2009, the jurisdiction signed a commitment letter with the OECD on 3 April 2002, agreeing not

[51] see Table 8.3.

[52] See Table 8.3

[53] See the International Cooperation (Tax Information Exchange Agreements) Act, 2005.

[54] See the Corporate Service Provider Business Act, 2012.

[55] See the USA-Bermuda Tax Convention Amendment Act, 2015.

[56] See the International Cooperation (Tax Information Exchange Agreements) Act, 2005 and the International Cooperation (Tax Information Exchange Agreements) Common Reporting Standard Regulations, 2017.

[57] See Table 8.4. Refer to the Proceeds of Criminal Conduct Act, 1997.

**Table 8.3** Bermuda: Legislation implemented to counter tax evasion

| *Prior to 2000* | *2000–2009* | | *2010–2016* |
|---|---|---|---|
| *Transparency Bermuda* | | | |
| The Trusts (Special Provisions) Act, 1989 | International Cooperation (Tax Information Exchange Agreements) Act, 2005 | EOIR | International Cooperation (Tax Information Exchange Agreements) Act, 2005 |
| The Companies Act, 1981 | | EOIR | The Corporate Service Provider Business Act, 2012 |
| The Trust Companies Act, 1991 | | EOIR | |
| | | EOIR | |
| | | US and UK FATCA | Model 2 intergovernmental agreement |
| | | US FATCA | The USA-Bermuda Tax Convention Amendment Act, 2015 |
| | | CRS | Multilateral Competent Authority Agreement |
| | | CRS | The International Cooperation (Tax Information Exchange Agreements) Common Reporting Standard Regulations, 2017 |
| | | CRS | The International Cooperation (Tax Information Exchange Agreements) Act, 2005 |
| | | CRS | Guidance Notes |
| *Effective exchange of information* | | | |

| *Prior to 2000* | *2000–2009* | | *2010–2016* |
|---|---|---|---|
| The Criminal Justice (International Cooperation) (Bermuda) Act, 1994 | The International Cooperation (Tax Information Exchange Agreements) Act, 2005 | | |
| The Proceeds of Crime Act, 1997 | | CRS and UK FATCA | The International Cooperation (Tax Information Exchange Agreements) Act, 2005 |
| The Proceeds of Crime (Designated Countries and Territories) Order, 1998 | | UK FATCA | Multilateral Competent Authority Exchange on Automatic exchange of Financial Account Information |
| US Tax Exchange of Information Treaty | | US FATCA | Model 2 intergovernmental agreement |
| The Bermuda (Evidence) Order, 1987 | | EU Code of Conduct | Multilateral Convention on Mutual Administrative Assistance in Tax Matters by extension from the UK |

*Source* Bermuda Monetary Authority Annual Report, 2001–2017 to continue existing practices or implement new initiatives considered as harmful tax practice pursuant to the OECD Report inter alia. The BVI also enacted a piece of legislation to facilitate the exchange of tax-related information between the US and BVI.[58] Subsequent amendments were made to empower the Central Authority to have access to relevant information. However, the impact of the standards established to counter tax evasion is more evident between 2010 and 2016.[59] For example, the BVI used an existing law[60] to implement EOIR, and enacted another piece of legislation to make provisions to establish the regulatory framework for the investment business sector to comply with EOIR.[61] In addition to these measures, the jurisdiction also introduced an Order[62] to provide for the implementation of both US FATCA and UK FATCA, and signed Model I Intergovernmental Agreements for both. To satisfy its obligations under CRS, the jurisdiction become party to the Convention on Mutual Administrative Assistance in Tax Matters by extension from the UK in 2014, a signatory to the Multilateral Competent Authorities Agreement, and passed the Mutual Legal Assistance (Tax Matters) (Amendment) Act, 2015. Further to these measures, it issued guidance notes for US FATCA, UK FATCA and CRS. To enhance its preventative measures under EOIR, the jurisdiction amended several Acts,[63] and also passed two additional Acts.[64] These measures also facilitated the effective exchange of information under US FATCA, UK FATCA and CRS. Through the use of existing legislation, information exchange was provided for under EOIR, and by becoming party to the Multilateral Convention on Mutual Administrative Assistance in Tax Matters by extension from the UK (OECD 2020), the jurisdiction satisfied the criteria for the EU Code of Conduct.

The impact of international policy initiatives against tax evasion on offshore financial centres in the Caribbean is most evident during the period 2010–2016. This conclusion is drawn based on the numerous

[58] See the Mutual Legal Assistance (Tax Matters) Act, 2003.

[59] See Table 8.4

[60] See the Mutual Legal Assistance (Tax Matters) Act, 2003.

[61] See the Securities and Investment Business Act, 2010.

[62] See the Mutual Legal Assistance (Tax Matters) (No. 4) Order, 2014.

[63] See the Anti-Money Laundering and Terrorist Financing Code of Practice and the Business Companies Act.

[64] See the Partnership Act and the Mutual Legal Assistance Act.

**Table 8.4** The BVI: legislation implemented to counter tax evasion

| *Prior to 2000* | *2000–2009* | | *2010–2016* |
|---|---|---|---|
| *Transparency* | | | |
| The Proceeds of Criminal Conduct Act, 1997 | The Mutual Legal Assistance (Tax Matters) Act, 2003 | EOIR | The Mutual Legal Assistance (Tax Matters) Act, 2003 |
| | | EOIR | The Securities and Investment Business Act, 2010 |
| | | US FATCA | Agreement to Improve International Tax Compliance with the US 2014 (Model I IGA) |
| | | UK FATCA | Agreement to Improve International Tax Compliance with the UK 2013 (Model I IGA) |
| | | US FATCA and UK FATCA | Amendment to the Mutual Legal Assistance (Tax Matters) Act, 2003 |
| | | US FATCA and UK FATCA | The Mutual Legal Assistance (Tax Matters) (No. 4) Order, 2014 |
| | | US FATCA and UK FATCA | Guidance Notes |

(continued)

**Table 8.4** (continued)

| *Prior to 2000* | *2000–2009* | | *2010–2016* |
|---|---|---|---|
| | | CRS | The Convention on Mutual Administrative Assistance in Tax Matters by extension from the UK 2014 |
| | | CRS | Signatory to the Multilateral Competent Authorities Agreement |
| | | CRS | The Mutual Legal Assistance (Tax Matters) (Amendment) Act, 2015 |
| | | CRS | Guidance Notes |
| *Prevention* | | | |
| | | EOIR | Amended the Anti-Money Laundering and Terrorist Financing Code of Practice in 2012 |
| | | EOIR | Amended the Business Companies Act in July 2012 |
| | | EOIR | The Partnership Act |
| | | EOIR | The Mutual Legal Assistance Act |
| *Effective exchange of information* | | | |
| | | US FATCA | Agreement to Improve International Tax Compliance with the US |

| *Prior to 2000* | *2000–2009* | | *2010–2016* |
|---|---|---|---|
| | | UK FATCA | Agreement to Improve International Tax Compliance with the UK |
| | | US FATCA and UK FATCA | Amendment to the Mutual Legal Assistance (Tax Matters) Act, 2003 |
| | | US FATCA and UK FATCA | The Mutual Legal Assistance (Tax Matters) (No. 4) Order, 2014 |
| | | US FATCA and UK FATCA | The Mutual Legal Assistance (Tax Matters) Order |
| | | CRS | Signatory to the Multilateral Competent Authorities Agreement |
| | | EU Code of Conduct | Party to the Multilateral Convention on Mutual Administrative Assistance in Tax Matters by extension from the UK |

*Source* BVI Financial Service Commission Annual Report, 2001–2017 legislative measures undertaken by each jurisdiction during this period compared to the other two periods analysed. Overall, the findings conclude that of the four jurisdictions, the BVI has been impacted the most by these internationally policy initiatives, followed by the Cayman Islands, The Bahamas and Bermuda during the period 2010 to 2016, in the order of most to least impacted jurisdictions.

## 8.9 Conclusion

International policy initiatives against tax evasion on the legal systems and institutions of OFCs in the Caribbean region have been beneficial in many ways. An enhancement of their legislative systems is evident, in addition to the creation of institutional frameworks and the implementation of enhanced supervisory, monitory and management systems in each jurisdiction have been observed. Further, the ongoing peer review process ensures that the legal systems and institutional frameworks in these jurisdictions are properly maintained to remain effective in countering tax evasion.

International policy initiatives have also resulted in increased preventative measures, particularly in the area of reporting obligations and due diligence procedures, employed by each jurisdiction as backstopping mechanisms to mitigate the risks associated with tax evasion. These initiatives have also given rise to a significant number of information exchange mechanisms implemented by each jurisdiction, and as a result, have strengthened their capacity to provide mutual legal assistance in international cooperation.

Another outcome observed, as a result of international policy initiatives, is a marked shift from the use of the term "offshore financial centre", to "financial centre", to remove any association with tax evasion by these jurisdictions. The rationale behind this move was that each jurisdiction had undergone the necessary measures to comply with international standards set by the Global Forum, the US and EU. By using the term financial centre, these jurisdictions have been able to project a clean, transparent image equivalent to that of other financial centres located onshore.

However, international policy initiatives have also had adverse effects on these newly termed financial centres. In the next chapter, we will review the consequences of these policy initiatives on the offshore business sector and economies of financial centres in the Caribbean region.

## References


Burke-White, W. W. and Anne-Marie Slaughter. 2006. The Future of International Law is Domestic (or, The European way of law). Faculty Scholarship at Penn Law, 962. https://scholarship.law.upenn.edu/cgi/viewcontent.cgi?article=1958&context=faculty_scholarship.

Cayman Island Monetary Authority. 2013. Annual report 2013. Cayman Island Monetary Authority. https://www.cima.ky/annual-reports.

Cayman Islands Tax Information Authority. 2015. Guidance Notes on the International Tax Compliance Requirements of the Intergovernmental Agreements Between the Cayman Islands and the United States of America and the United Kingdom. Cayman Islands Tax Information Authority. https://www.ditc.ky/wp-content/uploads/2020/06/FATCA_Guidance_Notes.pdf.

Council of Europe. 2016. Criteria and Process Leading to the Establishment of the EU List of Non-Cooperative Jurisdictions for Tax Purposes. Council of the European Union, FISC 187, ECOFIN 1014. https://data.consilium.europa.eu/doc/document/ST-14166-2016-INIT/en/pdf.

Council of Europe. 2017. Notification of Declaration. Public international law and treaty office division. https://rm.coe.int/notification-jj8419c-tr-127-243-united-kingdom-cayman-islands-declarat/1680726f99.

Department of International Tax Cooperation. 2020. Cayman Islands International Exchange of Information Instruments. Department of International Tax Cooperation. https://www.ditc.ky/wp-content/uploads/2020/06/International_Exchange_of_Information_Instruments.pdf.

Government of Bermuda. 2019. The Common Reporting Standard or Automatic Exchange of Financial Account Information in Tax Matters Guidance. Government of Bermuda. https://www.gov.bm/sites/default/files/Bermuda-CRS-Guidance-Version-2.0-2019.pdf.

Government of Bermuda. 2020. Update on Bermuda's Bilateral TIEAs and DTAs. Government of Bermuda. https://www.gov.bm/sites/default/files/Update%20on%20Bermuda%E2%80%99s%20Bilateral%20TIEAs%20and%20DTAs.pdf.

Internal Revenue Service. 2020. FATCA User Guide. Internal Revenue Service. https://www.irs.gov/pub/irs-pdf/p5118.pdf

International Tax Authority. 2019. Guidance Notes on the Common Reporting Standards and Requirements of the Legislation Implementing the Common Reporting Standards in the Virgin Islands. International Tax Authority. https://bviita.vg/file/2020/05/BVI-Updated-Guidance-Notes-for-Common-Reporting-Standards.pdf.

BVI Ministry of Finance. 2015. Guidance Notes on the International Tax Compliance Requirements of the Legislation Implementing the Intergovernmental Agreements between the British Virgin Islands and the United States of America and the United Kingdom to improve international tax

compliance. International Tax Authority. https://bviita.vg/file/2020/05/guidance_notes_20-3-15_-_final_2.pdf.
OECD. 1998. *Harmful Tax Competition an Emerging Global Issue*. OECD Publishing. https://read.oecd-ilibrary.org/taxation/harmful-tax-competition_9789264162945-en#page1.
OECD. 2003. *Peer Review: A Tool for Co-Operation and Change*. OECD Publishing. https://www.oecd-ilibrary.org/docserver/dcr-2002-6-en.pdf?expires=1615360132&id=id&accname=guest&checksum=2B3ECDDF1248AFDF24C14B8A697E5366.
OECD. 2010. *Promoting Transparency and Exchange of Information for Tax Purposes*. OECD Publishing. https://www.oecd.org/newsroom/44431965.pdf.
OECD. 2011a. *Global Forum on Transparency and Exchange of Information for Tax Purposes Peer Reviews: Virgin Islands (British) 2011 (Supplementary Report)*. OECD Publishing. https://www.oecd.org/countries/bermuda/peerreviewreportofbermuda-phase1legalandregulatoryframework.htm.
OECD. 2011b. *Peer Review Report of Bermuda, Phase 1: Legal and Regulatory Framework*. OECD Publishing. https://www.oecd.org/countries/britishvirginislands/global-forum-on-transparency-and-exchange-of-information-for-tax-purposes-peer-reviews-virgin-islands-british-2011-supplementary-be7a5054-en.htm.
OECD. 2012. *The Global Forum on Transparency and Exchange of Information for Tax Purposes Information Brief*. OECD Publishing. https://www.oecd.org/ctp/harmful/43757434.pdf.
OECD. 2013. *Global Forum on Transparency and Exchange of Information for Tax Purposes Peer Reviews: The Bahamas 2013*. OECD Publishing. https://www.oecd-ilibrary.org/fr/taxation/global-forum-on-transparency-and-exchange-of-information-for-tax-purposes-peer-reviews-the-bahamas-2013_9789264202795-en.
OECD. 2014. Standard for Automatic Exchange of Financial Account Information in Tax Matters. OECD Publishing. https://read.oecd-ilibrary.org/taxation/standard-for-automatic-exchange-of-financial-account-information-for-tax-matters_9789264216525-en#page1.
OECD. 2016. *Exchange of Information on Request: Handbook for Peer Reviews 2016–2020*. OECD Publishing. http://www.oecd.org/tax/transparency/global-forum-handbook-2016.pdf.
OECD. 2017. *Global Forum on Transparency and Exchange of Information for Tax Purposes: Bermuda 2017 (Second Round): Peer Review Report on the Exchange of Information on Request*. OECD Publishing. https://www.oecd-ilibrary.org/taxation/global-forum-on-transparency-and-exchange-of-information-for-tax-purposes-bermuda-2017-second-round_9789264280083-en.

OECD. 2018. *Country-by-Country Reporting—Compilation of Peer Review Reports (Phase I): Inclusive Framework on BEPS_ Action 13, OECD/G20 Base Erosion and Profit Shifting Project*. OECD Publishing. https://www.oecd-ilibrary.org/taxation/country-by-country-reporting-compilation-of-peer-review-reports-phase-1_9789264300057-en.

OECD. 2020. *Jurisdictions Participating in the Convention on Mutual Administrative Assistance in Tax Matters Status*. OECD Publishing. https://www.oecd.org/tax/exchange-of-tax-information/Status_of_convention.pdf.

OECD. 2021. *Members of the OECD/G20 Inclusive Framework on BEPS*. OECD Publishing. http://www.oecd.org/tax/beps/inclusive-framework-on-beps-composition.pdf.

The Bahamas Ministry of Finance. 2021. *Tax Information Exchange Agreements (TIEAs)*. Retrieved April 14, 2021. https://www.bahamas.gov.bs/finance.

The Bahamas Ministry of Finance. 2015. Guidance Notes on The International Tax Compliance Requirements of the Intergovernmental Agreement between The Bahamas and the United States of America. The Bahamas Ministry of Finance. https://www.taxreporting.finance.gov.bs/wp-content/uploads/2015/04/Bahamas-FATCA-Guidance-Notes_5-11-2015.pdf.

UK Statutory Instruments. 2014. *The International Tax Compliance (Crown Dependencies and Gibraltar) Regulations 2014*. UK Government, 520. https://www.legislation.gov.uk/uksi/2014/520/made.

US Senate and House of Representatives. 2010. Hiring Incentives to Restore Employment Act. Public law 111–147, US Government. https://www.govinfo.gov/content/pkg/PLAW-111publ147/pdf/PLAW-111publ147.pdf.

CHAPTER 9

# The Consequences of Global Policy Initiatives Against Money Laundering, Terrorist Financing and Tax Evasion on Financial Centres in the Caribbean Region

*Don D. Marshall and Aretha M. Campbell*

## 9.1 Introduction

The aim of this chapter is threefold: (i) it probes the dis-articulation and mis-portrayals of "offshore"; (ii) in the light of the new age of transparency, it raises questions of the knowledge produced about the international financial ecosystem; and (iii) seeks to present an analysis on the summary impact of major re-regulatory measures and compliance standards on a select group of Caribbean international financial centres. The conflation of lawful tax avoidance, illegal tax evasion, money laundering and terrorist finance perpetuates a pernicious geographic privileging and de-privileging in international policy reports and academic writing that mis-align opinions, obscures coercive and imperial relations of power and pollute quests for inclusive input in the shaping of global norms and standards for tackling crimes against the economy.



A. M. Campbell, *Money Laundering, Terrorist Financing, and Tax Evasion*, https://doi.org/10.1007/978-3-030-68876-9_9

## 9.2 "Offshore" and the International Financial Ecosystem

Ultimately we question validity claims of normative rightness and understandability of IFCs, particular those considered OFCs, of which the Commonwealth Caribbean financial centres are often described. These claims, and the employment of such terminology, have become problematic as they animate negative predicates that cling to particular geographies of global finance with distortionary effects on their competitiveness, public policy autonomy and sovereignty rights. To be sure, when we refer to an offshore financial centre/jurisdiction and an onshore financial centre/jurisdiction the intent is to situate all as part of the global geography of shores and jurisdictions offering a range of financial services and products to corporate and high net worth individuals. In a word, these all make up International Financial Centres—across shores in the Global North and those in the Global South although the North–South dualism does not strictly mark the field. For example, Liechtenstein, Monaco, Switzerland and Austria on the one hand, and Guernsey, Isle of Man and Jersey on the other offer discrete financial services while enjoying unique diplomatic relationships within the European Union and Britain, respectively. Within core countries a number of juridical districts or enclaves have been accorded "onshore" status to offer services that mimic those offered by "offshores" that proliferate in the Caribbean, South-east Asia and wider Pacific, as well as the aforementioned in wider Europe. London, Paris, New York, Dubai, Tokyo, Hong Kong and Singapore for example constitute a tier that also offers "offshore-type" services and too form a part of the IFC value chain.

Secondly, we deem it entirely important as knowledge producers in the political economy of capital mobility, to guard against the reproduction of geospatial inequalities. Currently the international financial architecture (IFA) comprises the G7, the G20, the Basel Committee on Banking Supervision, the IMF, the OECD, a slew of Western-based and Western-derived institutions and committees set up by the OECD and the European Commission to tackle global minimum taxation, money laundering and terrorist financing, fiscal and financial transparency and an international solution for taxation of the digital economy. On matters to do with international tax competition and information exchange the IFA interaction structure features a post-panoptic in terms of how financial centres are "watched over". This is in the metaphorical sense where shifting technologies, far-reaching reform efforts and assessment methodologies lead to surveillance regimes of categorizing and exclusion. It is now common place for countries to appear in black, grey and white lists emanating from the OECD while simultaneously differently situated in corresponding listings from the EU. In effect the major bodies feature mechanisms of surveillance power that create and perpetuate the "ban" or scarring of jurisdiction reputation.

While the OECD Global Forum on Transparency and Exchange of Information for Tax Purposes (Global Forum) is an organization that seeks to craft and monitor international tax law, practice and policy, the great powers in global tax governance are—the United States of America, Britain, the OECD and the G20.[1] The international policy directives aimed at increasing transparency and raising regulatory standards are not promoted and enforced across the IFC landscape. Indeed, what obtains is the uneven compliance enforcement across the IFCs, and its discriminatory application across shores, districts, cities and jurisdictions. It is about unequal relations of power and the problem constellation is that of OFCs held to be as lax jurisdictions susceptible to abuse, requiring reforms and surveillance of their re-regulatory frameworks and their Anti-Money Laundering/Combating the Financing of Terrorism (AML/CFT) regimes.

Following the global financial downturn of 2008, unprecedented levels of global scrutiny of the international financial architecture obtained. By 2009, the prior concerns about money laundering and terrorist financing quickly merged with a global concern about volatility and instability in the international financial system. The role of select international financial centres (IFCs)—mainly OFCs—and the conduct of multinational corporations and their executives came under scrutiny. Media stories that treated "corporate tax planning" as minimizing the tax exposure of large corporations affected the social reputation of companies (May 2015). Quite apart from the legal issues relative to the distance between tax avoidance and tax evasion, the political issue around social reputation mattered for corporations. Indeed, with the several sea changes in international tax governance underway, taxation would become part of corporate brand management.

[1] The Global Forum comprises 135 countries and 15 observers representing a number of tax and non-tax global entities.

The two major changes in global tax governance of the second decade of the twenty-first century were piloted by the G20 and the OECD. First, the adoption of an automatic exchange of banking information (AEoI) as a new global standard against tax evasion in 2014, more familiarly known as the OECD's common reporting standard (CRS). The second was the 2015 Base-Erosion and Profit-Sharing (BEPS) project on taxation of multinational companies that aims to constrain their aggressive tax minimizing strategies.

On the pages of academic journals, international policy reports and in multilateral fora some leading scholars and international non-governmental organizations argued that "offshore finance centres" continued to pose systemic risks to international financial stability and their existence threatened to undermine global cooperation in tax governance given their opacity and propensity to engage in calculated ambiguity (Sharman 2010a; Sharman 2010b; May 2015). This echoed the work of several scholars and consultants (Sikka 2003; Suss et al. 2002). Such ambiguity, they add, extends to tax planning techniques such as transfer pricing manipulation and or thin capitalization.[2] Here the concerns refer to complexities associated with the microphysics of power, positionality and interaction between multinational corporations and financial centres. The actors (i.e. financial industry advisors and jurisdiction lawmakers) in such conduit locations understand the co-constitutive nature of their role in facilitating trade flows and price competition. Their erstwhile counterparts in tax revenue departments value the interstitial relations and institutions governing the bilateral tax treaty provisions. Experts within trade law understand that legal advisors will seek to ensure some measure of tax neutrality for their clients. Indeed, the intricate dialectic between offshores and multinational companies is mirrored in the metropolis between onshores and corporates. The presiding contradictions within studies and reports keen on scrutinizing offshores in areas of tax avoidance, together with routine evaluations of the territories' AML/CFT regime while ignoring onshores and banking cities speak to levels of surveillance and techniques of truth production that require

[2] Calculated ambiguity, for Sharman, means "the ability to give diametrically opposed but legally valid answers to the same question from different quarters". For more on this, see the online article, J. Sharman (2010b) 'Offshore and the New International Political Economy'. International campaigns against tax avoidance measures have been led by international NGOs such as Tax Justice Network, Oxfam and Christian Aid.

urgent address. It is either we are worlding offshore or trading in disparagement reflective of the "financial hideaway" discourse of Hollywood and the forms of reporting that followed the release of the "Panama Papers" in 2016 and the "Paradise Papers" in 2017.

Caribbean economies with robust international business sectors are especially reliant on the success of their offshore financial business for the foreign exchange it generates and for how it frames its own domestic tax policy. For each of the four islands we review, the more robust and resilient the offshore business, the greater its refraction in economic growth rates. Negative portrayals of their OFC operations amount to economic threats. Of equal import are the colonial tropes so employed and put to work, both that of the wayward child and deviant feminine (Marshall 2009). This distinguishes the impact of the disparagement for the Caribbean when compared to Liechtenstein, Switzerland, Vanuatu and other financial centres in the Western core and Eurasia. The offshore and tax haven iconography is that of a holiday island resort of regulatory laxity and illicit money. The financial services industry is in turn beset by paradox; Caribbean OFCs are among the leading international financial centres and tax minimization or avoidance is a key element of wealth planning. It is the appeal of financial advisors as they seek to woo high net worth clients. Take the corporate advertiser "Offshore Protection" for instance. Part of the promotion of the City of London's offerings goes—"Though the UK is not commonly associated as an **offshore** tax haven it has most all the same features as a traditional **offshore** jurisdiction, yet remains a modern **financial centre**" (emphasis in the original)?[3] Of course the many conjurings and imaginings of the City of London insulates it from the realm of degeneracy long figured and imaged in colonial portrayals of the Caribbean. London anonymizes money but a regulatory forebearance is presumed.

Too often ignored in critiques of OFCs is the co-constitutive character of financialized capitalism, one where offshore is no longer a place but rather a set of capabilities, mimicked too by onshore financial centres. The scourges of money laundering, tax evasion and terrorist financing require an address of the grey world of finance itself. If its intricate dialectics amount to opacity, again this is much to do with the subject field, the material force of capital markets, financial trading and the several

[3] See International Offshore Jurisdiction Review—UK as a Tax Haven.

competitive tax regimes that abound. Altogether these dynamics were set in motion by postwar accretions arising from inter-imperial contests to facilitate international tax competition, trade and capital flows; quests on the part of multinational firms to "go global"; the bestowal of "science" on risk and financial engineering; capital formation dynamics—all leading to what Gullen describes as the force of complexity and tight coupling (among pairs of countries) at the level of both the network and the node that enhances global risks (Gullen 2015). The kind of offshore-onshore dualism that abides allows the media, financial specialists and global financial bodies to base assumptions on a jurisdiction's perceived classification rather than its regulatory systems, legal framework and performance against legitimate standards.

Historically, the provision of wealth and financial services in the Anglophone Caribbean extend back to the role of interlinkage zones of, for example, Nassau in The Bahamas, Belize, the Cayman Islands, Barbuda and Anguilla, each part of the co-constitutive British Atlantic trading system. There was the warehousing of the ships' cargo, the re-exporting of same, sea-faring activities and conduits of credit, commerce and services that shaped accumulation quests and the socio-economic fabric of those islands not marked by plantation economy features and influences. The predilection towards entrepot services, long a part of the merchant capital legacy of parts of the Anglophone Caribbean, meant some could adapt and emulate the strategy of offering a variety of wealth management services for a non-resident clientele when the opportunities arose in the 1960s and 1970s (Marshall 2009). The decolonization movement of the time featured debates about the secure of self-reliance and the viability of the national option. For British overseas-dependent territories, self-government was infused with identity and economic reproduction questions. The consensus among the islands elites in government, economy and emergent professions held that holiday-resorting and offshore financial services could serve as new niches for economic growth and development (Suss et al. 2002; Williams et al. 2005). Over time, the international financial service sector of The Bahamas, the Cayman Islands, Bermuda and the BVI comprises a range of offshore business to such a degree that it became an important contributor to the gross national product of these countries (IMF 2017).

Prior to 2000, these jurisdictions had operated their offshore financial sectors with nominal or zero taxes on income, no withholding taxes, and prevailing banking confidentiality provisions. These provisions were buttressed by networks of double taxation treaties, mutual legal assistance treaties (MLATs) and continuous updating of legislation in order to refine comparative and competitive advantage and to participate in what was an evolving, harmonized global framework of supervision following the Revised Basle Concordat of 1983. By this time policy harmonization was seen as vital to attenuating waves of deregulation in onshore financial environments, rising concerns of money laundering arising from the narcotics trade and USA concerns with tax evasion. The first MLAT was signed with the Cayman Islands in 1987, then with The Bahamas, Antigua and Barbados. The earliest forms of information exchange agreements appeared in the 1980s where the US applied pressure on Caribbean jurisdictions offering OFC services to agree to information exchange where drug funds were suspected to be in circulation. Prevailing depositor-protection requirements, the political and economic stability of Caribbean OFCs, the low-tax, low-friction ease of establishing business as well as the agility of authorities to adjust to changing international regulations constituted the characteristics that made them popular in attracting capital flows from wealthy individuals and companies from core countries and developing countries in emerging markets.

Increasing concerns surrounding the proliferation of money laundering, terrorist financing and tax evasion and the role presumably played by OFCs in facilitating these financial crimes placed them in the spotlight of global policy initiatives aimed at countering such crimes. As earlier stated, the OECD in 2014 through the Global Forum moved to have adopted, the AEOI or the common reporting standard. This dismantled aspects of banking confidentiality provisions around bank-account data, allowing for greater transparency. This led to a reduction in bank deposits held in IFCs around the world (Ahrens and Bothner 2019; O'Reilly et al. 2019; Johannesen and Zucman 2014; Menkhoff and Miethe 2019; Casi et al. 2018). The Base-Erosion and Profit-Shifting (BEPs) project introduced in 2015 was geared to ensure more adequate taxation of multinational companies. This was the outcome of work undertaken by the Committee on Fiscal Affairs of the OECD in 2011 and 2012, and later the UN Committee of Experts on International Cooperation in Tax Matters (hereafter referred to as the Committee). At root were proposals for a new withholding tax on cross-border business, ergo further taxing rights for "source states". Tax minimizing strategies by IFCs had been figured as eroding the tax base of source countries. The BEPS project has not fetched far-reaching cooperation because it left intact the "arms-length standard" which relies on the multinational company to value the intra-firm transactions between different subsidiaries as if they were being handled by a third independent party at market prices (Lips 2019). Not only was the OECD's Model Double Taxation presented at the Tenth Session discredited, 3000 new bilateral treaties were signed in 2015 alone to both update tax minimizing standards and to take advantage of still dysfunctional onshore legislation. Further, the BVI hosted a BEPS Conference in 2016 featuring a dialogue exchange between Caribbean industry officials and the OECD Global Forum on the question of joining the Inclusive Framework on BEPS. While the consensus held that there was little value of so doing, the BVI and 9 other Caribbean jurisdictions joined the Inclusive Framework citing reputation concerns (Smith 2016). The EU would use membership of the Inclusive Framework for its criteria to determine non-cooperative jurisdictions (read blacklisting) by the end of 2017.

Indeed, international standards placed upon financial centres in the Caribbean region have been instrumental in shaping the offshore business of these centres and beneficial to some degree. They have resulted in major legislative system reforms to ensure conformity with new transparency and accountability standards,[4] and responsibility in the region. The rate of compliance to international standards remains superior to that of onshore jurisdictions (Allred et al. 2017; Findley et al. 2014; Morriss and Henson 2019; Sharman 2010a). Take for example the 2016 EU directive to the UK and its Member States with regard to a beneficial ownership register. This was part of an attempt by the EU to expand the scope of its anti-money laundering directives. The Cayman Islands had for over a decade before then had provisions requiring 10% beneficial ownership to be recorded on all Cayman Island entities. In essence Cayman Island's beneficial ownership information was kept to a higher standard than what was previously obtained in the UK's Criminal Finances Act. The UK standard for disclosure of 25% of beneficial owners through the revised legislation and other intermediate vehicles is not being followed by the Cayman Islands. The regime maintains and insists on the legitimate right to privacy and the register is available only to tax authorities

[4] Ibid.

and law enforcement but not members of the public, journalists or others with "no legitimate interest" (Travers 2017).[5]

However, the cost of the range of compliance measures has come at a high price for jurisdictions in the region caught as they are in battlefields of contending representations and threats of counter measures from the OECD and some of its member countries, such as the USA and EU. The last decade of re-regulatory adjustments has led to some declines in some aspects of offshore business and an uptick in others. The collapse as some scholars and advisors anticipated did not occur (Garcia-Bernardo et al. 2017; IMF 2017). But the impact of the sector has had notable collateral consequences for the economic growth of the region's economies. In Barbados for example, its precipitous decline in economic growth from 2010 onwards was linked to its over-reliance on Canadian business. Changes in Canada's online environment as it relates to de-risking threats saw Canadian banking entities moving to end their correspondent banking relationships with the country and others in the region (CFATF 2019).[6] To determine the results of global policy initiatives on the business of the offshore sector in The Bahamas, the Cayman Islands, Bermuda and the BVI, a comparative quantitative analysis is conducted using data obtained from the central banks and various governing institutions in each country. The segments which will be examined include banking and fiduciary services, corporate services, securities and investment services, and insurance services. A further quantitative analysis is also undertaken to determine the effects of the offshore banking sector on the local economies of these jurisdictions. This analysis will be carried out by examining the impact of the offshore banking sector on data related to employment, spending by offshore operations within the domestic economies, and government revenues generated from the offshore sector in these countries. Conclusions are drawn based on the results of these two analysis.

[5] Apart from an outline of the distinctions, reference is also made to the proceedings in the debate in the House of Lords on 25 April 2017.

[6] For more on this, see, Caribbean Financial Action Task Force, "'De-risking' in the Caribbean Region".

## 9.3 The Impact of International Policy Initiatives

### 9.3.1 *Banking and Fiduciary Services*

#### *9.3.1.1 The Bahamas*

International regulatory initiatives against money laundering, terrorist financing and tax evasion have affected the offshore business of financial centres in the Caribbean in a number of ways. For example, in the banking and fiduciary segment, the region experienced a substantial decline in the number of licensees during the period 2011 to 2019. The Bahamas saw a steady decline which resulted in a 21% (57 licensees) reduction in the number of regulated entities, from 278 licensees in 2011 to 221 licensees in 2019 (Central Bank of The Bahamas (CBB) 2012; CBB 2020). Of this decline, the number of banks fell by 40% (16 licensees), banks and trust companies fell by 29% (20 licensees), while trusts decreased by 13% (21 licensees) (CBB 2012, 2020). These numbers represent a significant decline in a segment, which historically has been the dominant part of the offshore industry for The Bahamas (IMF 2017). According to the CBB, domestic tax reform policies, including the introduction of common reporting standards (CRS) and other regulatory changes, have adversely impacted the assets held by international supervised financial institutions in the jurisdiction (CBB 2019). These regulatory reforms have contributed to some private banks reorganizing or curtailing their offshore business within the jurisdiction (IMF 2017). Based on analysis conducted by the IMF, measures such as consolidation of business services, standardization of processes, outsourcing and automation of various functions were undertaken by licensees to reduce costs (IMF 2017). A total of 23 outsourcing agreements between international banks located in the jurisdiction and parent banks, and in some cases third parties, were approved by the CBB during the period (IMF 2017). A total of 11 mergers and acquisitions took place in the jurisdiction in 2016, and a number of US international banks (12 between 2011 and 2016), and European private banks exited the market (IMF 2017).

While Trusts remained the dominate type of regulated entity in the market in 2019, accounting for 147 licensees, registered Private Trust Companies (PTCs) steadily increased during the period, resulting in 142 licensees at the end of 2019, nearly equivalent to the number of Trust licensees (CBB 2013; CBB 2020). According to The Bahamas Financial Services Board, with PTCs client information is maintained by the Registered Representative only. Such information is shared with the Central

Bank or Bahamas Government only on the basis of a triggered event. This rise in the use of PTCs corresponds to the notable increase in supervised financial institutions (25 at the end of 2019) obtaining approval from the CBB to act as Registered Representatives of PTCs in the jurisdiction (CBB 2020).

#### *9.3.1.2 The Cayman Islands*

In the Cayman Islands, the number of licensed banks and trusts between 2011 and 2018 decreased by 15%. This decline was attributed mainly to licensed banks which significantly decreased by 50% (125 licensees) (CIMA 2012; CIMA 2020). Of this number, the largest decline occurred in Category B,[7] representing a loss of 48% (112 licensed banks). The most significant decrease occurred between 2015 and 2016, resulting in a reduction of 20.7% (38 licensees) (CIMA 2017). Between 2011 and 2017, there was a notable decrease of 11.4% each in licensed banks originating from both North America and Europe (CIMA 2012; CIMA 2018). During the same period, a substantial increase of 19.3% was observed in the number of licensed banks in the jurisdiction originating from the Caribbean and Central America, including Mexico (CIMA 2012; CIMA 2018). Similar to The Bahamas, banks undertook initiatives to consolidate and restructure their operations to reduce costs and enhance their management and governance of operational risks (CDB 2018b; CIMA 2020). According to the Cayman Island Monetary Authority (CIMA) and the Caribbean Development Bank (CDB), changes in global laws and regulations were considered the contributing factors for these reductions. The ongoing de-risking exercise by correspondent banks in the US was also a contributing factor (CIMA 2018). Additionally, given the increasing costs in global compliance, many US and European international banks withdrew from certain markets, product lines, customers and customer segments (CIMA 2018).

Fiduciary services in the Cayman Islands experienced a slight increase during the same period. The total number of trust licenses increased by 6% (22 licenses) from 371 in 2011 to 393 in 2018 (CIMA 2012; CIMA 2019). This increase was attributed mainly to the 130% (73 new licenses) growth in PTCs, and a 66.7% (18 additional licenses) rise in controlled

[7] Category A banks are allowed to conduct business in the international and domestic market, and category B banks are restricted to carrying out international banking and limited domestic business.

subsidiaries between 2011 and 2017 (CIMA 2012; CIMA 2018). These structures, as they are not required to be licensed by law, allow for client's privacy and confidentiality to be maintained through the completion of an initial registration with the CIMA, and the filing of an annual declaration, listing the names and addresses of directors and shareholders of the PTC, either of whom can be nominees or entities (Stoute 2017).

#### 9.3.1.3 *Bermuda*

Bermuda, on the other hand, has a very small banking and fiduciary business sector compared to the other three jurisdictions. During the period 2011 to 2019, the jurisdiction experienced a decrease of 15% (5) in fiduciary licensees from 33 in 2011 to 28 in 2019 (BMA 2012; BMA 2020). This decline was due to two surrendered licenses in 2016, one in 2017, and another in 2018 (BMA 2017; BMA 2018; BMA 2019), though the reason for surrendering these licenses is uncertain. Similar to The Bahamas and the Cayman Islands, Bermuda also experienced growth in the number of registered PTCs. This particular segment grew by 100% during the period, from 6 new PTCs in 2011 to 12 PTCs in 2019 (BMA 2012; BMA 2020). Like the other two jurisdictions, this vehicle offers clients similar features with respect to confidentiality and privacy rights pertaining to information sharing (Carey Olsen 2019).[8]

#### 9.3.1.4 *The BVI*

Similar to the other three jurisdictions, the British Virgin Islands (BVI) also experienced a decline in its banking and fiduciary sector during the period. The total number of banking and fiduciary services licensees fell sharply by 25% (89 licensees), from 351 in 2011 to 262 in 2019 (BVIFSC 2012b; BVIFSC 2020). The reasons for this decline include the cancellation of restricted class II trust licensees, which were restructured as PTCs, in addition to business consolidations between parent entities and their subsidiaries, mainly originating from Europe (BVIFSC 2012b). Another contributing factor was the acquisition of a number of trust companies, in addition to trust and corporate services providers by venture capital firms between 2011 and 2012 (BVIFSC 2013). The most significant decline

[8] For example, documents which are available to the public for inspection, such as the register of directors, officers and members, the law permit corporate entities and nominees to be appointed. Whereas, the register of beneficial ownership is filed with the BMA, therefore, it is not accessible for public inspection.

of 47.4% (212 licensees) occurred in the jurisdiction between 2012 and 2013 (BVIFSC 2013; BVIFSC 2014). According to analysis conducted by the BVI Financial Services Commission, this decline stemmed from mounting pressures to establish a central registry for beneficial owners of corporate entities and trusts, to adhere to the FATF Recommendations and the US Foreign Accounts Tax Compliance Act (FATCA) (BVIFSC 2013). These factors, coupled with the financial centre's negative publicity, adversely affected the jurisdiction's attractiveness for its financial products and services (BVIFSC 2013). Additionally, the jurisdiction also faced challenges and delays during Phase II of the Global Forum Peer Review process, which resulted in intense media scrutiny internationally in connection with the records and systems of two licensed service providers (BVIFSC 2013).

The cancellation of restricted Class II trust license holders also accounted for the decline in 2014, as six of the nine cancellations related to the restricted class II trust licensees (BVIFSC 2015). Three of which continued as PTCs in the BVI, while the others continued in another jurisdiction (BVIFSC 2015). Additionally, a number of licensees were also reclassified to better reflect the nature of their business conducted within the jurisdiction (BVIFSC 2015). Similar to The Bahamas, the Cayman Islands and Bermuda, an increase in the use of PTCs in the jurisdiction over the past four years (BVIFSC 2015) was observed. Between 2015 and 2018 the decline in the banking and fiduciary sector continued at a slower paste. One contributing factor to this decline was due to legislative changes enacted by the jurisdiction to provide for subsidiaries listed under regulated entity to comply with regulatory obligations, including the appointment of directors. This resulted in a reduction of 10% of its licensees listed under regulated firms (BVIFSC 2019).

#### *9.3.1.5 Region*

Overall, the banking and fiduciary sector of the offshore industry in the Caribbean region lost a significant number of licensed entities during the period. The BVI experienced the largest loss of 25% (89 licensees) in this sector (BVIFSC 2012b; BVIFSC 2019), followed by The Bahamas with 21% (57 licensees) decrease (CBB 2012; CBB 2020), the Cayman Islands with 15% decline, of which licensed banks contracted by 50% (125 licensees) (CIMA 2012; CIMA 2019), and Bermuda with a 15% (5 licensees) reduction (BMA 2012; BMA 2020). However, the Cayman Islands experienced a slight growth of 6% (22 licensees) in the number

**Table 9.1** Number of licensed banks & trust companies by jurisdiction

| *Year* | *2011* | *2012* | *2013* | *2014* | *2015* | *2016* | *2017* | *2018* | *2019* | *Change (%)* |
|---|---|---|---|---|---|---|---|---|---|---|
| Bahamas | 278 | 268 | 267 | 254 | 249 | 248 | 242 | 231 | 221 | (21) |
| Cayman | 621 | 625 | 607 | 592 | 597 | 571 | 546 | 526 | n/a | (15) |
| Bermuda | 33 | 30 | 30 | 29 | 29 | 28 | 28 | 27 | 28 | (15) |
| BVI | 351 | 447 | 235 | 226 | 218 | 211 | 206 | 177 | 262 | (25) |

*Source* CBB (2011), CBB (2014), CBB (2017), CBB (2020), CIMA (2015), CIMA (2020), BVIFSC (2012), BVIFSC (2013), BVIFSC (2014), BVIFSC (2015), BVIFSC (2016a), BVIFSC (2017), BVIFSC (2018), BVIFSC (2019), BVIFSC (2020), BMA (2012), BMA (2013), BMA (2014), BMA (2015), BMA (2017), BMA (2018), BMA (2019), BMA (2020)
*Note* The number of licensees for Bermuda reflect the number of trust licensees only

of trust licenses between 2011 and 2018 (CIMA 2012; CIMA 2019), due mainly to an increase use in PTCs. Similar growth in PTCs were also observed in The Bahamas, Bermuda and the BVI. At the end of 2018, the number of licensed banks and trust companies stood at 526 in the Cayman Islands (CIMA 2019), 231 in The Bahamas at the end of 2019 (CBB 2020), 177 in the BVI (BVIFSC 2019) and 28 licensed trusts in Bermuda (BMA 2020; see Table 9.1). Regulatory reforms spurred by international regulatory initiatives related to transparency are cited as the main cause for these declines in three of the four jurisdictions. These reforms resulted in structural changes, such as restructuring and consolidation of banking operations within this particular sector of the offshore industry.

As a result of these international policy initiatives, total assets reported in the offshore sector declined significantly in The Bahamas and the Cayman Islands (IMF 2019).[9] In The Bahamas, the banking and fiduciary services segment represents the principal component of its offshore business (IMF 2017), whereas in the Cayman Islands, assets and liabilities in its specialized niche intra-bank market, accounts as a major component of the sector (IMF 2010).[10] Between 2011 and 2019, total assets held by international banks in The Bahamas sharply declined by an estimated

[9] Data related to asset value is not available for Bermuda and the BVI.

[10] Asset values in relation to the losses of licensees in the banking and fiduciary segment of the offshore sector for the Cayman Islands, Bermuda and the BVI were not available. Note that Cayman Islands and the BVI experienced the largest losses of 41% each compared to 13% in The Bahamas and 6.7% in Bermuda.

66% (US$332b) from its peak of nearly US$500 billion in 2011 (IMF 2017) to B$$167.85 billion in 2019 (CBB 2020). The most substantial decrease in assets of roughly 41.5% (US$207.4b) (CBB 2012; CBB 2013) occurred between 2011 and 2012, while subsequent declines of 20.4% (US$60b) took place between 2012 and 2013 (CBB 2013; CBB 2014). Another significant fall of 25.7% (US$62b) occurred between 2014 and 2015 (CBB 2015; CBB 2016). Per the IMF, increased cooperation between authorities in The Bahamas and OECD countries, in addition to tax amnesty initiatives offered to clients by their home countries, attributed to these declines (IMF 2019).

Similar to The Bahamas, the Cayman Islands also experienced significant losses in its intra-bank market,[11] one of the core components of its offshore business sector (IMF 2019). The total cross-border assets[12] of licensed banks decreased by approximately 59% (US$978b) from US$1.65 trillion in June 2011 and to US$672 billion in December 2018 (CIMA 2012; CIMA 2019). Between the period of June 2011 to June 2018, total cross-border liabilities decreased by 61%, representing a US$1.029 trillion loss for the jurisdiction (CIMA 2012; CIMA 2019). The most significant losses of 16.7% (US$24b) and 29% (US$27b) took place from 2015 to 2016 (CIMA 2016; CIMA 2017) and between 2017 and 2018, respectively (CIMA 2018; CIMA 2019). As most of the banks licensed in the jurisdiction are subsidiaries or branches of onshore international banks, the loss in intra-bank assets and liabilities are attributed to international regulatory reforms designed to incentivize onshore banks to satisfy liquidity requirements and maintain overnight deposits at home, in addition to a reduction in economic growth globally, and legislative reforms aimed at reducing de-risking and restructuring activities by banks (CIMA 2016). As a result of its most recent losses, the jurisdiction fell in rankings from eight to twelfth place in the world in both cross-border assets and cross-border liabilities categories as of 31 December 2018 (CIMA 2019).[13]

[11] Data relating to the market value of assets lost for the banking and fiduciary segment in the Cayman Islands was not available.

[12] Cross-border assets and liabilities consist of cross-border position in both domestic and foreign currency, as well as domestic positions in foreign currency.

[13] Assets for this segment of the offshore financial industry were not available for Bermuda and the BVI.

### 9.3.2 *Corporate Service Providers*

#### 9.3.2.1 *The Bahamas*

Corporate service providers (CPSs) in the region experienced a substantial increase overall, with the exception of the BVI. The Bahamas experienced a steady increase in the total number of registered financial and corporate service providers. During the period, an increase of 22% (64 licensees) was observed from 289 registrants in 2011 to 349 in 2019 (Securities Commission of The Bahamas (SCB) 2013; SCB 2020). Of this sector, CPSs accounted for 60%, while financial services providers represented 30%, and providers offering both services made up 10% of the sector (SCB 2020). Between 2018 and 2019, a 20% (53 licensees) decrease was noted in the number of providers which offered corporate services only (SCB 2019; SCB 2020), in addition to a 36% (17 licensees) reduction in the number of providers which offer both financial and corporate services, whereas a 136% (61 licensee) increase was noted in the number of providers which offered financial services only (SCB 2019; SCB 2020). This shift coincides with the migration away from private banking and wealth management services to investment banking activities by licensees in the jurisdiction (IMF 2017).

#### 9.3.2.2 *The Cayman Islands*

In the Cayman Islands, a similar trend was also observed in the number of corporate services providers, which rose by 54% (49 providers) during the same period (CIMA 2012; CIMA 2020). A steady upward trend was observed in the number of CPSs during the entire period. Additionally, the number of licenses granted to company managers increased by 40% (33 licenses) up from 82 in 2011 to 115 in 2018 (CIMA 2012). Consistent growth was also noted throughout the entire period. This increase corresponds with the growth in investment regulated funds, as corporate vehicles are used to facilitate investments in these, as well as other types of funds.

#### 9.3.2.3 *Bermuda*

In Bermuda, on the other hand, the corporate services sector was previously unregulated. In July 2016, the jurisdiction introduced a new Corporate Service Provider Regulation, which made provisions for the licensing and regulation of CSPs by the Bermuda Monetary Authority (BMA). The results of this new regulation led to the licensing of 62 CSPs in 2017 (BMA 2018). Between 2017 and 2019 the number of CSPs grew by 53% (33 licensees) from 62 in 2017 to 95 in 2019 (BMA 2018; BMA 2020). This growth coincides with a notable increase in the investment and insurance sectors between 2018 and 2019 in the jurisdiction (BMA 2020).

#### *9.3.2.4 The BVI*

Whereas in the BVI, based on available data, the number of CPSs in the jurisdiction stood at 33 licensees in 2014, which represented a 65% increase over the previous year (CIMA 2015). However, the most important observation was in the number of company incorporations which sharply declined in the jurisdiction. The total number of BVI Business Company Incorporations significantly fell by 60% during the period 2011 to 2019, resulting in a total decreased of 38,579 incorporations (BVIFSC 2012b; BVIFSC 2020). Three notable periods of decline took place between 2012 and 2013 with an estimated fall of 16.8% (10,770 incorporations) (BVIFSC 2013; BVIFSC 2014), between 2015 and 2016 resulting in a 29% (12,983 incorporations) reduction (BVIFSC 2016a; BVIFSC 2017), and between 2018 and 2019 leading to a 30% (11,265 incorporations) drop (BVIFSC 2019; BVIFSC 2020). The decline noted in 2011 and 2012 was attributed to slowed growth in new company registrations globally (BVIFSC 2012b; BVIFSC 2013). Per the BVI Financial Services Commission, growth was noted in only one offshore jurisdiction, which recorded a 1% increase year on year. Subsequent declines between 2015 and 2016 were partly attributed to the enactment of the BVI Business Companies (Amendment) Act, 2015, and the Anti-Money Laundering (Amendment) Regulations, 2015, which subjected licensees to obtain beneficial ownership information (BVIFSC 2017). Whereas between 2018 and 2019, this decline was due to the new economic substance regulations which subjected companies to maintain a physical presence in the jurisdiction (Caribbean Development Bank (CDB) 2020).

According to analysis by the BVI Financial Services Commission, other contributing factors, which affected both trusts and corporate service providers alike, included the implementation of a new Secure Search (Beneficial Ownership) System Act (BVIFCS 2018), the signing of a MMOU with the Group of International Financial Centre Supervisors (GIFCS), and the introduction of new fees, in addition to an increase in several existing fees in the jurisdiction in 2017 (BVIFSC 2018). Other factors included the passage of Hurricane Irma and Hurricane Maria,

**Table 9.2** Number of corporate service licenses by jurisdiction

| *Year* | *2011* | *2012* | *2013* | *2014* | *2015* | *2016* | *2017* | *2018* | *2019* | *Change (%)* |
|---|---|---|---|---|---|---|---|---|---|---|
| Bahamas | 289 | 289 | 309 | 311 | 322 | 325 | 341 | 353 | n/a | 22 |
| Cayman Islands | 91 | 97 | 108 | 113 | 119 | 133 | 143 | 140 | n/a | 54 |
| Bermudà | n/a | n/a | n/a | n/a | n/a | n/a | 62 | 92 | 95 | 53 |
| BVI | 18 | 21 | 20 | 33 | n/a | n/a | n/a | n/a | n/a | 83 |

*Source* CIMA (2019), SCB (2011), SCB (2014), SCB (2017), SCB (2020), BMA (2017), BMA (2020)

which both disrupted services offered in the financial sector (BVIFSC 2018). As a result of these declines, company revenues generated from incorporations during the period decreased by 9% (US$16.4m), from US$191.7 million in 2011, to US$175.3 million in 2018 (BVIFSC 2012b; CDB 2019).

*9.3.2.5 Region*

Region wise, increased growth in the number of licensees was observed overall in three of the four jurisdictions.[14] The Bahamas experienced the most significant growth of 22% (64) new licensees (SCB 2020), followed by the Cayman Islands with an increase of 54% (49) new CSPs (CIMA 2019), whereas Bermuda's initiative to regulate its CSP's sector resulted in the registration of 62 CSPs in July 2016, and a 53% (33) growth between 2016 and 2019 (BMA 2017; BMA 2020). On the other hand, based on available data, 33 licensees were noted in the BVI in 2014 (BVIFSC 2015).[15] However, the BVI experienced a significant decrease of 60% in the number of company incorporations during the period 2011 to 2019, its main product offering. This decline is attributed to global anti-money laundering rules and the EU's economic substance regulations. As at the end of 2017, The Bahamas accounted for 353 licensed CSPs (SCB 2020), the Cayman Islands held 140 licensees (CIMA 2019), Bermuda stood at 95 licensees (BMA 2020) and the BVI accounted for 33 licensees as at the end of 2014 (BVIFSC 2015, see Table 9.2).

[14] This data was not available for the BVI.

[15] Data for the remaining period was not available.

### 9.3.3 Securities and Investment Services

#### *9.3.3.1 The Bahamas*

A marked shift from banking and fiduciary services towards the securities and investments sector was explicitly observed in The Bahamas, the Cayman Islands, and the BVI. The securities segment in The Bahamas expanded during the period 2011 to 2019. A noted increase of 24% (32) in the number of registered securities firms was observed from 132 in 2011 to 164 in 2019 (SCB 2013; SCB 2020). The total number of individuals registered under the Securities Industry Regulation (SIR) was 1095 as of 31 December 2019, in comparison with 471 at the end of 2012, representing an increase of approximately 132% (624 persons) (SCB 2013; SCB 2020). These numbers reflect the shift in private banking and wealth management services to investment banking activities (IMF 2017), specifically, a move from private banking to more specialized non-bank wealth management products, such as professional funds and Specific Mandate Alternative Regulatory Test Funds (SMART Funds) (IMF 2017). For example, SMART Funds increased by 51% (157) from 305 in 2011 to 462 in 2019 (SCB 2012; SCB 2013). These numbers also coincide with the increase in PTCs and family offices in the jurisdiction (IMF 2017). Overall, a 13% (90) increase in the number of investment funds licensed and registered in the jurisdiction was observed during the period 2011 to 2019 (SCB 2012; SCB 2013). An increase in net assets of 7% (B$8.9b) was also noted between 2013 and 2016, from B$127.9 billion to B$136.8 billion, respectively (SCB 2014; SCB 2017).[16] Per the IMF, it is unclear whether global regulatory changes or market innovation contributed to these increases.

#### *9.3.3.2 The Cayman Islands*

The securities and investment sector in the Cayman Islands also experienced an overall increase. In the securities investment category, the total number of investment regulated funds increased by 19% (1734 funds) between 2011 and 2018 (CIMA 2012; CIMA 2019). Of this increase, hedge funds contributed the most with an estimated increase of 50%, followed by equity funds with a 45% increase. Overall, total assets rose by 31% (US$1.745t) (CIMA 2012; CIMA 2019).

[16] This information is not available for 2017, 2018 and 2019.

In the investment category, the total number of regulated (mutual) funds registered with the CIMA rose by 17% (1583 funds) during the same period (CIMA 2012; CIMA 2019). Of this increase, Master Funds accounted for 70% (2946 new funds) between 2012 and 2018 (CIMA 2013; CIMA 2019). Total asset value corresponded with a significant increase of 203% (US$4.9t) from US$2.4 trillion in 2011 to US$7.35 trillion in 2018. The most significant rise of 92% (US$2.4t) was observed between 2012 and 2013. This increase was due in part to the signing of the European Securities Markets Authority Cooperation Agreement between securities regulators of the European Union (EU) including Croatia, Liechtenstein, Iceland and Norway, the Cayman Islands, and 33 other countries on 22 May, 2013 (CIMA 2014). This Agreement allowed for Cayman Islands funds to continue to be promoted in Europe upon commencement of the unified regulatory regime for alternative investment fund managers and funds within the EU (CIMA 2014).

At the end of 2018, the number of mutual funds stood at 10,992, representing a 4% (433 funds) increase over 2017 (CIMA 2019). Total assets also increased by 6%, while net assets fell by 3% over the previous year (CIMA 2019). The jurisdiction reported a net loss of US$30 billion, which was offset by asset appreciation during the course of the year, in addition to a decline of US$117 billion in total net assets and dividends, which was US$2 billon lower compared to 2017 (CIMA 2019). According to CIMA, this decline occurred due to a sharp selloff across asset classes during the last quarter of 2018, amidst increasing concerns related to the tensions in US-China trade, tightening of financial conditions, and growing indications of a slowing global economy, as an estimated 69% of Cayman Islands funds are managed by US firms (CIMA 2019).[17] By the end of December, the jurisdiction remained the premier choice for the domiciliation of funds (CIMA 2018).

#### 9.3.3.3 *Bermuda*

Unlike The Bahamas and the Cayman Islands, Bermuda experienced a decline in the investment business during the period. A 15% (9) decrease in the number of registered licensees was observed between 2012 and 2019 (BMA 2012; BMA 2020). The total number of investment funds

[17] Per the CIMA, an estimated 69% of funds based in the Cayman Islands are managed by US firms. Together, New York and Delaware make up 48% (3,425) of all (4,972) US managed funds.

declined substantially by 32% (247 funds) from 872 in 2011 to 638 in 2019 (BMA 2012; BMA 2020). Aggregate total assets held under management also fell by 8% (US$15m) during the period (BMA 2013). According to the Bermuda Monetary Authority, this decrease was due to the decline in the financial markets during the latter half of 2011, as a result of the Eurozone debt crisis (BMA 2013).

The number of investment funds continued to decrease steadily during the period up to 2018, despite initiatives undertaken by the jurisdiction to boost its investment business.[18] Of the aggregate asset under management, 75% related to investors in the European Union (BMA 2016). Between 2018 and 2019, a 24% (125 funds) increase in the number of investment funds was observed. Net asset value of investment funds corresponded with an increase of 11% (US$18m), which represents an overall increase of 2.98% in the value of total net assets. This increase is attributed mainly to strong profitable performance, in addition to an increase in subscriptions (BMA 2020). During this time, of the total aggregate asset under management, 73% pertained to clients in the European Union (BMA 2020).

#### *9.3.3.4 The BVI*

Similar to The Bahamas and the Cayman Islands, the BVI also experienced an increase in its securities and investment sector between 2011 and 2019. The total number of BVI funds registered and recognized in the jurisdiction rose by 29% (337 funds) (BVIFSC 2012b; BVIFSC 2020). A large increase of 59% (827 funds) was noted between 2012 and 2013 (BVIFSC 2013; BVIFSC 2014). According to the BVI Financial Service Commission, this increase was due to the Approved Investment Managers (AIM) initiative introduced in the jurisdiction during the latter part of 2012 (BVIFSC 2013). The AIM initiative provided investment managers with an alternative option to conduct investment business with less regulatory restrictions. A significant number of new licenses were issued due to its popularity per the Commission. However, notable declines of 21%

[18] The Investment Funds Amendment Act 2013 was enacted, which made provisions for two new classes of exempted funds, aimed to facilitate speed to the market. The jurisdiction also made the European Union's Alternative Investment Fund Managers Directive effective during the previous year and also signed a cooperative agreement with EU Member States to allow for its fund and fund managers to continue to conduct business in the EU without any competitive disadvantages.

(419 funds) between 2015 and 2016 (BVIFSC 2016a; BVIFSC 2017) and 7.1% (115 funds) (BVIFSC 2017; BVIFSC 2018) between 2016 and 2017 were observed, although the reasons for these declines were not noted by the Commission. In terms of new investment funds, a significant increase of 40% (44 funds) occurred between 2012 and 2013, which coincides with the introduction of the AIM initiative by the Commission during the period (BVIFSC 2013; BVIFSC 2014). Although small declines were noted between 2015 and 2016 by 12.1% (20 funds), and from 2016 to 2017 by 6.2% (9 funds) (BVIFSC 2016a; BVIFSC 2017), the total number of investment funds incorporated during the period increased by 13% (14 funds) (BVIFSC 2012b; BVIFSC 2020).

Per the Commission, the increased growth in investment funds came at the expense of the jurisdiction's traditional investment business, particularly mutual funds. Between 2011 and 2018, mutual funds declined significantly by 43% (1125 funds) in the jurisdiction (BVIFSC 2012b; BVIFSC 2019). A notable decrease of 10.5% (272 funds) was observed between 2011 and 2012 (BVIFSC 2012b; BVIFSC 2013). This declined was attributed in part to the global underperformance of fund, due to the increasing uncertainty related to the Eurozone crisis (BVIFSC 2012b). Another contributing factor was investors preferences, in addition to their demand for liquidity and transparency, which contributed to the marginal growth experienced in the industry (BVIFSC 2012b). These factors depressed new business in the local market, however, existing business was described as buoyant, particularly in the private sector, due to compliance, reorganizations and closures (BVIFSC 2012b). Liquidations and cancellations also contributed to the decline in the total number of funds in the jurisdiction (BVIFSC 2012b). Some of the main factors which attributed to these measures included the global reduction in new hedge fund startups, loss of confidence in the investment space by the market, the demand for more transparent products, increased competition from new markets in other offshore centres and in Europe, and the perception of a newly enhanced regulatory regime (BVIFSC 2012b). In 2017, although the number of cancellations were lower than the previous year, they were substantially higher than the number of new funds and recognized funds applications. This resulted in a continued decline in the number of regulated funds (BVIFSC 2018).

As mutual funds continue to be the largest category of licenses granted in the investment business, annual revenues declined consecutively for the fourth year, due to the fall in the number of mutual funds (BVIFSC

2017). However, as a result of fines levied against licensees by the Commissions' enforcement team for failure to file financial statements among other breeches, actual revenues exceeded the projected revenues (US$2,702,700) for the Enforcement Division (BVIFSC 2017).

#### *9.3.3.5 Region*

Overall, the region experienced tremendous growth in the securities and investment sectors of their offshore financial industry with the exception of Bermuda, and to a greater degree, the BVI. The most notable increases in the securities segment were observed in the Cayman Islands with a growth of 19% (1734 funds) in the total number of investment regulated funds between 2011 and 2018 (CIMA 2012; CIMA 2019). Increased growth was also observed in the BVI of 29% (337 funds) (BVIFSC 2012b; BVIFSC 2020), and in The Bahamas by 13% (90 funds) during the period 2011 to 2019, whereas in Bermuda, a substantial decline of 32% (247 funds) was observed during the same period.

In terms of mutual funds, the most significant increase was noted in the Cayman Islands with an estimated growth of 17% (1583 funds) between 2011 and 2018 (CIMA 2012; CIMA 2019). In contrast, the BVI experienced a significant decline of 43% (1125 funds) between 2011 and 2019 (BVIFSC 2012b; BVIFSC 2019). At the end of 2018, the total number of regulated funds in the Cayman Islands stood at 10,992 (CIMA 2019), which was 7 times that of the BVI which held 1502 funds (BVIFSC 2019), 14 times that of The Bahamas which had 803 funds (SCB 2019), and 21 times that of Bermuda with 525 funds (see Table 9.3) (BMA 2019). Although the IMF notes that it is not certain whether the increase in The Bahamas is attributed to regulatory changes or product innovation, per the CBB, the increase is due in part to the

**Table 9.3** Number of regulated funds by jurisdiction

| *Year* | *2011* | *2012* | *2013* | *2014* | *2015* | *2016* | *2017* | *2018* | *Change (%)* |
|---|---|---|---|---|---|---|---|---|---|
| Bahamas | 713 | 652 | 750 | 830 | 885 | 859 | 812 | 803 | 13 |
| Cayman | 9258 | 10,841 | 11,379 | 11,010 | 10,940 | 10,586 | 10,554 | 10,992 | 19 |
| Bermuda | 772 | 762 | 698 | 647 | 630 | 567 | 560 | 525 | (32) |
| BVI | 1160 | 1411 | 2238 | 2142 | 2033 | 1614 | 1499 | 1497 | 29 |

*Source* CIMA (2016), CIMA (2019)

**Table 9.4** Net assets of investment funds (US$ in trillions)

| *Year* | *2011* | *2012* | *2013* | *2014* | *2015* | *2016* | *2017* | *2018* | *2019* | *Change (%)* |
|---|---|---|---|---|---|---|---|---|---|---|
| Bahamas | n/a | n/a | 0,128 | 0,135 | 0,200 | 0,137 | n/a | n/a | n/a | 7 |
| Cayman | 2,423 | 2,599 | 5,000 | 5,605 | 5,707 | 6,142 | 6,936 | 7,35 | n/a | 203 |
| Bermuda | 0,159 | 0,187 | 0,176 | 0,164 | 0,144 | 0,137 | 0,161 | 0,157 | 0,175 | 11 |
| BVI | n/a | n/a | n/a | n/a | n/a | n/a | n/a | n/a | n/a | n/a |

*Source* SCB (2014), SCB (2017), CIMA (2019), BMA (2011), BMA (2014), BMA (2017), BMA (2020)

demand for its SMART Fund, particularly among Brazilian clients. With regard to the Cayman Island and the BVI signing on to the AIM initiative, global market conditions are attributed to their growth during the period, whereas Bermuda, although it successfully introduced the AIM mandate in its jurisdiction, financial market conditions due to the Eurozone debit crisis, resulted in a substantial decline, given its high concentration of roughly 75% in AUM which pertained to European clients.

Significant growth in asset value was also observed in the region. In the Cayman Islands asset values grew by roughly 203% (US$4.9 trillion) (CIMA 2013; CIMA 2020). Of this amount, hedge funds accounted for US$1.3 trillion, equity funds for US$415 billion, funds of funds for US$113 billion and fixed income funds for US$83 billion (CIMA 2013; CIMA 2020). In The Bahamas, net assets increased by 7% (B$8.9b) between 2013 and 2016 (SCB 2014; SCB 2017),[19] whereas in Bermuda, despite the decline in the number of funds held by the jurisdiction during the period, the total asset value of regulated funds increased by 10% (BD$16m) (BMA 2012; BMA 2020). At the end of 2018, the Cayman Islands held net assets valued at approximately US$7.35 trillion (CIMA 2019). The Bahamas at the end of 2016 held an estimated US$137 billion in assets (SCB 2017), and Bermuda held roughly US$175 billion in assets at the end of 2019 (BMA 2020; see Table 9.4).[20]

[19] Net asset values are not available for 2017, 2018 and 2019.

[20] Asset value data was not available for the BVI. Asset value was not available for the BVI. The assets values noted for The Bahamas and Bermuda are indicated in local currency. As both currencies are pegged (1 to 1) with the US dollar, for comparative purposes, the assets values for these two jurisdictions are noted in US dollars.

### 9.3.4 *Insurance Services*

#### *9.3.4.1 The Bahamas*

The insurance segment of the offshore financial sector in the region experienced significant growth, particularly in Bermuda, where it is a principal component of its offshore business. In The Bahamas, the total number of captive insurers increased by 1560%, from 10 captive insurers in 2011 to 166 captive insurers in 2019 (ICB 2012; ICB 2020). Between 2013 and 2014, a notable growth of 43% was observed. This growth is attributed mainly to the popularity of the captive product as a cost-efficient alternative for small and medium size businesses, which use the vehicle to manage and control the insurable risks of their parent entities (the Insurance Commission of The Bahamas (ICB) 2018). Between 2017 and 2019, the sector experienced various small declines in the number of captive insurers. Per the Insurance Commission of The Bahamas, these declines were due to the challenges faced in the international insurance market as a result of global tax reform initiatives (ICB 2019). Despite these declines, total assets held by external insurers increased by 87% (US$616 million), from US$713.5 million in 2011 to US$1.33 billion in 2018 (ICB 2012; ICB 2020).

#### *9.3.4.2 The Cayman Islands*

Unlike The Bahamas, the insurance sector in the Cayman Islands experienced a small decline of 3% (22) in the number of insurance licensees during the same period. Licensees fell by 5% (41) between 2014 and 2015. This decline is attributed to an exercise carried out by the CIMA to cancel licenses which were previously surrendered (CIMA 2015). Between 2015 and 2016, the number of licensees fell by 2% (14) due to slowed growth experienced in the sector caused by challenges related to increased competition in the captive insurance market by newer captives domiciles in the US (CIMA 2016). The introduction of the Patient Protection and Affordable Care Act in the US, coupled with a continued soft market, and uncertainty surrounding the US elections, further contributed to this downward trend (CIMA 2016). This trend continued between 2016 and 2017. The reasons cited by the CIMA for this decline included novation/commutation of liabilities, ceding/reinsurance companies, maturing catastrophe bonds, and mergers and acquisitions by healthcare captives (CIMA 2018). Between 2017 and 2018, a slight increase was noted in the number of insurance licensees.

This increase was attributed to the formation of companies in Class B(iii) insurers category, which allows insurers to underwrite unrelated business, as well as incorporation of commercial reinsurance companies as start-ups, in addition to re-domestication of insurers to the jurisdiction (CIMA 2019). Between 2018 and 2019, a small decline was noted in the number of captives, due to a reconciliation exercise undertaken by the CIMA around that time (CIMA 2020).

Despite these declines, total assets of international insurer licensees increased by 20% (US$11.5b) during the period (CIMA 2020). This increase allowed the jurisdiction to claim second place as the largest domicile for captive insurance companies, and the leading domicile for healthcare captives in the world (CIMA 2020).

#### *9.3.4.3 Bermuda*

Similar to The Bahamas, Bermuda's insurance sector also experienced substantial growth. An estimated growth of 30% (292) in the number of insurance licensees was noted between 2011 and 2018. This growth is attributed to an increase in the number of new registered insurers in the jurisdiction (Bermuda Insurance-Linked Securities (ILS) Market Report (BILSMR) 2013), but mainly to a surge of 21% in the number of special purpose insurers (SPI) in the market (BILSMR 2013). In 2013, the number of new captives doubled the recorded number in 2012, while a record number of SPIs was established (BMA 2014). Per the BMA, the rapid growth in SPIs registration is attributed to Bermuda's rising reputation as a global centre for the formation, listing and servicing of insurance-linked securities (ILS), which represented US$15.1 billion (60%) of the global ILS issuance by the end of 2014 (BILSMR 2014). Another factor mentioned by the BMA pertains to the fact that Bermuda's ILS is directly linked to its stock exchange market (BSX). In April 2013, the BSX introduced its NASDAQ OMX's X-stream trading platform, which allowed it to expand its trading to over 70 marketplaces in 50 countries (BMA 2014). This new trading platform further enhanced the jurisdiction's position in this space.

Another factor noted by the BMA is that Bermuda obtained its qualified jurisdiction status by the National Association of Insurance Commissioners (NAIC) at the end of 2013. This approval allows reinsurers licensed and domiciled in the jurisdiction to be eligible for reduced collateral requirements in accordance with the NAIC Credit for Reinsurance Model Law (BMA 2014). The NAIC qualified jurisdiction status became effective on 1 January 2015 (BMA 2016). Additionally, the jurisdiction also signed cooperation agreements with Member States of the EU in 2013, making way for its commercial insurance and reinsurance sector to be equated as equivalent to Europe's Solvency II system, which went into force on 1 January 2016 (BMA 2016). This ruling removed any competitive disadvantages for the jurisdiction's licensees to carryout cross-border business in the EU. Another point noted by the BMA is that the jurisdiction was not added to the EU's blacklist in 2017 (BMA 2018). Between 2015 and 2016, ISL issuance contracted due in part to a global decline in ISL issuance, and a migration towards the use of "cat bond light" platforms (BILSMR 2016; BILSMR 2017). This resulted in the overall number of insurance licenses declining by 8% (96) (BMA 2016; BMA 2017), however, growth continued in subsequent years by 6% (93 licenses) and 5% (64 licenses) respectively, due to ISL issuances (BILSMR 2018; BMA 2019).

Insurance-linked securities showed tremendous growth equivalent to 450% (US$7.2b), from US$1.6 billion in 2011 to US$8.8 billion in 2018 (BMA 2012; BMA 2019). The total net premiums of captive insurers corresponded with an increase of 127% (US$136.4b) (BMA 2012; BMA 2019), in addition to total assets by 117% (US$528b) during the period (BMA 2012; BMA 2019). The jurisdiction remains the world's leader in the issuance of catastrophe bonds with insurance-linked securities (BILSMR 2018).

#### *9.3.4.4 The BVI*

Like the Cayman Islands, the BVI also experienced a decline in its insurance sector between 2011 and 2019, however the decline in the BVI was significant. The total number of licensed captive insurers substantially fell by 66% (115 licensees) during the period (BVIFSC 2012b; BVIFSC 2020). The captive market consists mainly of single captive insurance companies originating from the USA (BVIFSC 2012b). The declined noted in 2011 was due to the re-domiciliation of a number of licensees to onshore and offshore jurisdictions, in addition to the liquidations and cancellation of others (BVIFSC 2012b). The market proved difficult for smaller insurers due in part to anomalies contained in the Insurance Act 2008, which entered into force on 1 February 2010 (BVIFSC 2012b). At that time, amendments were proposed to correct them. The captive market continued to experience challenges in 2012, as the number of cancellations surpassed the number of new licenses, resulting in a further decline in the market (BVIFSC 2013). This decline continued in 2013, as cancellations continued due mainly to entities liquidating or re-domiciling to other jurisdictions (BVIFSC 2014).

In 2015, limited growth was recorded due to the reduced applications in the number of new captive insurers (BVIFSC 2016a). Between 2016 and 2017, a notable decrease of 19% (26 licensees) was observed (BVIFSC 2017; BVIFSC 2018). This decrease was attributed mainly to external market forces (BVIFSC 2017). By that time, the jurisdiction had amended its Insurance Act 2008, which provided additional flexibility to captive insurers, and at the same time, introduced two new classes of captives (BVIFSC 2017). Between 2017 and 2018, the number of licensees in the captive market continued to decline due in part to the slow reception to these amendments (BVIFSC 2018; BVIFSC 2019). This trend continued between 2018 and 2019 due to the same reason (BMA 2019; BMA 2020).

#### 9.3.4.5 *Region*

The region experienced significant growth in the offshore insurance segment with exception to the Cayman Islands and the BVI. The number of licensees in Bermuda's insurance sector grew by 30% (292 licensees) between 2011 and 2018 (BMA 2012; BMA 2019), compared to 1560% (156 licensees) in The Bahamas (ICB 2012; ICB 2020), whereas losses of 3% (22 licensees) occurred in the Cayman Islands between 2011 and 2018 (CIMA 2012; CIMA 2019), and 66% (115 licensees) in the BVI between 2011 and 2019 (BVIFSC 2012b; BVIFSC 2019). At the end of 2018, the number of licensees in Bermuda was 1262 (BMA 2019), in the Cayman Islands 703 (CIMA 2019), and in The Bahamas 166 (ICB, 2020), followed by the BVI with 59 licensees at the end of 2019 (BVIFSC 2019; see Table 9.5).

Several reasons which attributed to Bermuda's growth in this particular sector included: i) the growth in ISLs due to its reputation as a leader in the insurance space; ii) the launch of the NASDAQ OMX X-Stream trading platform and the signing of cooperation agreements with EU Member States, which both expanded and diversified its market across regions; iii) the obtainment of qualified jurisdiction status by the NAIC in the US; and iv) not being listed on the EU's blacklist in 2017 (BILSMR 2014; BILSMR 2016; BMA 2014; BMA 2016; BMA 2018). In The Bahamas, the increase was attributed to the cost effectiveness of its captive product, whereas periods of declines were accredited to global

**Table 9.5** Number of insurance licensees by jurisdiction

| *Year* | *2011* | *2012* | *2013* | *2014* | *2015* | *2016* | *2017* | *2018* | *2019* | *Change (%)* |
|---|---|---|---|---|---|---|---|---|---|---|
| Bahamas | 10 | 11 | 82 | 117 | 148 | 173 | 165 | 172 | 166 | 1560 |
| Cayman | 725 | 731 | 750 | 764 | 723 | 709 | 696 | 703 | n/a | (3) |
| Bermuda | 970 | 1046 | 1119 | 1130 | 1231 | 1135 | 1198 | 1262 | n/a | 30 |
| BVI | 174 | 157 | 147 | 145 | 146 | 137 | 111 | 73 | 59 | (66) |

*Source* ICB (2011), ICB (2013), ICB (2017), ICB (2020), CIMA (2015), CIMA (2018), BMA (2006), BMA (2010), BILSMR (2014), BMA (2017), BILSMR (2018), BVIFSC (2012a), BVIFSC (2011), BVIFSC (2012b), BVIFSC (2013), BVIFSC (2014), BVIFSC (2015), BVIFSC (2016b), BVIFSC (2017), BVIFSC (2018), BVIFSC (2019)

tax reform (ICA 2018). In the Cayman Islands and the BVI, the cause for the declines was market driven, as both are highly concentrated in insuring risk in the US market (CIMA 2016; BVIFSC 2017) with both the Cayman Islands and the BVI being 90% and 100% concentrated in the US market, respectively.

In terms of assets, Bermuda had the most robust growth in total assets, followed by the Cayman Islands and The Bahamas. From 2011 to 2018, total net assets in Bermuda increased by 117% (US$528b) (BMA 2014; BMA 2019), compared to a 20% (US$11.3b) in the Cayman Islands (CIMA 2018) and an 86% (US$616m) in The Bahamas between 2012 and 2018 (ICB 2011; ICB 2019). As at the end of 2018, Bermuda held roughly US$980b in total assets (BMA 2019), the Cayman Islands held US$68.7b (CIMA 2018), The Bahamas held US$1.33b (ICB 2019) and the BVI held an estimated US$1.18b at the end of 2017 (BVIFSC 2018; see Table 9.6).

**Table 9.6** Total assets of external insurers by jurisdiction (US$ in billions)

| *Year* | *2011* | *2012* | *2013* | *2014* | *2015* | *2016* | *2017* | *2018* | *Change (%)* |
|---|---|---|---|---|---|---|---|---|---|
| Bahamas | 0,714 | 0,684 | 0,766 | 1,06 | 1,08 | 1,05 | 1,36 | 1,33 | 86 |
| Cayman | 57 | 79 | 83 | 55 | 54 | 58 | 61 | 69 | 20 |
| Bermuda | 452 | 505 | 607 | 583 | 631 | 764 | 838 | 980 | 117 |
| BVI | n/a | n/a | n/a | n/a | n/a | n/a | 1,18 | n/a | n/a |

*Source* ICB (2011), ICB (2013), ICB (2017), ICB (2019), CIMA (2018), BMA (2006), BMA (2010), BILSMR (2014), BMA (2017), BILSMR (2018)

## 9.4 Impact of the Offshore Financial Sector on the Local Economies in the Caribbean Region

### *9.4.1 The Bahamas*

The impact of the offshore financial sector on the local economies in the Caribbean region has been broadly negative, with the sector's contribution to total GDP generally declining during the period 2011 to 2019. In The Bahamas, for example, the local economy grew by 1.5% in 2018, over the previous year (IMF 2019). This growth is attributed to the output of the tourism industry and foreign direct investment project under construction, combined with rebuilding efforts in the wake of the passage of Hurricane Dorian (CBB 2019). Unemployment increased to 10.7% in 2018, up 0.6% from 2017 (IMF 2019). The CBB attributes this increase to the dislocation in workforce and halt in business operations on two islands due to the destruction caused by Hurricane Dorian (CBB 2019). According to a special report issued by the CBB, employment in the offshore banking sector fell by 8.9% (97 persons) to 996 in 2017 over the previous year (CBB 2018). Per the report, total economic contribution in terms of expenditure by the offshore financial sector within the local economy decreased by 9.29% (B$25.18m) to B$245.8 million in 2017 (CBB 2018), whereas in 2011, expenditure was B$231.7 million, almost equivalent to that of 2017 (IMF 2013). Overall, the offshore sector accounted for 1,976.9% of GDP as of June 2018 (IMF 2019), compared to 2,021.2% at the end of 2016 (IMF 2017) and 4,012.7% at the end of 2013 (IMF 2019). Of this percentage, banks, and banks and trust companies attributed 1,300.9%, external insurers contributed 8.1%, and investment funds made up 667.5% as of June 2018 (IMF 2019).

### *9.4.2 The Cayman Islands*

Compared to The Bahamas, the economy in the Cayman Islands grew by 3.2% in 2019, slightly down from 4.1% in 2018 (Government of the Cayman Islands Economics and Statistics Office (ESO) 2020). In 2016, the offshore financial sector contributed 14.3% to GDP, while its overall contribution, including its indirect contribution to GDP, was just above 40% in 2016 (Caribbean Development Bank (CDB) 2018b). These numbers compared to a direct contribution of 19%, and an indirect contribution of 48% in 2007, reflect a decline in the sector's overall contribution to GDP (CDB 2018b). This decline is observed again in 2017. While the offshore financial sector remained a major contributor to GDP, it attributed 35% in 2017, down by an estimated 5% from the prior year, while growing at roughly 1.8% (CDB 2018b). The sector has also indirectly impacted other segments of the jurisdiction's economy, such as wholesale and retail trade, which attributed 0.3 pp, and construction, 0.2 pp to the island's GDP. In 2018, although the financial sector continues to be the largest contributor to GDP, it attributed 25.5% to GDP, roughly 9.5% less than the previous year (CDB 2018b; CDB 2019).[21] In 2019, it remained the most important contributor to GDP, with growth of 1.7%, a 0.1% lower than the prior year (CDB 2020). The rate of unemployment fell to 4.1% in June 2017, up by 0.1% over 2016 (CDB 2018b). In 2018, the unemployment rate fell to 3.4%, representing a 0.7% decline over the prior year (CDB 2019). Although the rate of unemployment shows a downward trend, it is uncertain to what extent the financial sector contributed to this decline. The same with Government revenues, which was recorded at CI$653.5 mn in 2018, up 7% over the previous year (CDB 2020).

### *9.4.3 Bermuda*

Bermuda's economy grew between 1.0–2.0% in 2019, compared to 0.1% in 2018 (National Economic Report of Bermuda (NER)). The value added by the international business sector increased by 0.3% or $4.5 m, excluding financial services. This sector was the highest contributor to total GDP with 25.2% in 2019, compared to 23.8% during the previous year. In 2017, the international business sector remained the largest contributor to total GDP with an attribution of 26.1% to total GDP, representing a 0.7% ($8.2m) increase in value added (Government of Bermuda Department of Statistics 2018). The sector continued to remain the largest contributor to total GDP in previous years, representing 26.3% in 2016 (Government of Bermuda Department of Statistics 2017), 28.0% in 2015 (Government of Bermuda Department of Statistics 2016) and 27.1% in 2014 (Government of Bermuda Department of Statistics 2015). In 2019, this sector contributed 3,995 jobs to the local economy out of the total number of jobs (34,303), reflecting a 0.3% increase over the

[21] This percentage represents the domestic and offshore banking centre.

previous year. Within this sector, foreign exchange earnings increased to $1.53b, which represents a 4% ($59m) growth (GOB 2020). Businesses in the sector involved in insurance management services showed marginal increases, while the reinsurance business generated $0.6b in gross profit. In addition to job provision, the sector contributes to the local economy by way of expenditures among local businesses, it adds value to the tourism industry through business visits, and it generates government revenue through fees and taxes (GOB 2020).

### 9.4.4 *The BVI*

In the BVI, the local economy expanded by 2.1% in 2019, down compared to 3.3% in 2018 (Caribbean Development Bank (CDB) 2020). The unemployment rate in the BVI stood at 2.9% as of 31 December 2017. This rate has consistently been under 5% for almost a decade, and participation in the labour force has averaged 90% during the same period (CDB 2018a). In 2018, fees collected for the financial services sector was $260m (BVIFSC 2018). This revenue represents a substantial increase over 2017, due to a number of fees and taxes implemented by the BVI Government in 2017 (CDB 2019). However, despite this increase, government revenue was down by US$30 million during the year (Klein 2019). Whereas in 2017, fees collected was equivalent to $197.8m, of which $175.4m was transferred to the BVI Government (BVIFSC 2018). According to the Caribbean Development Bank, all government sources of revenue fell in 2017, except for taxes levied on goods and services which increased by 2.5%, due to increase expenditures by financial services operators. In 2016, the BVI Financial Services Commission recorded revenues of $193.8m (BVIFSC 2017), representing a 6% decline compared to $205.7m in 2015 (BVIFSC 2016a). In 2014, $207.9m (BVIFSC 2015) was collected in total revenue, $208m in 2013 (BVIFSC 2014), $205m in 2012 (BVIFSC 2013) and $199m in 2011 (BVIFSC 2012b). These numbers show a steady decline commencing in 2013.

### 9.4.5 *Region*

Region wise, the economies in the four jurisdictions have exhibited minimal growth overall. This performance was markedly better in comparison with the negative, flat and 1% average growth rates for other Caribbean countries during the Great Recession. However, the economic contribution of the offshore financial sector to the total GDP in the four jurisdictions has been declining for the most part during the period 2011 to 2019. For instance, in The Bahamas, while the economy grew by 1.6% in 2018, which is the highest growth observed in the jurisdiction since 2012, the offshore sector contribution to GDP during this period dwindled. In 2013, the sector attributed 4,012.7% to GDP, compared to 2,021.2% in 2016, and 1,976.9% as of June 2018 (IMF 2019). Of this percentage, banks and banks and trust companies attributed 1,300.9% percent, followed by external insurers and investment funds (IMF 2019). In the Cayman Islands on the other hand, a slow growth in GDP has been noted since 2015, however, in 2018, the economy grew by 4.1% (ESO 2020). Although the financial sector remains the largest contributor to GDP, this sector has been on the decline in recent years. For example, in 2016 this sector attributed 40% to GDP, compared to 35% in 2017, and 25.5% in 2018 (CDB 2018b; CDB 2019). Whereas in Bermuda, GDP during the period has been broadly mixed. In 2019, a modest growth of 0.5% was noted, compared to a contraction of 0.4% in 2018 (GOB 2020). Since 2015, the jurisdiction's international business sector, the largest contributor to GDP, has been on the decline. This sector attributed 28% to total GDP in 2015, 26.3% in 2016, 26.1% in 2017 (Government of Bermuda Department of Statistics (GOBDOS) 2016; GOBDOS 2017; GOBDOS 2018), and 23.8% in 2018 (GOB 2020). Most recently however, the sector contributed 25.2% to total GDP in 2018, a 1.4% increase over the prior year (GOB 2020). However, it is not certain whether this first sign of upward trend will continue.

Similar to the other three jurisdictions, GDP in the BVI expanded by 2.1% in 2019, however, an increase of 3.3% was also observed in the prior year (CDB 2020). The offshore sector's contribution to GDP has been on a downward path since 2013. During that year, the jurisdiction recorded total revenue of $208m, which fell to $193.8m in 2016, with a small increase equivalent to $197.8m in 2017 (BVIFSC 2014; BVIFSC 2018; CDB 2018a). According to the Caribbean Development Bank, this slight increase is attributed to taxes levied on goods and services which increased by 2.5%, due to increase expenditures by financial services operators, while government fees fell during the year. In 2018, the BVI Financial Services Commission recorded revenue of $260m, however, the increase is credited to an increase in taxes and fees by the BVI Government during the prior year (BVIFSC 2018). Revenues collected represents 62% ($232m)

**Table 9.7** Real GDP by jurisdiction

| *Year* | *2011* | *2012* | *2013* | *2014* | *2015* | *2016* | *2017* | *2018* | *2019* |
|---|---|---|---|---|---|---|---|---|---|
| Bahamas | 1,6 | 1,8 | 0,7 | 0,7 | 0,6 | 0,4 | 0,1 | 1,6 | n/a |
| Cayman Islands | 0,9 | 1,4 | 1,2 | 2,1 | 2,8 | 3,1 | 3,1 | 4,1 | 3,2 |
| Bermuda | (4,4) | (3,9) | (2,4) | (0,4) | 0,8 | (0,7) | 3,6 | (0,4) | 0,5 |
| BVI | n/a | n/a | 5,4 | 1,3 | 0,8 | 7,1 | (3,7) | 3,3 | n/a |

*Source* IMF (2019), CBB (2014), ESO (2016), ESO (2015), ESO (2019), CDB (2019), Government of Bermuda Department of Statistics (2015), GOBDOS (2020)

of the total net revenue ($372.3m) to the BVI Government (BVI Government 2019), which reflects a $30m decline in the sector's contribution to total revenue (Klein 2019; see Table 9.7).

## 9.5 Comparative Analysis

A key objective of this chapter is to study the consequences of international policy initiatives on the offshore business of financial centres in The Bahamas, the Cayman Islands, Bermuda and the BVI, and the impact of the offshore business sector on the economies of their respective jurisdictions. Below, we have ranked each country in the order of most impacted to least impacted. The discussion which follows explains the rational for each jurisdiction's placement on the list.

### *9.5.1 The BVI*

Overall, the results reveal that global policy initiatives have had adverse effects on each of the principal sectors in the offshore business of financial centres in the Caribbean region, with the exception of Bermuda. The BVI was the hardest hit of the four jurisdictions as a result of these initiatives. The most significant impact experienced by the jurisdiction was a sharp decline in company incorporations by 60% or 38,579 incorporations, the principal sector of its offshore industry. The jurisdiction also saw a substantial reduction of 25% (145 licensees) in the total number of banking and fiduciary services licensees, another major component of its offshore business (BVIFSC 2012b; BVIFSC 2020). Coupled with these adverse effects, the number of captive insurers in its insurance sector fell by 66% (115 licensees), another important part of the jurisdiction's offshore business (BVIFSC 2012b; BVIFSC 2020). Further, although the BVI experienced an increase of 28% in the total number of BVI funds registered and recognized in the jurisdiction (BVIFSC 2012b; BVIFSC 2020), and a 13% growth in the number of investment funds, this growth came at the cost of its mutual funds business, a main component in its investment sector, which declined significantly by 43% (1125 funds) between 2011 and 2018 (BVIFSC 2012b; BVIFSC 2019).

While the jurisdiction's local economy expanded by 2.1% in 2019, down compared to an increase of 3.3% in 2018 (Caribbean Development Bank (CDB) 2020), government revenues contributed by its financial sector have been on the decline since 2013. Where revenue increases have been noted, such increased have been credited to increases in fees and taxes implemented by the BVI Government (CDB 2019). International policy standards instituted by the FATF related to money laundering and terrorist financing, and mounting pressures by the Global Forum, extending back to the introduction of FATCA by the US and the economic substance rule by the EU Code of Conduct Group related to tax evasion and tax avoidance—have been cited as the main causes for these declines experienced by the jurisdiction in its company incorporation business and its banking and fiduciary sector. Although new initiatives were undertaken by the jurisdiction in an attempt to boost its investment business, the global underperformance of funds due to increasing uncertainty in the Eurozone crisis (BVIFSC 2012b), combined with investors preference for liquidity and transparency, resulted in marginal growth in the sector, which came at the cost of its mutual funds business which declined by 43% (BVIFSC 2012b). These factors, in addition to the passage of Hurricane Irma and Hurricane Maria, which both disrupted services offered in the financial sector (BVIFSC 2018), contributed to the overall adverse impact experienced by the offshore business in the jurisdiction. Given the unfavourable effects of international policy initiatives on the jurisdiction's company incorporation business and its banking and fiduciary sector, the BVI is listed as the hardest hit country of the four jurisdictions (see Table 9.8).

It is also worth adding that the May 2016 publication of the "Panama Papers" which featured data leaks of 11.5 million files of high net worth and influential individuals, as well as other offshore holdings provided fodder for arguments that OFCs inhere shady dealings and provide shelter for the criminal underworld, corrupt public officials and firms keen on evading their erstwhile tax obligations. The International

**Table 9.8** Summary of country findings

| *Country* | *International banking* | *Corporate services* | *Securities & investments* | *Insurance services* | *Economy* | *Regulatory factors* | *Accolades* | *Overall ranking* |
|---|---|---|---|---|---|---|---|---|
| BVI | 25% decline in the number of licensed banks (145 licensees) from 2011 to 2019 | 60% decline in the number of company incorporation (38,579) from 2011 to 2019 | 29% increase in the number of investment funds (337) from 2011 to 2019 | 66% decline in captive insurance licensees (115 licensees) between 2011 to 2019 | GDP expanded by 2.1% in 2019. In 2018, GDP was 3.3% | FATF Recommendations, Common Reporting Standards | Leader in international business company incorporations | Most adversely affected |
| | | | 43% decline in mutual funds (1125 funds) for 2011 to 2018 | | Government fees was US$260 m in 2018, US$197.8 m in 2017 and US$193.8 m in 2016.[a] | US FATCA & EU Code of Conduct Group economic substance regulations | | |
| The Bahamas | 66% or US$332b decline in total assets between 2011 to 2019 | 22% (64) increase in the number of licensed corporate service providers from 2011 to 2019 | 24% increase in the number of securities firms from 2012 to 2019 | 1560% increase in captive cell companies from 2011 to 2019 | GDP grew by 1.5% in 2018 | US adoption of FATCA | | 2nd most adversely affected |

| *Country* | *International banking* | *Corporate services* | *Securities & investments* | *Insurance services* | *Economy* | *Regulatory factors* | *Accolades* | *Overall ranking* |
|---|---|---|---|---|---|---|---|---|
| | 21% (57) decline in the number of regulated entities from 2011 to 2019 | | 13% (90 funds) increase in investment funds 2011 to 2019 | 87% (US$616 m) increase in total assets from 2011 to 2018 | Financial services industry contributed 1,976,9 to GDP in June 2018, 2,021.2% in December 2016 and 4,012.7% in December 2013 | Tax amnesties offered by onshore jurisdictions | | |
| | | | 7% (B$8.9b) increase in assets from 2013 to 2016 | | | Introduction of Common Reporting Standard | | |
| Cayman Islands | US$978b decline in intra-bank cross-border assets from 2011 to 2018 | 54% (49) increase in the number of corporate service providers between 2011 to 2019 | 19% (1734) increase in the number of regulated funds from 2011 to 2018 | 3% decline in the number of insurance licenses between 2011 and 2018 | GDP grew by 3.2% in 2019 | Basel Committee on Bank Supervision Regulations | Premier choice for domiciliation of funds | 3rd most adversely affected |

(continued)

**Table 9.8** (continued)

| *Country* | *International banking* | *Corporate services* | *Securities & investments* | *Insurance services* | *Economy* | *Regulatory factors* | *Accolades* | *Overall ranking* |
|---|---|---|---|---|---|---|---|---|
| | US$1,029b decline in intra-bank cross-border liabilities between 2011 to 2018 | | 31% (US$1.745t) increase in total assets of regulated funds between 2011 to 2018 | 20% (US$11.5b) increase in assets of insurer licensees from 2011 to 2018 | GDP grew by 4.1% in 2018 | FATF - mandatory Register of Directors Filing | Top domicile of choice for hedge funds | |
| | 15% decline in banks & trusts. Licensed banks declined by 50% (125 licensees) from 2011 to 2018 | | 17% (1583) increased in mutual funds from 2011 to 2018 | | Financial services industry contributed 25.5% to GDP in 2018, 35% in 2017, and an est. 40% in 2016 | Common reporting standards | 2nd in world in number of international insurers | |

| *Country* | *International banking* | *Corporate services* | *Securities & investments* | *Insurance services* | *Economy* | *Regulatory factors* | *Accolades* | *Overall ranking* |
|---|---|---|---|---|---|---|---|---|
| | 6% increase in the number of trust licenses from 2011 to 2018 | | 203% increase in total assets of mutual funds (US$4.9t) between 2011 to 2018 | | | OECD Exclusive Framework on BEPS Country to Country Reporting | World leader in healthcare and group captives | |
| Bermuda | 15% (5) decline in license banks between 2011 to 2019 | 53% (33) increase in corporate service providers from 2016 to 2018 | 15% (9) decline in registered licensees in securities & investment sector from 2011 to 2019 | 30% (292) increase in insurance licensees from 2011 to 2018 | GDP grew by 1.0% to 2.0% in 2018 | FATF push for regulation & supervision | Global leader in insurance sector | Least adversely affected |
| | | | 32% decline in the number of regulated funds (247) from 2011 to 2019 | 450% (US$7.2b) increase in insurance linked securities segment from 2011 to 2018 | International business grew by 0.3% to US$4.5 m in 2018 | | World leader in catastrophe bonds issuance with Insurance-linked securities | |

(continued)

Table 9.8 (continued)

| *Country* | *International banking* | *Corporate services* | *Securities & investments* | *Insurance services* | *Economy* | *Regulatory factors* | *Accolades* | *Overall ranking* |
|---|---|---|---|---|---|---|---|---|
| | | | | 127% (US$136.4b) increase in total net premium of captive insurers & 117% (US$528b) increase in total assets from 2011 to 2018 | International business contributed 25.2% to GDP in 2019, 23.8% in 2018, 26.1% in 2017 and 26.3% in 2016 | | | |

*Source* IMF (2017), CBB (2012, 2017, 2018, 2019, 2020), CIMA (2012, 2018, 2019, 2020), CIMA (2016), BMA (2012, 2020), Government of Bermuda (2019, 2020)

[a]2018 revenue represents a substantial increase over 2017, due to a number of fees and taxes implemented by the BVI Government in 2017. Despite this increase, the sector's contribution to total revenue declined by US$30 m. Fees fell in 2017 except taxes levied on goods and services, which increased by 2.5%, due to increased expenditures by financial services operators resulting in an increase in fees collected over the prior year

Consortium of Investigative Journalists (ICIJ or Consortium) would have published the findings under the provocative byline—"The Panama Papers: Exposing the Rogue Offshore Finance Industry". The BVI was hard hit by the mis-characterization of its business reputation. The ICIJ identified approximately 114,000 BVI Business Companies Incorporated by Mossack Fonseca since 1977. The Consortium was aware that between 1985 and 1999, 90% of all BVI Business Companies Incorporated by this firm were inactive. The Consortium was also aware that the 30.000 active BVI Business Companies identified in the Panama Papers were legitimate vehicles being used to facilitate cross-border trade and investment. The ICIJ chose not to acknowledge how the BVI had innovated, improved and adopted the newer financial transparency standards to ensure high-quality benchmarks. It instead sought to showcase a BVI list of companies that included the "inactive", "discontinued", "dissolved" and the "defaulted" (Smith 2017).

### 9.5.2 *The Bahamas*

Similar to the BVI, The Bahamas also suffered significant losses due to the negative effects stemming from global policies on the offshore business of its financial centre. During the period 2011 to 2019, its international banking segment experienced a 66% reduction in total assets equivalent to US$332 billion (Central Bank of The Bahamas (CBB) 2020). This decline corresponds to a 21% (57 licensees) reduction in the number of regulated entities, most of which were banks (40%), and banks and trust companies (29%) (CBB 2012; CBB 2020), which is the dominant part of the industry for the jurisdiction (IMF 2017). On the other hand, the jurisdiction experienced growth in other segments of its offshore sector. In the corporate services sector, an increase of 21% (60 registered licensees) was observed (Securities Commission of The Bahamas (SCB) 2013; SCB 2020). Of this sector, corporate services providers accounted for 60%, while financial services providers represented 30% (SCB 2020). Additionally, in the securities sector, the number of registered securities firms increased by 24%, while the total number of individuals registered under the Securities Industry Regulation (SIR) grew by 132% (SCB 2013; SCB 2020). The investment sector also expanded by 4% in the number of investment funds licensed and registered in the jurisdiction during the period (SCB 2012; SCB 2020), which corresponds to an increase in net assets of 6.9% (B$8.9b) between 2013 and 2016 (SCB 2014; SCB 2017).

Further, the insurance sector also expanded by 1560% in the total number of captive insurers (ICB 2012; ICB 2020), which corresponds an increase of 87% (US$616m) in total assets held by external insurers between 2011 and 2018 (ICB 2012; ICB 2020).

Overall, the local economy grew by 1.5% in 2018, over the previous year (IMF 2019). This growth is attributed mainly to the output in the tourism industry and foreign direct investments, spurred by rebuilding efforts related to Hurricane Dorian (CBB 2019). However, despite the noted growth in its corporate services sector, securities and investment sector and insurance segment, the offshore sector's contribution to the jurisdiction's GDP continues to decline. As of June 2018, the sector accounted for 1,976.9% of GDP (IMF 2019), compared to 2,021.2% at the end of 2016 (IMF 2017), and 4,012.7% at the end of 2013 (IMF 2019). As the investment and insurance sectors in The Bahamas are relatively small compared to those in the other three jurisdictions, The Bahamas has not been able to fully recoup from the losses in assets experienced in its international banking segment during the period. Domestic tax policy reforms, including the introduction of common reporting standards, and other regulatory changes such as FATCA (CBB 2019), have been the main causes which led some private banks curtailing their offshore business within the jurisdiction (IMF 2017). Unlike the BVI, the jurisdiction saw a marked shift in private banking and wealth management services to investment banking activities (IMF 2017), which contributed to increases in its corporate services, securities and investment services and insurance services. As a result of the negative impact experienced by the banking and fiduciary sector of the offshore business in The Bahamas, the jurisdiction was hit to a lesser degree compared to the BVI and is ranked second most impacted from adverse effects due to international policy initiatives on its offshore business and domestic economy (see Table 9.8).

### *9.5.3 The Cayman Islands*

Similar to BVI and The Bahamas, the Cayman Islands was also adversely affected in one of the principal offshore segments in its offshore financial sector. During the period 2011 to 2018, the jurisdiction experienced a loss of approximately US$978 billion in intra-bank cross-border assets and an estimated US$1,029 trillion in cross-border liabilities (CIMA 2012; CIMA 2019). While the number of licensed banks also fell sharply by 50% (125 licensees), this was offset by a small increase of 6% in its fiduciary licensees (CIMA 2012; CIMA 2019), attributed mainly by a 130% (73 licenses) growth in PTCs, and a 66.7% (18 licenses) growth in controlled subsidiaries (CIMA 2012; CIMA 2018). Like The Bahamas, the Cayman Islands also experienced a marked shift away from the more traditional private banking and wealth management services to investment banking services. For example, in the securities sector, the total number of investment regulated funds increased by 32% (1592), attributed mainly to hedge funds and equity funds, resulting in a growth of 31% (US$1.745t) in total assets (CIMA 2012; CIMA 2019).

Mutual Funds also increased substantially by an estimated 17% (1583 funds) (CIMA 2012; CIMA 2019), spurred mainly by increases in master funds, resulting in a substantial increase of 203% (US$4.9t) in total asset value during the period 2011 to 2018 (CIMA 2013; CIMA 2019). Despite this increase, a US$30 billion in net loss was reported by the jurisdiction, which was offset by asset appreciation during the course of the year, in addition to a reduction of US$117 billion in total net assets and dividends, which was US$2 billon lower compared to 2017 (CIMA 2019). The increases in its securities and investment sector corresponded to the growth experienced by the jurisdiction in its corporate services sector (CIMA 2012; CIMA 2019). Unlike The Bahamas, the Cayman Islands experienced a small decline of 3% (22 licensees) in the number of insurance licensees in its insurance sector during the same period. Despite this decline, total assets held by international insurer licensees increased by 20% (US$11.5b) (CIMA 2012; CIMA 2019).

Overall, despite the major losses suffered by the jurisdiction in intra-bank cross-border assets and cross-border liabilities, and in its international banking segment, the impact of global policy initiatives has not impacted the Cayman Islands to the same extent as it had in the BVI and The Bahamas. One of the main reasons for this pertains its diverse product offering. For example, the jurisdiction has developed its securities and investment sector, as well as its insurance sector as principal segments of its offshore sector, in addition to its intra-bank niche market, and its banking and fiduciary segment. While the intra-bank market was directly impacted by international regulatory reforms, which subjected onshore banks to new liquidity requirements, and initiatives introduced to reduce de-risking by banks (CIMA 2016), the impact on its international banking segment was partly offset by a modest increase in its fiduciary business. Additionally, its securities and investment sector, in addition to its insurance sector, are driven mainly by market performance. The growth experienced in its securities and investment sector in turn boosted its corporate services business.

As a result of these factors, the jurisdiction fell in its world ranking from eight to twelfth place in 2017 (CIMA 2018), in both cross-border assets and cross-border liabilities categories (CIMA 2019). It remains the premier choice for the domiciliation of funds and is also considered one of the top domiciles of choice for hedge funds (CIMA 2016). The jurisdiction also maintains its second position behind Bermuda in the number of international insurers and is the leader in healthcare and group captives in the world (CIMA 2020). Additionally, the jurisdiction's economy grew by 3.2% in 2019, although it was slightly down from 4.1% in 2018 (Government of the Cayman Islands Economics and Statistics Office (ESO) 2020). Despite the fact that the percentage in contribution by the offshore financial sector to GDP has been on the decline for many years now, the sector remains a major contributor to GDP with a 25.5% contribution in 2018 (CDB 2019). Given the Cayman Island's product diversification in other sectors such as its securities and investment sector, and its insurance sector, which both experienced notable growth in total assets, the jurisdiction experienced less impact to its offshore business from international policy initiatives compared to the BVI and The Bahamas. As a result, it is ranked third in the extent to which adverse effects impacted its offshore business and domestic economy due to global policy initiatives (see Table 9.8).

### *9.5.4 Bermuda*

Bermuda on the other hand, experienced minimal loss due to the effects of international regulatory initiatives on its offshore financial sector, compared to the losses experienced by the other three jurisdictions. Although the number of banks licensed in the jurisdiction declined, this decrease was a mere 15% (5 licensees) (BMA 2012; BMA 2020), compared to a decrease of 25% (145 licensees) in the BVI (BVIFSC 2012b; BVIFSC 2020), 21% (57 licensees) in The Bahamas (CBB 2012; CBB 2020) and 50% (125 licensees) in the Cayman Islands (CIMA 2012; CIMA 2020). Additionally, this loss was offset by a 100% (6) growth in PTCs during the period (BMA 2012; BMA 2020). Unlike The Bahamas and the Cayman Islands however, the jurisdiction experienced a 15% (9) decline in the number of registered licensees in its securities and investment sector during the period 2012–2019 (BMA 2013; BMA 2020).

This was due mainly to declines in the financial markets as a result of the Eurozone debt crisis (BMA 2013), as its aggregate asset under management was 75% concentrated in the European Union (BMA 2016). Similar to The Bahamas, the jurisdiction experienced a significant increase in its insurance sector. The number of insurance licensees increased by 30% (292 licensees) during the period 2011–2018. This growth was attributed mainly to a surge of 21% in the number of special purpose insurers (SPI) in the market (BILSMR 2013), due to Bermuda's rising reputation as a global centre for the formation, listing and servicing of insurance-linked securities (ILS), which represented US$15.1 billion (60%) of global ILS issuance at the end of 2014 (BILSMR 2014). Another factor was due to the fact that Bermuda's ILS are directly linked to its stock exchange market (BSX), which expanded to include the NASDAQ OMX's X-stream trading platform, providing access to trading in over 70 marketplaces in 50 countries (BMA 2014). ILSs corresponded with significant growth equivalent to 450% (US$7.2b) during the period (BMA 2012; BMA 2019). The total net premiums of captive insurers increased by 127% (US$136.4b), in addition to total assets with growth of 117% (US$528b) (BMA 2012; BMA 2019). This growth coincides with the increase of 53% (33 licensees) in the number of corporate services providers between 2017 and 2019 (BMA 2018; BMA 2020).

Overall, Bermuda suffered the least losses in the region compared to the BVI, The Bahamas and the Cayman Islands, due to its relatively small banking and fiduciary sector. The jurisdiction is also highly concentration in the insurance sector of the market, particularly in its ILSs segment, which experienced significant growth during the period, despite a 15% decline in its investment and securities business. Today, the jurisdiction remains the world's leader in the issuance of catastrophe bonds with insurance-linked securities (BILSMR 2018). In 2019, its GDP grew by 1.0 to 2.0%, compared to 0.1% in 2018 (National Economic Report of Bermuda (NER)). The value added by the international business sector increased by 0.3% ($4.5m), excluding financial services during the year (GOB 2020). This sector remains the highest contributor to GDP, attributing 25.2% in 2019, compared to 23.8% during the previous year (GOB 2020). Given these factors, Bermuda was hit the least compared to the other three jurisdictions. As a result, it is ranked fourth as it is the jurisdiction which has experienced the least adverse effects on its offshore business and domestic economy due to international policy initiatives (see Table 9.8).

## 9.6 Summative Analysis

The industry which was once seen as an alternative means to diversify Caribbean economies away from traditional industries such as tourism and agricultural, and as a potential viable source to achieve real economic growth has proven to be a major contributor to the GDP of Caribbean economies (IMF 2017). Financial centres in offshore jurisdictions, perceived to be the major culprits for money laundering, terrorist financing and tax evasion, became the central focus of international policy initiatives, and as a result, have had to bear the high cost of compliance or face defensive counter measures from OECD countries, in addition to other measures taken by the US and EU with regard to their respective policies.

Financial centres in the Caribbean have had to endure increasing demands and make continuous stringent reforms to their legal systems and institutions, compared to the OECD countries. As a result, they have become transparent with superior compliance levels to global standards than OECD Member States themselves (Sharman 2010a; Findley et al. 2014; Allred et al. 2017). Having played by the very rules created by the OECD, these Caribbean financial centres have been placed at a competitive disadvantage, as the rules are not equally applied to OECD countries. Whether the rules pertain to money laundering, terrorist financing or tax evasion, the OECD has been more stringent and critical on financial centres in the Caribbean than those in their very own Member States, despite the fact that these types of financial crimes occur globally.

Added to this, the US and EU have increasingly placed additional demands on these jurisdictions to either comply with their very own measures, or face the consequences for non-compliance. These measures have placed heavier compliance costs on these jurisdictions and have further put them at a competitive disadvantage. All these measures have pushed business away from compliant jurisdictions such as these four Caribbean financial centres, to non-compliant ones (Johannesen and Zucman 2014; Johannesen, 2014; Hanlon et al., 2015; Caruana-Galizia and Caruana-Galizia 2016; Omartian 2016; De Simone et al. 2018). For example, low-tax jurisdictions, such as Delaware, Nevada and Wyoming, have attracted larger cross-border deposits compared to offshore countries (Casi et al. 2019 as cited in Chiocchetti). Increase investments in non-financial assets such as real estate, art works, collectibles, precious metals and cryptocurrencies, and the use of the non-reportable financial institutions category to bypass reporting requirements for CRS have also been noted by other authors (Casi et al. 2018; Knobel and Mienzer 2014).

In the midst of all this political bureaucracy, financial centres in the Caribbean not only have had to bear the full costs of compliance, but now have to deal with a shrinking industry that had become a critical essential component of their domestic economies. Added to this, they are facing the crippling economic effects of COVID-19, coupled with the ongoing efforts to rebuild after suffering the devastating effects of several major climate change related hurricanes (The Bahamas and the BVI). These factors have increased the importance of the offshore business sector's contribution to the success of Caribbean economies. This leads us to question the future of financial centres in the Caribbean, concern ourselves with what additional measures can be expected from the OECD, the newly elected president of the US and the EU, and ponder on how much longer will these political power giants be allowed to continue to pursue their very own political interests at the expense of small, fragile, powerless states.

## 9.7 Conclusion

International policy initiatives to counter money laundering, terrorist financing and tax evasion have come full circle. Financial centres in offshore jurisdictions continue to adopt and adapt to available international transparency standards, while some OECD Member States have not done so. The application of these standards continue to be applied vigorously in offshore jurisdictions, while a blind eye is turned for OECD Member States. In the midst of this convoluted political state, money laundering, terrorist financing and tax evasion continue to be prevalent global problems facilitated by noncompliant countries including OECD Member States.

What is clearly evident is that the business that was once enjoyed by financial centres in offshore jurisdictions is now flourishing in OECD Member countries. Offshore jurisdictions have been placed at a competitive disadvantage, notwithstanding the resilience and innovation at work, while OECD countries have become more attractive jurisdictions for the offshore business. This current state of being reveals the negative unintended consequences of international policy initiatives aimed at tackling financial crimes. These tilt the competition stakes in favour of online financial centres in OECD and other core jurisdictions in Eurasia, while displacing Caribbean OFCs. All this while the cost of compliance continues to increase for these jurisdictions, one local industry expert estimating the costs to have climbed by 58% over the two-year period 2016 to 2017 (Smith 2017).

In short, the offshore sector, which had become one of the main contributors to the GDP of each jurisdiction and currently remains a principal contributor, has been slipping for almost a decade now in at least three of the four jurisdictions. The COVID-19 world recession presupposes further economic jeopardy, and policy-makers are pinning their hopes on a rebound of the offshore sector as part of an overall economic recovery. It is also worth noting that COVID-19 has not affected the normative desirability of financialization. The need for specialized financial services remains as essential as ever.

Surely the challenges for the Caribbean are quite myriad, but ultimately political will and bargaining shall matter in the years ahead. There is no global governance body that manages international tax matters on a truly inclusive, multilateral basis. Caribbean OFCs require, as part of the Global Forum, inclusion in the deliberations that proliferate with regard to financial crimes and international taxation.

Scholars tracking these developments ought to ruse with the Western geographic privileging and de-privileging at work. The Caribbean as a region and others of the Global South have been evacuated in techniques of historical writing through the use of subordinate clauses, parenthesis or footnotes, their peoples, lives and customs never being a subject of the sentence, its tone or pitch of voice. The techniques extend to some studies of globality, particularly in the literature addressing the junction point between international taxation and global finance. These feature openness and closure, emphasis and neutrality, as well as meanings produced through an aggregate of cues and clues, rather than by agreed clear signs of what is legitimate business and tax planning and why competition across a global geography of service providers exist—and necessarily so. To wit Umberto Eco (Sondheim 1976), we need to reflect on the "undercode" of signs and meanings if we are to coherently and rationally address financial services governing regulatory standards, and their cascading effects on tax authorities, inter-company trades, bond markets, employer associations and security cooperation networks. What offshore **means** may inhere a kind of transnational business arrangement or process or legal terminology but when it comes to signify financial services especially emanating from the Caribbean, destabilizing insights of the meaning occur involving inflections and facile connections. To mobilize the stereotypes an undercode of indeterminate historical associations is made. Put differently, a study of the geographies of global finance cannot escape the semiotics at work, the tracing of genealogy, indeed the ambiguities, puns and equivocations in the knowledge produced about the shores themselves ranging from the increments of meanings of entrepots to that of financial districts.

## References

Allred, Brent B., Michael G. Findley, Daniel Nielson, and J. C. Sharman. 2017. Anonymous Shell Companies: A Global Audit Study and Field Experiment in 176 Countries. *Journal of International Business Studies* 48 (5): 590–619. https://link.springer.com/article/10.1057/s41267-016-0047-7?shared-article-renderer.

Ahrens, Leo and Fabio Bothner. 2019. The Big Bang. Tax Evasion After Automatic Exchange of Information Under FATCA and CRS. COFFERS EU Horizon 2020 Project, Wp3. http://uniset.ca/fatca2/the-big-bang.html.

Bermuda Monetary Authority. 2006. 2006 Annual Report. Bermuda Monetary Authority. https://www.bma.bm/publications/annual-reports.

Bermuda Monetary Authority. 2010. 2010 Annual Report. Bermuda Monetary Authority. https://www.bma.bm/publications/annual-reports.

Bermuda Monetary Authority. 2011. 2011 Annual Report. Bermuda Monetary Authority. https://www.bma.bm/publications/annual-reports.

Bermuda Monetary Authority. 2012. 2012 Annual Report. Bermuda Monetary Authority. https://cdn.bma.bm/documents/2018-12-28-04-03-39-Annual-Report-2012.pdf.

Bermuda Monetary Authority. 2013. Bermuda ILS Market Report. Bermuda Monetary Authority, Q4 2013, 1 (2). https://www.bma.bm/publications/bermuda-ils-market-report.

Bermuda Monetary Authority. 2013. 2013 Annual Report. Bermuda Monetary Authority. https://cdn.bma.bm/documents/2018-12-28-04-02-00-Annual-Report-2013.pdf.

Bermuda Monetary Authority. 2014. Bermuda ILS Market Report. Bermuda Monetary Authority, Q4 2014, 1 (2). https://www.bma.bm/publications/bermuda-ils-market-report.

Bermuda Monetary Authority. 2014. 2014 Annual Report. Bermuda Monetary Authority. https://cdn.bma.bm/documents/2018-12-28-03-59-49-Annual-Report-2014.pdf.

Bermuda Monetary Authority. 2015. 2015 Annual Report. Bermuda Monetary Authority. https://www.bma.bm/publications/annual-reports.

Bermuda Monetary Authority. 2016. Bermuda ILS Market Report. Bermuda Monetary Authority, Q4 2016, 3 (4). https://www.bma.bm/publications/bermuda-ils-market-report.

Bermuda Monetary Authority. 2016. 2016 Annual Report. Bermuda Monetary Authority. https://cdn.bma.bm/documents/2018-12-28-03-56-18-Annual-Report-2016.pdf.

Bermuda Monetary Authority. 2017. Bermuda ILS Market Report. Bermuda Monetary Authority, Q4 2017, 5 (4). https://www.bma.bm/publications/bermuda-ils-market-report.

Bermuda Monetary Authority. 2017. 2017 Annual Report. Bermuda Monetary Authority. https://www.bma.bm/publications/annual-reports.

Bermuda Monetary Authority. 2018. Bermuda ILS Market Report. Bermuda Monetary Authority, Q4 2017, 5 (4). https://www.bma.bm/publications/bermuda-ils-market-report.

Bermuda Monetary Authority. 2018. 2018 Annual Report. Bermuda Monetary Authority. https://www.bma.bm/publications/annual-reports.

Bermuda Monetary Authority. 2019. 2019 Annual Report. Bermuda Monetary Authority. https://www.bma.bm/publications/annual-reports.

Bermuda Monetary Authority. 2020. 2020 Annual Report. Bermuda Monetary Authority. https://www.bma.bm/publications/annual-reports.

Butkiewicz, J., and L. Gordon. 2013. The Economic Growth Effect of Offshore Banking in Host Territories: Evidence from the Caribbean. World Development, 44.

BVI Financial Services Commission. 2011. Annual Report 2010. BVI Financial Services Commission. https://www.bvifsc.vg/publications/bvifsc-annual-report-2010.

BVI Financial Services Commission. 2012a. Annual Report 2011. BVI Financial Services Commission. https://www.bvifsc.vg/publications/bvifsc-annual-report-2011.

BVI Financial Services Commission. 2012b. Annual Report 2012. BVI Financial Services Commission. https://www.bvifsc.vg/publications/bvifsc-annual-report-2012.

BVI Financial Services Commission. 2013. Annual Report 2012. BVI Financial Services Commission. https://www.bvifsc.vg/publications/bvifsc-annual-report-2012.

BVI Financial Services Commission. 2014. Annual Report 2013. BVI Financial Services Commission. https://www.bvifsc.vg/sites/default/files/annual_report_2013_revised_dec_3_with_ircp.pdf.

BVI Financial Services Commission. 2015. Statistical Bulletin. BVI Financial Services Commission. https://www.bvifsc.vg/sites/default/files/documents/Statistical%20Bulletins/1_2015_stats_bulletin_qtr_4_2015.pdf.

BVI Financial Services Commission. 2016a. Annual Report 2016. BVI Financial Services Commission. https://www.bvifsc.vg/sites/default/files/annual_report_2016.pdf.

BVI Financial Services Commission. Statistical Bulletin. 2016b. BVI Financial Services Commission. https://www.bvifsc.vg/sites/default/files/2016_statistical_bulletin_qtr_4.pdf.

BVI Financial Services Commission. 2017. Statistical Bulletin. BVI Financial Services Commission. https://www.bvifsc.vg/sites/default/files/documents/Statistical%20Bulletins/2017_statistical_bulletin_qtr_4_with_totals.pdf.

BVI Financial Services Commission. 2018. Statistical Bulletin Q4 2018. BVI Financial Services Commission. https://www.bvifsc.vg/sites/default/files/documents/Statistical%20Bulletins/q4_2018_statistical_bulletin.pdf.

BVI Financial Services Commission. 2019. Annual Report 2019. BVI Financial Services Commission. https://www.bvifsc.vg/library/publications/bvifsc-annual-report-2019.

BVI Financial Services Commission. 2020. Statistical Bulletin Q4 2020. BVI Financial Services Commission. https://www.bvifsc.vg/sites/default/files/q4_2020_statistical_bulletin_.pdf.

BVI Government. 2019. Budget in Brief 2019 Transitioning Towards Sustainable Growth. BVI Government. https://bvi.gov.vg/pub/2019%20Budget%20Address.pdf.

Carey Olsen. 2019. The Bermuda Private Trust Company Guide. Carey Olsen. https://www.careyolsen.com/briefings/bermuda-private-trust-company-guide.

Caribbean Development Bank. 2018a. Country Economic Review 2017 British Virgin Islands. Caribbean Development Bank. https://www.caribank.org/publications-and-resources.

Caribbean Development Bank. 2018b. Country Economic Review 2017 Cayman Islands. Caribbean Development Bank. https://archive.caribank.org/publications/featured-publications/country-economic-review-2017-cayman-islands.

Caribbean Development Bank. 2019. Country Economic Review 2018 Cayman Islands. Caribbean Development Bank. https://www.caribank.org/publications-and-resources.

Caribbean Development Bank. 2020. Country Economic Review 2019 Cayman Islands. Caribbean Development Bank. https://www.caribank.org/publications-and-resources.

Caribbean Financial Action Task Force. 2019. '"De-Risking" in the Caribbean Region.' Retreived April 21 2021. https://www.cfatf-gafic.org/documents/resources/13667-de-risking-in-the-caribbean-region-a-cfatf-perspective.

Caruana-Galizia, Paul and Matthew Caruana-Galizia. 2016. Offshore Financial Activity and Tax Policy: Evidence from a Leaked Data Set. *Journal of Public Policy* 36 (3): 457–488. https://econpapers.repec.org/article/cupjnlpup/v_3a36_3ay_3a2016_3ai_3a03_3ap_3a457-488_5f00.htm.
Cayman Island Monetary Authority. 2012. Annual Report 2011. Cayman Island Monetary Authority. https://www.cima.ky/upimages/publicationdoc/AnnualReportandAu_1499163695.pdf.
Cayman Island Monetary Authority. 2013. Annual Report 2012. Cayman Island Monetary Authority. https://www.cima.ky/upimages/publicationdoc/AnnualReportandAu_1499163437.pdf.
Cayman Island Monetary Authority. 2014. Annual Report 2013. Cayman Island Monetary Authority. https://www.cima.ky/upimages/publicationdoc/AnnualReportandAu_1499163115.pdf.
Cayman Island Monetary Authority. 2015. Annual Report 2015. Cayman Island Monetary Authority. https://www.cima.ky/annual-reports.
Cayman Island Monetary Authority. 2016. Annual Report 2015. Cayman Island Monetary Authority. https://www.cima.ky/upimages/publicationdoc/AnnualReportandAu_1499162240.pdf.
Cayman Island Monetary Authority. 2017. Annual Report 2017. Cayman Island Monetary Authority. https://www.cima.ky/annual-reports.
Cayman Island Monetary Authority. 2018. Annual Report 2017. Cayman Island Monetary Authority. https://www.cima.ky/upimages/publicationdoc/AnnualReportandAu_1532104978.pdf.
Cayman Island Monetary Authority. 2019. Annual Report 2018. Cayman Island Monetary Authority. https://www.cima.ky/upimages/publicationdoc/AnnualReportandAu_1575903466.pdf.
Cayman Island Monetary Authority. 2020. Annual Report 2019. Cayman Island Monetary Authority. https://www.cima.ky/upimages/publicationdoc/AnnualReportandAu_1613507422.pdf.
Casi, Elisa, Christoph Spengel, and Barbara Stage. 2018. Cross-Border Tax Evasion after the Common Reporting Standard: Game Over? ZEW—Centre for European Economic Research Discussion, Paper No. 18–036. https://www.sciencedirect.com/science/article/abs/pii/S0047272720301043?via%3Dihub.
Chiocchetti, Alice. 2020. *The Effects of Automatic Exchange of Information on Evaded Wealth*. http://piketty.pse.ens.fr/files/Chiocchetti2020.pdf.
Department of Statistics. 2015. Gross Domestic Product 2014 Highlights. Government of Bermuda. https://www.gov.bm/government/reports-and-statistics.
Department of Statistics. 2016. Gross Domestic Product 2015 Highlights. Government of Bermuda. https://www.gov.bm/government/reports-and-statistics.

Department of Statistics. 2017. Gross Domestic Product 2016 Highlights. Government of Bermuda. https://www.gov.bm/government/reports-and-statistics.

Department of Statistics. 2018. Gross Domestic Product 2017 Highlights. Government of Bermuda. https://www.gov.bm/government/reports-and-statistics.

De Simone, Lisa, Rebecca Lester, and Kevin Markle. 2020. Transparency and Tax Evasion: Evidence from the Foreign Account Tax Compliance Act (FATCA). Retreived September 13 2018. Available online: https://papers.ssrn.com/sol3/papers.cfm?abstract_id=3037426.

Economics and Statistics Office. 2020. The Cayman Islands' Annual Economic Report 2019. The Government of the Cayman Islands. https://www.eso.ky/quarterlyandannualeconomicreports.html#3.

Findley, Micheal, G., Daniel, L. Nielson, and Jason, C. Sharman. 2014. Causes of Noncompliance with International Law: A Field Experiment on Anonymous Incorporation. *American Journal of Political Science*. https://onlinelibrary.wiley.com/doi/10.1111/ajps.12141.

Garcia-Bernardo, Javier, Jan Fichtner, Eelke M. HeemSkerk, and Frank W. Takes. 2017. Uncovering Offshore Financial Centers: Conduits and Sinks in the Global Corporate Ownership Network. *Scientific Reports* 7(6246). https://www.nature.com/articles/s41598-017-06322-9.

Government of Bermuda. 2020. National Economic Report of Bermuda 2019. Government of Bermuda. https://www.gov.bm/sites/default/files/NATIONAL%20ECONOMIC%20REPORT%202019_Web.pdf.

Gullen, Mauro F. (2015). *The Architecture of Collapse: The Global System in the 21st Century*. Oxford University Press.

Hanlon, Michelle, Edward L. Maydew, and Jacob R. Thornock. (2015). Taking the Long Way Home: U.S. Tax Evasion and Offshore Investments in U.S. Equity and Debt. *The Journal of Finance* 70 (1): 257–287. https://doi.org/10.1111/jofi.12120.

IMF. 2004. The Bahamas: Assessment of the Supervision and Regulation of the Financial Sector—Review of Financial Sector Regulation and Supervision. International Monetary Fund, Country Report No. 04/318. https://www.imf.org/en/Publications/CR/Issues/2016/12/31/The-Bahamas-Assessment-of-the-Supervision-and-Regulation-of-the-Financial-Sector-Review-of-17773.

IMF. 2008. Bermuda: Assessment of Financial Sector Supervision and Regulation. International Monetary Fund, Country Report No. 08/336. https://www.imf.org/external/pubs/ft/scr/2008/cr08336.pdf.

IMF. 2013. The Bahamas: Financial Sector Stability Assessment. International Monetary Fund, Country Report No. 13/101. https://www.imf.org/en/

Publications/CR/Issues/2016/12/31/The-Bahamas-Financial-Sector-Stability-Assessment-40475.

IMF. 2017. The Bahamas Selected Issues. International Monetary Fund, Country Report No. 17/315. https://www.imf.org/en/Publications/CR/Issues/2017/10/06/The-Bahamas-Selected-Issues-45311.

IMF. 2019. The Bahamas Financial System Stability Assessment. International Monetary Fund, Country Report No. 19/199. https://www.imf.org/en/Publications/CR/Issues/2019/07/02/The-Bahamas-Financial-System-Stability-Assessment-47068

Johannesen, Niels, and Gabriel Zucman. 2014. The End of Bank Secrecy? An Evaluation of the G20 Tax Haven Crackdown. *American Economic Journal: Economic Policy*, 6 (1). http://gabriel-zucman.eu/files/JohannesenZucman2014.

Klein, Micheal. 2019. BVI Government Sees Financial Services Revenue Fall Sharply. Cayman Compass. https://www.caymancompass.com/2019/12/20/bvi-government-sees-financial-services-revenue-fall-sharply/.

Knobel, Andres, and Markus Meinzer. 2014. "The End of Bank Secrecy"? Bridging the Gap to Effective Automatic Information Exchange. An Evaluation of OECD's Common Reporting Standard (CRS) and its alternatives. Tax Justice Network. https://www.taxjustice.net/wp-content/uploads/2020/11/TJN-141124-CRS-AIE-End-of-Banking-Secrecy.pdf.

Lane, Philip, and Gian Milesi-Ferretti. 2010. Cross-Border Investment in Small International Financial Centers. International Monetary Fund. https://www.elibrary.imf.org/view/IMF001/10747-9781451962833/10747-9781451962833/10747-9781451962833_A001.xml?language=en.

Lips, Wouter. 2019. Great Powers in Global Tax Governance: A Comparison of the US Role in the CRS and BEPS. *Globalizations* 16 (1): 104–119. https://www.tandfonline.com/doi/full/10.1080/14747731.2018.1496558.

Marshall, Don, D. 2009a. Gender Tropes and Colonial Discourses in the Turbulence of Global Finance. *Contemporary Politics* 54 (19): 413–427. https://www.tandfonline.com/doi/full/10.1080/13569770903441743.

Marshall, Don D. 2009b. The Path to "International Finance": Bringing (Caribbean) Offshore Financial Centres In; Attenuating the Western Grand Narrative. In *The Diplomacies of Small States: Between Vulnerability and Resilience Palgrave MacMillan*, ed. A.F. Cooper and T. Shaw, Chapter 13, 219–243.

May, Christopher. 2015. *Global Corporations in Global Governance*. Routledge.

Menkhoff, Lukas, and Jakob Miethe. 2019. Tax Evasion in New Disguise? Examining Tax Havens International Bank Deposits. DIW. https://www.diw.de/documents/publikationen/73/diw_01.c.574066.de/dp1711.pdf.

Morriss, Andrew P., and Clifford C. Henson. 2019. Regulatory Effectiveness & Financial Centers. *Virginia Journal of International Law*, 53, 417. https://

scholarship.law.tamu.edu/facscholar/325/?utm_source=scholarship.law.tamu.edu%2Ffacscholar%2F325&utm_medium=PDF&utm_campaign=PDFCoverPages.

Offshore Protection. 2021. International Offshore Jurisdiction Review—UK as a Tax Haven. Retreived April 27 2021. https://www.offshore-protection.com/united-kingdom-tax-havens.

Omartian, Jim. 2016. *Tax Information Exchange and Offshore Entities: Evidence from the Panama Papers*. Researchgate. https://www.researchgate.net/publication/315647151_Tax_Information_Exchange_and_Offshore_Entities_Evidence_from_the_Panama_Papers.

O'Reilly, P., K. Parra Ramirez, and M. A. Stemmer. 2019. *Exchange of Information and Bank Deposits in International Financial Centres*. OECD Publishing, OECD Taxation Working Papers, No. 46. https://doi.org/10.1787/025bfebe-en.

Sharman, Jason, C. 2010a. Shopping for Anonymous Shell Companies: An Audit Study of Anonymity and Crime in the International Financial System. *Journal of Economic Perspectives* 24 (4): 127–140. https://www.researchgate.net/publication/227363207_Shopping_for_Anonymous_Shell_Companies_An_Audit_Study_of_Anonymity_and_Crime_in_the_International_Financial_System.

Sharman, Jason, C. 2010b. Offshore and the New International Political Economy. *Review of International Political Economy* 17 (1): 1–19. https://www.tandfonline.com/doi/abs/10.1080/09692290802686940.

Sikka, Prem. 2003. The Role of Offshore Financial Centres in Globalization. *Accounting Forum* 27 (4): 365–399. https://ssn.com/abstract=467682.

Smith, L. 2016. Tax Transparency: The Gamechanger. IFC Review, 17–18.

Smith, L. 2017. Above Board: We Actually Do It Right. IFC Review, 12–13.

Sondheim, Alan. 1976. Umberto Eco, A Theory of Semiotics. *Art Journal* 36 (2): 180–186. https://www.tandfonline.com/doi/abs/10.1080/00043249.1977.10793351.

Stoute, Graham. 2017. Cayman Islands Private Trust Companies. Carey Olsen. https://www.careyolsen.com/briefings/cayman-islands-private-trust-companies.

Suss, Esther C., Oral H. Williams, and Mendis Chandima. 2002. *Caribbean Offshore Financial Centers: Past, Present, and Possibilities for the Future*. International Monetary Fund, IMF Working Paper WP/02/88. https://www.researchgate.net/publication/5124060_Caribbean_Offshore_Financial_Centers_Past_Present_and_Possibilities_for_the_Future.

Travers, Anthony. 2017. *Offshore and Well off the Mark—The Facts and the Fantasy*. IFC Review, 2017/18, 9–11. https://www.traversthorpalberga.com/downloads/pdf/IFCAnnualReview2017.pdf.

The Central Bank of The Bahamas. 2011. 2010 Annual Report. Central Bank of The Bahamas. https://www.centralbankbahamas.com/publications?cat=113&stub=main.
The Central Bank of The Bahamas. 2012. 2011 Annual Report. Central Bank of The Bahamas. https://www.centralbankbahamas.com/publications/annual-reports/annual-report-statement-of-accounts-2011?N=N.
The Central Bank of The Bahamas. 2013. 2012 Annual Report. Central Bank of The Bahamas. https://www.centralbankbahamas.com/publications/annual-reports/annual-report-statement-of-accounts-2012?N=N.
The Central Bank of The Bahamas. 2014. 2013 Annual Report. Central Bank of The Bahamas. https://www.centralbankbahamas.com/publications/annual-reports/annual-report-statement-of-accounts-2013?N=N.
The Central Bank of The Bahamas. 2015. 2014 Annual Report. Central Bank of The Bahamas. https://www.centralbankbahamas.com/publications/annual-reports/annual-report-statement-of-accounts-2014?N=N.
The Central Bank of The Bahamas. 2016. 2015 Annual Report. Central Bank of The Bahamas. https://www.centralbankbahamas.com/publications/annual-reports/annual-report-statement-of-accounts-2015-publication?N=N.
The Central Bank of The Bahamas. 2017. 2016 Annual Report. Central Bank of The Bahamas. https://www.centralbankbahamas.com/publications?cat=113&stub=main.
The Central Bank of The Bahamas. 2018. 2017 Annual Report. Central Bank of The Bahamas. https://www.centralbankbahamas.com/publications/annual-reports/central-bank-of-the-bahamas-2017-annual-report-publication?N=N.
The Central Bank of The Bahamas. 2019. 2018 Annual Report. Central Bank of The Bahamas. https://www.centralbankbahamas.com/publications/annual-reports/annual-report-statement-of-accounts-2019?N=N.
The Central Bank of The Bahamas. 2020. 2019 Annual Report. Central Bank of The Bahamas. https://www.centralbankbahamas.com/publications/annual-reports/annual-report-statement-of-accounts-2019?N=N.
The Insurance Commission of The Bahamas. 2011. 2011 Annual Report. The Insurance Commission of The Bahamas. https://www.icbbahamas.com/wp-content/uploads/2017/02/2011-ICB-Annual-Report.pdf.
The Insurance Commission of The Bahamas. 2012. 2012 Annual Report. The Insurance Commission of The Bahamas. https://docs.google.com/a/icb.gov.bs/viewer?a=v&pid=sites&srcid=aWNiLmdvdi5ic3xpY2ItbmV3c2l0ZXxneDoxNDBjZWZlNmNiYzQ0Zg.
The Insurance Commission of The Bahamas. 2013. 2012 Annual Report. The Insurance Commission of The Bahamas. https://insurancecommissionbahamas.com/publications/publications-annual-reports/.

The Insurance Commission of The Bahamas. 2015. 2014 Annual Report. The Insurance Commission of The Bahamas. https://insurancecommissionbahamas.com/publications/publications-annual-reports/.
The Insurance Commission of The Bahamas. 2017. 2016 Annual Report. The Insurance Commission of The Bahamas. https://insurancecommissionbahamas.com/publications/publications-annual-reports/.
The Insurance Commission of The Bahamas. 2018. 2017 Annual Report. The Insurance Commission of The Bahamas. https://docs.google.com/a/icb.gov.bs/viewer?a=v&pid=sites&srcid=aWNiLmdvdi5ic3xpY2ItbmV3c2l0ZXxneDo1Y2M4ZWU3OTJmYmEyODg5.
The Insurance Commission of The Bahamas. 2019. 2018 Annual Report. The Insurance Commission of The Bahamas. https://insurancecommissionbahamas.com/wp-content/uploads/2019/07/2018-Annual-Report.pdf.
The Insurance Commission of The Bahamas. 2020. 2019 Annual Report. The Insurance Commission of The Bahamas. https://insurancecommissionbahamas.com/wp-content/uploads/2019/07/2018-Annual-Report.pdf.
The Securities Commission of The Bahamas. 2011. 2010 Annual Report. The Securities Commission of The Bahamas. http://www.scb.gov.bs/publications.html.
The Securities Commission of The Bahamas. 2012. 2011 Annual Report. The Securities Commission of The Bahamas. https://www.scb.gov.bs/wp-content/uploads/2018/04/2011-Annual-Report-Final-For-Website.pdf.
The Securities Commission of The Bahamas. 2013. 2012 Annual Report. The Securities Commission of The Bahamas. https://www.scb.gov.bs/media/publications/annual-reports/.
The Securities Commission of The Bahamas. 2014. 2013 Annual Report. The Securities Commission of The Bahamas. https://www.scb.gov.bs/wp-content/uploads/2018/04/AR2013-30AprilLIVE-w-1May14-transmittal-complete.pdf.
The Securities Commission of The Bahamas. 2015. 2014 Annual Report. The Securities Commission of The Bahamas. http://www.scb.gov.bs/publications.html.
The Securities Commission of The Bahamas. 2017. 2016 Annual Report. The Securities Commission of The Bahamas. https://www.scb.gov.bs/wp-content/uploads/2018/04/SCB-2016-AR-FINALwebsiteR1.pdf.
The Securities Commission of The Bahama. 2018. 2017 Annual Report. The Securities Commission of The Bahamas. http://www.scb.gov.bs/publications.html.
The Securities Commission of The Bahamas. 2019. 2018 Annual Report. The Securities Commission of The Bahamas. http://www.scb.gov.bs/publications.html.

The Securities Commission of The Bahama. 2020. 2019 Annual Report. The Securities Commission of The Bahamas. https://www.scb.gov.bs/wp-content/uploads/2020/07/SCB-ANNUAL-REPORT-2019.pdf.

Williams, Oral H., Esther C. Suss, and Chandima Mendis. 2005. Offshore Financial Centers in the Caribbean: Prospects in a New Environment. *The World Economy* 28 (8): 1173–1188.

**Don D. Marshall** acquired a Ph.D. in International Political Economy from the University of Newcastle-upon-Tyne in the U.K. in 1996 and shortly thereafter joined the Sir Arthur Lewis Institute of Social and Economic Studies (SALISES) at the University of the West Indies, Cave Hill Campus. He was promoted to Senior Fellow in August 2005 and to Professor of International Political Economy and Development Studies in May 2021.

# Index





A. M. Campbell, *Money Laundering, Terrorist Financing, and Tax Evasion*, https://doi.org/10.1007/978-3-030-68876-9

The manufacturer's authorised representative in the EU is Springer Nature Customer Service Centre GmbH, Europaplatz 3, 69115 Heidelberg, Germany. If you have any concerns regarding our products, please contact ProductSafety@springernature.com

Printed and bound by CPI Group (UK) Ltd, Croydon, CR0 4YY
30/09/2026
02225451-0017